TWENTIETH-CENTURY
READING EDUCATION:
UNDERSTANDING PRACTICES OF TODAY
IN TERMS OF PATTERNS OF THE PAST

Advances in Reading/Language Research

Peter B. Mosenthal, *Research and Language Arts Center, Syracuse University*, Series Editor
(formerly edited by Barbara A. Hutson, *Division of Curriculum and Instruction, Virginia Polytechnic Institute and State*)

Volumes 1-3: 1982-1986
  edited by Barbara A. Hutson

Volume 4: *Cognitive Science and Human Resources Management*, 1986, edited by Thomas G. Sticht, Frederick R. Chang, and Suzanne Wood

Volume 5: *Literacy Through Family, Community, and School Interaction*, 1991, edited by Steven B. Silvern

Volume 6: *Reconsidering the Role of the Reading Clinic in a New Age of Literacy*, 1999, edited by Dorothy H. Evensen and Peter B. Mosenthal

Volume 7: *Reconceptualizing Literary in the Media Age*, 2000, edited by Ann Watts Palliotet and Peter B. Mosenthal

Volume 8: *Twentieth-Century Reading Education: Understanding Practices of Today in Terms of Patterns of the Past*, 2000, by Gerard Giordano

TWENTIETH-CENTURY
READING EDUCATION:
UNDERSTANDING PRACTICES OF TODAY
IN TERMS OF PATTERNS OF THE PAST

by GERARD GIORDANO
Utah State University

JAI PRESS INC.
Stamford, Connecticut

CONTENTS

To Karen, with unqualified love

INTRODUCTION

Peter B. Mosenthal

"Time," wrote Henry David Thoreau, "is but the stream that I go fishing in." Many of us go fishing in that stream, content to focus on the currents of the here-and-now. We pay little heed to the currents that have gone before and we pay even less attention to the currents of the future. From time to time, some historians may dislodge our focus on the currents of the here-and-now and persuade us to ponder the stream that passed before we took up residence at our present fishing hole. In so doing, most of these historians have tended to portray the stream that has passed before us as a simple "chronology"—dividing the ebb and flow of the stream into precisely delineated dates. For instance, historians remind us that 1776 was the year in which the Declaration of Independence was signed, Gibbon published the *Decline and Fall of the Roman Empire*, the Scottish philosopher David Hume died, Fragonard completed one of his most celebrated paintings, the English landscape painter John Constable was born, Mozart conducted his "Haffner" Serenade, Adam Smith published the *Wealth of Nations*, and Cook made his third voyage to the Pacific. Similarly, historians characterize 1927 as the year when Lindbergh flew the Atlantic, Trotsky was expelled from the Communist Party, *Show Boat* opened in New York, Freud published *The Future of an Illusion*, Pavlov did his work on conditioned reflexes, Al Jolson starred in *The Jazz Singer*, the

German economic system collapsed, Thornton Wilder published *The Bridge of San Luis Rey,* and the Harlem Globetrotters basketball team was organized.

Such a static interpretation of history restricts the view of life events. Instead of seeing a broad stream consisting of many eddies whose patterns repeat over time, one may see the stream of life as little more than a set of fixed reference points. Hence, the Roman civilization "ended" when Alaric and the Visigoths sacked Rome in 410 A.D. Then the Dark Ages "began." For some, history is this simple.

In contrast to this approach to interpreting time, a few gifted historians have been able to chart patterns of change. Pierre Wack (1985) has illustrated this view of history in an article that was built upon Thoreau's metaphor of time as a stream. In his article, "Scenarios: Shooting the Rapids," Wack takes us back to the era when the pharaohs ruled Egypt. At this time, a temple stood far up the Nile, beyond the cataracts in Nubia, in the area that is now the northern deserts of the Sudan. Three tributaries joined together in that region to form the Nile, which flowed down a thousand miles to produce a miraculous event each year—the river basin flooding that permitted Egyptian farmers to grow crops in the hot, rainless midsummer.

Every spring, the temple priests would gather at the river's edge to check the color of the water. If it were clear, the White Nile, which flowed from Lake Victoria through the Sudanese swamps, would dominate the flow. Because the flooding would be mild and late, the farmers would harvest a small crop. If the stream appeared dark, the stronger waters of the Blue Nile, which joined the White Nile at Kartoum, would prevail. The flood would rise enough to saturate the fields and provide a bountiful harvest. Finally, if the stream showed dominance by the green-brown waters of the Atbara, which rushed down from the Ethiopian highlands, then the floods would be early and catastrophically high. The crops would usually be drowned and the Pharaoh would have to distribute reserved grain from his stores.

Each year, the priests sent messengers to inform the king of the color of the water. They also used lights and smoke signals to carry word down stream. The Pharaoh then knew how prosperous the farmers in this kingdom would be, how much he could raise in taxes, and whether he could afford a campaign to conquer additional territory. In this regard, the priests of the Sudanese Nile were among the world's first historians who, based on the events of the stream's past, forecast the conditions of life's stream in the future.

By understanding history as the lens for uncovering patterns of the past, we, like the pharaohs of old, are better prepared to deal with our future. Rather than being simply reactive, we can use this knowledge to plan for the future. As any good history shows us, the streams in our life histories are much more than unique events arranged between chronological benchmarks; instead, like history itself, these events repeat themselves in grand fashion. To uncover the patterns or themes of repetition is the true challenge for great historians.

Certainly the field of reading has been blessed with numerous histories (Graff, 1989; Kaestle, 1985; Resnick & Resnick, 1977; Shannon, 1990; Stedman & Kaestle, 1987; Venezky, 1984) that have attempted to move beyond the simple chronological ordering of the events that have comprised research, instructional practices, and policies. Yet these histories have been limited in their scope. In many instances, the histories have been written from a single ideological or theoretical perspective. To the extent that past practices were not consistent with the historian's ideology or theory of reading, they were portrayed as "undermining progress"; to the extent that past practices were consistent with the historian's ideology or theory, they were portrayed as "promoting progress" and serving as key elements for "real reform."

Rather than settling on a single theory or ideology for framing his history, Giordano, in his epic, *Twentieth-Century Reading Education: Understanding Practices of Today in Terms of Patterns of the Past*, portrays the history of reading in the United States over the past century as the interplay between four instructional approaches: skills-based, language-based, literature-based, and technology-based. Which of these approaches dominated at any time appears to have depended upon which of three questions educators, researchers, and policymakers focused. These questions were: "What is?" "What is possible?" and "What ought to be?"

When educators, researchers, and policymakers organize their broader intellectual and practical pursuits by focusing on the question of "what is," they are inclined to adopt the status quo and spend the larger part of their intellectual pursuit refining and extending current educational practices. In this mode, research is used to validate how reading is currently taught and evaluated.

After a period, educators, researchers, and policymakers change their preoccupation with "what is," shifting their attention to the issue of "what ought to be." By raising this question, they inevitably challenge the efficacy of current practices and open the way for new possibilities. At this point, research is used to demonstrate that the "best practices" of the present are flawed. This, in turn, opens the way for educators, researchers, and policymakers to explore questions about "what is possible" and related questions about which of the possibilities are the most effective.

In the possibility stage, all practices are viewed as viable candidates for inclusion on the list of "best practices." At this point, intense research, marketing, and political maneuvering take place to secure agreement as to which method is the most effective. As a consensus develops, this refocuses educators', researchers', and policymakers' attention back on the "what is" stage of the reform cycle.

In crafting his history, Giordano shows that, while the United States has run through several reform cycles, these cycles have consistently included the same four possibilities of instruction: skills-based, language-based, literature-based, and technology-based approaches. In this regard, Giordano persuasively demonstrates that, for over a century, the options for how educators, researchers, and policymakers might think about instructional approaches have been finite—not unlike the finite combinations of river colors that the pharaohs noted in the tributaries of the Nile many centuries ago.

While Giordano presents the summary of his work in the Foreword, he concludes his magnificent opus addressing the issue of how different multicultural groups have been taught reading over the past century in the United States. In so concluding, he avoids the broader speculative question, "Why is reform in education and reading so cyclical?" While this was not the author's intent to address this question, it is clear that Giordano has joined with a host of other historians and researchers (e.g., Carnoy & Levin, 1985; James & Tyack, 1983; Gould, 1987; Kaestle, 1972, 1985; Kirst & Meister, 1985; Kliebard, 1988; Presseisen, 1985; Schlesigner, 1986; Slavin, 1989) who have invoked the concept of the cycle to explain efforts at reform and general change in education. Indeed, as Cuban (1990) has suggested, answers to this question appear to be varied:

> Reforms return because policymakers fail to diagnose problems and promote correct solutions. Reforms return because policymakers use poor historical analogies and pick the wrong lessons from the past (Katz, 1987). Reforms return because policymakers fail, in the words of Charles Silberman two decades ago, "to think seriously about educational purposes" or question the "mindlessness" of schooling (Silberman, 1971, pp. 10-11). Reforms return because policymakers cave in to the politics of a problem rather than the problem itself. Reforms return because decision-makers seldom seek reliable, correctly conducted evaluation of program effectiveness before putting a program into practice (Slavin, 1989). In short, were policymakers to pursue a rationale course of analysis and decision making and, where fitting, use research and evaluation results properly, there would be no need for the same solutions to reenter the policy arena (p. 6).

While it is easy to blame policymakers for the lack of real reform, I am suggesting an alternative explanation—an explanation that closely complements Giordano's account of the changing nature of reading instruction. In short, Giordano's history of reading is really a history of different "agendas" (Mosenthal, 1999). Every agenda (be it a reading instruction, research, or policy agenda) has a goal. Goals are not neutral; they represent desired outcomes or conditions. As such, goals are outcomes or conditions that *should be* attained according to an individual's or group's beliefs, values, perspectives, or practices. As such, agendas enter Giordano's question cycle not at the level of "what is" or "what is possible," but rather at the level of "what should be." When a desired goal is blocked, a problem is said to exist. As such, problems represent undesired conditions or states—that is, conditions or states that *shouldn't be*. Moreover problems represent an impasse in one's ability to change "what is" into "what should be."

Second, agendas cannot be set by just anyone; rather, only certain individuals or groups have the prestige, ability, and power that are required to set agendas. Third, agendas are set to benefit some but not others. Fourth, agendas are designed to impact different levels of organization (e.g., the student, the classroom, the school district, the county, the state, or the nation). Fifth, the extent to which agendas can be carried out is limited by the amount of available resources, such as money, time, and human capital.

Sixth, to achieve goals or solve problems, agenda setters prescribe a set of actions to be taken. (In this regard, prescribed actions, like goals that should be and problems that shouldn't be, reflect values, for they are actions that *should be taken.*) Seventh, once actions have been prescribed, agendas then include actions taken. Eighth, actions taken result in outcomes actually realized.

Finally, agendas usually include some form of evaluation or assessment. On one hand, evaluation is used to determine the extent to which actions actually taken relate to actions prescribed. Evaluation is also used to determine the extent to which the outcomes of the actions taken represent successful goal achievement or problem solution. When taken together, these various features constitute agendas.

In applying the notion of agendas to Giordano's history, readers will find that the cycles of change are accompanied by changes in established agendas of reading research, practice, and policy. In most instances, change occurs when different individuals or groups obtain the predominant power needed to set agendas. As such, Giordano's book provides a remarkable chronicle of the individuals and groups who have set and implemented the major reading agendas over the past century. Moreover, as different individuals and groups assume power to change the reading agenda, so the goal of reading changes, as well as the actions prescribed for teaching reading. While these actions fall within the domain of Giordano's four instructional approaches, he provides a detailed account of how these approaches have differed over time. Moreover, as reading agendas have changed over the past century, so have the beneficiaries of these agendas. In his history of reading, Giordano shows how different agendas have tended to advantage (and, at times, disadvantage) different groups of readers within American society.

Throughout his book, Giordano shows that, while one agenda may rise to the fore, it still remains in competition with other agendas. As the vicissitudes of the times change, along with those who have the power to set the reading agenda, so the very nature of reading agendas themselves change. Through the lens of his book, we see that these changes cycle through four instructional approaches.

In closing, I am reminded of Cuban's (1990) plea for improved understanding of change in education:

> Reforms do return again, again, and again. Not exactly as before or under the same conditions, but they persist. It is of even greater importance that few reforms aimed at the classroom make it past the door permanently. It is important for policymakers, practitioners, administrators, and researchers to understand why reforms return but seldom substantially alter the regularities of schooling. The risks involved with a lack of understanding include pursuing problems with mismatched solutions, spending energies needlessly, and accumulating despair.... We can do better by gathering data on particular reforms and tracing their life history in particular classrooms, school, districts, and regions. More can be done by studying reforms in governance, school structure, curricula, and instruction over time to determine whether any patterns exist (p. 12).

Giordano's *Twentieth-Century Reading Education: Understanding Practices of Today in Terms of Patterns of the Past* is a book that should be read by policymakers, practitioners, administrators, and researchers alike. Few books so thoroughly and objectively chronicle the patterns of reading reform during the twentieth century.

Among the patterns of data that Giordano so assiduously presents lies the explanation for genuine reading reform.

REFERENCES

Carnoy, M., & Levin, H. (1985). *Schooling and work in the democratic state.* Stanford, CA: Stanford University Press.

Cuban, L. (1990). Reforming again, again, and again. *Educational Researcher, 19* (6), 3-13.

Gould, S. J. (1987). *Time's arrow, time's cycle.* Cambridge, MA: Harvard University Press.

Graff, G. (1989). *Professing literature: An institutional history.* Chicago: University of Chicago Press.

James, T., & Tyack, D. (1983). Learning from past efforts to reform the high school. *Phi Delta Kappan, 64,* 400-406.

Kaestle, C. (1972). Social reform and the urban school. *History of Education Quarterly, 12,* 211-229.

Kaestle, C. (1985). The history of literacy and the history of readers. *Review of Research in Education, 12,* 11-54.

Katz, M. (1987). *Reconstructing American education.* Cambridge, MA: Harvard University Press.

Kirst, M., & Meister, G. R. (1985). Turbulence in American secondary schools: What reforms last? *Curriculum Inquiry, 15,* 169-186.

Kliebard, H. M. (1988). Fads, fashions, and rituals: The instability of curriculum change. In L. N. Tanner (Ed.), *Critical issues in the curriculum* (pp. 16-34). Chicago: National Society for the Study of Education.

Mosenthal, P. B. (1999). Forging conceptual unum in the literacy field of pluribus: An agenda-analytic perspective. *Journal of Literacy Research, 31,* 213-254.

Presseisen, B. Z. (1985). *Unlearned lessons: Current and past reforms for school improvement.* London: Falmer Press.

Resnick, D. P., & Resnick, L. B. (1977). The nature of literacy: An historical exploration. *Harvard Educational Review, 47,* 370-385.

Schlesinger, A. M. (1986) *The cycles of American history.* Boston: Houghton Mifflin.

Shannon, P. (1990). *The struggle to continue: Progressive reading instruction in the United States.* Portsmouth, NH: Heinemann.

Silberman, C. (1971). *Crisis in the classroom.* New York: Alfred Knopf.

Slavin, R. (1989). PET and the pendulum: Faddism in education and how to stop it. *Phi Delta Kappan, 90,* 750-758.

Stedman, L., & Kaestle, C. (1987). Literacy and reading performance in the United States, from 1880 to the present. *Reading Research Quarterly, 22,* 8-46.

Venezky, R. L. (1984). The history of reading research. In P. D. Pearson, R. Barr, M. L. Kamil, & P. Mosenthal (Eds.), *Handbook of reading research* (Vol. 1, pp. 3-38). New York: Longman.

Wack, P. (1985). Scenarios: Shooting the rapids. *Harvard Business Review, 63* (6),139-150.

FOREWORD

Nineteenth-century educators attempted to ensure that their students would not fail in reading. And they provided help to those learners who were failing. Despite this attention, organized remedial reading approaches were not discernible until the twentieth century. This book examines the origin of four influential twentieth-century remedial reading approaches: skills-based, language-based, literature-based, and technology-based. As part of this investigation, the book identifies the social, emotional, physical, and cognitive factors that were linked by educators and psychologists to reading. Additionally, the issues related to remedial reading that overlapped with those in the general field of reading education are examined. These issues included testing, diagnosis, individualized education, textbooks, readability, multiculturalism, bilingualism, and disability.

The organization of this book is distinct from that employed typically in histories of education. Instead of presentation through a linear chronology, the material is organized in topics. As a result, individuals, events, and distinctive instructional materials from the same part of the twentieth century are sometimes reviewed in several different chapters. This organization enables each chapter to be read as an independent essay. Extensive quotations have been selected from thousands of primary sources and integrated into the text to provide a sense of intellectual involvement with scholars who wrote throughout the nineteenth and twentieth centuries.

Because remedial reading was the distinctive development that set twentieth-century reading education apart from the educational practices of the nineteenth century, this book employs remedial programs as its special vantage. But even though it did not emerge until the twentieth century, remedial reading was anticipated in the nineteenth-century trend to fiercely criticize schools, especially for their inability to reduce reading failure. Undeterred by such onslaughts, many tradition-minded educators did not abandon their loyalty to the prevailing pedagogy. However, just the unprecedented propagation of novel instructional methods during the nineteenth century was an indication of a sizable dissatisfaction with those prevailing instructional practices. Though the dominant pedagogy had been an alphabet-centered approach at the beginning of the 1800s, alternative approaches such as phonics, whole-word learning, and the sentence method were embraced zealously by nineteenth-century educators with distinctive philosophies.

In the middle of this search for an alternative pedagogy, some nineteenth-century educators began to experiment with individualized instructional techniques that could complement rather than replace the instructional approach with which learners were failing. These individualized techniques were the immediate antecedents of twentieth-century remedial reading programs. As the individualized techniques were refined, accompanying developments in testing enabled educators to efficiently isolate the factors that might be responsible for reading problems. Convinced that some of these factors were physical, educators suggested classroom activities to modify eye movements and neurological anomalies, two dysfunctions that they judged to interfere frequently with reading.

The fascination with the physical etiology for learning problems paralleled the development of elaborate diagnostic and remedial procedures. By the 1940s complicated clinical approaches for remedial reading had been patterned after medical procedures for evaluation and intervention. While many educators were drawn to such specialized programs, others demonstrated a diametrically opposed philosophy when they designed remedial lessons to be implemented with groups of students in their own classrooms. Although grouped reading lessons may have become popular in reaction to the pretentious demeanor that some remedial reading experts had begun to assume, they were also promoted as a response to escalating estimates of the numbers of students who could benefit from individualized reading instruction but who were unable to be accommodated.

Extremist political rhetoric became common during the 1930s. Convinced that the economic depression signaled the end of capitalist society, political activists adjured teachers to participate in an inevitable revolution. Just a decade later, teachers were prodded by conservative political forces in the opposite direction, illustrating a dialectic pattern that would continue throughout the century. For example, skills-based reading programs, even though they continuously dominated instruction, were castigated when politically liberal philosophies were popular. However, the regulation inherent in skills-based programs was viewed as a complement to national security during both world wars and the cold war. Part of a broad initiative to promote efficiency through standardization, skills-based programs structured learning through materials that were arranged sequentially, connected to a hierarchy of skills, based on an explicit curriculum, and linked to textbooks.

The textbooks with which skills-based programs were associated became caught in the political fray when they were attacked by liberal educators because of inherent inadequacies and because of the proclivity of teachers to rely excessively on them. However, textbooks were defended with equal passion by conservative educators who viewed them as a resource with which to guarantee that students were learning skills that were academically critical and essential for national security. The political turmoil encompassing textbooks extended to other controversies with which the general field of reading education was being buffeted.

Some persons who opposed skills-based instruction were attracted to language-based approaches because these liberated themselves from textbooks by means of an emphasis on the experiences and functional language of children. In contrast to the increased criticism of skills-based instruction that was apparent during periods when liberal values reigned, the popular support for language-based activities achieved its climax during such eras. Despite these non-concentric patterns of popularity, language-based instruction was at times linked with skills-based programs. For example, during the 1960s language-based activities were regularly supplemented with skills-based exercises. However, this type of interdependence decreased as language-based activities polarized into the politically liberal whole language programs.

While educators argued about the respective impact of skills-based and language-based instruction on remedial learners, literature-based programs were also attracting their own special audience. These programs were a response to the conviction that the content of reading materials influenced both learning and character development. Searching for books that would be responsive to learners who had already encountered problems, some educators aspired to use books themselves as part of analytical procedures patterned after psychological therapy. Others educators attempted to mold reading instruction into a preventative bulwark that could shield readers when they eventually encountered problems.

A fourth major category of reading lesson that was apparent during the twentieth century was technology-based. Developed originally toward the end of the 1800s, some of the initial activities involved supplementary mechanical and electronic devices. These were followed by activities that were enriched through radio, cinema, and television. As personal computers became more accessible during the 1970s, the popularity of technology-based reading activities increased concomitantly. However, the use of technology-based reading activities expanded even further during the 1980s and 1990s when computers were employed to expedite personal communication and to access the vast banks of information available through the Internet.

The rudimentary stages of skills-based, language-based, literature-based, and technology-based instruction were discernible during the 1800s. Another motif that had appeared during the 1800s but which still resounded throughout the twentieth century was a concern about teaching reading to special groups, such as persons with disabilities. Despite some pioneering nineteenth-century efforts that demonstrated that individuals with disabilities could develop literacy skills, most educators assumed that the curricula for this group should reinforce nonacademic learning and be implemented in isolated institutions. Nonetheless, schools began to hire specially trained teachers to instruct the many children with disabilities who could not be accommodated in institutions. In a similar turn of events, increasing numbers of children with disabilities were fully integrated into regular education classrooms when their numbers exceeded the opportunities for placements in the public schools' special classrooms. Exposed to academic curricula, those learners with disabilities who were placed in regular classrooms created a demand for programs that would help them become literate.

Another special group of learners with whom educators became concerned were students who were culturally, ethnically, or linguistically diverse. Partly because of fears that unassimilated foreigners would undermine America's traditions, efforts to educate immigrants had been initiated during the 1800s. Many of these efforts were designed for implementation in segregated classrooms. Similar to the case for learners with disabilities, the many non-English-speaking students who could not be accommodated in segregated classes had to be placed in regular education classrooms. Nineteenth-century and early twentieth-century educators debated whether speakers of other languages should be taught to read with English or their native language. They also argued about the relative effectiveness of different formats for lessons when teaching reading to speakers of other languages. These politically charged issues continued to be controversial throughout the twentieth century.

Chapter 1

THE ROLE OF READING IN A
BESIEGED EDUCATIONAL SYSTEM

The inadequacy of the old conception of education to meet the demands and the doubts has become such a prolific source of disquietude and dissatisfaction that ere long a new one must needs be constructed (Young, 1906).

Though remedial reading did not emerge as a formal area of emphasis within education until the twentieth century, it was anticipated in nineteenth-century trends such as increased criticism of the schools. However, the criticism of the schools that was evident throughout the nineteenth century seemed mild and isolated in contrast with the widespread storm of vituperation that formed at the end of that century. Arguing for progressive educational techniques that were language-based and child-centered, reform-minded teachers questioned whether their tradition-minded colleagues had not maintained a greater allegiance to the economic and social establishment than they had to children's interests. Even when this criticism did not come from instructors who wished to advance progressive educational practices, it predisposed teachers toward such practices simply because these represented an alternative to an educational system that had been portrayed as moribund. Defiant to these rhetorical onslaughts, defenders of the schools came together as a secure phalanx. This academic tumult was especially relevant to reading education because of a consensus among traditional educators, the general public, and most progressive instructors that reading was a critical skill for which the schools were accountable.

*   *   *

Writing in the 1905 *Preface* to his *History of Education*, Monroe explained his reasons for assembling the exhaustive information in this book. He argued that an educator needed "to acquire a sufficient body of fact concerning the educational practices of the past," "to develop an ability to interpret that experience in order to guide his own practice," and "to exercise his judgment in estimating the relation existing between various theories and corresponding practices" (pp. vii-ix).

1

However, Monroe used baroque language to describe the most important reason for studying historical information, which was "to obtain a conception of the meaning, nature, process, and purpose of education that will lift him above the narrow prejudices, the restricted outlook, the foibles, and the petty trials of the average schoolroom, and afford him the fundamentals of an everlasting faith as broad as human nature and as deep as the life of the race" (pp. vii-ix). Converting this last remark into more current parlance, Monroe had hoped that historical information could help persons see the broad context for the crises that were being confronted almost a century ago. He was convinced that once teachers had glimpsed the expansive context for their problems, they might respond to education issues more effectively.

Monroe's rationale for examining the past is as appropriate today as it was during the time he wrote it. However, questions about a cursory examination of the recent discussions among educators about learning to read highlights continuing divisiveness in their attitudes toward even the most practical issues, such as which strategies and materials should be employed. Contemporary educators have also disagreed about the research methods that are appropriate for resolving disputes, the psychological foundations that support behavior, the philosophical assumptions required to explain learning, the range of evidence that is relevant to reading, and the political restrictions imposed on learners by schooling. As such, Monroe's remarks may not only be valid today but they may generalize from the wider field of education to the specialized context of reading education. If this is the case, educators can examine the extent to which the current furor about reading education has been anticipated in earlier dialogues as well as the possibility that past dialogues may still be relevant to the issues being confronted today.

CRITICISM OF EDUCATION

Like the general history of modern education, the history of reading education has been a series of confrontations among disputants who have respectively attempted to defend or discredit the schools and public education. Aware of the opportunities to buttress the credibility of their scholarly work by making rhetorical appeals outside those disciplines, many educational critics attempted to enlist support from parents and the general public. For example, William Smith's 1884 novel, *The Evolution of Dodd*, was subtitled *A Pedagogical Story*. Similar to the impact that *Uncle Tom's Cabin* had on popular attitudes toward slavery prior to the Civil War, Smith's eloquent writing helped to persuade readers about the abuse of learners in the schools. Smith described the "trackless Sahara" of the young Dodd's experiences as he was pushed by the schools toward juvenile delinquency. He signaled readers about his attitudes toward the school system when he described the weather on Dodd's first day at school as "a leaden morning in November, when the mud was the deepest and the first snow was shied through the air, whose sharpness cut like a knife" (p. 14). At school Dodd met Miss Stone, a teacher who "being somewhat dull intellectually, and detesting severe study, she abjured all paths that would lead her to teach the high branches of learning, and bent her rather spare and somewhat stale energies to fitting herself for primary work" (p. 17). Smith concluded the novel with a call for "personality, individuality, and character, in every teacher and pupil in the public schools, and freedom of each to develop his own way, and not after a pattern made and prepared by a pattern maker" (p. 245).

A decade later, William Stead (1964) published his immensely successful book *If Christ Came to Chicago*. This 1894 book's title was derived from a rhetorical question that Stead asked continually: What would Christ do, were he to return to earth to visit this city and observe its injustice, evil, and suffering? Among the many inequities that were documented in this report of more than 400 pages was the taxation system supporting the schools of Chicago:

> If Christ came to Chicago and took any practical interest in the establishment of His Kingdom in the city, the assessment system would be radically reformed. This is not a question of politics or of administration of finance. It is a question of elementary morality. For the assessment system is based on a lie. It is worked by perjury, and it has as its natural and necessary results injustice, corruption, and the plunder of the poor. Its continuance for another year would be a practical recognition of the devil's dominance and ascendancy in Chicago, which it is idle to attempt to counterbalance by such lip worship and devout genuflections as we blasphemously dignify by the name of Divine service in our churches (Stead, 1964, p. 207).

Though increased criticism of education was more noticeable during the latter part of the 1800s than during the first 50 years of that century, that criticism accelerated even further in the first decade of the twentieth century. Henderson (1902) pointed out that "in every high school, the land over, one sees this constant falling out of line" and that "perhaps only one third or one quarter of the children remain to graduate" (p. 112). He concluded that "surely an educational process is failing lamentably, when it succeeds with so small a percentage of its materials" (p. 112). Eight years later, Gillette (1910) alerted his readers about a revolt in education when he wrote that "there is on foot an educational movement almost amounting to a revolution" (p. 1). As to the source of the criticism that was responsible for the educational revolution, Gillette identified "files of the United States Educational Reports, those of the proceedings of the National Education Association, those of the various educational and other periodicals, the daily press, practical experiments conducted by teachers' training institutions, [and] books on education" (p. 1). And as regards the objects of educational criticism, Gillette pointed to "waste in education" and the "useless material contained in our school curricula."

G. Stanley Hall was an influential psychologist who was one of the founders and then the first president of the American Psychological Association. In addition to encouraging the use of experimental techniques in psychological research, he wrote extensively about all aspects of child growth, including education. In his voluminous two-volume exploration of problems in education, Hall (1911a, 1911b) included an 83-page chapter on "Some Defects of our Public Schools." The defects he reviewed were organized into 21 topics that ranged from *lack of professional training in teachers* to *feminization of [the] teaching force.* Hall wrote that "until lately" criticism of education had been restrained "partly because it was deemed essential that the confidence of the public that taxes itself for its support be not jeopardized" (1911b, p. 570). However, he observed that "a literature of recent censure, and even condemnation, is now large and growing" (p. 570). Once the restraints on criticism had been removed, Hall himself did not hesitate to join critics because he thought that "our prevalent *methods of teaching* are open to very grave criticism" (p. 609). Hall also gave an example of inadequate curriculum when he noted that "perhaps the chief and most just criticism of our common-school system is that there is a vast body of things learned that are forgotten when school life ends" (p. 617). Sympathetic to much of this criticism, he admitted that "our curriculums, methods, and ideals are still to quite an extent inherited heirlooms from the past" (p. 617).

Though much of the criticism of education was a broadside directed at national institutions and practices, schools in large industrial cities were particularly vulnerable. As part of an inquiry into the New York City educational system, Hanus (1913b) objected that "the actual work of the schools, in large part, both in its spirit and in its detail, cannot be commended" (p. 11). Although he acknowledged that exceptions could be found, he also concluded that "the quality of the teaching and supervision is, in general, not good" (p. 11). As a final condemnation, Hanus observed that "this adverse judgment of the spirit that dominates the actual work of the schools...extends also to the course of study and the syllabi" (p. 11).

Even Chicago, which was regarded as a city with one of the best school systems in the country, was not insulated from attacks. For example, Rice (1893) had not concealed his disappointment with Chicago's educational practices during the 1890s when he wrote that "I found the instruction, in general, so unscientific that in judging them by the minimum requirement I should regard their standard as very low" and that "some of the teaching was by far the most absurd I have even witnessed" (p. 202). Writing during the 1920s, Counts (1971) certainly increased rather than reduced the anxiety of his readers when he attempted to document that nonacademic personnel had been tampering with Chicago's schools. After identifying industrial and commercial kingpins who had been espousing cost-efficient programs to promote vocational training, basic skills, and civic awareness, he warned his readers about the negative consequences of their intrusion into education.

Ample evidence was readily available to substantiate Counts's allegations about the interests of the commercial community in Chicago's schools. For example, business persons had commissioned the publication of professional books on vocational education. Such sponsorship was apparent in the foreword to

Kerschensteiner's (1911) text on vocational education when he reported that "the Commercial Club of Chicago, recognizing the imperative need of practical, vocational training to supplement present public school courses, has engaged Dr. Edwin G. Cooley, formerly Superintendent of Schools of Chicago, to investigate the industrial education systems of Europe, with a view to learning what place such courses of study should have in the public school systems of America" (p. vii).

One of the most eloquent urban critics of this period was Upton Sinclair (1906), who had gained national attention with *The Jungle*, an exposé of disease, corruption, and inhumane working conditions within Chicago's meat processing industry in the early 1900s. As an indication of Sinclair's commitment to social reform, he had attempted to establish a socialist community in New Jersey a year after *The Jungle* had appeared and he dedicated this book "to the workingmen of America." In a 93-chapter book on higher education, Sinclair (1922) referred to America as "the plutocratic empire." Buttressing his writing with research citations to prevent it from being dismissed as another of the many editorials that were being written about crises in education, Sinclair depicted universities as components of an unfair school system designed to sustain special privileges for an elite class and "to keep America capitalist" (p. 18).

Writing during the great depression, Kilpatrick (1932) recognized that his readers were preoccupied with that economic crisis. But he counseled them that "the ills from our present serious business depression, serious as they are, are in themselves not so significant [as the educational issues before the country]" (p. 3). He warned that the public dishonesty created by bad business practices was nullifying the beneficial impact of education and that the "mis-educative effects of business challenge education's essential reason for being" (p. 83). He railed against prevalent business practices in which "graft becomes common," "crime becomes an occupation," and "politicians become corrupt" (p. 83).

Woelfel (1933) also deplored the influence of industry and business on education. He wrote enthusiastically about the expanding role of organized labor associations "which during the present economic depression are gathering to themselves large cohorts of discontents" (p. 11). He dedicated his book "to the teachers of America—active sharers in the building of attitudes—may they collectively choose a destiny which honors only productive labor and promotes the ascendancy of the common man over the forces that make possible an economy of plenty" (p. v). Woelfel's biased view of capitalism was apparent when he compared business persons to racketeers and predicted that rising socialism would banish them from both society and education. Three years later, Langford (1936) wrote a book about the interrelationship of education and social conflict in which he indicated that "Marx's description of the development of human societies as the history of class struggles has been fought more and more bitterly by capitalism" because "it has been recognized as the theoretical weapon of the rising proletarian class, which is destined to supersede the present rulers of society just as they themselves superseded the feudal barons" (p. 2).

Lynd and Lynd (1929, 1937) exhaustively recounted the social changes in a typical, medium-sized American city during the era from 1885 to 1935. In the portion of this record that covered the period from 1925 to 1935, they described the debates within this mainstream community about the philosophy needed to undergird education:

> On the one hand, there is the belief, a natural outgrowth of the American individualist and democratic tradition, that the schools should foster not only free inquiry but individual diversity, and that they best serve their communities when they discover, and equip the individual to use, his emotional and intellectual resources to the fullest extent, in however diverse ways. Although professional educators are still searching for ways in which this can be done, this philosophy has gained wide acceptance among them, and is in some cases used as a defensive bulwark against repressive forces. It inevitably runs counter to another philosophy, far more often found in human societies, namely that the function of the educational system is the perpetuation of traditional ways of thought and behavior, the passing on of the cultural tradition, and, if need be, the securing of conformity by coercion (Lynd & Lynd, 1937, p. 234).

The Lynds could not conceal their distress when the community they were investigating eventually turned away from the progressive philosophy with which they personally sympathized. Using an understated, professorial style for their writing, they noted sadly that "there is no sector of our culture where the efficiency of large-scale routines is capable of being more antithetical to the spirit of the social function to be performed than in education" (p. 241).

ADVOCACY FOR EDUCATION

Testimonials by conservative and liberal educators who were criticizing education were apparent throughout the nineteenth and early twentieth centuries. However, advocacy for established practices in education was also evident. McAndrew (1878) decried those newspaper editorialists who had depicted schools negatively and applauded those who "have shown by their pens that it is naughty to knock the schools" (p. 552). He quoted remarks from Joseph King, president of the national News Enterprise Association, in which he explained his enthusiasm for the schools:

> Schools are our best public service. Newspapers and schools should both be working for the same thing: progress, advancement, a living less forlorn. It isn't fair to our teachers to represent them as unattractive to children. American boys and girls have no better friends than the public-school teachers. It is absurd to suggest that children dislike school. Even if it were true it would be poor public policy to advertise it. That would make it harder to cure. But it isn't true. American teachers have made the schoolhouse the favorite resort of children; their friends are there, their interesting work, their jolly play (King, quoted by McAndrew, 1878, pp. 551-552).

In a history of education that he published originally in 1886, Painter (1901) wrote about the positive achievements and strong sense of direction that he saw for future schools. He concluded that "a strong interest in education exists in every section of our country; and, under the impulsion of this feeling, every effort is made to advance the public schools" (p. 321). Five years later, Shoup (1891) proclaimed to his readers that "no other nation of the earth has ever had so large a proportion of reading writing, thinking men and women as has our country at the present time" and that "these qualities are due to the beneficent influence of the common school" (p. 302).

Even some of the criticism that was expressed about education was delivered in a fashion that was designed to simultaneously reassure persons about the overall soundness of the system that was being castigated. In an early twentieth-century report (Commission on Industrial and Technical Education, 1906), the authors wrote of "a growing feeling of inadequacy of the existing public school system to meet fully the need of modern industrial and social conditions" or of "a vague feeling of dissatisfaction with results" (p. 5). However, the report's authors were quite clear about the supportive attitudes of the critics who were making such comments, assuring readers that their remarks "did not imply hostility" because "everywhere the Commission found the people loyal to the purpose of the schools, and proud of the advanced position which the State has held, and they do not complain of the cost" (p. 5).

Many of the books about education written after 1900 were addressed specifically to parents and members of the general public rather than to professional educators. In the preface to his book on the social implications of education, Dutton (1900) observed that at one time educational books were "not seriously studied except by teachers" because "education was regarded as a matter belonging exclusively to the school." But he boasted that this earlier period had ended and that "to-day there is no subject that excites greater public interest" and that "fathers and mothers are anxious to understand the aims and methods of the school" (p. vii). An example of a book written for a general audience was that by Mowry (1908) in which he recollected his career as a New England educator. He began this autobiography with an assurance that "there is no better place to bring up a boy than on a farm, especially if that farm is located in the midst of an intelligent community with a good rural school" (p. 9). Although he called attention to problems that the schools were confronting, he prefaced these remarks by observing that "without doubt it is safe to say that no greater progress is apparent in any direction than in the processes and results of our American system of education" (p. 265). (Mowry warned that a dire problem arose from immigrants with "extreme differences" in "language, social life, morals, and religion" and who maintained views of government that were "totally un-American" [p. 276]. Even in the face of this situation that was "fraught with great danger," Mowry had "no misgivings as to the result." He tried to allay parents' fears by confiding that "I believe that this entire foreign population is to be rapidly assimilated" [p. 278].)

In another classic autobiography written for a general audience, Swett (1911) described his years as an educator in California. Recalling that he would visit schools after he had been elected state superintendent of public instruction in 1891, he wrote that he "found many things to commend" and that "the essentials to be learned by children...were well done in the classes that I visited" (p. 246). In one of the final chapters, he reassured his readers that "our whole public-school system, from primary schools to the State University, is keeping even pace with our rapid increase in wealth, in population, in science, in art, and in literature" and that "at the beginning of this century all the omens are auspicious" (p. 258).

Though advocates for the schools remained firm in their support for the traditional models of education, this support was often coupled with an admission of increasingly frequent and fierce attacks upon the schools. For example, Denison (1912) admitted that the number of school problems that were unresolved was indicated by "the mass of criticism and even abuse aimed continually at our schools" (p. 7). Though she paraphrased some of this hostile criticism, noting that "a principal declares that a revolution is necessary in present methods of education," or that "a physician writes that schools are physical menaces to children," she still counseled her readers that "all this criticism does not alter the firm tradition that our schools are the bulwarks of democracy" (p. 8). After reviewing critical remarks about education by the president of Harvard University, King (1914) observed that neither these criticisms, nor "even severer indictments of current education" had diminished his confidence in the schools:

> This is not to be taken to mean that our schools are less efficient absolutely than those of past generations, but rather that they are relatively less able to cope with the demands of their age. If it could be possible to transfer them to the social conditions of even a generation ago we have reason to think they would prove superior to the schools of that day in meeting the demands made upon them. But even so recently as the past generation, much of the work now being loaded upon the school was performed by other institutions. Moreover, in that day, with a less crowded population and cheaper living, the problem and the need of the schools' taking up various specialized types of education, such as industrial and vocational, did not present itself (p. 4).

IMPORTANCE OF READING

John Dewey (1898) described reading as a nineteenth-century fetish, which had become obsolete. He observed that literacy had once been viewed as the door to learning and to success in life at a time "when ability to read and write marked the distinction between the educated and the uneducated man, not simply in the scholastic sense, but in the sense of one who is enslaved by his environment and one who is able to take advantage of and rise above it" (p. 316). Dewey wrote that reading and writing were "regarded as more or less arbitrary tasks which must be submitted to because one is going to the mysterious thing called a school" (p. 317). Carefully using the past tense when he described "the curriculum of the three R's," Dewey noted that "to learn to read and write was an interesting, even exciting thing; it made such a difference" (pp. 316-317). Dewey expressed his annoyance at traditional teachers who employed instructional strategies to teach lessons through "all manner of pretty devices and tricks in order that the child may absorb them unawares" (p. 317). The only concession that he made to the continued viability of literacy was an observation that "there are undoubtedly rural regions where the old state of things still persists" (p. 317).

Dewey identified the societal changes that he thought had contributed to this decline in the importance of reading:

> The capital handed down from past generations, and upon whose transmission the integrity of civilization depends, is no longer amassed in those banks termed books, but is in active and general circulation, at an extremely low rate of interest. It is futile to try to conceal from ourselves the fact that this great change in the intellectual atmosphere—this great change in the relation of the identification to accumulated knowledge—demands a corresponding education readjustment. The significance attached to reading and writing, as primary and fundamental instruments of culture, has shrunk proportionately as the immanent intellectual life of society has quickened and multiplied. The result is that these studies lose their motive and motor force. They have become mechanical and formal, and out of relation—when made dominant—to the rest of life (1989, p. 317).

In addition to his concerns about children being required to develop archaic skills, Dewey was worried about reading because "physiologists are coming to believe that the sense organs and connected nerve and motor apparatus of the child are not at this period [i.e., the first two years of school] best adapted to the confining and analytical work of learning to read and write" (p. 319). Observing that reading was a type of symbolic reasoning, he also questioned whether "the child of six or seven years [is] ready for symbols to such an extent that the stress of educational life can be thrown upon them" (p. 320).

Stanley Hall (1911b) cited the 1900 census to corroborate that "the percentage of illiterates over ten years of age in this country ranged all the way from 2.3 per cent in Nebraska which led, to 5.9 per cent in Massachusetts, the twenty-fifth state, and ending with Louisiana, the forty-ninth, with 38.5 per cent" (p. 443). (Hesseltine [1936] had reported that "in 1890, 30 per cent of the Southern population could not read or write" but that in the wake of popular demands for the states to adequately support public education "the extent of illiteracy dropped 50 per cent during the succeeding decade" [pp. 707-708].) Hall reported the rates of illiteracy among different ethnic groups, noting that "illiteracy, according to the latest available statistics, is 4.9 per cent of the native whites, 11.5 per cent of the foreign whites, and 47.4 of the negroes [sic], as against a fraction of 1 per cent in lands like Prussia and Norway" (p. 596). Despite such alarming statistics, Hall was not unduly concerned, speculating that "perhaps we are prone to put too high a value both upon the ability required to attain this art and the discipline involved in doing so" (p. 443).

Dewey's and Hall's attitudes were not shared by most educators. Hall himself admitted that some of his personal opinions did not represent those held generally by the public because "parent and child both realize that position and effective-ness in adulthood depend pretty directly upon success in school" (p. 617). Patri (1917) indicated that he was personally inspired by Dewey's opinions while teaching in New York City in the late 1800s. However, he acknowledged that the "average parent thinks of education largely in terms of books" and that "the poorer the people are the more apt they are to over-value the traditional work of the schools" instead of "music, cooking, stories, dramatics, dancing, wood, [and] clay" (p. 50). He lamented that many parents, "from the highest to the lowest," believed that "the book and the book knowledge shall save you" and that "this is education" (p. 57). This perception of a direct link between success in school and success in later life was focused on reading to a greater extent than any other type of learning. In his cultural history of education, Butts (1947) indicated that suc-cess in reading was the primary goal of elementary education during the 1800s.

Writing about the warnings of educational commentators during the 1800s, Graff (1991) noted that even though literacy was perceived as a road to education and moral improvement, "some fiction, however, was considered potentially dan-gerous, appealing to emotions and sentiments and undercutting morality" (p. 355). Despite some warnings during the 1800s about reading as a path to moral perdition, educators continued to view it as a useful academic subject, a valuable vocational asset, and a necessary tool for extracting the wisdom from virtuous books such as the Bible.

Writing about the growth of the reading public in England, Williams (1961) observed that the 1700s sustained "an important expansion which both created regular journalism and changed the social basis of literature" and that "in the nine-teenth century there was a major, and at time spectacular, expansion in reading" (p. 156). In the introduction to Taylor's history of the Ohio School System, Bar-ney (1857) wrote that an objective of this book had been to document "the educa-tional spirit and tendency of the age." With regard to this spirit, Barney described in flourishing style the persons who would benefit from expanded literacy:

> Who reaps the benefit of it? Those whose lives are protected by the virtue and regard to law which a good education always inspires,—those whose property is rendered more valuable by the industry and skill which a good education always imparts,—those who sleep in peace, because education and the virtue of which it is the handmaid, have extinguished the torch of the incendiary,—those who enjoy quiet and security, because education has disarmed the rob-ber and assassin (1857, p. ix).

Most of his contemporaries would have supported Hinsdale's confident 1896 assertions that "the primary teacher's first duty is to enlarge and clarify the child's mental store" and "her second duty is to enlarge and clarify his vocabulary" (p. 76). Hinsdale added a comment that "the teacher's great instrument in the accom-plishment of these goals is reading" (p. 76). In his teaching methods textbook, Boyer (1908) began a section on the *History of Reading* with the statement that "reading has always been the fundamental school study in all the civilized nations" (p. 120). He used ornate language to describe reading as a process that "opens the door to all the centuries, and makes it possible for a good reader to become the veritable 'heir of all the ages'" (p. 119). In a book about classroom management that was published originally in 1907, Bagley (1916) described a procedure in which students would monitor each other during oral reading and point out errors. He wrote that "by adopting this device, the teacher can assure himself that every pupil in the class will give the lesson his undivided attention, and that every pupil who reads will strive as strenuously as he can to avoid mistakes" (p. 6). Bagley was convinced that such zealous attention to reading was appropriate because "an accurate mastery of the mechanics of reading may be assumed as essential to the educated individual" (p. 6).

Charters (1913) agreed with the majority of persons during the late 1800s and early 1900s who were confident that reading was critical to success in school, employment, and life. As a consequence of this widely shared perception, parents looked to reading programs as weather vanes with which to confirm that their children's educations were being blown by nurturing winds. As the criticism of schools increased to hurricane force during the 1900s, parents and educators maintained keen attention on reading education. Their uncompromising conviction about the importance of learning to read was to a large extent the basis for whether a crisis siren would be sounded. The remedial reading programs that were eventually developed during the twentieth century were largely the response to such an emergency wail.

SUMMARY

Although critics had pointed to inadequacies in education during the 1800s, the number and intensity of these attacks increased during the 1900s. The offensives against general education were accompanied by criticism of reading. In most cases, those educators who supported traditional models for education also supported the popular skills-based programs that were associated with traditional education. And those educators who were calling for fundamental reforms in education espoused alternative instructional strategies. Not only was the public alarmed by this debate, but educators themselves, who agreed with the public about the critical importance of reading, began to question whether students were learning to read effectively. As a consequence of the aggitation created by persistent challenges about the effectiveness of reading education, teachers began to search for alternatives to the prevalent instructional programs of the nineteenth and early twentieth centuries.

Chapter 2

EARLY CONTROVERSY ABOUT LITERACY EDUCATION

A larger bibliography has been worked out for the teaching of reading than for the teaching of any other subject (Charters, 1913).

Although all children were learning to read by a single method at the beginning of the nineteenth century, many diverse approaches were used by the end of that century. Each of the emerging reading approaches was embraced by zealous educators who were searching for the optimal program that would be effective with all learners. However, the proliferation of approaches, as well as the subsequent emergence of eclectic types of instruction, indicated the inability to employ any single approach as an avenue to universal literacy. By the end of the 1800s educators had begun to devise individualized instructional approaches that foreshadowed some of the twentieth-century approaches for helping with reading difficulties.

* * *

In 1894 Martin observed that "some of us perhaps are looking back to the district school with jealous fondness; to the academy and to the older days at college or to a time when school work and school discipline were more severe and formal" (1902, p. 276). He ruminated poetically that "the process of evolution has in it necessarily an element of sadness" because "when old things pass away, we miss them even if we would not have them stay" (p. 276). Such emotional pining for the vanished practices of yore would have been misplaced in the case of reading education. For the instructional procedures employed in reading education at the end of the twentieth century were very much like those that were popular a century earlier. With the exception of the remedial reading approaches, which did not emerge until the twentieth century, nineteenth-century educators had already implemented the instructional strategies that would be employed during the next era.

As an example of progress in reading education during the late 1800s, some instructors were teaching children to search for semantic and grammatical context clues to help them decipher unfamiliar vocabulary. Other instructors used transcripts of students' own language as reading materials to ensure that the vocabulary, grammar, and level of abstraction within instructional passages were suited to children's level of development. Not only were methods and materials for teaching reading in the 1800s comparable to those employed today, but many of the issues that were controversial during the 1800s are still controversial today. And many of the questions asked during the 1800s, such as those about the materials that were most suitable for reading instruction, are still being asked today.

NINETEENTH-CENTURY CONTROVERSY OVER READING MATERIALS

Arguments from the first half of the 1800s in Massachusetts indicate the longevity of the controversies about reading methods and materials. Because it had historically placed an unusually strong emphasis on education, Massachusetts had a reputation as a standard-setter among the states (Harper, 1939). In an 1894 preface to Martin's history of education in Massachusetts, Harris wrote that "almost all educational problems have been agitated at one time or another in Massachusetts" (1902, p. vii). He noted the significance of this agitation by observing that "the experience of 'the Bay State' has thus been vicarious, serving not only for itself but in a measure for all the other New England States, and also for the new communities in the West, settled in great part by emigrants from New England" (p. vi). Writing a decade after Harris but from a complementary perspective, Munroe (1911) indicated that "for the greater part of the nineteenth century, there is no question that Massachusetts, Connecticut and New York were in the van of educational advance, and that among these three Massachusetts stood first" (p. 299). He wrote poetically of Massachusetts that "on her sterile hills has been enacted practically the whole drama of American educational progress" (p. 303).

Horace Mann was state superintendent of instruction in Massachusetts for 12 years beginning in 1837. In the introduction to his book on educational problems, Hall (1911a) had written that Mann had started the "great movement" in educational reform. Munroe (1912) described the situation at which this reform had been directed:

> Mr. Mann found, when he entered upon his duties, that 42,000 children in Massachusetts did not attend school at all, that of those who did, the average attendance was only seventeen weeks. He found those children housed in school buildings scarcely fit for swine. He discovered most school committees to be ignorant and slothful, most teachers to be ill-trained and worse paid. There was little but chaos in the curricula and more than chaos in the methods and means of teaching. He found the schools rent by sectarian jealousies, and, most serious of all, he found the towns divided into hostile camps, each district spending its pittance as it pleased,

choosing its teachers by methods worse than haphazard, and opposing all change and improvement with the fanatic fierceness of a puffed-up ignorance (p. 301).

One of the key provisions in the reforms that Mann advocated was the substitution of the whole word method for the analytical alphabet approach that was prevalent in Massachusetts and the other New England states. This intellectual clash between Mann and the teachers of Massachusetts a century and a half ago is only one of many nineteenth-century incidents that shadowed the debates about reading education that would dominate the twentieth century.

Though the Massachusetts controversy about reading education was centered about reading methodology, robust and often hostile criticism was directed at reading materials as well. As an example, Eliot was president of Harvard University in 1890 when he advised that "it would be for the advancement of the whole public school system if every reader were hereafter to be absolutely excluded from the school." Eliot explained that he opposed reading textbooks because "they are not real literature; they are but mere scraps of literature" (Eliot quoted by Wells, 1915, p. 587). Huey was another opponent of the prevailing reading education materials. Although acknowledging their aesthetic qualities, he observed in 1908 that "next to the beauty of the primers, the most striking thing about at least three-fourths of them is the inanity and disjointedness of their reading content" (1968, pp. 278-279). The following passage from Mandeville's 1849 *Primary Reader* may be the type of passage to which critics such as Huey and Eliot had referred with disdain:

> Every tame parrot was once a wild parrot in the woods.
>
> Some men have several parrots in the same cage against the wall, but this man has but one.
>
> Every tiger is not young, but some tigers are old tigers. Camels are high, long, large, and strong. The camel is not wild and fierce like the tiger in the cage on the cart, but tame and wild.
>
> Some parrots can talk like any boy or girl. No one should put his hand or his head in the cage of the fierce tiger (Mandeville's 1849 *Primary Reader*, quoted by Johnson, 1935, p. 263).

However, the same primary reader from which this passage was taken contained meaningful stories that were sure to engross students. The following passage, in which Mandeville hyphenated some words as an aid to pronunciation, introduced a four-paragraph story with a moral that is readily discernible:

> Two boys went out in-to the snow, with a lit-tle sled. One was na-med James, the oth-er was na-med Sam-u-el. James said to Sam-u-el, "You dare not go on that pond with your sled." Sam-u-el said, "Yes, I dare, but it is wrong; be-cause fa-ther said we must not do it." Then James laugh-ed and said, "What of that? Fa-ther can-not see us; for he is at work in the shop" (Mandeville's 1849 *Primary Reader*, quoted by Johnson, 1935, p. 264).

Not only did many reading textbooks contain stimulating passages, but the instructional manuals that accompanied them included suggestions for extremely creative activities that were synchronized to the passages. For example, the teacher's manual for the 1890 series of reading books by Silver, Burdett & Company suggested that the following activity, which occurred in the level-three reader from a series of six graded textbooks, be linked to an illustrated textbook passage about workers who were processing rubber:

Material: Rubber and many articles made of rubber. Turtle shell and palm nuts.

Lead children to describe the picture.

Have them write after the oral description is given.

Have them read their descriptions.

Lead them to tell the story which the picture suggests.

Lead them to tell the story on paper.

Have the children read their stories.

Tell them of the country in which rubber trees grow.

Have them read the book lesson silently before reading it orally.

Have pupils reproduce the lesson without reference to the book (Todd & Powell, 1899, p. 77).

Four years later Hinsdale (1896) was extremely positive when he referred to the textbook as "'the walking-beam' of the intellectual life." Writing 17 years after Hinsdale, Charters (1913) concluded that "no other subject has books so well adapted to its pupils as primers and first readers" (p. 104). Charters's high estimate of progress in reading was evident when he noted that "the excellent results attained in this subject lead us to have increasing hope of a similar excellence in all subjects (p. 104). This high estimate was restated by Samuel Parker in 1923 when he noted that "the technique of teaching beginning reading has been very highly perfected" and that "hence it is described here in detail as an example of the fine art of teaching" (p. 72). Many other nineteenth- and early twentieth-century educators shared these positive views toward early reading materials. Kiefer (1948) expressed these sentiments with tenderness in her history of the American textbooks that were used from 1700 to 1835. She wrote that "it is impossible to reproduce adequately, even to a sympathetic reader, the soul of these little books and the message imparted by their very physical make-up" (p. 4).

McGuffey Readers

Though he had criticized the standardized reading materials from the early 1900s, Huey did not challenge their attractiveness or aesthetic appeal. Referring specifically to the beauty of the McGuffey readers, Mulcahy and Samuels (1987) recounted that as early as 1840 a shift was apparent in textbooks as a result of which they became more attractive and easier to use:

> The cover of an 1879 edition of *McGuffey's First Eclectic Reader, Revised* is decorated with elaborate swirls and designs, and the title of the book preceding the first lesson is embellished with an elaborate type. Though the content of this reader is simplistic, the illustrations are beautifully drawn and retain an almost photographic appearance, smaller illustrations accompanying the text. The book is amply illustrated with superb artwork (p. 38).

As an example of this beauty, Figure 2.1 is an elaborate embellishment that decorated one of the chapter numerals in a McGuffey primer.

McGuffey's series were by far the most popular reading materials of the nineteenth century, selling more than 122,000,000 copies before 1920 (Lindberg, 1976). The period of greatest sales was from 1870 to 1890, when more than 60 million copies were purchased (Clifton, 1933). This astounding rate of adoption had begun to wane by 1900. As an indication of the decline, a more modest 15 million copies were sold during the three decades following 1890. But the McGuffey series continued to be used widely. Vail (1911) reported that "for more

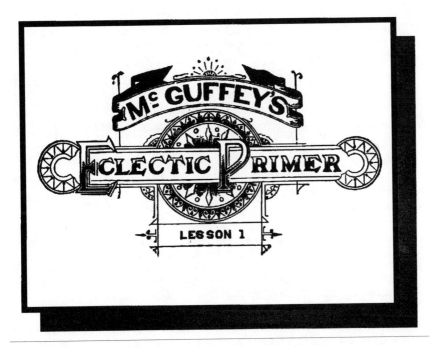

Figure 2.1.   Embellishment Accompanying an Initial Lesson in
the Popular McGuffey Series First Published in 1836

than seventy years the McGuffey Readers have held high rank as text-books for use in the elementary schools, especially throughout the West and South" (p. 4). A quarter of a million copies were sold from 1920 to 1963 (Carpenter, 1963) and the series was still being used during the 1970s (Lindberg, 1976).

Writing more than a century after the series had been introduced, a descendant of McGuffey concluded that the reading series had "more influence on nineteenth-century American culture than any other books except the Bible" (McGuffey-Ruggles, 1950, p. 129). Though her familial ties may have biased her admiration for these textbooks, few historians would challenge McGuffey-Ruggles's appraisal of the cumulative influence of the series. In their history of Ohio, Roseboom and Weisburger (1934) wrote ingenuously that "despite the smiles of the more sophisticated youth of today and the criticism of educational authorities, few of the older generation brought up on these familiar manuals will concede that Ohio schools improved their standards when the old [McGuffey] textbooks were put aside" (pp. 431-432).

Fullerton (1927) indicated that adults who wished to commemorate the personal impact of this reading series organized scores of "McGuffey clubs" throughout the Midwest. However, these clubs were also magnets for political conservatives. An introductory document in Vail's *A History of the McGuffey Readers* (1911) contained a statement that "all members of [the McGuffey Society] must be native born Americans; believe in the established order of government for the people and by the people; believe that there has come the Twilight of the Kings; believe that the government of the United States has upon its shoulders the salvation of the world and the perpetuation of the civil and religious liberties of all peoples; and promise to read—at least once a year—the Declaration of Independence and pledge themselves also never to miss an opportunity to induce any citizen of the United States to do likewise (prefatory document, p. 2).

The following reminiscence from a rural learner who had used the McGuffey readers during the late 1800s indicates the patriotic association that students formed with the books as well as the style of instruction with which the books were identified:

> We read the books over and over. The reading was oral. We vied with each other in intonation, in inflection, in interpretation. We thundered Rienzi's address to the Romans, Spartacus to the Gladiators, Webster's Reply to Hayne, and all the fine selections that characterized these choice readers. We committed to memory and "spoke" dozens of the pieces we liked (Laylander, quoted by Fuller, 1982, p. 14).

In his history of American education, Cubberly (1947) asserted firmly that the McGuffey readers had resulted in significant educational changes, one example of which was that this sequenced set of books had "helped to establish the graded school, with its class organization" (p. 294). Agreeing with this assessment,

LESSON X.
The Sun is Up.

See, the sun is up. The sun gives us light. It makes the trees and the grass grow.

The sun rises in the east and sets in the west. When the sun rises, it is day.

When the sun sets it is night.

This little boy was up at five. He saw the sun rise, and heard the sweet songs of birds on every bush.

Do you know who made the sun ?
God made it.

Figure 2.2.   A Page from an Early Textbook Indicating
Emphasis on Religion

Kliebard (1986) concluded that the McGuffey readers created a "profound stan-
dardizing influence on the curriculum of the nineteenth-century schools" (p. 2).

Although Huey had criticized standardized reading materials for inadequate
content, he did not precisely substantiate his negative evaluation. As an example of a contrasting view, Vail (1911) characterized the McGuffey readers as
books which were "recognized as formers of good habits of action, thought,
and speech for three quarters of a century, which have taught a sound morality
to millions of children without giving offense to the most violent sectarian" (p.

Figure 2.3. Illustrations from the Popular McGuffey Reading Series

3). However, Commager (1950) noted 40 years later that "what children have learned in school is not to be taken too seriously as an index to their character, but it is an almost infallible guide to the moral system that adults approve, and when that approval persists for three generations, it attains almost constitutional dignity" (p. 38). He then described how the McGuffey readers taught "industry, obedience to parents, kindness to the old and to animals, temperance, generosity, promptness, and the inevitable triumph of the virtuous over the wicked" (pp. 39-40). Figure 2.2 is a page from the 1837 edition of a McGuffey reader that exemplified the emphasis that was placed on morality and religion in this and other reading books of the period.

Butts (1947) admitted that the McGuffey readers had taught religion, morals, and literacy; but he judged that the readers had exhibited social and practical lessons as well. Figure 2.3 contains examples of illustrations from the McGuffey readers that were not only elegant but interest-provoking. The content accompanying passages reinforced these intriguing pictures. For example, the following passage was synchronized to the illustration of the three boys contained within Figure 2.3:

> Under a great tree in the woods, two boys saw a fine, large nut, and both ran to get it. James got to it first, and picked it up.
>
> "It is mine," said John, "for I was the first to see it."
>
> "No, it is mine," said James, "for I was the first to pick it up." Thus, they at once began to quarrel about the nut. As they could not agree whose it should be, they called an older boy, and asked him.
>
> The older boy said, "I will settle this quarrel." He took the nut, and broke the shell. He then took out the kernel and divided the shell into two parts, as nearly equal as he could. "This half of the shell," said he, "belongs to the boy who first saw the nut. And this half belongs to the boy who picked it up. The kernel of the nut, I shall keep as my pay for settling the quarrel. This is the way," said he, laughing, "in which quarrels are very apt to end."

Moral lessons such as those in the preceding passage were typical in the McGuffey readers. Fullerton (1936) characterized the ethical content of the McGuffey readers when he wrote that "virtue always triumphed and wickedness always was punished" (p. vi). Figure 2.4 is a middle nineteenth-century illustration that accompanied a passage about the righteous behavior of the young George Washington after chopping down a cherry tree. Stories of moral deeds by heroes, especially Washington, were common in reading textbooks. Figure 2.5, which is from a reader published in the late 1800s, illustrates a child helping an elderly person across a treacherous street after the child has realized that this person should be given the same respect as her own mother.

Figure 2.4. Illustration for a Middle 1800s Reading Passage about the Moral Behavior of George Washington

Popularity of Other Reading Series

The emphasis on meaningful content that marked the McGuffey readers was typical of other readers from the 1800s as well. Carpenter (1963) described the McGuffey readers as books without "noticeable innovations and nothing radically different from other readers current at the time" (p. 79). Identifying 11 basal reading series in addition to the McGuffey readers that were popular during this

Figure 2.5. Illustration from an 1890 Passage about
Respect for Mothers

period, Carpenter attributed the prospering of the McGuffey series to several factors, the most important of which was an aggressive sales and advertising campaign. Lindberg (1976) also estimated that the McGuffey readers were not "markedly different from most other reading textbooks of the time" and attributed their success to clever marketing rather than distinctive content.

During the middle portion of the 1800s the McGuffey readers were certainly the most popular textbooks on the market. Sales for this series were particularly robust in western states. Nonetheless, after he had reviewed other textbooks that were popular during the middle and late nineteenth century, Vail (1911) concluded that "at no time in the history of [the McGuffey readers] have they been without formidable competition" (p. 61). Vail noted that the Goodrich Readers "were perhaps the most constant competitors with the McGuffey Readers in the early years throughout the states of the Mississippi Valley" and that the Wilson Readers "were vigorously pushed into the schools of Ohio and Indiana about 1867" (pp. 62-63). Referring to the school textbook trade in general, Branham (1930) reported that during the decade beginning in 1870 "competition among publishers became so keen and so expensive that it was a very real menace to their prosperity" (p. 59). Carpenter (1963) indicated that sales for several of these series totaled in the millions. Sanders wrote a frequently adopted series. Nietz (1961) reported that Sanders's series was the dominant set of textbooks in the eastern states. Like the McGuffey readers, Sanders's books highlighted morality while discussing a wide range of topics.

Judd (1918b) addressed the great number of reading materials available to teachers during the late 1800s and early 1900s when he wrote that "the volume of this kind of publication has become so great that one can hardly keep up with the readers which appear each year" and that "since 1880 there has also been a flood of books classified as supplementary readers" (pp. 4-5). Reporting about the extensive materials that he used to write his book on reading pedagogy, Huey noted that he had located more than one hundred "texts, manuals, and systems for teaching children to read...representing the best that could be found" (1968, p. 276). Clearly, additional resources were available to Huey that he chose not to review.

Although Richey (1931) examined the professional affiliations of authors of reading textbooks, he limited the reading materials for this analysis to books published as parts of graded series. Even with this limitation, he was able to locate 28 series of reading education materials that had been published just between 1876 and 1886. Richey respectively identified 27, 41, 53, and 55 reading series for the succeeding four decades. Though some of these series were revised editions, one cannot help but be impressed that Richey was able to identify 204 reading series that had been published between 1876 and 1926. Robinson (1930) conducted an exhaustive review of reading materials from 1775 to 1930. He examined only 85 reading books published between 1775 and 1825, but then 481 published between 1875 and 1915. Classifying the content of those book by categories, he found that the most frequently occurring topic for reading passages in the books from 1825 to 1875 was *morals and conduct*, accounting for 16 percent of the passages in 481 readers. The second most frequent topic was *animals and birds* (16%), followed by *nature study* (8%). The categories for the most frequently occurring topics changed in the 588 readers published from 1875 to 1915. In that more recent group of textbooks, passages about *boys and girls* occurred most often (18.5%). (*Boys and girls* had accounted for only 3% of the passages in the books from 1825 to 1875.) Passages about *animals and birds* (15%) and *nature study* (8%) still remained second and third in frequency. But passages about *morals and conduct* had dropped to 5 percent. Additionally, Robinson calculated that 14.5 percent of the selections in readers from 1825 to 1875 were poetry, and that this percentage increased to 18.5 percent in the readers from the next 40-year period. Sixteen years later, Minnich (1936) analyzed the content of 33 readers from the 1800s and found that the three most frequently occurring topics were *ethics*, *God*, and *death*.

Robinson (1930) thought that the reading books published between 1875 and 1915 had exhibited a respect for literary objectives. He judged that books published before 1875 had contained "scraps" of articles by respected authors whereas the books from this later period contained complete stories, essays, and poems. But even reading books published before 1875 aspired to promote an appreciation for literature. This aspiration was indicated by the subtitles of popular textbooks. For example, the 1836 edition of Cobb's *The North American Reader* was described as "containing a great-variety of pieces in prose and poetry from very highly esteemed American and English writers." As an indication of this textbook's popularity, Caldwell and Courtis (1925) referred to an 1845 survey of the Boston school system indicating that the Cobb readers were being used in all of that city's schools. Minnich (1936) reviewed the sixth reader in the McGuffey series and determined that "one hundred and eleven of the great authors were quoted" (p. 72). He also counted more than 125 poems from the eighteenth century that were incorporated into the fifth- and sixth-level readers.

EARLY FUNCTIONAL READING MATERIALS

For more than two centuries some educators argued that reading materials should be preeminently practical. The link between reading materials and religious texts was the most pervasive example of such a belief. In an 1838 article, Barnard had observed that "the schools of [Connecticut] were founded and supported chiefly for the purpose of perpetuating civil and religious knowledge and liberty, as the early laws of the colony explicitly declare" (1965, p. 136). Huey (1968) observed in 1908 that religious reading materials had dominated reading instruction for several centuries. Briggs and Coffman (1911) described the first primer, which had appeared in Germany in 1419, as "wholly religious in character" (p. 25). Hall (1897) noted that the reading primer was named after "a little religious book used at prime or dawn" (p. 11). Writing about education in Pennsylvania, Wickersham (1886) observed that "about the only branch attempted to be regularly taught in the earliest schools was Reading, and this instruction was mainly given as a preparation for learning the catechism and taking part in other religious exercises" (p. 191). Wickersham wrote that "the first Primers were quite as much church books as school books, containing hymns, prayers, creeds, and catechisms, as well as the Alphabet and elementary reading lessons" and that "as soon as a child had fairly mastered the reading lessons of the Primer, he was expected to learn the Catechism, and, in connection therewith, to read the Psalter and possibly portions of the Bible, commencing with the New Testament" (pp. 191-192). Vail (1911) reported that the *New England Primer* was "strongly religious and fully in accord with the faith of the people" and that "it served as a first book in reading and was followed by the Bible" (p. 45). Jensen (1931) wrote of the *New England Primer* that "it contained about eighty pages of New England puritanism [sic], savage theology, contempt of joy and tenderness, sturdy self-reliance, and noble emphasis on right living" (p. 2).

Since the educational needs of females were generally regarded as incidental to those of males, the link between reading and religion may have been an even more significant factor for explaining the acquisition of literacy among females than it was for males. Alice Palmer wrote that in the early years of the 1800s "the common schools were the only grades of public instruction open to young women" and that even in the progressive schools of Massachusetts "girls were allowed to go to school only a small part of the year, and in some places could even then use the schoolroom only in the early hours of the day, or on those afternoons when the boys had a half-holiday" (Palmer & Palmer, 1908, pp. 337-338). Writing about his years as a schoolmaster during the late 1800s, Stableton (1900) inadvertently revealed his prejudice against female learners by his consistent choice of biased language, noting, for example, that "with superintendents who are in close sympathy with boys, and are ardent students of boy life, and the right kind of principal and of teachers in the higher grades, our high schools would be full of boys, and the girls too, would still be there" (p. 8). Whereas reading was perceived as necessary to acquire knowledge of religion, writing was seen as a portal to employment and general self-development. Wickersham (1886) reported that "when instruction in Writing was first introduced into the early schools, it was confined wholly to boys" because "such an accomplishment was deemed unnecessary for girls " (p. 192). Wickersham added with regret that even in 1886 "so deep rooted was this prejudice, that men could be found who entertained it, almost down to the present day" (p. 192).

Unlike the McGuffey readers and the series of textbooks that had emerged later during the nineteenth century, neither the vocabulary items nor passages in earlier reading textbooks were sequenced in progressive difficulty. Passages in the *New England Primer* and competing readers were selected primarily because they reinforced religious values. Jensen (1931) wrote that these books were not actually reading books at all but rather "religious manuals, with creeds and prayers in keeping with the beliefs of the religious sects which published them" (p. 2). In his examination of the content of four reading texts that were published prior to 1775, Robinson (1930) calculated that 70 percent of the passages concerned religion and another 6 percent involved morals and conduct. As an example of the religious character of these materials, one of the passages in the *New England Primer* described how a controversial minister was burned at the stake in view of his wife and children:

> Mr. John Rogers, minister of the gospel in London, was the first Martyr in Queen Mary's reign, and was burnt at Smithfield, February 14, 1554.—His wife, with nine small Children, and one at her breast following him to the stake; with which sorrowful sight he was not in the least daunted, but with wonderful patience died courageously for the Gospel of JESUS CHRIST (passage from the *New England Primer*, cited by Johnson, 1935, p. 83).

Figure 2.6 contains illustrations for the passage about Rogers' burning that appeared in three different editions of the *New England Primer*.

Commenting on the connection between literacy and religion during the 1800s, Graff (1991) observed that "one of the most common and important uses of

Figure 2.6. Illustrations for a Passage about a Minister Being Burned at the Stake from Three Different Editions of the *New England Primer*

literacy was in extending the moral bases of society" (p. 355). Though the connection between literacy and religion in the schools was not abandoned, the practice of using explicitly religious materials decreased during the 1800s. Writing toward the end of the 1800s, Martin observed that "early in the present century the catechism, the Psalter, and the Bible were almost universally displaced by the Spelling Book and the Reader" (1902, p. 99).

After citing passages from Horace Mann's twelfth report as Secretary of the Massachusetts State Board of Education, Wise (1964) called attention to the convincing arguments that Mann had made against the maintenance of sectarian religions in the public schools. Intending to combat sectarianism without diminishing the role of religion in education, Mann boasted that he had rekindled a resurgence of Bible reading in schools. Since Mann's narrow view of religion enabled him to classify the Bible as nonsectarian, he did not consider his support for the Bible to infringe on his public opposition to sectarian religions in public education. But Wise concluded that the rhetoric Mann directed against sectarianism, when combined with personal biases that enabled him to equate a general approach to Christianity with nonsectarianism, inadvertently led to a diminishment of religion in the schools. Wise summarized these changes, noting that "since [Mann] did not wish a denominational religion in his schools, and since the pluralistic approach did not occur to him, religion increasingly disappeared from the curriculum" (p. 378). One indication of the retirement of explicitly religious materials was the appearance of textbooks that taught "reading by object lessons" during the early part of the nineteenth century. Briggs and Coffman (1911) gave examples of object lesson readers that included an agricultural reading textbook published in 1824 and a historical reading textbook published in 1827.

Though series of reading materials had appeared during the initial half of the nineteenth century, none of the nineteenth-century reading series achieved the popularity of the six-volume edition of McGuffey readers that was published in 1850. Reeder (1900) wrote that "McGuffey's series has probably attained the largest sale and widest distribution of any series yet produced in America" and that "in range of subject–matter it swept almost the entire field of human inter-est—morals, economics, politics, literature, history, science and philosophy" (p. 51). Reeder applauded the practical value of the McGuffey readers and provided general advice to teachers about the need for reading instruction to be functional. He counseled that "rational progress in educational theories and methods is usually promoted by drawing on life's actual experiences outside the highly organized institution known as the school" (pp. 89-90).

Shaw (1904a) described a program in the Winnebago County, Illinois schools in which academic skills were integrated with information about agriculture in the learners' community. She wrote approvingly that "such work adds to the chil-dren's power to use their text-books" (p. 4892). She indicated that in addition to farming materials, the children maintained bookkeeping records and diaries recounting their agricultural experiences. With regard to the reading centers stocked with magazines that had been placed in her schools, she asked "where else will you find in a rural school a reading table whose magazines are bought by the district?" (p. 4893). Although Shaw applauded this community-based func-tional literacy program because of its "application of good sense to public educa-tion," she reminded her readers that such an application of common sense in the schools "is so rare as to seem a miracle when it is found" (pp. 4893-4894).

Remarks from a chapter titled *A Typical First Lesson* by Briggs and Coffman (1911) illustrated an approach to reading that emphasized relevant topics. Many teachers today might evaluate as progressive the approach they employed almost a century ago:

> Children will be trained in reading without the necessity of the teacher giving any extensive drills in pronouncing.... Some plans require the learning of eighty, others of two hundred words, before the children are allowed to do any actual reading. Such methods certainly can possess little intrinsic interest for the children.... It seems far better to have the class really *read* something the very first day...every sentence is accompanied by the suggested physical activity on the part of the child or teacher, but the children do not *pronounce* any of the words written on the board. The teacher speaks those she cannot act (Briggs & Coffman, 1911, pp. 51-52).

Changes in Attitudes During the Late 1800s

Though religious content was one of the factors contributing to the popular-ity of reading series during the 1800s, the identical feature could have been responsible for the rejection of those same series by a more secular society in the 1900s. In a classic study about the changes in the lives of college students, Sheldon (1901) wrote extensively about college religious customs, trends, and organizations. A strong proponent of religion who referred with sarcasm to the period during which he was writing as the "present enlightened age," Sheldon observed that religious customs had begun to be dismissed by college students as early as the 1880s when these were viewed as "superannuated survivals of medievalism." Although he predicted that a new generation of students would rediscover these discarded religious customs, he also admitted that an equally large number of students were "fast giving way" to "acute dislike [of religious customs]" (p. 285). Aware of the contradiction in these observations, Sheldon speculated philosophically that such contradiction "is one of the striking signs of the complexity of modern forces" (p. 286).

In his history of education in Massachusetts, Martin (1902) wrote of the shift from religious reading materials during the 1800s that "the importance of this change in the New England schools can not be overestimated" and that "its influence was deep and abiding" (p. 101). He wrote eloquently that "the showy scene-painting in the narratives of Scott for the simplicity of the gospel story of the life of Christ—such a substitution could not take place without modifying subtly but surely, all the life currents of the community" (pp. 101-102).

In his influential book on the changes in culture, politics, and attitudes at the beginning of the twentieth century, Sullivan (1927) identified prevalent attitudes that were shared by both religious and nonreligious segments of society. One of these attitudes was a civil libertarian belief that church and state should be separated. In the preface to Alder's textbook on moral instruction of children, Harris (1892) wrote that "the demand of the age to separate Church from State becomes more and more exacting" and that "religious instruction has almost entirely ceased in the public schools" (p. x).

Butts (1947) had also noted growing secularism in the last two decades of the 1800s. Although he attributed this change to factors such as industrialism and urbanization, he thought that the spread of secularism was also fanned by emerging scientific concepts associated with the theory of evolution. When combined with emerging secularism, this latter shared belief may have been sufficient to undermine the support for the McGuffey series and other religious readers. In his biography of Ella Flagg Young, who after the Civil War had taught for a half-century in the Chicago schools, McManis (1916) observed that "as an age of scientific interest and discovery, the period when Mrs. Young began to teach was unique" and that "the world was ablaze with controversy" because "Darwin had but recently published his treatise" (p. 33). Though McManis conceded that many educators provided little more than "lip serve to the new doctrines of science," he still discerned "attempts on the part of those in the schools to carry over to educational activities the questions raised by scientists" (p. 33). Childs (1931) was a prominent leader in the progressive education movement. He was influenced by the attributed connection of science to education. Pointing to the interaction between the theory of evolution and ideas about society that were developed by progressive intellectuals whom he referred to as "experimentalists," he wrote that "the theory of evolution as formulated by Darwin has made a profound contribution to the thought of the experimentalists" (pp. 14-15).

Functional Reading in the 1900s

Although she was not a teacher, Jane Adams (1897) wrote about the educational implications of her experiences with the Italian youths who resided near Hull House in Chicago. She warned of the dangers of Chicago's downtown area "whither the boy longs to go to sell papers and black boots; to attend theaters, and, if possible to stay all night, on the pretense of waiting for the early edition of the great dailies" (p. 108). Adams counseled educators that "if a boy is once thoroughly caught in these excitements, nothing can save him from overstimulation, and consequent debility and worthlessness, but a vigorous application of a compulsory education law" (p. 108). The compulsory education law that would be enforced would ensure that boys were placed in schools for which "the ultimate aim is to modify the character and conduct of the individual, and to harmonize and adjust his activities; that even the primary school should aim to give the child's own experience a social value" (p. 105).

Adams's opinions about the social goals for general schooling would be repeated by other educators who saw it as appropriate for literacy learning as well. Shaler (1904) was one of these educators. He explained that "the first aim of the common schools—that which gives them the name of common schools—is to give to the mass of the people a training which will serve the needs of citizenship." The following passage by Shaler (1904) about the common schools elaborated the minimal standards that were to be set in the "common school" curriculum:

> The essential object of a school system is to give all youths a sufficient amount of training to enable them to read and write and use the arithmetic which is required in common life, and a supplement to these simple things a clear idea of geography and of general history, with a special knowledge of that of his own country. To this it is desirable to add some acquaintance with the elements of natural science, as well as some training in signing. With this foundation the citizen is ready to continue his education by reading and observation, as he heeds do for all his life (pp. 174-175).

In a chapter on reading that he included in his book on social education, Scott (1908) had noted that "learning to read means the use of a language for the eye, and that the way in which a child learns the spoken language may throw some light on the way in which he can best acquire the written one" (p. 199). As he investigated the way in which spoken language was learned, Scott concluded that it "is primarily a social phenomenon" and that the motivation to read "is principally social, and that service gladly given and eagerly received is the mainspring of progress in learning to read" (p. 201).

Swift (1916) adjured educators that the schools "have a higher function than merely to teach the three R's" and that "one of the purposes of elementary and secondary education is to train children in such activities as will organize the mental processes so as to strengthen the social will" (p. 127). Swift recommended that these social objectives be achieved by organizing the school "on a social basis so that its activities will call out the responsibility of social relations" (p. 127).

Marietta Johnson (1931) was a progressive educator who wrote 15 years after Swift. She observed that "childhood is not a preparation for adult life" and that "the school must satisfy the interests of childhood" (p. 692). She even advocated that the use of books be delayed until children were eight or ten years old and that learners in the early elementary grades instead be occupied with "singing, dancing, hand work, nature, free play and stories."

The attitudes that Johnson defended in 1931 were very much like those that John Dewey had exhibited 40 years earlier and that were the foundation for his Chicago-based laboratory school. The psychological as well as the physical atmosphere of Dewey's school was indicated in a report that was published in the *University of Chicago Weekly* several days after Dewey's laboratory school had opened:

> The primary school connected with the pedagogical department of the University opened Monday morning with twelve children in attendance, and twice that number of parents and visitors. The building, No. 389 Fifty-seventh street, is a new house; has large windows, sunny rooms, and is surrounded by a playground. The work of the first morning began with a song, followed by a survey of the premises to test the knowledge of the children regarding the use of garden, kitchen etc., as well as their powers of observation. They were then seated at tables and provided with cardboard. At the end of the morning each child had completed a paper box for pencils and other materials. A story was told by one of the children and physical exercise concluded the program ("The Model School," 1896, p. 707).

Commenting specifically on reading education, Dewey (1898) himself had warned against approaches where "the child learns to read not for the sake of what he reads, but for the mere sake of reading" for "when the bare process of reading is thus made an end in itself, it is a psychological impossibility for reading to be other than lifeless" (p. 322).

Burstall (1909) described the "self-organized group work" approach that was "related to the Dewey movement and to industrial education" (p. 170). Explaining that this approach had been formally implemented in the Boston schools beginning in 1906, Burstall gave examples of learning activities in which "the class is formed into self-directive groups; the children determine what they shall study and how" (p. 169). She cautioned that in this program "the teacher must not assert authority: it is an example of the contrast between the kingdom of law and the kingdom of grace" (p. 170). She wrote with satisfaction that in spite of the seemingly confused situations in which the "self-organized group work method" was employed, "it is clear that this method saves time and effort, because the pupils really know and remember what they have worked up" (p. 169).

Like Burstall, Finley (1913) identified student interest as the key element in school learning. But Finley described a personalized approach to instruction that used blackboard work adapted for individual learners:

> The *human* interest, or the interest in people and what they are doing, is the *dominating interest* of the child and the one that *all children have in common.* One child will have wider experiences with animal life and in all the stories he reads about animals he is constantly interpreting from the standpoint of his human experience.... The teacher's best preparation for teaching the first steps in reading, therefore, will be to learn what experiences a child of six has had in his home.... When we start with the experiences of the child, the *vocabulary* should be so chosen as to prepare him to take up his first book (1913, pp. 1-2).

Finley summarized several initial reading lessons that exhibited a pedagogical structure that could be replicated. He was confident that teachers who modeled these lessons would be successful because they were based on a fundamental principle of effective instruction, the principle that "if *sufficiently interested* in the words and phrases [the learner] *will master them*" (p. 9).

Nila Banton Smith (1934) described the reading books that were popular from 1880 to 1918 as designed to develop "appreciation for and permanent interest in literature" (p. 185). In contrast to these earlier academic materials, she thought that school texts published from 1918 to 1924 had a progressively practical orientation. By 1925 she judged that the orientation of reading books had changed again and were aimed at preparing individuals for "well-rounded living." Social and functional goals within reading materials remained evident during the 1930s.

Stone (1937) thought totally literary readers had dominated the schools during the early part of the twentieth century but that the situation had changed to one with "a strong trend to make the reading content in the primary grades that of the social studies, and this trend is being felt in the intermediate grades also." Stone worried that this trend had been implemented to such an extent that the schools were in danger "of throwing overboard entirely literary selections in our enthusiasm for materials on the social studies" (p. 15).

William Gray (1939) documented the concerns of teachers about functional reading when he wrote about their "efforts to develop curriculums based on the needs of individuals in contemporary life" and their enthusiasm for materials that reflected "personal problems, home life, group living, social issues, vocational problems, and personal philosophy" (p. 7). Writing the following year, Durrell's (1940) view about the need for practical reading materials was apparent when he warned about "an overconcern on the part of the teacher about literary objectives" (p. 11). He thought that such an overemphasis could retard the development of lifelong reading habits, causing a negative backlash against an educational system that learners would perceive as coercing them to study literature. Durrell even suggested that "it is possible that 'good literature' may be acquired only by a selected minority, just as are delights in certain musical and artistic forms" (p. 11).

NINETEENTH-CENTURY CONTROVERSY ABOUT METHODS OF READING INSTRUCTION

The volume of professional writing about reading education during the late 1800s was impressive. By 1913 Charters was able to boast that the bibliography for reading education was larger than that for the other areas of education. Writing originally in 1886, Hall (1897) wrote that "how to teach children to read, and what they should read, are two of the oldest and most complicated, as well as most important problems of pedagogy" (p. 1). The size of the professional literature about approaches for teaching reading was in proportion to the amount of disagreement about the effectiveness of specific methods. For example, vitriolic debate between advocates and opponents of skills-based approaches was discernible throughout the 1800s. Discussing models of teaching in a passage first published in 1847, Page had warned of the "pouring-in" approach in which teachers identified key information and then forced this information into students:

> It is as if he should provide himself with a basket of sweetmeats, and every time [the teacher] should come within reach of a child, should seize him and compel him to swallow—regardless of the condition of his stomach—whatever trash he should happen first to force into his mouth.... How many teachers are just such misguided caterers for the mind. They are ready to seize upon the *victims* of their kindness, force open their mental gullets, and pour in, without mercy and without discretion, whatever sweet thing they may have at hand, even though they surfeit and nauseate the poor sufferer (1885, pp. 108-109).

In his famous book, *Recollections of a New England Educator*, Mowry (1908) described his career during the latter part of the 1800s when the "A-B-C method" was being supplanted by modern methods "called the word method, the sentence method, the thought method and several phonetic systems" (p. 20). When Mowry became superintendent of a Massachusetts school district in 1891, he required all 12 elementary schools in that district adopt the "thought method." However, he was disappointed that the holistic approach he supported needed to be used in conjunction with skills-based reading textbooks because "the Board had already furnished to the schools six primary readers" (p. 201).

Multiple records described the reading approaches that were used during the nineteenth century. Paul Passy was a French traveler who provided a detailed account of the holistic word method's implementation in the United Sates during the early 1880s:

> Here is how our instructor teaches the word method. She draws a cat on the blackboard; then she asks the students what it is. "A Cat," they say. Then the instructor writes the word *cat* under it. She pronounces it and has the students repeat. Then she tells them about cats—their nature, their habits—from time to time adding one or two words to the blackboard.... The next day they begin with a dog. When the students know enough words and small phrases, it is possible to put a book in their hands. They will almost always read it without stopping (Passy, quoted by Finkelstein, 1989, p. 295).

Finkelstein (1989) documented the recollections of a nineteenth-century student who described the use of sand tablets to learn the alphabet:

> The primary class was called the "sand class." This had white sand spread out on edges to keep from spilling on the floor; and on this economical sort of stationary...the least advanced scholars exercised their intellectual and artistic powers, learning at the same time, how to name and draw the letters of the alphabet (anonymous, quoted by Finkelstein, p. 43).

Recounting the history of reading education in 1886, Hall described the conflicts among educators about the different methods. He pragmatically noted that no single method by itself could be the optimal approach because if a child "is especially apt in the use of the hand, he learns to read largely by its agency; if chiefly visually-minded, through the eye" (1897, p. 9). Having reviewed several disparate approaches, he argued reassuringly that no strategies "which a tactful teacher knows well can fail to help her and her pupils" (p. 16). He discouraged teachers from attempting to select a single method from the many that were available because "if the proportions of the different partial methods are duly adjusted, all doors are knocked at, and all parts of the mind working consistently" (p. 9). Citing Huey, Hall noted five approaches to reading instruction as well as "combination methods." He especially applauded the eclectic approaches because "the true teacher will not entirely neglect any of these methods." In a later work, he deplored both educators and publishers who had laid "absurd stress" upon petty variations of the different instructional approaches and materials, scolding that "primary reading should no longer be made a fetich" (1911b, p. 417).

Possibly more than any other city, Chicago was famous as the site where many progressive instructional innovations had been implemented. DeWeese (1902) wrote that "for three years past the eyes of the educational world have been upon Chicago" and that "it is doubtful indeed if any city on the continent has made such marked progress in two years toward the realization of those aims that are regarded by advanced educators as essential to efficient school administration, and to the attainment of the highest standards in popular education" (p. 325). Although Dewey's experimental school contributed to the innovative practices that were being implemented in Chicago, innovative practices were not confined to his school. Rice (1893) observed the multiple methods that were used to teach reading in the elementary schools of Chicago during the early 1890s, a period well before Dewey had initiated his school in January of 1896. He noted that "the methods employed in teaching reading vary in the different schools" and that "in some instances the pupils are taught by the word method, in others by the sentence method, and in still others by a variety of methods, including phonics and word-building" (p. 202). In her history of Chicago, Pierce (1957) wrote that a considerable improvement over the purely *memoriter* form of learning was especially noticeable during the 1880s, reading in particular, by the fourth grade being pointed beyond the mere ability to read to "a nicer discrimination in the use of words" (p. 384). She observed that "the abandonment of old-time procedures was recommended" and that in the grammar grades the aims of instruction were focused on "the application of the knowledge, the facts acquired, to the business of life" (p. 385).

Charters (1913) discerned five established approaches to the teaching of reading: the alphabet method, the word method, the phonic method, the natural method, and the sentence method. One of the approaches to which Charters had referred was the "sentence method." Luke (1931) documented that multiple educators in Europe had advocated the sentence method as early as the 1700s. Even though Hall had written in 1886 that he personally supported drilling, he also noted that most teachers "now assume that knowledge should always precede practice" (1897, p. 14). Hall attributed this consensus among teachers to a belief that "children love wholes and.... abhor elements, details, abstractions" and that "they find, at least in the vernacular, sentences easier than words" (p. 14). McKee (1934) indicated that the sentence method was used frequently in the United States after 1890. Schmidt (1929) described an instructional procedure that was characteristic of the sentence method:

> The teacher begins by engaging the children in an interesting conversation, asking questions about some object and letting them answer. When a thought basis has thus been established, she writes a child's statement on the board, tells the class what she has written, and lets them "read" it. She writes another sentence and they "read" that also. Other sentences are added that involve changes of a word here and a word there, and thus the pupils are led to identify the individual words (p. 152).

Although Charters had simply referred to approaches that were based on children's oral language as the *sentence method*, Schmidt (1929) differentiated this from the *story method*, in which an entire passage was elicited and then used as the opportunity for instruction. He thought this latter approach could "avoid the insipid, disconnected type of subject matter that characterizes the sentence-method reading material" (p. 153).

The emerging attitudes of educators were resolved in their focus upon the linguistic abilities, cognitive aptitudes, and personal experiences that children brought to the learning process. In the late nineteenth century, Hinsdale (1896) wrote about the nonacademic foundation for the language-based learning such as that involved in the sentence method:

> We must keep clearly in mind the preparation to read that the child who has never looked into a book brings to school. First, he has a certain store of facts, ideas, and images gained by observation, reflection, and conservation, which serves to interpret to him, through the process called apperception, the new facts and ideas of the printed page—the extent and nature of this preparation depending upon the quickness of his mind, the character of his environment, natural and social, and particularly upon the cultivation of his home. Secondly, he has at command a certain store of oral language by which he both receives and conveys ideas, which

preparation is also relative in both quantity and quality, being determined by the activity of his mind and the speech that he is accustomed to hear (p. 86).

Also writing in the nineteenth century, Eliot (1898) had advised teachers to expose learners to a wide range of literature during reading instruction. In a lecture about *The Grammar School of the Future*, he encouraged teachers to "realize that every subject needs to be illustrated, for both teacher and pupil, by many and various books" (p. 304). Like Eliot, McMurry (1903a) advised teachers to expand instruction beyond the limits of a single reading textbook. He sponsored an approach which he labeled "primary reading through incidental exercises and games." He gave numerous examples of opportunities to develop reading skills "offered by the other studies, by school movements and games in primary classes" (p. 137). He wrote enthusiastically about the rationale for incidental literacy activities and the general structure with which these were to be implemented:

> It is assumed that the more closely the written or printed words and sentences are related to the children's activities, or the more dependent these activities are made upon a knowledge of the word-forms, the quicker and more natural will be their mastery. To put it briefly, the teacher abstains from the use of oral speech to a considerable extent and substitutes the written forms of the words on the blackboards in giving directions, in games, and in treating topics in literature and science (McMurry, 1903a, p. 137).

With regard to his suggestion that play be used as a technique for learning to read, McMurry acknowledged that some teachers in single-room schoolhouses had objected that the games were "too noisy and attract the attention of the children who are busy at their seats." Undeterred by this criticism, he responded that "often it would be a good thing for these children to watch the younger ones at their games" because "it would rest them and put them into closer sympathy with the little ones" (p. 143). He assured his readers that "it is our purpose, so far as possible, to make use of this natural bent of the child to insure interest in his reading, as well as to give him the free exercise, which he needs, of his muscles" (p. 143).

Rice (1893) was a proponent of language-based strategies who did not conceal his negative biases against phonics when he described the instruction in a Chicago elementary school during the early 1890s:

> The teacher made an attempt to teach phonics, but while the pupils had learned the sounds of the letters they did not possess much power to combine them, so that after sounding all the letters in a word they frequently remained unable to name the word. When the pupils began a new lesson they pronounced all the words in the column placed at the top of the lesson before going to the text. In pronouncing these words each child was obliged to go through a set formula, thus: "That word is 'moon,'" "That word is 'dark,'" etc. When a pupil simply named a word without repeating the formula, "That word is," the teacher said "Well, tell me so," whereupon the child would say, "That word is 'mice,'" or whatever it happened to be (p. 203).

Publishing pedagogical histories respectively in 1900 and 1908, Reeder and Huey were both especially attentive to the emergence of phonics instruction in their accounts of reading materials and instruction throughout the 1800s. Reeder (1900) noted that "the phonics plan spells words by the succession of sounds instead of by letters" (p. 80). Although he lacked confidence in it, he still acknowledged that "the strength of the phonic method lay in the independent power it gave to the child in mastering new words" (p. 80). Reeder's admission was echoed less than a decade later by Huey, who also conceded that "if the child is able to successively reproduce the sounds of the letters as they stand in a word, he can learn for himself to pronounce new words as they appear" (1968, p. 260). Francis Parker was a nineteenth-century opponent of phonics who, like Reeder and Huey, still admitted that its goal had been "developing the power of associating, independently, the sounds of words with the letters, and by this means gaining independent recognition of words" (1937, p. 162).

Parker, Reeder, and Huey were influential educators who agreed that phonics approaches, if used at all, should have only restricted applications. They thought that the poor correlation between the sounds of words in English and the spellings of those words justified such restrictions. Reeder and Huey both described the nineteenth-century creation of alternative alphabets. Through the addition of special characters and the elimination of silent letters, these alphabets were used to create phonetically consistent passages that facilitated learners' verbalization of the words in those passages. Balmuth (1982) indicated that the most successful alternative alphabet had been the *Pronouncing Orthography* developed by Edwin Leigh in 1864, a system in which original spellings were preserved but subtle variations in letters provided cues to variations in pronunciation. For example, silent letters were retained but printed in fonts that were thinner than those used for the letters to be pronounced.

Reeder and Huey classified alternative alphabets as strategies with which to create materials for programs that they referred to as *phonetic*. They viewed the phonetic alphabets as desperate responses by frustrated educators who had refused to admit the hazards posed by the inconsistency between the spellings and pronunciations of English words. Reeder questioned whether students would later generalize those skills that they had developed with eccentric phonetic materials to passages that contained words with standard spellings. Reeder also wrote that he had withheld his support for phonetic educational materials because he believed that "English must be learned and read as it is from the start, consistencies and inconsistencies included" (1900, p. 72).

Highlighting the similarity between the sounds of letters and sounds in nature was a component of several phonics approaches popular during the late 1800s and early 1900s. Reeder (1900) reviewed the *Pollard Synthetic Sound System*, noting that "no theory has ever had more ardent supporters or been promulgated by more zealous advocates" (p. 83). In this approach, "an effort is made to have the child discover these sounds in nature—in the bleating of the lamb, a, the puff of the

2 And both Jesus was called, and his disci'-
ples, to the marriage.

3 And when they wanted wine, the mother
of Jesus saith unto him, They have no wine.

4 Jesus saith unto her, Woman, what have
I to do with thee? mine hour is not yet come.

5 His mother saith unto the servants, What-
soev'er he saith unto you, do it.

6 And thare were set thare six waterpots of
stone, after the manner of the purifying of
the Jews, contain ing two or three firkins
apiece'.

7 Jesus saith unto them, 'Fill the waterpots with water. And thay filled them up to
the brim.

8 And he saith unto them, Draw out now,
and bear unto the governor of the feast.
And thay bare it.

Figure 2.7. An Illustration of the Phonetic Approach to Reading from
a Textbook used During the early 1870s

steam-boat, p, the kitty's hiss, f, the growl of the dog, r" (p. 83). Writing 26 years
later, Klapper (1926) was less complimentary than Reeder in his description of
the Pollard method:

> In Pollard's Synthetic Method of Reading and Spelling, one finds a scheme that is purely pho-
> netic, "almost arrogantly so." The mechanical mastery of words; the constant use of diacritical
> marks; the use of sound games and phonics pictures, (*f* is the symbol of cats at war, *sh* of a child
> being put to sleep); the personification of the letters (some letters are boys, while capitals are
> men, etc.); all these are typical of the archaic devices and organization to which this method
> has constant recourse (pp. 63-64).

As an indication of the popularity of reading approaches that emphasized
sounds in nature, both Huey (1968) and Reeder (1900) identified several

Wuns, Rip Van Win'-kl went up
a-mung' the hilz, hwār hî sē
cwîr lit'-l men plê'-ing bēl.
The gêv Rip sum -thing tū drink,
hwich put him tū slîp.
Hî slept twen'-ti yîrz, and hwen hî wōk up
hî wez an ōld man with grê hāɪ and bîrd.
Hî went hōm.   Nō wun niū him at ferst.
Hî wez tōld hwet had hap'-nd
hwail hî wez a-slîp' a-mung' the hilz.

Figure 2.8.   An Illustration of the Scientific Alphabet, a Phonetic
Approach to Reading Used During the Early 1900s

programs that relied on this strategy. In 1913 Finley still recommended that the association of letter sounds with sounds in nature be established through individualized blackboard work comprising stories with the distinctive vocabulary and experiences of the learners. (Examples of sounds in nature that Finley highlighted included *t*—the sound of a watch, *m*—the sound of a telegraph wire, and *h*—a tired dog panting.)

Figures 2.7 through 2.11 illustrate some of the types of reading materials that were used during the late 1800s and early 1900s. Figure 2.7 is a page from a reading methods book from the 1870s. Figures 2.8 and 2.9 are pages from reading materials used in the early 1900s. The book from which Figure 2.9 was extracted also encouraged picture reading, a technique that integrated pictures with printed text. Figure 2.10 illustrates a picture reading unit and Figure 2.11 is an example of picture reading applied to early twentieth-century materials about the Bible.

ECLECTIC APPROACHES

Although remedial reading activities were not evident until the twentieth century, educators were certainly aware that no single approach to instruction would universally teach all children to read. Rather than propose supplementary activities

1. Once upon a tim¢ there were two little dogs. They were nām¢d Jippỹ and Jimmỹ. They lĭv¢d in a lŭmber yard. It was nẽảr the rĭver by a dŏck.

2. The mother of the puppĭ¢s was an Īrish sĕtter. She was kĕpt in the yard, be eạu̶s¢ ẞhe was a good watch-dog. She was chặỉn¢d to her kĕnn¢l. This was a home for her and her children.

3. The puppĭ¢s play¢d clōs¢ by. They never thôu̶ḡht of running a way. They had never seen any thing but lŭmber. They did not ƙnow̶ there was any thing ĕls¢ to see.

Figure 2.9. A Page from a Phonetic Reading Textbook in Which Special Markings Were Introduced to Facilitate Pronunciation of Unfamiliar Words

and materials to remedy the limitations in any specific approach, educators attempted to make up for the deficiencies in one approach by combining it with a complementary reading program. Though these types of procedures became increasingly popular toward the end of the nineteenth century, they were discernible in the beginning of the 1800s. For example, Briggs and Coffman (1911) described the early nineteenth-century Grafer approach in which writing and reading were integrated so that the manual exercise in writing could reinforce the learning that had transpired during the reading portions of lessons.

Eclectic instruction like that modeled in the Grafer approach eventually became so popular that it was incorporated into textbooks. The 1836 edition of the McGuffey readers encouraged learners to use several types of strategies, including word attack skills and context, to decipher the meaning of unfamiliar vocabulary. By the time the 1879 edition was published, teachers were being explicitly directed to use eclectic instructional strategies. For example, advice in the 1879 edition indicated that the most effective sequence for combining instructional strategies was "first teaching the words in each lesson *as words*; then, the elementary sounds, the names of the letters, and spelling" (instructions to teachers in a McGuffey reader, quoted by Fries, 1963, p. 21). Like the McGuffey readers, the *New American Readers* published by Sargent and May in 1871 were eclectic. The authors described the series as possessing "all the advantages of the word method, the Phonic System, the A B C Method, and Objective-Teaching" (quoted by

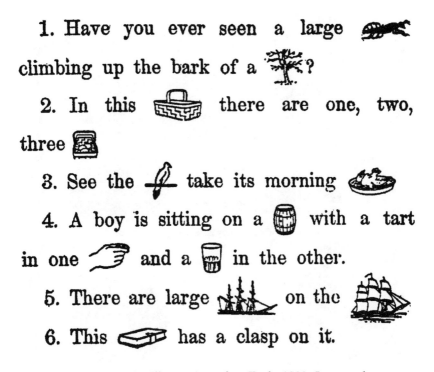

Figure 2.10. An Illustration of an Early 1900s Lesson that Integrated Print with Pictures

Nietz, 1961, p. 91). The objective-teaching approach to which Sargent and May referred involved the reading of functional passages, such as those concerned with agriculture or history.

The founder of the *International Phonetics Society*, Paul Passy had reported in 1882 that both phonic approaches and whole word approaches were being implemented in schools. Despite his personal commitment to phonics, Passy recognized the special opportunities for learning afforded by the whole word method. After describing these benefits, he noted that "whatever the advantages of the word method, it is most often combined with the phonic method" and that "this mixed method can be used without much difficulty and one can learn the words when the orthography doesn't conform to the pronunciation" (Passy quoted by Finkelstein, 1989, pp. 295-296). Writing in 1886, White recommended a mixed approach to initial reading instruction that included three stages. Though children were taught to recognize words holistically in the initial stage, a period of instruction with the sentence method followed, and both the phonics and the alphabetic method were incorporated into the final stage. The approach recommended by

Figure 2.11. Picture Reading Lesson from Early Twentieth-Century Reading Materials about the Bible

White had similar features to the popular *rational method*, which incorporated activities from the whole word, phonic, and sentence methods.

In the teacher's manual that accompanied a popular set of reading textbooks, Todd and Powell (1899) gave precise instructions about using phonetically grouped words to teach the sounds of short and long vowels. However, they thought that integrated activities could enable teachers to ensure that "the children's language lessons and reading lesson are on the same subject" (p. 67). Consequently, they also provided advice for holistic, language-based activities that were linked to the pictures in basal reading series:

> Obtain the subject of the picture from the pupils and write it on the board. Have pupils tell what they see. Write one of the sentences given. Have pupils read it. Erase. Write the new words. Erase, and have pupils write the words from memory. Write the sentence again and have pupils read it. Continue the work by having the children (*a*) see, (*b*) say, (*c*) write, (*d*) read. After the whole description is written have it read as a unit. Erase, and send pupils to the board to write the description. In a following lesson the children may be led to tell the story suggested by the picture. Read the book lesson (Todd & Powell, 1899, p. 66).

Hughes (1912), who had defined four "fundamental laws" for teaching reading, was more reluctant than some of his fellow educators to excoriate phonics. Two of his laws were holistic, encouraging teachers to develop reading through independent activities and reliance on learners' interests. But the other two laws reflected skills-based philosophies, encouraging teachers to employ repetition and to "overcome a related sequence of well graded difficulties" (p. 30). Although he identified five approaches to reading (the whole word, alphabet, phonic, phonetic, and sentence methods), Hughes insisted that "it matters not how the child has been taught" (p. 52). Despite his alleged indifference to the five approaches, he admired phonics because after a student "has learned to recognize new words independently he has in some way gained the power of automatically associating the letter forms with the various positions of the vocal organs in producing oral language" (pp. 52-53). But Hughes incorporated language-based as well as skills-based activities into his instructional approach. For example, he encouraged teachers to build lessons on students' interests while simultaneously establishing a structured set of skills that the students would master. Instead of designating a monolithic set of reading materials that embodied a single approach to instruction, he counseled that "it was wise to have as great a variety of good primers as possible" (p. 123). He also encouraged teachers to use fairy tales, folk stories, myths, and nursery rhymes as part of instruction. However, he pursued this recommendation one step further, advising that the best reading materials were home-made transcriptions of students' own language that could in turn supplement a diverse collection of basal readers.

Kendall and Mirick (1915) decried an overemphasis on memorizing letters of the alphabet and the spelling of disconnected words by students who were forced to stand with "copper-toed shoes ranged along the guide-line of a convenient crack in the schoolroom floor" (p. 11). They noted that it was appropriate to use phonics, but in ways that avoided the "evil of mechanical repetition" (p. 15). In a similarly reconciliatory tone, McFee (1918) adjured disputing educators that "it does not matter whether the phonic, word, synthetic, or other method is used—all have been known to produce excellent results, if only interest is kept at a white heat" (p. 67). In the introduction to a textbook on reading published in the early 1920s, the editor advised readers that teachers who had split into "warring camps" about the value of phonics were "about to swing back again, not to any old extreme, but to the position, important but subordinate, which phonics ought to have in the teaching of reading in the first two or three years of school life" (Dougherty, 1923, pp. vi-vii).

The editor listed seven reasons why phonics should be incorporated into reading instruction, the most convincing of which may have been that "it becomes a matter of economy to the child, and to the teacher as well, to cease memorizing the sound of sight words, for this must be done steadily and carefully in the presence of the teacher, and to begin to discover for himself a way to get the correct pronunciations of the print before him" (Dougherty, 1923, p. ix). In the book from which the preceding introductory remarks were extracted, Dougherty recommended phonics while she simultaneously assured her readers that it should be taught "as a means, not as an end" (p. 3).

Nila Banton Smith (1934) described the *Story Hour Readers*, a set of reading books that were used widely in the early 1900s. The authors of these readers recommended that teachers use a five-stage approach for instruction: storytelling, dramatization, blackboard recording of children's language, analysis of blackboard recordings, and reading from the book. In the fourth stage, analysis of blackboard transcripts of language, teachers encouraged learners to examine the oral language transcriptions in increasingly more refined detail. Smith indicated that this multistage approach, in which students progressed from thought groups to sentences, phrases, sight words, and finally phonetics, was typical of other reading programs. Klapper (1926) had also admired the eclectic features of the *Story Hour Readers*:

> The books that are put into the hands of the children are artistic in illustration and design, and offer literary content more varied than in the average reading system. The progress that is made is rapid, but graded so that each step gives the child a thorough foundation on which he builds growing knowledge and increasing power. The method owes much of its effectiveness to its skillful inclusion of the worth-while principles and devices of the best systems of primary reading, and to its rational balance between the literary and the mechanical elements that make up a reading method for the introductory school years (p. 100).

DISPUTES AMONG ZEALOTS

Although the persons who adjured teachers to use strategies eclectically may not have exhibited an ardent partisanship to any specific approach, zealous advocates for approaches that they thought should be used exclusively were also evident during the early 1900s. Huey believed that learners should rely on context skills when they encountered words with which they were unfamiliar. He warned against the use of phonics as a reading strategy because "it is simply obstructive of habits of natural reading and speaking to interrupt the reading with thoughts of letter sounds" (1968, p. 351). He recommended that the phonic analysis of any word in a passage be taught "before the reading is attempted, and with the word in isolation, so that the child will not come to think of such learning as 'reading'" (p. 351). Huey's advice was similar to that of Finley (1913), who thought that phonics "should be used as a LAST RESORT only" because the holistic recognition of words in semantic contexts was "the right habit of self helpfulness" (p. 16). Finley also advocated the development of syntactic contextual skills through word cards that would be manipulated to "build sentences on the floor" (p. 13).

Mathews (1966) chronicled the disputes between advocates of the alphabet and whole word approaches in his report about educational arguments from the 1820s through the 1960s. He noted that the alphabet approach, which had been the only approach to reading instruction prior to the 1800s, continued as the most popular approach to reading instruction for most of the early nineteenth century. In his history of education in Pennsylvania, Wickersham (1886) paraphrased a passage from a treatise on teaching that was completed by Christopher Dock in 1750. In that manuscript, Dock had written about the alphabet method that "the A–B–C's were taught by requiring the pupil to name them in order after the teacher and by himself, but he was also required to point them out and name them miscellaneously" (Dock, quoted by Wickersham, 1886, p. 223). Wickersham added that "as an exercise in Spelling the pupil named the letters and the teacher pronounced the words, and then the process was reversed, the teacher naming the letters and the pupil pronouncing the words" (p. 223).

In a book published originally in 1893, Hale (1927) stated that he had only limited recollections about learning to read with the alphabet method after he entered a Boston school in 1824, when he was two years old. But he did remember that "there was a little spelling-book called 'The New York Spelling-Book,'" and that some of the additional reading books he used included "Mrs. Barbauld's 'First Lessons,'" "Come hither, Charles, come to mamma,"; and "'Popular Lessons,' by Miss Robbins" (p. 10).

Peabody (1836) provided detailed recollections of a teacher in Boston who used the alphabet method to teach reading and writing during this same period. She described how the kindly teacher would examine the initially unintelligible attempts to reproduce letters while "betraying no misgivings as to the want of resemblance" but rather "took the writing for what it was meant to be; knowing that practice would at once mend the eye and hand; but that criticism would check the desirable courage and self-confidence" (p. 6). Peabody speculated about the reasons why this method was so effective:

> Reading and writing are begun simultaneously; and the former will be very much facilitated, and the latter come to perfection in a much shorter time than by the usual mode. By copying print, which does not require such a sweep of hand as the script character, a clear

image of each letter is gradually fixed in the mind; and while the graceful curves of the script are not attained till afterward, yet they are attained quite as early as by the common method of beginning with them; and the clearness and distinctness of print, is retained in the script, which, from being left to form itself so freely, becomes also characteristic of each individual's particular mind (1836, pp. 5-6).

Writing about rural education in the Middle West during the late 1800s, Fuller (1982) also provided reminiscences of persons who had learned to read with the alphabet method:

> Reading, of course, was the first subject they learned, and not all of them remembered how they learned it. Those who did explained that their teachers had first taught them the ABC's, then tried to show them how these letters were combined into words. It was a laborious process, requiring much self-discipline, for although textbooks offering the phonic and sight methods of teaching reading had been published as early as 1878, they remembered that they had to combined letters into words without reference to the sound of letters. Only those fortunate enough to have *McGuffey's Pictorial Eclectic Primer*, which contained pictures representing each letter, *a* for ax, for example, might learn to associate a letter with a sound (p. 11).

Though many authors expressed their admiration for the alphabet method, critics were apparent as well. Martin (1902) wrote unsympathetically about the schoolmaster-dominated system of education with which the alphabet approach was associated that "the schoolmaster is impaled upon the pen of every satirist; the trident is not more inseparable from the conception of Neptune in art, nor the organ form the pictures of Saint Cecilia, than is the rod from the portrait of the schoolmaster" (p. 239). Though Thompson (1853) had written a half-century earlier about a kindly teacher who the students held in reverence, even he still had added that the students wished to "gain his approbation" not only because of his positive qualities but also "doubtless, from the belief they still entertained, that his displeasure would be attended with fretful consequences to themselves" (p. 86).

In a novel written originally in 1871, Eggleston (1889) wrote about the alphabet method. Though Eggleston indicated in the preface that the work was not biographical, he still considered it to be the "result of the experience and observation of the writer." He did not disguise his disapproval of this approach:

> There is one branch diligently taught in a backwards school. The public mind seems impressed with the difficulties of English orthography, and there is a solemn conviction that the chief end of man is to learn to spell.... It often happens that the pupil does not know the meaning of a single word in the lesson. That is of no consequence. What do you want to know the meaning of a word for? Words were made to be spelled, and men were created that they might spell them. Hence the necessity for sending a pupil through the spelling-book five times before you allow him to begin to read, or indeed to do anything else (Eggleston, 1889, pp. 24-25).

Writing about the frequency with which the *New England Primer* had been used as a reading textbook in North Carolina prior to the Civil War, Knight (1916) reported that this book had contained pictures accompanied by jingles, "which was a very old method of teaching the alphabet" and that "the jingles were doubt-less thought to lend themselves to teaching certain religious beliefs" (p. 195). Knight wrote that spelling books were used extensively throughout North Carolina to teach reading because "spelling-books during the *ante-bellum* period were not intended primarily for the purpose of teaching spelling, but served the three-fold purpose of spellers, readers, and moral instructors" (p. 1940). Describing the unsuitable classroom procedures with which the alphabet method was employed, Knight cited an 1850 document in which an unidentified author wrote that "the method of teaching was extremely primitive; to look on the book and make a decent droning noise of any kind, not out of the common key, would insure immunity from the all-potent rod, while this habit of noise, pleasant as it is as a reminis-cence, because it was the music of our early years, was anything else than an advantage to those who really wished to bend their minds to study" (anonymous, quoted by Knight, 1916, p. 152).

Late nineteenth-century educators agreed about the universality of the alphabet method during the early 1800s and its remarkable longevity throughout the nineteenth century. At the beginning of the twentieth century Reeder (1900) wrote that "from the earliest period of modern development...until within quite recent times, the alphabet or spelling method has been almost universally employed" (pp. 62-63). Reeder's negative biases were revealed in his description of a set of lessons taught with the alphabet method:

> When the alphabet was learned, two-letter syllables were taken up and learned by spelling, then three-letter syllables, like bla, cla, fla, etc., and monosyllabic words. Several of the first pages of the old spelling books were filled with such nonsense columns. It was assumed that there was a necessary connection between naming the letters of a word and pronouncing the word. No other approach to the pronunciation of the printed symbol was imagined by the great majority of teachers. So universal was this opinion that it passed into proverb: "You must spell before you can read," expressed the idea of inexorable sequence. In every school, children might be seen at all hours of the session laboriously working through the words of the reading or spelling lesson, letter by letter, whispering each letter in turn. The spelling habit once learned, remained with the pupil for many years (1900, p. 6).

In a book published originally in 1833 about schools during the first quarter of the nineteenth century, Burton (1929) described his personal experience learning to read with the alphabet method at a school he began to attend in 1804, when he was only three and a half years old:

> My first business was to master the A B C, and no small achievement it was; for many a little learner waddles to school through the summer, and wallows to the same through the winter, before he accomplishes it, if he happens to be taught in the manner of former times. This might have been my lot, had it not been for Mary Smith. Few of the better methods of teaching, which now make the road to knowledge so much more easy and pleasant, had then found their way out of, or into the brain of the pedagogical vocation. Mary went on in the old way indeed; but the whole exercise was done with such sweetness on her part, that the dilatory and usually

unpleasant task was to me a pleasure, and by the close of that summer, the alphabet was securely my own (p. 9).

Burton wrote of a prevalent custom in which the teachers of this period presented books to students. He described this practice in a chapter with the title "Little Books Presented the Last Day of the School":

> The next summer, my present was the "Death and Burial of Cock Robin." I could then do something more than look at the pictures. I could read the tragic history which was told in verse below the pictured representations of the mournful drama. How I used to gaze and wonder at what I saw in that little book! Could it be that all this really took place; that the sparrow really did do the murderous deed with his bow and his arrow? I never knew before that birds had such things.... I went on puzzled and wondering, till progressive reason at length divined its meanings.... I had a similar present each successive season, so long as I regularly attended the summer school. What marvels did they contain! How curiosity and wonder feasted on their contents! They were mostly about giants, fairies, witches, and ghosts (Burton, 1929, p. 31).

Burton concluded a chapter about reading instruction with the following parenthetic remarks:

> It ought not to be omitted, that the Bible, particularly the New Testament, was the reading twice a day, generally, for all the classes adequate to words of more than one syllable. It was the only reading of several of the younger classes under some teachers. On this practice I shall make but a single remark. As far as my own experience and observation extended, reverence for the sacred volume was not deepened by this constant but exceedingly careless use (p. 55).

Writing about education in England in a book published originally in 1892, Sharpless (1902) observed that "the schools are divided into 'infant schools' and 'schools for older scholars'" and that "the division takes place nominally at the age of 7, though it is a matter of advancement rather than of age" (p. 30). Sharpless noted that the children in infant school, many of whom were not yet three years old, "could read, such as I saw, with considerable fluency easy sentences" (p. 30). Making observations about reading instruction in Great Britain more than 30 years after Sharpless, Winch (1925) noted that teachers were using phonic, syllable, and look-and-say methods. But he also noted the continued use of the alphabet method, though it had "suffered an eclipse in infants' departments during the last fifteen or twenty years." But Winch added that "teachers of senior schools maintain [the alphabet method] almost universally" (p. 59). Winch's pragmatic advice for helping teachers select a reading method was evident in the following passage:

> Whatever method is to be employed, it must satisfy two practical conditions...it must be a method usable by teachers under ordinary school conditions...and it must be suitable to the mental development, or lack of development, of the children with whom it is to be employed. An alphabetic–syllabic–spelling method does satisfy these practical conditions.... In my judgment, however, there is little ground for the wholesale overthrow of the alphabetic method, except of course, change of fashion—which I do not deny is a most potent force, perhaps as potent in education as in dress (1925, p. 59).

After examining the reading pedagogy that had developed during the nineteenth century in reaction to the alphabet method, Reeder (1900) questioned whether fundamental philosophical principles had influenced these developments. A proponent of language-based approaches to reading education, he concluded that "the development of method in English reading has sprung from two main sources—the one having its origin in the inherent peculiarities of English notation, the other in the psychology of the process of learning to read" (p. 70). One of the influences on methods of teaching reading identified by Reeder was the inconsistency with which phonic principles could be applied to written English. This inconsistency spurred the transformation of phonic programs into "phonetic" programs that employed expedient alphabets. Although some of these temporary, learning alphabets were quite complex, a set of phonetic reading books published in 1894 by Silver, Burdett & Company used simple diacritical marks to indicate the pronunciation of words. For example, horizontal lines over letters indicated long vowels and slashes through letters indicated silent letters (N. Smith, 1934). The use of alternative alphabets enabled proponents of phonics approaches to empower students so that they could read any type of material rather than only those in which words exhibited consistent phonic patterns. Still, critics such as Reeder saw practical disadvantages to the materials in phonetic programs because "the necessity for using peculiarly printed books, and the variation given to the word form, making them more or less trying to the eyes, were obstacles which were not overcome by the advantages claimed for the system" (p. 82).

The other factor contributing to the emergence of alternative reading materials was a "wholeness theory" which postulated that since the final act of reading was a unitary process, pedagogy should be based on a progression from wholes to parts. The whole word method had been the initial manifestation of the wholeness theory. However, not all educators were enamored of the whole word method. In his autobiography Sheldon (1911) described his personally distressing experiences as a student learning to read with the whole word method during the early 1800s:

> Every child, old or young, had for his stock reading the old English reader. There was little in it that I understood, but I had gone over it so many times, having the words pronounced for me and hearing others pronounce them, that I had learned everything by heart; and being of the opinion that the one that read the fastest was the best reader, I used to rattle it off as fast as I could make my tongue go. Not understanding the meaning of anything I read, and having caught wrong pronunciation from hearing others read, I discovered, later in life, that I had made some very ridiculous mistakes. One I remember, in a quotation from the Bible which reads, "Is thy servant a dog that he should do this thing?"—but which I always read at school, "Is thy servant *bedaubed* that he should do this thing?" This I suppose I must have read, or more properly recited, so rapidly, that the teacher never discovered the mistake. I do not remember to have been directly taught anything or to have received criticism on anything (p. 25).

The wholeness theory on which the whole word method of reading instruction depended was embraced by educators who believed sentences and stories to be the optimal starting point for reading instruction. In his textbook on the sentence method that had been first published in 1881, Farnham (1895) identified an explicit connection between instruction and a philosophical proposition about wholeness:

> The first principle to be observed in teaching written language is that "things are recognized as wholes." Language follows this law. Although it is taught by an indirect process, still, in its external characteristics, it follows the law of other objects.... The sentence...will be understood as a whole, better than if presented in detail.... A second principle is, we acquire a knowledge of the *parts* of an object by first considering it as a whole.... That words are no exception to this rule is obvious from the almost universal practice of writing out the word and looking at it as a *whole* to determine whether it is properly spelled.... The sentence, when properly taught, will, in like manner, be understood as a whole, better than if presented in detail.... The third principle is that while language, oral or written, follows the laws of other objects so far as its material characteristics are concerned, it differs from other objects studied for their own sake. While it is to be recognized, it must be so recognized as to make the thoughts expressed by it the conscious object of attention.... In oral speech this is already the case. The written language is to be so acquired that the same results will follow (pp. 17-20).

However, not all educators agreed with Farnham. Instead of interpreting nineteenth-century confrontations among proponents of the word, phonic, and alphabet methods as responses to a wholeness principle, Reeder (1900) judged that whole word and phonic approaches were both pragmatic experiments that lacked a philosophical base. He concluded that "like the word method, [the phonics method] developed from no particular center, but was tried as an experiment" (p. 80). Farnham himself disapproved of phonics not only on philosophic grounds but because he thought it was impractical. After describing an experiment in which a phonics approach had been used in a school system, he conceded that "for a time it was thought that the true method of teaching children to read had been discovered" (p. iii). But he then disclosed the long-term results:

> After a trial of five years, however, it was seen that while pupils learned to read by this method in much less time than usual, and attained a high state of excellence in articulation, their reading was nearly as mechanical as before, and few of them became good spellers. The two systems of analysis, phonic and graphic, had so little in common that permanent confusion was produced in the mind (Farnham, 1895, p. iv).

Though he underscored the impracticality of phonics instruction, Farnham was eloquent in his praise for language-based approaches:

> The teacher goes to the board, and in a clear, bold hand writes a sentence, as: "I have a knife." The pupils see the writing, but of course do not know what it means. The teacher will call a pupil and put a knife into his hands, and the pupil in response to the impulse which is the result of previous training will instantly hold up the knife and say, "I have a knife." The teacher writes another sentence, as, "I have a pencil," and puts the object in the hands of another child, who will respond, "I have a pencil." The teacher will proceed in the same way until several children have objects in their hands, representing as many sentences upon the board (p. 30).

Another indication of Farnham's progressive insights was his conviction that reading and writing should be taught in an integrated fashion. Although he rationalized this conviction with an argument that it was instructionally "economic" to combine the two types of learning, he anticipated instructional techniques for which language-based instructors would advocate decades later.

> It will be seen that reading, writing, spelling, and composition are simultaneous operations by this method, and that all are subordinated to the thought gained and expressed. In this way much time is gained, and the multitude of classes in ungraded schools is diminished. These subjects are all related to each other, and are dependent upon thought; and to treat them separately is to destroy this relation and dependence (pp. 50-51).

Although Farnham may have been the most explicit advocate for language-based reading instruction, he was not the first. For the holistic strategies that Farnham advocated had been fermenting in Europe throughout the nineteenth century. Curtis (1967) wrote about the instructional approach of David Stow, a teacher in Scotland who had recommended in 1840 that children should use "picturing out" when learning to read. Stow recommended that children should "never commit words to memory until the meaning is previously analyzed and understood" (Stow, 1840, quoted by Curtis, p. 216). John Wood, also a Scottish teacher, had written 20 years before Stow about alternative approaches to reading instruction. Even at this early date, Wood thought changes in reading instruction were needed because "the children were taught, indeed, to read, but the doubt was, whether they had been made such masters of their own language, as in future life to give them any pleasure in reading, or to enable them to derive much profit from it" (Wood, 1820, quoted by Curtis, p. 217).

In the United States, Chicago's "Colonel" Francis Parker was the most famous advocate for holistic, experience-based reading instruction. Vandewalker (1908) characterized Parker as a scholar who "probably did more than any other single individual in the United States" to bring about the adoption of progressive practices in the elementary schools. In his history of elementary education, Samuel Parker (1912) described Francis Parker as "the most influential personal factor during a quarter of a century in securing an adoption of the Froebelian theory in elementary school work" (p. 471). With regard to Samuel Parker's connection of Francis Parker to Friedrich Froebel, Samuel Parker had identified the fundamental principle of Froebel's theory as a conviction that education should take place "through motor expression and social participation" (p. 471). Francis Parker delivered a set of lectures in 1891 that became the most persuasive testimonial in support of the wholeness principle. The following syllogism illustrates Parker's logic about the relevance of this principle to reading:

1. Every printed word must be learned by one or more acts of association.
2. The less the number of acts required to function a word, the greater the economy.

3. The greatest economy in learning a word would be, therefore, one act of association (F. Parker, 1937, p. 150).

McCaul (1959) wrote that during the late 1800s "almost every education controversy eventuated in a bitter clash between the pro- and anti-Parker factions of the city" and that "invariably the doughty Colonel emerged the victor, and invariably his enemies would have at him again the next year" (p. 270). McCaul provided examples of such clashes:

> Each autumn when Parker presented his budget to the Board, his enemies would slash it to ribbons in hopes of maneuvering him into resigning.... Sometimes Parker's enemies on the Board would construct tests and administer them to the children of his practice school. The results would be published in the newspapers, and a great clamor would arise about "glorified mudpie making." Parker's friends would counterattack by polling schoolmen to show that the tests were unfair and the interpretation of the results illogical; while Parker himself would strike back by proclaiming with suitable embellishments that the child, not subject matter, should be the center of instruction (1959, p. 270).

McCaul observed that "Parker had decided to come to Chicago because he expected the city to become the 'education storm center' of the nation" and that a witty colleague had later responded that Parker "had labored industriously that the prophecy which he had made might be fulfilled to the uttermost" (p. 270).

Parker did not disapprove of phonics for pragmatic reasons. He admitted that "phonetic methods can be used with great facility and great apparent results" (p. 163). He worried instead that by the use of such a method "a fixed habit of attention to the forms [of words], and the forms alone, is the inevitable result" (p. 163). Parker warned that when phonics generalizations were employed, "the spontaneous unity of action is broken and can be regained only with the greatest effort on the part of the victim" (p. 163). He pursued the analytical-holistic argument to its final, philosophical resolution, stipulating that the act of reading itself was a holistic phenomenon that would be perverted by the introduction of analytical learning strategies.

Impassioned arguments by educators of the early and middle 1800s had focused on whether reading could be learned more efficiently through the synthesis of letters into spelling patterns or through memorization of entire words. By the end of the nineteenth century, the arguments had shifted to questions about the usefulness of analytical or holistic methods. Alternative strategies that were progressively proposed were linked to letter sounds, phonetically transcribed passages, whole words, sentences, or entire passages. Francis Parker was aware of the dynamic interaction between these progressively developed theories when he noted in 1891 that "the phonic-method, which succeeded the alphabet-method... was the first attempt to improve the latter method" (p. 162). But Parker did not respect the phonic or alphabet methods, which he judged as two examples of "formal methods which have little and sometimes no relation to the thought itself" (p. 161). In an 1890s discussion that had been published in the *Journal of Education*, he stated bluntly that since "reading is thinking, it should be educated thinking" (1895, p. 165).

Changes in reading instruction during the 1800s did not transpire without social and political commotion. Parker, Reeder, and Huey adduced historical information selectively to explain why the alphabet method had lost its popularity. But they had an ulterior motive for documenting the demise of the alphabet method and predicting a comparable fate for phonics instruction. That ulterior motive was to convey a sense of *manifest destiny* for the language-based style of reading instruction that they supported. These debates between proponents of the alphabet, word, and phonics methods led to shifts in the attitudes and practices of teachers. The word method and phonic method challenged and then supplanted the alphabet method, becoming popular with both teachers and the public. But these approaches were in states of dynamic development, continually being modified as a result of confrontations by hostile opponents. Because critics pointed to the limited range of instructional materials in the schools that were strictly compatible with phonics generalizations, phonics approaches were transformed into phonetic approaches in which alternative alphabets could be employed. In a similar demonstration of adaptability, the word method mutated into the sentence method after the former was criticized for being not sufficiently interesting to young learners.

As support for the whole word and phonics methods grew, the alphabet method lost popularity. His contemporaries agreed with Huey when he wrote in 1908 that the alphabet method "which was nearly universal in America until about 1870, is now chiefly of historical interest" (1968, p. 265). In contrast, the word method had blossomed during the late 1800s. Reeder (1900) wrote that "the word method made but little headway previous to 1870" but that "progressive teachers and students of method in different parts of the country gradually came to see that as the child uses words but knows nothing of their elements, so should he learn the printed symbols without analysis or synthesis" (p. 78). After the alphabet method had been retired as the prevailing approach to reading, it was replaced in most cases by whole word or phonic programs. Though more holistic than the alphabet method, the phonics approach was still dismissed as fundamentally analytical by some educators. For example, Reeder (1900) not only disapproved of phonics but expressed skepticism about the phonetic approaches that employed alternative alphabets:

> The strength of the phonic method lay in the independent power it gave to the child in mastering new words, in which respect it was far superior to the alphabet method and squarely met the weak point in the word method, which was the main cause of its development. Its weakness lay in the fact that it straightened the natural tendency...to spell by sound.... As a remedy for this defect, the Phonetic method was devised, which is but a modification of the Phonic method (p. 80).

Each modification of the analytical approaches resulted in a more confrontational stylization of the holistic rhetoric. This tumultuous dispute precipitated changes in pedagogy that were very much like those that would transpire a century later. For example, Huey (1968) described examples of innovative, language-based lessons which had been implemented in the schools of Chicago during the late 1800s but which were similar to current procedures. These lessons included activities where children "read and correct their own statements, and often these are printed by some of the older children and returned as a printed story of what has happened" (pp. 297-298). How widespread were such language-based teaching procedures? At Francis Parker's funeral in 1902, Dewey chastised those who thought Parker a "faddist" and defended him because the "things for which he stood are taken today almost as a matter of course, without debate, in all the best schools of the country" (Dewey, 1902, cited by Cuban, 1984, p. 33).

INDIVIDUALIZED INSTRUCTION

Twentieth-century remedial reading instruction has been associated with the emergence of several corollary initiatives, such as the movements toward expanded use of assessment, diagnosis, and eclectic instruction. However, individualized instruction in the classroom was the movement with which remedial reading was most closely associated. Despite this connection, the extensive literature on individualized approaches to remedial reading did not emerge until the 1920s and 1930s. Irwin and Marks (1924) described the relationship between special education programs during this period and attitudes about individualized instruction:

> The classes for mental defectives, although originating within the school system, were at first regarded as an expedient for the welfare of normal children. The defectives were segregated for the same reason that bruised apples are taken out of one barrel and put into another, for the sake of the sound apples that are left behind. Although this was far from the point of view of their originators, it was the idea which made headway with the public and the school authorities, by whom the special classes were accepted as a receptacle for "seconds." Their true educational value was not at first generally recognized. It consisted in the simple but significant fact that here for the first time, the school was consciously trying to study the human material in its hands and to adapt the school program to the actual limitations of the pupil. In time we shall see that this spirit must underlie the education of all the children in the schools and not that alone of the small minority of the immature and handicapped (p. 3).

A year earlier, Buswell (1923) had summarized three salient characteristics of the individualized programs for "mentally exceptional children" to which Irwin and Marks referred:

> Such an "individual system" involves, first, a detailed statement of the curriculum in terms of definite unit assignments which can be readily interpreted by the pupil; second, an opportunity for individual progress at varying rates of speed, a new assignment being given only when the old one is satisfactorily completed; and, third promotion to a higher grade whenever the work of a given grade is finished.... There are no failures in the ordinary meaning of the term, the pupil being required to work on each assignment until it is mastered. There is a possibility, with such an individual system, of modifying the general character of the curriculum as well as the rate of progress, thus providing definite variations in assignments to meet the ability of all types of pupils (pp. 683-684).

The remedial individualized education initiatives that were clearly visible during the 1920s were synchronized with more amorphous but still discernible student-centered developments in the general field of education. O'Shea (1924) wrote that "during the past two decades, an enormous amount of experimental work has been undertaken by American psychologists and educators for the purpose of developing serviceable methods for determining the intellectual capabilities of individuals, particularly children of school age, and also for the purpose of devising ways and means of measuring achievement in school work" (p. xxiii). From a complementary perspective, Chadsey (1924) observed that "probably the majority of the problems with which the educational world has been concerned during the last thirty years have centered around the necessity of breaking down in as many ways as possible the tendency towards uniformity of treatment of the individual pupil" (p. v).

Brueckner and Melby (1931) began their book on diagnostic teaching by noting that "during the past three decades a large amount of information has been assembled showing that the schools have failed in many cases to adapt the curriculum and methods of teaching to the differences in ability, interests, and needs of individual pupils" (p. 1). They concluded that "in an attempt to remedy the conditions revealed by these studies" schools had implemented individualized instructional programs that "in many cases greatly improved the situation" (p. 1). Sixteen years later, Butts (1947) assessed that during the first two decades of the twentieth century only "a few voices here and there began to urge the claims of individual development." However, Butts did report that "in the 1920's the tempo of interest in individual development was accelerated" (p. 642).

Even though individualized instruction did not become popular until the twentieth century, it was entwined in some of the educational writings of the 1800s. In his 1912 history of elementary education, Samuel Parker discussed individualized instruction in England during the 1800s. Figure 2.12 is an illustration that Parker included in his textbook and which was described simply as the "Old-Time Method of Individual Instruction" (p. 101). Figure 2.13 is from the early 1800s and depicts children teaching other students who had been formed into ability groups. Reigart (1916) extensively described the reliance on volunteer student monitors and paid adult monitors within the Lancasterian system of instruction that was popular in the New York City schools during the nineteenth century.

In a British report about advances that had been made in U.S. schools, Mark (1901) wrote that one of the focal points for "almost the whole of American school problems" was the "problem of individuality in education" (p. 1). He then identified the two objectives of individualized educational curricula as "reaching of the individual learner in the mass, meeting him at the point of his attainment, and helping him in his special difficulties" and "building up of individuality" (p. 6). After reviewing examples of individualized instructional techniques, Mark explained that "these instances have been quoted to show ways in which the life

Figure 2.12. Illustration from Parker's 1912 History of Elementary
Education and that was Titled
"Old-time Method of Individual Instruction"

of the school-room is brought into touch with the individual interests and
activities" (pp. 102-103).

In 1903 Shaw published an exposition of educational practices in the New York
City public schools in which she wrote with disapproval of a reading lesson that
was not individualized:

> Every child could and did pronounce his reading words with unusual distinctness. The chant in
> which recitations were delivered was as uniform as everything else. "*Wren, w* is silent. The
> ónly sound of *r*; the sécond sound of *e*; the ónly sound of *n*," was as near the heavy accentua-
> tion as I can get. It was the best and the worst school I ever saw. The best because no pains, no

Figure 2.13. Early Nineteenth-Century Illustrations of Children
Teaching Younger Students Who Have Been Divided into Ability Groups

time, *nothing* has been spared to bring it up to the principal's ideal; and the effort had been crowned with entire success. The worst because it ignored absolutely any individuality in the pupils and fitted them for nothing more than a mechanical obedience to another's thinking (1903, pp. 4210-4211).

In a book about the ideal school written two years later, Search (1905) included an entire chapter on the rationale for individualized instruction and another on methods to be used during individualized instruction. After remarking that renowned inventors had not developed their genius as a result of conscientious attention to school activities, he wrote that "the great teacher is he who early discovers the innate germ and gives it opportunity for expression" (p. 7). Search suggested that reading be individualized as an alternative to the "poverty-stricken primary exercise" that was common in the elementary schools:

With departmental organization it would be a good thing if the pupils, as individuals or in small numbers, could pass in turn to an adjoining room for drill in reading at the hands of a specialist, with exercises much longer than the brief line which a child usually reads, the other pupils, in the meantime, being occupied with other work. If this is inconvenient, then the teacher may well gather the children around her in smaller groups, vitalizing the exercise by closer help and by the children's more fruitful attention (1905, p. 214).

A year after Search's book had appeared, Gilbert (1906) published an early work on educational administration in which he chastised teachers who resorted to the "mass teaching" that he judged to be "like shooting at a flock of birds with an old-fashioned smooth-bore, 'scattering' shot-gun" (p. 41). As an alternative, he suggested an individualized approach to instruction that was based on the arrangement of students within classes into small groups.

Washburne (1924) indicated that he had implemented a fully individualized curriculum before 1920 within the school district at which he was superintendent. He noted that "the most difficult part of the entire curriculum to individualize is beginning reading" (p. 68). The approach that Washburne initiated allowed students to begin learning at different levels and then proceed according to personalized schedules:

> Children are promoted as individuals whenever they finish a grade's work in any subject.... A child may be promoted to fourth grade in reading while he is still doing third grade arithmetic. He may be promoted in one subject in November, in another subject in February, in another subject in April or May—it makes no difference what time of the year, what the condition of his other subjects, or what the work of other pupils. Each child is an individual, moving through the course of study at his own natural rate (p. 179).

Washburne (1932) later summarized the instructions that were given to teachers in his district about how such an individualized approach was to be implemented for reading:

> Find out, through tests, what the child's reading ability is; give him plenty of books to read that fit his ability; let him read aloud to you alone, or in small groups...check up, when necessary, on the books he has read, by a brief oral test, or by letting him write a book review or give an oral book report; and when he has read enough books to bring his reading score to the next grade's standard, allow him to read books from the next grade's list (pp. 66-67).

After examining progress in education from 1845 to 1923, Caldwell and Courtis (1924) predicted the traits they thought would characterize future schools. The initial prediction was that "schools of the future will pay far more attention to individuals than the schools of the past" (p. 155). They also predicted that standardization in schools would diminish so that each child could learn "at a rate natural to his ability and effort" (p. 156).

Writing a year earlier, McGregor (1923) stated that "it has always been essential to successful teaching that provision be made for meeting individual needs corresponding to individual differences among pupils" (p. 6). She elaborated an approach to instruction that she termed *supervised study* and that rested on the belief that "the work of the school is properly to supervise and direct the individual while he teaches himself" (p. 3). In the introduction to McGregor's book,

Hall-Quest (1923) defined supervised study as "a procedure that seeks to prevent retardation and failure" and in which "the individual is given careful diagnosis and treatment," "the classroom is chiefly a laboratory or a workshop," and "types of instruction or lesson plans are employed as means toward selected supervisory aims" (p. xii).

Thayer (1928) included a chapter on individualized instruction in his textbook about the waning of the recitation approach to learning. He acknowledged that a form of individualized instruction had followed in the wake of Thorndike's research on measurement. But he lamented that Thorndike's approach had resulted in the use of intelligence for "segregation" of pupils. He thought that the damage done by this procedure was compounded because "tests thus far devised are limited because they do not accurately measure the traits they center upon measuring, and because they do not center upon all of the traits that are significant in producing results" (p. 89). Thayer spoke in favor of a more democratic approach to individualized learning:

> Individual instruction, therefore, in contrast with the normal curve theory of learning, enables pupils to progress at their own rate, but insists that each child come up to an approved level of efficiency as a condition for advance. The mastery of one assignment is the prime requisite for undertaking another. A partial answer in a recitation will not do, nor will the happy failure of a teacher to ask an embarrassing question enable a pupil to "get by." Each pupil must perform the entire assignment and his ability to do so is tested objectively and individually (1928, p 204).

Just as Thayer misrepresented Thorndike and his followers, he also made unfair generalizations about the incompatibility of individualized instruction and the recitation method. In 1901 Mark had published the Gilchrist Report in England, dedicating it to William Torrey Harris "in grateful remembrance of many words and deeds of welcome from American educators." Mark quoted from an article in which Torrey had written that "the first object of his recitation is to draw out each pupil's own view of the subject-matter of the lesson" and that "our teacher probes beneath the mere first statements for the more comprehensive phases which should lie in the pupil's mind if he understands what he is reciting." Harris added that "now begins the real work of the recitation: this pupil shall now supplement or perfect his own views by those of others" (W. T. Harris, quoted by Mark, 1901, p. 87). Mark had concluded that elementary schools should be required to "make the utmost use of the recitation as an individualizing instrument" (p. 86).

After reviewing individualized instructional programs implemented between 1888 and 1932, Ruediger (1932) concluded that the popularity of individualized instruction was still growing and cautioned that "all learning, and consequently all teaching, is ultimately individual" and that "in no case is it desirable to have the slow student and the rapid student chained together" (pp. 391-392). That same year, Judd (1933) wrote that "various methods of individual instruction have been adopted in recent years" as a result of which "pupils have been classified according to ability and instruction" (p. 356). However, he warned that "individual teaching is sometimes carried a step farther," and gave the following example:

> Each pupil is thought of as so distinctly different from all other pupils that he is allowed to exercise his initiative not only with regard to methods of study but with regard to the topics to be studied. Class organization and the coherent sequences which have characterized the traditional courses of instruction are sometimes abandoned and the individual is encouraged to discover and follow his personal intellectual or practical interests (Judd, 1933, p. 356).

Judd observed that "extreme reconstructions of the education program" of the type he had described were "found in small private schools rather than in ordinary schools" and that "it is quite certain that no movement to abandon a systematic curriculum can be successful" (p. 356).

After reviewing teachers' manuals and published courses of university studies during a nine-year period beginning in 1925, Nila Baton Smith (1934) estimated that a significant increase had transpired in the number of publications emphasizing individualized instruction. She wrote that "the number of teachers' manuals and courses of study...which made...recommendations [about ability grouping, diagnostic tests, and remedial work] prior to 1925 was exceedingly limited" and that "since that date practically every publication of either of these types has devoted considerable space to a discussion of these topics" (p. 225). Searching for changes within school textbooks rather than teachers' manuals, Schorling and Edmonson (1931) pointed to the changes in materials published during the 1920s that were linked to individualized instruction. They concluded that "one of the main achievements of the science of education in recent times is the presentation of evidence causing teachers to recognize the problem of individual differences" (p. 43). They gave examples of the textbook activities that they thought incorporated individualized instruction:

> In drill materials some authors have adopted a pattern of drill with the following features in both textbooks and supplementary drill booklets: (a) a uniform period of time for all drill units, (b) a series of preliminary inventory tests followed or supported by a small number of "feeding" practice tests which gifted pupils may omit, provided they have shown a high degree of skill on the inventory test, (c) diagnostic tests including a narrow range of difficulties, and (d) provision of three goals, or levels of achievement, corresponding to the gifted, the average, and the slow student (Schorling & Edmonson, 1931, p. 43).

After reviewing examples in which texts had been adapted to the individual needs of learners, Schorling and Edmonson concluded that "the literature on individual differences is very extensive" and assured their readers not to "doubt that these studies have materially affected the writing of recent textbooks" (p. 44). Five years later, Hildreth (1936) wrote firmly that "reading instruction is individualized more than formerly" (p. 117). She noted that the basis for this individualization was a general awareness that "no two children of the same age and experience may be equal in achievement at any time, even under similar practice conditions" (p. 344). She concluded that remedial reading should be individualized and that "remedial instruction is more successful than ordinary teaching for this reason if for no other" (p. 676).

Initial Sense of Identity for Remedial Reading

With an emphasis on assessment, empirical validation, and the correction of precise skills, early twentieth-century remedial reading programs were sometimes viewed as the antithesis of the child-centered, progressive educational approaches with which they competed. In 1936 Mayhew and Edwards (1966) wrote a detailed account of the most famous progressive educational program, the laboratory school that John Dewey had supervised in Chicago from 1896 to 1903. In an introduction to their book, Dewey himself indicated that their history was "so adequate" that it was unnecessary for him to add any clarifying remarks to the authors' descriptions of the methods used at his school. Mayhew and Edwards described how instructors at Dewey's school disagreed with the practice in which "literacy, interpreted as the ability to read, write, and figure, has laid the responsibility upon the teacher of developing early proficiency in the child's use of these tools." They explained that such an emphasis on teacher-directed instruction was predicated on the inappropriate assumption that reading was "considered necessary before the child could help himself from the storehouse of learning books" (pp. 379-380). In contrast to the traditional approaches to literacy instruction, the teachers at Dewey's school resolved to delay the teaching of reading until the learners "exhibited readiness" for that instruction:

> It was found, for instance, that when a child was interested in an activity just for the sake of the activity, when he played miller without being interested in what the miller did, it was an indication, in general terms, that he was at the stage of growth when he did not separate means from ends. At that stage therefore he certainly would not be interested in learning how to read as a means to an end. If, however, as is characteristic of the seven-year-old, when playing miller he could remember what a miller does and could plan what he must do in the character of a miller, then he would be ready for and would be interested in using language as a means to a specific end (Mayhew & Edwards, 1966, p. 380).

With such an amorphous approach to reading education, it was not surprising that some children attending Dewey's school did not develop adequate literacy skills. Despite the institutionalized progressive philosophy, some of the teachers did recognize the prevalence of reading problems and attempted, with the approval of their students, to develop remedial activities:

> As class and teacher grew acquainted, many in the group were found deficient in ability to read or write with ease and proficiency. In consequence and after discussion, the group decided to give, for a period, much time and attention to collateral reading.... Writing lessons were also begun, supplemented with drill exercises on words or construction that troubled them (Mayhew & Edwards, 1966, p. 167).

Although a perceived need for remedial reading activities could be discerned in the 1900s, it was not until two decades later that remedial reading instruction became firmly established. It was clear that remedial reading was developing an initial sense of identity when William Gray (1919) wrote a chapter on "scientific" principles for teaching reading in which he encouraged teachers to be attentive to methods of reading, content of passages, the editorial format of instructional materials, and the goals of learners. Three years later, Gray (1922) wrote an influential book about diagnosis and treatment in reading that he based on an estimate that "there are thousands of boys and girls in school each year who make little or no progress because of inaccuracies and personal handicaps which could be eliminated" (p. 2). As an indication of the variability among the estimates by contemporary educators about the number of students who would benefit from remedial reading instruction, Sutherland (1922) wrote in that same year that "if the feeble-minded and those handicapped by other conditions and disabilities, such as defective vision and chorea, are eliminated, a careful study of the remaining pupils of a grade will show that 30 to 35 per cent of the pupils are retarded in their development because of failure to 'use their minds' in reading" (p. 37).

Although his early conjecture was significantly less than Sutherland's, Gray's estimates of the number of persons requiring remedial instruction would escalate dramatically over the next two decades. But even at this early date, Gray (1922) accurately predicted that the remedial approach to reading was growing because "during the last year more than thirty cities have made detailed reports of diagnostic and remedial studies" and "progressive teachers and supervisors of many other cities have reported that they have given a considerable amount of time to remedial instruction" (p. 3). Having forecast that a field of "diagnostic and remedial studies" was emerging, Gray identified four areas on which this new field should center: "important types of remedial cases," "appropriate instruction for remedial cases," "the technique of diagnosis," and the preparation of "teachers who are thoroughly trained to engage in diagnostic and remedial work effectively" (pp. 3-4). Two years later, Maddox (1924) reported that the field of remedial instruction had grown to such dimensions that courses on remedial instruction were being offered in colleges of education. He wrote confidently that this new field was "the most significant movement in education that has yet arisen" and characterized it as "the most encouraging evidence to scientists in other fields that education is itself a science and in the near future will base its procedure on rational grounds, on facts discovered, verified under control, and continually refined in practice" (p. 164).

SUMMARY

Disconcerted by persistent questions about whether children were learning to read adequately, teachers began to search for alternatives to the prevalent instructional programs of the nineteenth and early twentieth centuries. The various literacy approaches that were endorsed relied on letter identification, whole word learning, phonics, alternative alphabets, and the personal language of individual learners. Disputes erupted among educators as the alphabet approach waned and the popularity of phonics, whole word learning, and language-based approaches expanded during the latter part of the 1800s. These alternative programs developed in response to a widely held conviction that reading was so important that all persons needed to be literate.

It was obvious to some educators that no single method of instruction could by itself be a solution to the schools' literacy problems. These educators anticipated remedial reading activities when they recommended that materials, learning activities, and instructional strategies from the distinct approaches be joined eclectically to guard against the weaknesses inherent in any single program. Although the combination of methods could supplement for the deficiencies in those individual methods, the equation for an effective mixture of approaches did not seem to be forthcoming.

As had been the case during the period when eclectic approaches had been proposed, the strife among the warring factions seemed to be reducing when both educators supporting holistic approaches and those advocating for skills-based reading agreed that instruction should be individualized. A direct extension of the movement toward individualized instruction, remedial reading emerged not as another distinct approach to instruction but rather as a method that could complement and enhance the other approaches. As such, it was not based on philosophic convictions about an optimal model of learning but rather on expedient considerations designed to raise the probability that children would learn to read, irrespective of the primary approach with which they might have begun instruction. However, just as disagreements had developed about the most effective approach to general reading education, divisive arguments erupted about the best way to teach remedial reading. Many of the issues that that were pretexts for this early divisiveness continued to be contentious throughout the twentieth century.

Chapter 3

SEARCH FOR PHYSICAL FACTORS

The widespread interest in the movement for measurement in education is rapidly giving many investigators a new point of view (Courtis, 1915).

During the early 1900s academic testing expanded. These tests indicated physical factors such as visual perception that correlated with reading. Although many educators concluded that aberrant eye movements were merely the result of inappropriate reading strategies, some advocated ocular exercises as a cure for reading problems that they thought had been caused by the faulty eye movements themselves. In a parallel fashion, some educators who thought they had discovered neurological disorders that were interfering with reading suggested classroom activities to modify those dysfunctions.

* * *

Beginning in the late 1800s physicians and psychologists had begun to search for physical factors that might be causing learning problems. Impressed by these investigations, some educators developed diagnostic procedures as well as remedial exercises that were sensitive to physical factors. Even in those cases where the development of diagnostic procedures and the searches for the physical causes of reading failure were not directly related, the two types of investigations were still mutually supportive in that the emerging diagnostic procedures facilitated the systematic examination of physical factors. Conversely, the scientific attitudes that persuaded some educators to posit physical explanations for reading problems predisposed them toward new diagnostic procedures. Even though both of these scientific and diagnostic initiatives were both germinating among educators during the late 1800s, they did not flower until the first quarter of the 1900s.

BEGINNING OF INDIVIDUALIZED DIAGNOSIS

Near the end of the 1800s, Hinsdale (1896) had recognized that not all children were learning to read successfully in their classrooms. But he did not consider this problem of sufficient significance to require an extraordinary type of instruction. He wrote that although "the ease or difficulty with which children learn to read, in the real sense of the word, differs greatly with different children," that nonetheless "quick-witted children brought up in intelligent homes, where they hear from birth good reading and talking, will, under good tuition, learn to read almost as naturally as a thrush learns to sing" (p. 92).

Less complacent than Hinsdale, Ayres (1909) was alarmed because studies conducted during the early 1900s showed that the percentage of students who could not keep up with their peers ranged from 5 to 50 percent. The large number of students that were being "held back" was just one indicator of the academic problems that he had highlighted. Ayres recommended that these problems be addressed through administrative procedures such as "better medical inspection, courses of study which will more nearly fit the abilities of the average pupil, more flexible grading, and a knowledge of the facts [i.e., that Ayres was presenting in his book]" (p. 7). Given the precise emphasis of the title for Ayres's book, *Laggards in Our Schools*, readers cannot help but be struck by his infrequent references to remedial instruction. Ayres did note "two disquieting characteristics of the courses of study in vogue in our city school systems," that the curricula were designed for the "unusually bright pupil" and "better fitted for the girl than for the boy pupils" (p. 218). Other than such general references, he steered away from problems of instruction and restricted his suggestions for improvements to administrative antidotes.

Although educators such as Hinsdale and Ayres were either not aware or not attracted to the concept of individual diagnosis, some of their contemporaries demonstrated different attitudes. Before the turn of the century, Francis Parker had advised teachers that "the central factor of class teaching consists in watching closely the mind of each pupil" (1937, p .269). In a similar fashion, Allen (1890) had recommended that teachers make observations to enable them to "determine the temperaments" of students and adjust instruction accordingly. Allen counseled teachers that such analytic observations should include attention to students' "physical characteristics and mental peculiarities" (p. 55). Even in 1897, Warner had written explicitly about "methods of mental examination in schools" that included techniques organized under the following categories: "the pupil reads aloud," "the pupil reads to himself quietly," "the teacher reads to the pupil," "the pupil recites from memory," "the pupil talks of the passage read," "class recitation of the passage read," "repeated recitation of the passage pupil knows best," and "answers to general questions on the passage" (pp. 134-135).

Increased Popularity of Academic Testing

The increasing popularity of diagnosis, like the accelerated spread of academic testing in general, was abetted by the expansion of the scientific perspective in education. In an article about "scientific common-school education," Adams

(1880) had documented a movement "that began several years ago" in which education was progressing "away from mechanism, and toward science." He wrote with approval of a "practical educationist" in Massachusetts who had written a unique report that "presents not theories, inferences, and conclusions, but a mass of raw material; it shows exactly what the common schools examined by him do" (p. 934). He explained that "this is done by means of a series of lithographic reproductions of the written exercises handed in by the children" and that as a result "any one who cares to do so is enabled to judge for himself of the quality and value of the educational staple which is being supplied" (p. 934).

In a history of education that he published before 1900, Shoup (1891) had also noted the emergence of "empiricism" in education. Comparing innovative educational methods with the techniques that had been responsible for early developments in medicine, Shoup informed his readers that "such a system of practice—practice based on the results of observations rather than on scientific investigation of principles—is styled EMPIRICISM; the person who employs it is said to be an EMPIRIC; and his methods are said to be EMPIRIC or EMPIRICAL" (p. 9). A decade later, Ware (1901) wrote from Great Britain that the United States was a country in which the science of education commands "attention from men of first-rate abilities; and probably during recent years the world owes more to the original research of the Americans in this branch of science than to that of any other people" (p. 262).

Judd (1933) indicated that "exact measurements of the achievements of pupils were first made in the nineties and the early years of the present century" (p. 378). He explained that the early procedures that were employed were "tests of the ability of pupils in various school systems to spell and to solve problems in arithmetic." He also noted that "since 1900 much energy has been devoted to the extension of the testing movement" (p. 378). Judd concluded that the testing developments were part of a larger movement characterized by "a growing tendency to guide all kinds of educational activities by carefully conducted analyses and by measurements of results" and felt so positive about this movement that he described it as "the most hopeful aspect of the administration of schools" (p. 378).

Like Judd, the members of the American Historical Association's Commission on the Social Studies (1934) were struck by the rapid growth of testing during the initial third of the twentieth century. Although they did attribute the expansion to systemization in education, they identified other factors that were responsible:

> The rapid rise of this testing or measurement movement was due no doubt to a number of factors or conditions—to the demonstrated defects of the traditional modes of testing; to the great popularity and prestige of natural science; to the sustained effort on the part of a number of able young men to convert education into a science; to the rise of quantitative and mechanistic psychology; to the growth of city school systems of great complexity demanding new forms of administration; and to the borrowing by school men of ideas of control and efficiency from large business enterprise (American Historical Association's Commission on the Social Studies, 1934, pp. 88-89).

In a book published originally in 1907, Bagley (1908) had advised teachers that "the efficiency of instruction may be tested by a careful application of the method of formal examinations" (p. 249). But he also noted the drawbacks of the informal procedures he had described. Despite these limitations, he assured his readers that a test "is far better than no test at all, and it may be made more and more effective by gradually improving the technique of examination questions, and by adopting a scale of grading more elastic that the numerical system affords" (p. 249). With regard to the "numerical system," Bagley judged that "except in mathematics or some similar branch of exact science, it is impossible to apply an exact scale of marking" (p. 248).

Writing in his history of elementary education, Samuel Parker (1912) made predictions about early twentieth-century developments in education that were especially noteworthy. He predicted expansion of a "tendency to measure accurately the results of instruction by precise objective, scientific methods as a means of testing its value" (p. 489). The testing movement to which Parker referred had grown since the early 1900s. Scott (1908) wrote that if the school was to be accountable to the public "it is necessary that there should be some measurement of its efforts" and that "indications of this need are already seen on every hand, but much remains to be done to render the tests proposed suitable, as well as scientific and exact" (p. 23). Writing five years later, Hanus (1913a) also testified that "methods of exact measurement are still in process of evolution" and that "except for arithmetic and penmanship, 'standard scores' or standard achievements are not available for measuring the quality of the results actually attained by the schools" (p. viii).

Morgan (1914) gave numerous examples of informal tests that instructors could administer in an effort to identify "backwards children." She described a general set of procedures by which teachers could gather assessment information in the least obtrusive manner and then subsequently make records that they could analyze. In a book about delinquency, Healy (1917) also advised teachers to use informal assessment strategies when he observed that "if a child has been going to school for a certain number of years and has failed to learn what has been taught during that period...this is an indication of personal defect" (p. 57). He cautioned that teachers should hesitate before classifying children as retarded because of potentially extenuating factors such as inadequate instruction, bad companions, poor hygiene, sensory defects, inappropriate nutrition, and the inherently noninteresting nature of much school work. Nonetheless, Healy concluded that students should be tested because this was "the common way of evaluating the individual's ability" (p. 57). He recommended that teachers estimate reading ability "by general observations during the giving of tests" and that "further tests with reading, and estimation of the vocabulary, and the flow of ideas, can be made as necessary" (p. 67).

Burgess (1921) reported that "the inception of the modern movement for scientific measurement in education dates from 1910 and was marked by the publication of the first of the modern scales for the measurement of classroom products" (p. 14). The test to which she referred had been developed by Edward Thorndike to measure handwriting. Burgess noted that "this earliest scale was rapidly followed by others for measuring the classroom products in different subjects and by numerous reports of extensive applications for these new educational adjuncts." By 1921 she detected "more than a hundred standardized tests and measuring scales, and over a thousand reports on the results secured by using them" (p. 15).

Burgess had credited Thorndike with having publicized the first academic test. Thorndike had written a classic text on measurement in 1904. In a later edition of that book, *An Introduction to the Theory of Mental and Social Measurements*, Thorndike (1913) wrote that "since the first edition of this book appeared the literature related to methods of measuring mental and social facts has been enriched by a number of investigations in which they have been used" (p. vii). In the preface to a mammoth book on measurement that was published almost a decade later, McCall (1923) observed that the use of assessment had grown "at such a phenomenal rate in the last few years as to make this movement for the mental measurement of children the most dramatic tendency in modern education" (p. v). Although he acknowledged persons who strenuously opposed the use of measurement in education, McCall judged them to be "an ever-dwindling group." Two years later, Irwin and Marks (1924) began their textbook about individualized instruction with the confident assertion that "the use of psychological and standardized tests in public education is a self-evident outcome of scientific progress" (p. 1). In a similarly confident tone, Baker (1927) concluded that "mental measurement is a familiar topic to all teachers and to school administrators" and that tests had become so popular because they were viewed as "definite and objective" (p. 3).

Increased Popularity of Individualized Reading Tests

William Gray (1925) described the years from 1911 to 1915 as a transitional period in reading characterized by "the introduction of a new instrument of investigation" (p. 6). The new instrument to which Gray referred was the reading test. He recalled that "by the close of 1915, scientists, administrators, and teachers were measuring the results of instruction in reading" (p. 6). In a frequently cited research report, Zirbes (1918) indicated that she had become aware of "modern methods of measurement in education" in 1914, but that she "straightway became a conscientious objector." However, she did eventually accept the new diagnostic procedures which led to "a thorough revision of the theory and practice" of her teaching in the classroom. In a two-part report about recently emerging tests of reading, William Gray (1916a, 1916b) had specified that tests were needed to assess "rates of reading" and "reproduction and interpretation." He presented detailed procedures for measuring reading speed and introduced teachers to techniques for assessing oral and silent comprehension. He clearly identified the assessment of comprehension as a measure that was "necessary to secure certain facts which are not ordinarily noted in the schoolroom" (1916a, p. 232). Four years later, Wilson and Hoke (1921) were unqualifiedly enthusiastic about the progress they observed in the testing and diagnosis of both reading skills and reading comprehension:

> The subject of reading has been receiving marked attention from psychologists and other educational experts during recent years. The importance of reading in every child's development justifies this attention. This interest has resulted in sufficient scientific information in the form of standardized tests, scales, and standards of achievement which enable every classroom teacher to determine accurately the ability of her children in reading. Every teacher now in a classroom or coming fresh from the training school should be sufficiently familiar with a test or several tests so that she can justify her instruction in reading by scientific facts as well as by opinion (p. 154).

Not all educators were as positive toward reading tests as Wilson and Horke. Five years after Gray had called for improved measures of comprehension, Courtis (1921) noted that those teachers who were following Gray's counsel were mistaken. For Courtis insisted that assessment be restricted to "skill in the mechanics of reading" and that comprehension, if tested at all, should be referred to by a distinct term, such as "scanning" or "intensive reading." Writing that same year, Burgess (1921) refrained from criticizing reading tests that emphasized skills or comprehension, but she did disapprove of those that pandered to the standardized curricula that many teachers had implemented. She discouraged the use of such "teacher-centered" tests in favor of child-centered assessment that was designed "to make it possible to study education by finding out what the children can do" and to "proceed by measuring the accomplishment of the pupil, rather than by analyzing the methods of the teacher" (p. 15).

In a book that concentrated on silent reading methods, Watkins (1922) avoided the opportunity to cast a vote in favor of skills-based or comprehension-based assessment and instead indicated her optimism about the value of general diagnostic testing which could enable a teacher to "determine the degree of skill possessed by the pupils under her charge in any or all of the various qualities which make up good reading" (p. 5). McCall (1922) also declined to vote on the issue of whether skills or comprehension should be emphasized in assessment. In a chapter on educational diagnosis within a 400-page book on measurement, she listed 14 different types of assessment data that were needed to guide instruction in reading. Among the categories of information in this list were reading scores, reading ages, reading quotients, mental ages, and intelligence quotients.

In the early 1920s William Gray (1922) was able to identify 13 reading tests. Gray had himself developed one of the first diagnostic oral reading procedures in 1915. In this early system of assessment, teachers employed symbols to create written records on a copy of a passage that a learner was reading orally. This annotated transcription indicated any oral alterations to the passage made by the reader. So popular was Gray's informal diagnostic procedure that virtually every textbook on remedial reading from that time to the present has included information about it. Robinson (1985) wrote that "what is surprising is that, with only minor revisions, this test became the most popular oral reading test available and remained so, without revisions, until 1963" (p. 25).

Clarence Gray (1922) quoted from the instructions for William Gray's original, early test:

> If a word is wholly mispronounced, underline it.... If a portion of a word is mispronounced, mark appropriately.... Omitted words are marked [by placing a circle around the omitted words]; substitutions [by writing above the original words in the text]; insertions [by the use of the ^ symbol with the inserted word or phrase written above the caret]; and repetitions [by the use of underlining with the letter R above the underlined word or phrase]. Two or more words should be repeated to count as a repetition. It is very difficult to record the exact nature of each error. Do this as nearly as you can. In all cases where you are unable to define clearly the specific character of the error, underline the word or portion of the word mispronounced. Be sure you put down a mark for each error. In case you are not sure that an error was made, give the pupil the benefit of the doubt. If the pupil has a slight foreign accent, distinguish carefully between this difficulty and real errors (W. Gray, 1915, quoted by Clarence Gray, 1922, p. 285).

The preceding passage about William Gray's diagnostic oral reading strategies was recorded by Clarence Gray, who had recommended that diagnosis be implemented as a component of an individualized approach that was necessary for effective remedial reading instruction. He wrote that "individual diagnosis, then, leads to the individualizing of methods" and "affords individual instruction based upon the needs of the individual" (p. 9).

Writing in Great Britain, Cyril Burt (1922) noted that "in America, there has risen an eagerness to supplement traditional examinations by psychological tests, and to apply the new statistical methods to the survey of educational systems" (p. 257). However, Burt worried about "perhaps too great an eagerness" for teachers to employ assessment because it seemed to him plausible "that teachers need no assistance from psychologists in assessing educational attainments" (p. 257). When diagnostic tests were employed, Burt counseled that "the aim of such tests and surveys should not be to criticize" because these tests were intended "to serve the teacher, not to rule him; to enable him, in fact, to do more easily what already he desires to do, but can now do only with difficulty, or not at all: that is, to assess—independently of all personal or subjective standards, whether his own or those of an external scrutineer—the comparative level of his individual pupils or of his class taken as a whole" (p. 257).

Pointing out that both teachers and test creators "can find something to learn from the other," Burt (1922) wrote in his unctuous style about opportunities for reducing teacher bias through formal tests:

> Tests are time-savers. They cannot pretend to greater accuracy than the considered sentence of the observant and experienced teacher, judging his own pupils. But observation is slow, and

experience an affair of years. The young teacher who has not yet based his expectations on pro-longed experience, the new teacher who had not yet had opportunity for protracted observa-tion, may by means of such devices be helped swiftly to some provisional conclusion. To the verdicts even of the shrewdest judge the method may have something to contribute: for without such a method we possess in educational measurement no personal equations—no formula measuring the estimate of one teacher against the estimate of a different. The lack is crucial. It is like the option of twenty francs or twenty marks when one is ignorant of the rate of exchange (p. 261).

To facilitate individualized instruction, Burt recommended that teachers attend to two complementary procedures, diagnostic testing and diagnostic teaching. He wrote that diagnostic testing "may reveal what in a given child are the mental capacities we may most successfully rely upon, and what we cannot entirely trust" and that diagnostic teaching "consists of individual instruction carried out by con-stantly varied devices and by widely diversified methods." He cautioned that diagnostic teaching was "to be accompanied always by a close observation of the child's spontaneous method of attack and by a detailed study of the ways which the child can, does, and will by preference, follow and adopt in learning a given piece of work; and it is to be succeeded always by an intensive training in the most defective operations by means of the least defective mental channels" (p. 268).

With regard to reading, Burt (1922) advocated that teachers assess "mechani-cal" skills as well as comprehension. He recommended that "among younger bor-derline cases, it is the mechanical aspect of the reading process—uttering a certain sound on seeing a certain sign in print—that in general calls for testing" whereas comprehension was for older children "by far the most noteworthy element to test" (pp. 269-270). Burt (1922) explained the various types of tests that were available to help teachers:

Tests in reading may be usefully classified in various ways according to procedure. They may, in the first place, be either group tests or individual tests. If the children are to read silently, they may conveniently be tested simultaneously and in class. If they are to read aloud, each must be tested singly, privately, and in succession.... There is a further classification. The mat-ter read may be either continuous or discontinuous. In the second case, the test sheet contains a list of disconnected words: it provides what may be termed a vocabulary test. In the former case, the test-sheet usually consists of a connected passage of prose. Lastly, in degree of diffi-culty, either kind of test may be uniform or graded, according as the words throughout are equally easy, or become progressively harder (p. 270).

Clarence Gray (1922) identified Uhl as "one of the first" persons to use diag-nostic procedures to evaluate reading ability. In the study that had made such an impression on Clarence Gray, Uhl (1916) had concluded that tests, though they were effective, should be supplemented with alternative measures of academic achievement and records about remedial instruction. Uhl also recommended that remedial instruction be individualized and that it be taught by specially desig-nated teachers. In a textbook on reading that he published several years later, Uhl (1924) gave notice that "the days of the untrained practitioner are numbered" and that "public policy as well as individual interests require teachers to discover the reading ailments of pupils and then prescribe remedies for the curable cases" (p. 264). However, Uhl was concerned about the increased demands that expanded remedial teaching would make on classroom teachers. He wrote that "it is far more practicable for the teacher to arrange remedial work in such a way that the entire class can profit by it" and reassured teachers that "specific training given to the entire class does not necessarily decrease the individual differences of the pupils" (p. 292).

At the beginning of the 1930s, Sangren (1932) began his book on the use of tests in reading with an observation that "remarkable advances" had recently been made in reading assessment. But he judged that the average classroom teacher had been left "far behind." On the first page of this book he admonished those teachers who doubted the value of assessment:

> Efficient teaching is always preceded by some type of testing or examination which will, as completely as possible, describe the pupils and their abilities and locate their strengths and weaknesses, the sources of their difficulties and the causes of their deficiencies. The teacher who expects to give adequate and effective training in silent reading to pupils merely on the basis of their promotion to a certain grade or in terms of the adopted text book for the grade is, in most cases, headed for failure. Efficient teaching and supervision of silent reading will follow and be based upon the most thorough study of the pupils and their abilities that existing measuring devices and means of investigation will permit (Sangren, 1932, p. 5).

Progressive educators who had embraced child-centered, experiential approaches were reluctant to implement the diagnostic procedures that were being developed during the 1920s. Stone (1931) summarized the philosophy of progressive educators when she noted that "the teacher's first responsibility toward her group is to provide conditions for real living together" and that "activities resulting from the children's interests and the teacher's guidance serve as the basis of a natural and meaningful approach to reading" (p. 564). As opposed to the skills-based types of assessment that had become increasingly popular, she suggested an individualized, naturalistic approach to diagnosing reading problems:

> The first grade teacher soon discovers that the art of teaching reading does not lie alone in the skillful manipulation of materials, but that it lies as much in studying each child individually and in early detecting that specific limitation which may be impeding his progress. The obstruction may be a lack of confidence in attacking any new problem; it may be confusion resulting from parental pressure; it may be due to an overstimulating program outside of school (Stone, 1931, p. 564).

Despite the reluctance of progressive educators such as Stone, individualized diagnosis had become a regular feature of remedial instruction by the end the 1920s. Brueckner and Melby (1931) wrote that "at present there are approximately five hundred standardized tests available" and that "estimates of the number of standardized tests sold each year vary from fifteen million to twenty-five million" (p. 64). Additionally, they noted that "the necessity of supplementing the standard test by exercises more closely adapted to the local curriculum has resulted in the development in many school systems of informal objective tests quite similar in form to the exercises found in standard tests" (p. 64).

LINK TO VISUAL PERCEPTION

In addition to their practical value, diagnostic reading procedures may have been attractive because of the scientific validation they provided and which some judged to have secured the same precise level of screening that was attributed to medical practice. For this same incidental reason, some educators may have been attracted to research that linked reading to the physical factors involved in visual perception. Hollingworth (1923) recounted that the "first cases of inferiority in reading were reported by ophthalmologists, who, upon discovering nothing wrong with visual apparatus of the child brought for examination, pronounced the difficulty to be word blindness or 'congenital alexia'" (p. 63). Hollingworth indicated that the initially recognized instance of alexia was reported in 1896.

Like Hollingworth, Judd (1918b) reviewed the medical literature for cases of nonreaders and concluded that "congenital word-blindness, inability to learn to read, or dyslexia" was a condition "first recognized in 1896" (p. 121). Though allegations of a link between reading disability and perception had been made during the late 1800s, these suspicions increased progressively during the initial decades of the twentieth century. In a book on the psychology of disability that was published in 1917, Bronner observed that "many experimenters have investigated the question of eye movements and the economics of perception" (p. 76). In a chapter about the relationship of reading material and eye movements to success in reading, Clarence Gray (1922) not only noted an increased interest but predicted that "reading teachers will lay greater stress upon such investigations" (p. 173).

This interest in reading materials and eye movements was part of a general movement in which the health of the eye had been promoted. Allport (1896) warned that "the deleterious influence of education and intellectual advancement upon the human organism can not be questioned" and that "the eye is no exception to the principle involved in this statement" (p. 125). In his book on eye care, Allport included an entire chapter on the damage to vision that occurred in the schools. He was convinced that many visual problems were the result of detrimental environmental factors because "the eyes of a people engaged in rural and pastoral occupations will demonstrate few, if any errors of refraction; and in races of a barbaric or semi-barbaric nature, such pathologic conditions may be said to be positively unknown" (p. 125). He concluded that "unquestionably, therefore, school-life is disastrously prolific of refractive errors, and should be controlled with every means that is possible by those who have such matters in charge" (p. 126). Allport pointed to building lighting, the design of desks, blackboards, textbooks, and even the angle of vision during penmanship exercises as factors responsible for a decline in students' vision.

In his classic nineteenth-century study of children and school, Warner (1897) wrote about the relationships between children's eye movements and their educational development. Not only was Warner convinced that children needed to make appropriate eye movements to achieve their full educational potential, but he advised teachers to use eye-training exercises to reduce educational problems.

Hygiene of Reading

Pointing out the dangers of insufficient lighting in schoolrooms, Shaw (1901) noted that adequate lighting was "not the only care that must be exercised to prevent impairment of eyesight" because "the size of the letters in the text of school books, if below a certain standard, will prove harmful" (pp. 170-171). This latter observation was part of an academic topic that was referred to as the "hygiene" of school and reading. Writing in England, Kerr (1897) defined school hygiene as "all that makes in school for a balanced mind and a healthy body" (p. 613). Among the factors that he thought should be subsumed beneath school hygiene were heating, ventilation, lighting, visual acuity, hearing ability, furniture, methods of instructional drilling, medical conditions, administrative policies, domestic conditions, and school activities.

Concluding a book about "the educative process" that was published in the United States in 1905, Bagley (1922) devoted an entire chapter to hygiene. He observed that "in the sense that it departs from the primitive lines of life, education is an artificial process" and that "it demands a readjustment for which the body is not *naturally* adapted" (p. 335). Bagley considered "educational hygienic" to be the antidote for such problems. In his attempts to develop a hygienic environment, he advised teachers to be attentive to light, temperature, ventilation, and learner fatigue. With regard to fatigue, Bagley warned that "there is probably a seasonal variation in work capacity, the curve...reaching its highest points in December and January and its lowest point in July" (p. 342). Though Bagley thought educational hygiene was relevant to all aspects of school work, he counseled teachers that it was "in connection with reading and writing that there is probably the greatest danger of evil consequences from a violation of hygienic laws" (p. 342). To ensure appropriate learning, he advised instructors to be attentive to the postures of their students as well as the size of print employed within their scholastic materials.

In his 1908 textbook, Huey (1968) included an entire section on hygienic requirements. He explained that "all books and papers shall be printed in such type and arrangement as shall fall within certain recognized limits" (p. 406). Of these recognized limits, he thought that "the size of the type is perhaps the most important single factor" (p. 406). The following passage illustrates the specificity with which Huey (1968) detailed hygienic requirements:

The thickness of the vertical strokes of the letters should not be less than .25 millimeter, according to Cohn; preferably .3 millimeter, according to Sack. This thickness of the letters has been found by Javal and others to be a very important factor in increasing legibility, and thus in decreasing fatigue. Griffing and Franz found, however, that hair lines might form parts of the letter without decreasing the legibility provided the other parts were thick. They find it possible, however, that such hair lines may increase fatigue. The minimum of thickness stated above should be insisted upon on the main lines (p. 407).

Even more precise was a 1914 report from the Illuminating Engineering Society that concentrated on papers and inks used in printing. In the introductory paragraph, the authors indicated that "this report covers printed papers; mat, semi-glossy, glossy; sizings, fillers, inks; writing papers and inks, typewriter papers, inks and carbons; drawing papers and inks; tracing papers and cloths; blue print papers; photostat papers" and that "data are given for specular and diffuse reflecting power and brightness, diffuse transmission and opacity, contrast ratio, back reflection, entrant and exit scatter and other properties" (p. 379). With regard to each of these topics, the authors provided extremely precise information to assist publishers in their quest for reading hygiene. The following passage summarizes the advice on the specular reflecting power of different types of paper:

The proportion of light specularly reflected varies from practically nothing up to 5 per cent in the case of the highly glazed paper. There is a wide variety of half gloss papers. When the surface is dulled by putting a thin mat overcoat on a glossy paper, the specular angle is small and the paper has a subdued brilliancy and gives but slight glare. On the other hand, paper that is heavily filled and calendered but unglazed has a wavy surface that gives a bad glare on account of the wider angle of specular reflection (Illuminating Engineering Society, 1914, p. 379).

In view of such reports, it was hardly unanticipated when Klapper (1914) advised teachers of "an unmistakable and unvarying law for size of type, viz., as the type of decreases in size optic fatigue increases" (p. 13). After conducting research about the hygiene of reading, Blackhurst (1922) classified five categories of factors affecting reading: the reader, environment, experiences preceding reading, ability of the learner, and features "which belong to the print, such as size of type, length of line, leading, [and] regularity of margin" (p. 697). With regard to print, Blackhurst advised that 24-point type be employed in materials intended for first and second graders. But he thought that 18-point type was the optimal size for third and fourth grade learners because "with respect to smaller type, the material becomes less and less readable as we recede from 18-point" (p. 700).

After reading the various reports about the hygiene of reading, Uhl (1924) advised teachers that several hygienic factors could influence reading. He disagreed with Huey about the relative impact of the size of print, concluding instead that the most important hygienic factor was "the quality of the paper upon which the content is printed" (p. 94). Other recommendations that Uhl made about techniques for increasing legibility were that "letters should be relatively wide," "the face of letters should be relatively heavy, clear, and well defined," and that "letters should be surrounded by a sufficient amount of white space" (p. 95).

Although interest in discovering a link between visual perception and reading remained fervid, progressively fewer references to hygienic factors were made during the two-decade period that ended in 1940. Though Traxler (1941) was convinced that teachers should remain interested in information about the size and style of type and about print contrast, he was able to report only several relevant studies that had appeared during the entire 1930s.

Diagnostic Interest in Eye Movements

Even as early as 1918, investigators such as Judd questioned the validity of much of the literature on reading hygiene. Woelfel (1933) wrote that Judd had called upon teachers to "avoid latter-day speculative vagaries about education" and instead be impressed by "the steady accumulation of language, science, and technical discovery" (pp. 81-82). Judd (1918b) used these focal points identified by Woelfel to aid him in conducting research about the effects of different sizes of print on eye movements. But he concluded disappointedly that "only slight differences in fixation appear when the type is enlarged or when it is reduced within wide limits" and that "the unit of recognition in reading is very little affected by changes in the sensory content" (p. 53). By the 1930s a consensus had developed that hygienic features were not responsible for success in reading. Most educators had turned their attention to eye movement, eye dominance, letter perception, and word perception as factors that exhibited greater potential for explaining reading problems.

On the other hand, some early twentieth-century educators had anticipated the interest in a correlation between eye movement and reading. For example, Freeman (1916) recounted that "for the accurate study of eye movements it is necessary to resort to some mechanical means of recording them, such as the mechanical recording device described by Huey, or some photographic method" (p. 95). After noting that two researchers had "merely observed the eye through a telescope," Freeman suggested that "instead of using a telescope we may observe the eye movements in a mirror from behind the subject" (pp. 95-96). Figure 3.1 illustrates the type of apparatus to which Freeman referred.

Freeman (1916) gave explicit instructions for teachers to calculate the reflected eye movements that learners exhibited while reading:

> Each individual should calculate the average number of pauses per line and per unit length of line; the average number of words per line, and the average number of words perceived during one reading pause.... The average number of pauses made per second and the number of words read per second should also be calculated.... The general report should include a table in which these facts are brought together in such a way that individual differences and averages shall appear. These results should then be interpreted (pp. 97-103).

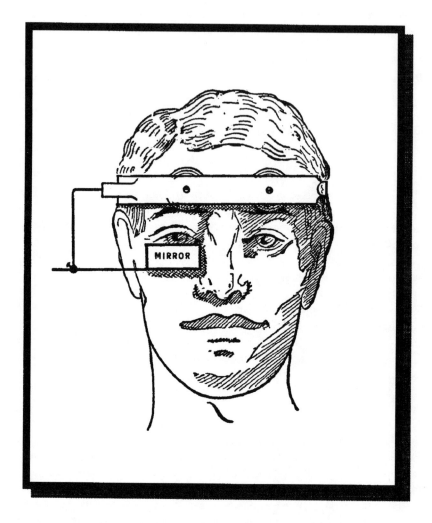

Figure 3.1. Illustration from a 1916 Textbook of a Device with Which to Observe Eye Movements During Reading

Freeman also recommended that the pauses made by the eyes during reading be analyzed. "Since a reading pause consists in a very brief fixation of the eye, we may artificially produce reading pauses by exposing reading matter for a brief interval of time, and thus study the successive reading acts in isolation" (p. 110). As in the case of eye movements, Freeman (1916) suggested an apparatus to assist in this analysis:

The apparatus is one of a number which have been devised to expose objects to view for a brief time. Because of the fact that the exposure is made by a falling screen, the apparatus is called a fall tachistoscope. An opening in the screen exposes the stimulus card for a length of time depending on the size of the opening and the height from which the screen drops (p. 111).

As was the case with the recording of eye movements, Freeman gave advice about how data related to eye pauses could be summarized for interpretation. "The results may be made comparable by dividing in each case the number of objects (letters or digits) exposed by the number of exposures necessary to recognize them, to give what we may for convenience call the average number of objects recognized per exposure" (p. 112).

Dodge (1900) had noted that the studies of eye movements during reading that had been done during the 1800s had relied on self-reports by participants. But he concluded that "all self-observation of the eye movements and fixation pauses is utterly unreliable" and that "direct observation by an assistant is by far the simplest and least questionable control" (pp. 454-455). O'Brien (1921) recounted that Huey "became one of the most prominent investigators through devising and perfecting a mechanical apparatus which registered, with some degree of success, the movements of the eyes during the reading process" (p. 5). Although it is true that Huey had used a mechanical device to investigate the correlation between reading and eye movements more than a decade before such choices became popular, Huey required that a sensing apparatus be attached directly to the eye itself. Clarence Gray (1922) described Huey's procedure:

This method requires that a small plaster-of-Paris cup be attached to the cornea of the eye. To this small cup was attached a delicate string. This ran over a small pulley and was then attached to a pointer. Any movements were recorded upon a moving drum (p. 177).

Discussing the technology that had been employed by Huey, Betts (1936) concluded prudently that it had not "found popular favor with investigators" because it was inaccurate and could "cause permanent damage to the eye" (p. 136).

Departing from those educators who had employed Huey's hazardous apparatus, Buswell (1922) became an early proponent for new technology that enabled researchers to correlate reading with photographs of eye movements:

A satisfactory method of studying growth of reading habits must rest upon the measurement, either directly or indirectly, of some aspect of the actual process or reading. Furthermore, this method must be objective in character, rather than dependent upon the subjective judgment of even a superior teacher. The method which most fully meets these requirements is that of photographing the eye movements of a pupil during the process of reading (p. 7).

An ardent proponent of progressive education, Eugene Smith (1924) discouraged attention to "mechanical" aspects of reading because "in general, it is the reader who spends no appreciable time on the mechanical process of reading, whose whole mind is on the content, who gets the information most readily"

(p. 43). Despite such critical opinions about reading mechanics, Smith was not prepared to dispute the relevance of efficient eye movements to reading. In fact, he was convinced that a skills-based program was dangerous precisely because it encouraged inefficient eye movements. He warned teachers that "the child who knows the alphabet is, then, handicapped for life if poor eye-habits are formed on account of this knowledge" (p. 39).

Washburne, the superintendent of Illinois's Winnetka school district from 1919 to 1943, was another progressive educator. As an indication of his progressive attitudes, he was described in the *About the Author* section of one of his books (Washburne, 1926) as a person "brought up from early childhood with the influence of John Dewey and Colonel Francis Parker permeating his home and school life" (p. vi). Although he deferred to liberal educational theory, Washburne was convinced that "many remedial readers are below average because they have the wrong kind of eye habits" and that "instead of their eyes taking in a considerable group of words with one fixation and then moving on to the next group, their eyes make many stops, see only a few letters at a time or perhaps a word, move backward as well as forward" (1932, p. 64). He informed readers that "this whole subject has been thoroughly investigated at the University of Chicago" and he endorsed "special drill material to overcome this type of weakness" (p. 64).

Inskeep (1930) had warned of the need to maintain eye health in general classroom activities and during recreation as well as during reading instruction. For example, he wrote that "blackboard writing is frequently too light and too small to be read easily by children" (p. 224). Inskeep also cautioned about the harmful impact of movies, advising parents and teachers to be worried about, glare, flicker, rapidity of motion, and excessive concentrated attention. He suggested that "since colored movies and the black with *less vivid contrasts* are not as trying on the eyes they should be more frequently used at junior matinees" (p. 225). With regard to eye movement during reading, Inskeep noted that "if the book is too heavy to be held *steadily* by the little hands the muscles that move the eyeball become tired trying to move the eyes across the page in perfect alignment and a tendency to cross-eyes results" (p. 224). He also noted that reading "requires that the eyes be focused on letters that are smaller than anything probably the child has ever looked at carefully and constantly before" and that additional strain resulted because "the eye must run along a line with closest attention to detail" (p. 221).

Writing the same year as Inskeep, Storm and Smith (1930) provided three reasons to explain the intense interest of many reading educators in eye movements. They wrote that the movements "are a fundamental element of the reading process, they are reliable because they are not easily controlled by the individual, and they yield clearly objective evidence" (p. 101). Storm and Smith gave advice on the instructional implications of the eye-movement research when they described classroom activities to increase perceptual span, decrease the number of regressions, and reduce the vocalizations made during silent reading. Worried that teachers might not view such activities as relevant, they assured them that eye

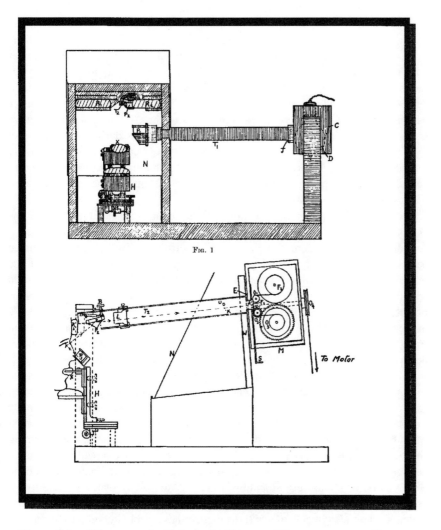

Figure 3.2. Diagram of a Relatively Compact Eye-movement Camara
Illustrated in a Textbook from the 1930s

movements maintained "a very close relationship to reading" and that this relationship had been documented by professionals who had "devoted some study to
this phase of reading" (p. 83).

In his 1936 textbook on reading readiness, Harrison listed factors connected to
physical development that could foster reading. Not only eye dominance but lateral and vertical eye muscle balance were included among these factors. Betts

(1936) assured his readers that "the earliest and most intensive research in the field of reading had to do with eye-movements" and that "few books on reading methodology or reading disabilities fail to include chapters on the work of the eyes in reading" (p. 169). He included an appendix on eye-training exercises with the stereograph, a special mechanical device for developing efficient eye movements. Betts was convinced that "children can profit physically by the incidental exercises and eye recreations" (p. 383). The stereograph was not as bulky as other pieces of equipment intended to assist readers. As an indication of how unwieldy some diagnostic eye-movement equipment was during this era, a picture in Betts's 1936 book depicted an eye-movement camera that was roughly the size of a pickup truck. Taylor (1937) presented multiple illustrations of comparably massive apparatuses. In contrast, Figure 3.2 illustrates a relatively compact device from the 1930s.

Dolch's book on remedial reading (1939) contained an appendix on the "Ophthalmograph" and the "Metrononoscope." The Ophthalmograph was a "compact" eye-movement camera and the Metrononoscope was an automated device for flashing words and phrases to students. Although he thought the research base for such devices was sound, Dolch warned of problems that could result from the disruption that the machines might cause in schools. He also worried that teachers might have a tendency to rely excessively on them. Dolch's immensely practical book exhibited a great deal of the savvy he had gained from observing children in their classrooms. In the preface he emphasized that he was not writing about students "whose difficulties are so complicated that they must be studied and helped by a reading clinic" (pp. v-vi). Instead, he developed assessment and instructional activities intended for "the great majority, who can be taken care of by the classroom teacher or by a special teacher who has given some study to remedial reading" (p. v). Dolch's pragmatism and independence were apparent when he disputed prospects for devising a single, optimal approach for teaching word-attack skills. He advised that "the three habits of attack in reading should all be present and...the child should recognize by sight, he should guess words from context, and he should use sounding" because "to do any of these three to the exclusion of the other two makes a poor reader" (p. 67). Despite such pragmatism, Dolch's acknowledgments of eye movements' inescapable importance to reading programs revealed the prevailing attitudes during the 1930s.

Remedial Eye Training

In the early part of the twentieth century, Hall (1911b) had reported about "manifold and fruitful investigations" into the "psycho-physic processes involved in the act of reading" (p. 409). On the basis of these investigations, he advised that the length and uniformity of printed lines in books should be controlled so as to enable readers to make the optimal number of fixations in each line of print. After observing that "some cultivated adults read from two to four times as fast as others just as cultivated," he concluded that "there is some indication that for more practiced readers, the anticipatory work to the right of the fixation point increases and that the space between the eye and the focus which is always changing is greatest in most rapid readers" (p. 413). Three years later Klapper (1914) advised that "the teacher must realize how much care must constantly be exercised if children are to be kept free from eye ailments that follow in the wake of reading and study" (p. 9). He counseled teachers to help learners "develop motor habits of breaking the lines into a given number of regular pauses and moves, each line showing the same number of stops and sweeps" (p. 9).

During the 1920s educators continued to give advice about eye training to improve reading. O'Brien (1921) recommended that "short exposure exercises, in which the amount of materials exposed is gradually increased...tend to develop speed in reading" (p. 273). Pennell and Cusack (1924) warned teachers that "a child cannot get thought from his reading, no matter how great his desire or love for reading may be, unless he has command over the mechanics of reading." Identifying information about eye movements as one of the most valuable types of information about the mechanics of reading, they recommended that children be instructed about efficient eye movements in order to "decrease the eye-strain caused by the artificial reading process and increase the speed of silent reading" (p. 50). The primary exercise they advocated was "widening of the perceptual span" through the use of phrases or short sentences to facilitate "quick exposure." Leonard (1922) wrote a textbook in which he recommended that teachers carefully select materials based on whether the content would motivate students to read. Despite this literature-based focus, he attempted to reconcile his program with the eye-movement research when he wrote that exposure to diverse reading materials not only stimulated learners but was "actually found to do all that is necessary for most children in forming essential right habits of eye-sweep" (p. 170).

Cole (1934) strongly encouraged teachers to use eye-movement-based reading activities. For example, she instructed teachers to monitor whether students were making the ideal number of eye movements in each grade (16 fixations per line in first grade and four in fourth grade). In the preface to a remedial reading textbook that she wrote several years later, Cole (1938) assured readers that her book was relatively brief because she had confined its contents to "objectively proven facts." Within a chapter on remedial exercises for increasing the speed of reading, she illustrated a set of drills for training the eyes to make efficient movements. In one of her examples she explained how learners could use a template that contained geometric shapes arranged on a page:

> The pupil who is reading is told to look at the first dot on the first line, then to slide his eyes along the line to the right until he comes to the second dot, look at it, and again slide his eyes to the right until he come to the third dot. He then brings his eyes back, along the diagonal to the second line; he stops at each of the three crosses on this line and then brings his eyes back to the beginning of the third. He proceeds in this way down the page (Cole, 1938, p. 98).

Although Cole described eye-training exercises that incorporated the use of the *lantern* (i.e., slide projector) she concentrated on nonmechanical materials such as flash cards and worksheets. In a later edition of their popular textbook on reading education, Pennell and Cusack (1935) also gave examples of nonobtrusive activities to promote appropriate eye movements. They provided examples of adaptations to standard reading practices that teachers could implement to help readers' eyes form "the habit of making regular, long eye-jumps along the line" and to encourage "avoidance of regressive movements" (p. 42). So convinced were Pennell and Cusack of a connection between efficient eye movements and appropriate reading instruction that they used the heading "Eye Training" to introduce the section about phonics.

Not all educators agreed that eye-training activities needed to be nonobtrusive. Seltzter (1933) wrote that "lateral muscle imbalance" was responsible for "mirror-reading, as well as the type of reading disability characterized by reversing the order of letters, omitting letters, and supplying letters not needed" (p. 93). Although he acknowledged that his therapeutic suggestions were "bitterly opposed" by "oculists," Seltzter proposed physical, conditioning activities that could be performed by students while looking through prisms. A pamphlet published four years later about the use of eye-training devices in the classroom (American Optical Company, 1936-1937) advised teachers that "prism-reading as a corrective technique, either in the office of the eye specialist, or in the reading clinic under the supervision of the eye specialist, furnishes an effective method for dealing with many cases of reading disability which are associated with visual inefficiencies" (p. 42).

Earl Taylor (1937), who worked for the company that had manufactured some of the most popular reading machines on the market in the 1930s, endorsed "prism-reading" because it could "bring about efficient reading, the essential features of which, in addition to comfortable vision, are few fixations, few regressions, rapidity, rhythm, and maximum comprehension" (p. 252). Taylor added that "desirable eye habits are induced by reading exercises which control the eye-movements of children who are learning to read, and by remedial training of this nature for both children and adults who have reading disabilities" and that "at least one-half of the students in our public schools and other education institutions, and of the adult population as well, might benefit from this type of training" (p. 252). Unlike those colleagues who had shown hostile reactions to eye specialists, Taylor judged that "specialists in this country at the present time are giving and recommending various types of orthoptic training, since they have come to realize that, by the use of prism exercises, it is possible to take care of certain visual anomalies which do not respond to other corrective measures" (p. 254). Concluding that monitoring of eye movements was essential to the implementation of corrective reading activities as well as to reading diagnosis, Taylor wrote that an "eye-movement photograph or reading-graph is indispensable in any comprehensive visual or reading examination" and that such photography "is the only *objective information* which permits comparison between groups of individuals, and furnishes a definite prognostic test for checking corrective measures" (p. 323).

Criticism of Eye-Movement Research

During the early decades of the twentieth century many instructors were convinced of a critical connection between eye movement and successful reading. These instructors alluded to this connection as the rationale for diagnostic procedures that were designed to sort effective from ineffective readers. Some instructors went a step further, maintaining that certain patterns of eye movements were responsible for successfully learning to read. The teachers in this latter group recommended remedial activities to redress the deficient eye movements they had discerned. Although the popularity of these suggestions is well documented, some critics did challenge those suggestions. For example, Vernon (1931) reviewed data about reading eye movements that had been reported by Judd and Buswell at the University of Chicago. She questioned whether the variations in eye movements that had been recorded with different types of material "were due to differences in comprehension of the material, of familiarity with it, or of interest in it" and regretted that Judd and Buswell "unfortunately did not obtain any introspections on the subject" (p. 69). After reviewing her own experimental data, she concluded that many eye movements were simply "permanent ocular motor habits, unconnected with perception and assimilation of the reading content" (p. 96). With regard to incorporating data about eye movements into remedial reading, she advised educators that her own data presented "no definite experimental evidence as to how perception developed with sufficient detail and accuracy for reading purposes" (p. 177).

Hildreth was one of the reading educators who was prominent during the 1930s but who remained unconvinced of a critical relationship between eye movement and learning to read. In her 1936 textbook she indicated her disposition when she boldly titled a section "Meaning Dominates and Directs Perception." She gave examples of a student excited about a university class reunion who had read "college" for "cottage" in a passage unrelated to colleges and about another person who specialized in infant welfare who had read the title of a journal article, "Studies of Student Mortality," as "Studies of Infant Mortality." She referred to the features of words that were used by readers as "cues" and insisted that meaningful cues dominated perceptual cues. She wrote with confidence that "meaning dictates whether one should read 'b' or 'd,' 'abominable' or 'abdominal'" (1936, p. 87). Sure that meaning determined perception, Hildreth was also convinced that emotional attitudes influenced perception during reading because "words and phrases with high emotional tone appear to be easier for the child to learn than words lacking any special emotional significance" (p. 90). She gave examples of words that children had learned readily or failed to learn easily, suggesting that emotional factors had influenced their learning.

Gates (1935) had advised teachers during the 1930s to be guided by the psychological principle to not "separate a skill from the normal function it is intended to serve" (p. 269). This principle certainly influenced his attitudes toward the mechanical devices associated with eye-movement instruction. In the section of the book about features of the eye that could impair learning to read, he concluded that eye dominance was "a very minor source of difficulty" (p. 348). After expressing skepticism about the value of the eye-movement research, he also advised teachers that the equipment needed to discern eye movements was both expensive and impractical. Even in the original 1927 edition of his book on remedial reading, Gates had advised teachers that "knowledge of the exact nature of eye movements is at present chiefly interesting and useful in diagnosis" and that remedial activity "directed exclusively to correcting the eye movements might be expected to be futile" (pp. 233-234).

Writing after that decade in which critics such as Vernon, Hildreth, and Gates had questioned the value of eye-movement research, Traxler (1941) commented cautiously about teachers who believed that remedial activities could redress deficient eye movements. Though he reported that "the fact that the photographic technique for recording movements of the eyes during reading which has been in use for some twenty years has shown close relationship between reading skill and number and duration of fixations" he also conceded that "a considerable number of reading specialists have been critical of this type of training" (pp. 31-32).

Writing more than 10 years after Traxler had made these careful remarks, Spache (1953b) was still cautious. After characterizing eye movement as "the most widely studied of the physical factors" involved in reading, he concluded critically that the research was "inconclusive, even contradictory" (p. 50). Using a similar rhetorical tone, Anderson and Dearborn (1952) admitted that much of that which was known about the psychology of reading had been based on the eye-movement approach in which "research has not conclusively demonstrated that any lasting benefit is derived from eye-movement training as such" and that "the whole approach requires reexamination" (p. 131).

Like the little boy who could not conceal his commonsense observations in the fairy tale about *The Emperor's New Clothes*, Duncan (1953) was more candid when he observed that "while it is true that there are personal differences in eye-span...in actual practice no one uses eye-span mechanically" (p. 90). Duncan's remarks were similar to observations that had been made more than a decade earlier by ophthalmologists. For example, Irvine (1941) had presented a proposed ocular policy for public schools that had been developed by the ophthalmologists of the Los Angeles County Medical Association. With regard to the value of eye movements as a component of reading diagnosis, Irvine reported a consensus among the ophthalmologists that "results of research in this field [i.e., ophthalmology] have been completely negative" (p. 785). The ophthalmologists discouraged the examination of eye movements for diagnosing reading problems because "there is wide variation in eye movement among good readers according to subject matter" and because "the evidence indicates that eye movements are desultory because the subject cannot read, and not that the subject cannot read because eye movements are wandering" (pp. 785-786). After reminding educators that "not the eyes but the brain learns to read," the authors of the report concluded caustically that "measuring of eye movements seems to be so much wasted time" (p. 786).

Response to Criticism

Though many educators were criticizing eye-movement research at the end of the 1940s, some enthusiasts were reluctant to relinquish diagnostic procedures and training activities that had seemed earlier to be a secure foundation for instruction. Blair (1946) was a student of Gates who expressed an opinion in 1946 about eye movements that would become more and more prevalent. He wrote that "faulty eye movements are symptoms rather than causes of poor reading ability" and that "remedial work should therefore be directed toward causes rather than symptoms if satisfactory therapeutic results are to be accomplished" (1946, p. 30). However, Blair still made a list of machines that teachers could use to train the eye movements of their students.

Blair's disavowal of the usefulness of eye-movement research while paradoxically endorsing the machines that were based on that research reflected an ambivalence that other remedial reading specialists would exhibit. Having located a link to physiology that in some ways elevated their profession closer to the medical fields of which they were envious, educators were reluctant to part with the practical activities that were based on that link. This reluctance was apparent even after evidence indicated that the logical basis for that link was questionable. As another example of this intellectual ambivalence, Kottmeyer (1947) had succumbed to his emotions rather than logic when he acknowledged objections to eye-movement photography but still remonstrated that "however legitimate these and other criticisms may be, the fact remains that the photography of eye movements has increased our knowledge of how eyes behave during the act of reading and that graphs often provide information about the mechanics of a reading habit which cannot be ascertained in any other way" (p. 36). In the second edition of his book, Blair (1956) still expressed his conviction that "while the study of a pupil's eye movements during reading will give a measure of his reading ability, it is equally clear that the remedial work should not be directed toward the training of eye movements" (p. 23). But in a chapter about remedial teaching that appeared in that edition, Blair noted that "there is no reading skill which responds more readily to remedial treatment than that of speed" (p. 94). He then described the merits of the devices such as that used in the push-card method and in which "the teacher should begin moving a large card down the page one line at a time, and at a rate of speed that will force the pupil to read at a faster than usual tempo" (p. 97). In addition to the push-card, Blair recommended a group of machines to accelerate reading

Figure 3.3. Illustration from a 1956 Textbook of an Apparatus to Increase Reading Speed

speed. For example, he described the *reading board*, a device illustrated in Figure 3.3 and in which "gears driven by an electric motor push an aluminum cover down a page of print at various rates of speed."

In a report about tachistoscopes, Hamilton (1954) reviewed the work of a nineteenth-century teacher in Connecticut who had written about the effectiveness of drilling students with words printed on a revolving blackboard. Hamilton characterized this instructional approach as one that "was concerned primarily with the development of habits of quick perception, accuracy of perception, and ability to discriminate quickly" (p. 151). He indicated that even though current teachers recognized that educators and psychologists in the 1800s were skeptical of claims about the effectiveness of such perception-based systems of learning, they still persisted with the use of tachistoscopes in the hope of enhancing learning. Hamilton wrote of the research about the nineteenth-century Connecticut teacher that "in spite of the fact that many persons expressed doubt as to the validity of her claims for the method, one can see in it the background of many of the present-day aspects of tachistoscopic training" (p. 151).

In a textbook about basal reading instruction published a year later, Yoakam (1955) wrote that "modern theory holds that the teacher can do little directly to develop eye movements as such" and that efficient eye movements "grow as a result of general reading experience" (p. 51). Despite this disclaimer, Yoakam included detailed information about patterns of eye movements during reading, the typical number of fixations made per line by efficient readers, and the deleterious effect of visual regressions. Though he admitted that "the facts summarized concerning eye movement do not give us any direct guidance concerning what should be done, if anything," Yoakam still admonished that "a reasonable grasp of the perceptual process in reading will give a teacher a better understanding of the importance of good visual and of the difficulties involved when a child is learning to read" (pp. 51-52).

An appendix to Strang and Bracken's popular 1957 reading education textbook indicated the continuing popularity of assumptions about the connection of eye movements to reading. This appendix contained 11 *mechanical aids* for diagnosing and correcting eye problems associated with reading. These mechanical devices included the *rateometer* and *accelerator* as well as a *tachistoscope*, a *hand-eye coordinator*, a *pacer*, a *trainer*, and a *perceptascope*. In a textbook published four years later, Strang, McCullough, and Traxler (1961) admitted that reading machines continued to be popular. But they judged that the rationale for employing them had "shifted from attempting to increase eye span to the purpose of quickening the association between the visual impression of the printed symbol and its translation into meaning" (p. 442). They also observed that the use of machines to increase speed was "being modified in the direction of an emphasis on their motivational value" (p. 440).

Controversy about the relationship of eye training and learning was not confined to reading educators. Having developed an elaborate theory of perceptual learning, Kephart (1960) had recommended that preschool children employ perceptual readiness activities in order to achieve academic objectives. Convinced that academic objectives would elude students who did not use the perceptual activities he prescribed, he wrote optimistically that "if readiness can be achieved by giving such special attention early, many slow learners can fall in with the rest of their fellows and continue learning through the customary activities of the group" (p. viii). In a chapter titled "Training Ocular Control," he summarized some of the instructional activities that he had recommended:

> The general procedure is to move a target in front of the child and ask him to follow it with his eyes. Care is taken to watch the child's eyes carefully to see that he is following the target and that his eyes are moving smoothly and with coordination. In the event of any continued jerkiness or lack of control, the training is discontinued and some other means of helping the child is undertaken (Kephart, 1960, p. 241).

Reviewing the history of remedial reading, Roswell and Natchez (1971) employed a mixed metaphor when they noted that "the pendulum swings back and forth during the years, with each area enjoying the spotlight at different periods" (p. 6). They concluded that "in recent years, emphasis has turned back to cultural difficulties and perceptual disorders" (p. 6). As an indication of how rapidly that pendulum could complete a swing, the authors (Roswell & Natchez, 1977) withdrew their prediction about the return of an emphasis on perceptual disorders from the edition of their textbook that was published just six years later.

In the seventh edition of the textbook that Harris had originally published 40 years earlier, Harris and Sipay (1980) still maintained that eye-movement photography was a "reliable and valid" measure of reading performance. They referred to a 1946 study by Tinker to substantiate this observation. Despite Harris and Sipay's reliance on Tinker's research, Tinker himself had co-authored a 1957 textbook on remedial reading in which he and Bond questioned the usefulness of eye-movement research. Bond and Tinker had written that "examination of the available data reveals that eye-movement patterns...are symptoms of reading disability, not causes" (Bond & Tinker, 1957, p. 89). As an even more explicit indication of the chasm separating them from Harris on this issue, Bond and Tinker referred skeptically to professional books in which authors had continued to advocate for the use eye-movement patterns to diagnose reading problems. Among the works to which they referred was the 1956 edition of Harris's textbook on remedial reading. Bond and Tinker concluded that "the value of this practice is, in our opinion, doubtful" (1957, p. 200).

LINK TO NEUROLOGY

Clarence Gray (1913) published a study about the interrelation of breathing and reading in which he had made records with a "pneumograph," "kymograph," "Marey tambour," and "Jacquet chronometer." Although Gray indicated plans for subsequent studies (including an investigation of the extent to which "manner of dress has a certain effect upon the breathing of both adolescent girls and women"), this research never rivaled the popularity of investigations into eye movements. Nonetheless, both the studies about breathing and eye movements by early researchers revealed a propensity to seek physiological explanations to complex psychological problems. This propensity was also evident in the emerging research about neurological factors and reading. Dearborn (Lord, Carmichael, & Dearborn, 1925), a strong advocate of theories postulating that congenital and physiological factors contributed to reading disability, attempted to explain how congenital left handedness might contribute to reading disability:

> The outgoing movement of the left hand is from the centre of the body towards the left. The left handed person, possibly because he watches what his preferred hand does and thus establishes the habit, may show a preference for this same direction in his eye movements. The reading of "saw" as "was" is a very common observed error, although it is by no means confined to the left handed reader.... The confusion of letters which are the same in form but different in position, such as p, g; d, b; n, w; has been explained as due to the fact that our earliest memories of letters may be muscular. The eye movements may be quite as important as hand movements in fixing these memories (p. 3).

Dearborn later acknowledged that the conceptual ties between reading disability and physical aberrations was problematic because the concept had "become a catchall into which problems are indiscriminately dropped" (1939, p. 103). Despite this problem and "despite the recent consensus of contrary findings," he wrote that he still found "evidence to include, among the structural conditions [contributing to reading disability], deviations in the lateral dominance of hand and eye, especially change of handedness, and left-eyedness" (p. 104).

The reading reversals that fascinated Dearborn attracted other researchers as well. In 1934 Hildreth conducted a careful analysis of the reading and writing reversals made by children with reading problems and those made by children who were reading successfully. She also examined the number of reversals made by left-handed and right-handed children. She did not perceive significant differences in learners' tendencies to make reversals as a result of their handedness. But she did detect "some tendency for the poorest readers to make more reversals than good readers, just as the poorest readers made more kinds of all other types of errors than good readers" (p. 19). Hildreth assumed that this relationship was "associative" and that "the inconsistency of the reversal tendency prevents a conclusion that reversal tendency is a cause of poor reading" (p. 19).

Four years later Dolch (1939) reviewed research studies about reading and handedness and reported that "at first, there seemed to be a markedly greater number of left-handed children among poor readers than normal." But he cautioned that "later studies have tended to contradict this impression" (p. 15). Despite such cautionary warnings, books on remedial reading published in the 1930s (as well as during the decades that followed) contained advice to teachers about the need to assess features such as handedness because these could be indicators of neurological disorganization that interfered with reading. When Betts (1936) reviewed research relevant to remedial reading, he organized the reviews about several topics, the first of which was maturation. Subsumed beneath this topic were factors such as "defective cerebral development," "delayed cerebral development," and "confusion of cerebral development" (pp. 54-55).

Samuel Orton had published reports during the 1920s and 1930s about persons with learning disabilities, highlighting a disorder that he named *strephosymbolia.*

He indicated that *strephosymbolia*, which could not be predicted by the level of a child's general intellectual ability, was characterized by "confusion between similarly formed but oppositely oriented letters, and a tendency to a changing order in the direction of reading" (1989, p. 337). Gillingham and Stillman (1940) were students of Orton who later indicated that "it cannot be said how many people have this specific disability," but they quoted Orton who estimated the occurrence at "roughly somewhat over 10 per cent of the total school population" (p. 24). Orton concluded that such persons frequently exhibited "indications of developmental deviations in their acquisition of speech and motor patterns which bear out the belief expressed herein that the strephosymbolia syndrome can best be explained on the basis of confused cerebral dominance rather than abnormal vision" (1989, p. 308).

In 1946 Orton admitted that the neurological basis for his theory was far from secure even in his own mind. But he thought that the success of the instructional strategies that had been derived from his theory was sufficient to validate those strategies:

> Whether or not our theory is right, I do not know, but I do know that the methods of retraining which we have derived from that viewpoint have worked. I do not claim them to be a panacea for reading troubles of all sorts but I do feel that we understand the blockade which occurs so frequently in children with good minds and which results in the characteristic reading of the strephosymbolic type in childhood (S. Orton, quoted by J. Orton, 1966, p. 145).

Orton (1989) proposed a series of instructional activities to aid persons with learning problems that had a neurological origin. But he was wary of "overstandardization lest the procedure become too inflexible...which would clearly be unwise in view of the wide variation in symtomatology" (p. 96). Orton himself did provide several quite precise examples of the phonetic type of instruction that he viewed as beneficial. He wrote that "in teaching the phonetic units we have often found it convenient to use cards, each bearing a single letter or one of the more common digraphs, phonograms or diphthongs, printed by hand with fairly large rubber type in the lower case or small letter form" and that "these cards are exposed to the child one at a time with instruction in 'what it says' as well as its name, until he can give either the sound or name for any of the cards at sight" (p. 96).

Orton also provided examples of factors that correlated with the neurological anomalies that he judged to be the primary causes of reading problems, noting, for example, that "studies of laterality in the cases of developmental alexia have shown a very considerable number of crossed patterns between handedness and eyedness, as well as the other forms of motor intergrading" (p. 51). He carefully qualified these correlates when he wrote that such patterns were "by no means without exception and we have encountered extreme cases of the reading disability in children who were right-sided as well as in those who were completely left-sided" (p. 51). In a similar fashion, he warned teachers who were implementing writing instruction that though "in some individuals the use of the

wrong hand will lead to serious consequences," at the same time a "large number of left-handed individuals who have acquired a satisfactory writing with the
right hand demonstrates without question that this is possible in many
instances" (p. 269). Orton regularly provided such warnings because he anticipated that the principles he had defined might be overgeneralized.

In their book on reading education, Stanger and Donahue (1937) acknowledged
that their ideas had been built on the work done by Orton during the 1920s and
early 1930s. In the preface they discussed their own reliance on a theory of
"well-known neurologists." The underlying theory to which Stanger and Donahue
had referred concerned the need for one of the brain's hemispheres to establish
dominance. They indicated that several years of diagnosing children with reading
problems had enabled them to realize that "a very great majority of these children
presents evidence of confusion" (p. 16). The consequent confused cerebral dominance could be manifest as problems that were "auditory, visual, or kinaesthetic...or, as more often happens, a combination of any of these types" (p. 16).

In their attempt to investigate the effects of cerebral dominance, Stanger and
Donahue focused on early reading rather than remedial reading because they
were "not concerned with the remedial value of this theory, excellent as it has
proved itself" (pp. 16-17). They became concerned with the development of good
habits because "remedial work implies retraining, the erasing of bad learning
habits" (pp. 16-17). Instead of encouraging teachers to develop remedial reading
expertise, they thought that a more appropriate goal was for "every primary
teacher to eliminate the necessity of later remedial work." Stanger and Donahue
(1937) presented extremely detailed lessons that they encouraged teachers to
replicate punctiliously:

> The letter to be learned is first made by the teacher while the child is watching, and this is fur-
> ther reinforced by a clearly worded description of the successive strokes used. Then the letter,
> made several times on paper in its correct form, is given to the child for tracing. As each letter
> is traced, its name and sound should be given. Thus, very slowly, the child says as he traces the
> letter. "Capital *a* and the sound is...." Care must be taken in the tracing, that not only the fin-
> ished form is correct, but that the child makes the letter with his hand moving in the accepted
> direction (p. 126).

As an indication of the longevity of assumptions about a connection between
neurological dominance and reading, Robinson (1961) judged that dominance,
expressed through "left or inconsistent hand, foot and eye preference" was "probably of less importance" than other factors that had been associated with reading
failure. These other factors included school practices, emotional disturbances,
family relations, peer relations, hearing, and demonstrated brain damage. However, Robinson qualified these remarks, indicating that her advice to reduce the
emphasis on indicators of dominance did not apply to "seriously retarded readers"
(p. 365).

Early Criticism of Neurological Research

After he had reviewed specific studies on physiological aspects of reading, Traxler (1941) concluded that "although some persons hold very definite opinions, the sum total of the research literature to date does not warrant these opinions" (pp. 36-37). Gates (1947) reviewed the literature on eye and hand dominance six years later and concluded that "the extent to which these several characteristics contribute to difficulty in reading is by no means clear" (p. 107). Though he did not judge his review to be conclusive, he did observe a "tendency [that] seems to be definitely in the direction of minimizing the importance of the factors" (p. 107). Gates described his personal position as "skeptical of the importance of some of the 'organic characteristics,' such as left-handedness or left-eyedness as a source of reading defect" (p. 7). Even in an earlier edition of his remedial reading textbook, he had asserted confidently that "the idea that confused brain dominance or lack of dominance should be the cause of such reading difficulties was considered too speculative to be serviceable" (1935, p. 352).

Acknowledging his intellectual debt to Gates, Blair (1946) reviewed the literature about handedness and reading problems. Like Gates, he concluded that teachers "should not pay undue attention to the handedness of children who are in need of remedial work in reading" (p. 67). Initially, Spache did not discount the possibility that handedness had some influence on reading, but he still indicated his personal skepticism, remarking that his colleagues may have greatly exaggerated the role of such factors" (p. 7). Later Spache (1953b) took a stronger stance when he wrote that the "physical factors no longer generally accepted as causal [of reading problems] are those concerned with laterality, such as handedness, eye-hand dominance, cerebral dominance, and reversals [of letters by readers]" (p. 50). Vernon (1957) phrased a simple but cogent argument about the limitations of neurological explanations for reading disability when she noted that "all theories which attribute reading disability to some general lack of maturation are unsatisfactory in that they give no explanation as to why reading alone should be affected, and not other cognitive activities" (p. 109).

Continued Interest in Neurological Research

In 1939 Dearborn had stubbornly refused to accede to "the recent consensus of contrary findings" which had challenged the relevance of cerebral dominance information to reading. This stubbornness turned out to be a somewhat prudent reaction. Although the impact of theories of cerebral organization diminished after the 1930s, the general concept continued to attract some supporters. In latter editions of both Harris's book on remedial reading (Harris & Sipay, 1980) as well as that of Bond and Tinker (Bond, Tinker, & Wasson, 1979), studies about cerebral organization were cited from a multidecade period. Though some studies supported the view that cerebral organization was a cause of reading disability, others did not. The authors of these textbooks cautiously characterized the studies about cerebral organization with descriptions such as *controversial, puzzling*, and *equivocal*.

The most controversial reports about the neurological factors affecting reading may have been those of Delacato (1959, 1963). Delacato proposed his theory as an alternative to the prevailing beliefs that remediation should occur through instructional materials and procedures. When he boldly and unqualifiedly stipulated the neurological prerequisites for learning, Delacato made remarks that seemed to be less temperate restatements of those made several decades earlier by Orton:

> One-sidedness, which in turn reflects hemispheric dominance, is prerequisite to reading and complete speech, hence training at this level takes place within the pre-remedial period. One-sidedness means that one hand becomes the skilled hand, one foot becomes the skilled foot and one eye becomes the predominant eye. They must all be on the same side (Delacato, 1963, p. 122).

On the other hand, it was more than the tenor of his rhetoric that set Delacato aside from other educators who had supported neurological explanations for reading problems. The distinctiveness of his ideas was revealed when he described a series of gross motor activities to correct neurological dysfunctions that might interfere with learning to read:

> We have been able to take children who deviated from normal development (severely brain injured) and through extrinsic imposition of normal patterns of movement and behavior have been able to neurologically organize them sufficiently so that they could be placed within the human development pattern of crawling, creeping and walking. Finally, with man's unique lateral neurological function added to this structure, talking, reading and writing developed (Delacato, 1963, pp. 77-78).

In the numerous editions of his popular textbook on remedial reading, Harris had been reluctant to take a decisive stand about most controversial issues. But Harris was not reluctant to advise teachers about the limited benefits of Delacato's strategies, declaring that "reading specialists can safely ignore the Delacato approach" (Harris & Sipay, 1980, p. 296).

One of the strongest links between remedial reading and neurology was that posited by Smith and Carrigan (1959). They published a "chronicle of a search for the cause of severe reading disability" that carried them "into neurophysiology and from there into endocrinology" (p. vii). Smith and Carrigan termed this abstruse theory *the synaptic transmission model*. A clear understanding of this model may have been delayed rather than expedited by the introductory remarks with which they qualified the exposition of their model:

> During the following description, it would be kept in mind that synaptic transmission *model* and the specific neural *mechanism* are separate entities. The model is an analogue, an "as if"

construct. On the other hand, the neural mechanism which accounts for transmission has been advocated by neurophysiologists as a literal reality. In essence, it is thought that the model accounts for the behavioral data. If future investigators determine that the neural mechanism itself does not exist, the model will not be invalidated. So long as transmission occurs *as if* such a mechanism exists, the model remains adequate (Smith & Carrigan, 1959, p. 16).

On the basis of their research, they recommended that reading be promoted through vitamins and hormones. Since the children with whom they interacted were physically healthy, they acknowledged that "the use of medicine for essentially healthy people is not ordinarily recommended" (p. 70). However they thought that "the change in self-concept that occurs when [students] suddenly begin to read may justify the 'tampering'" (p. 70). After completing their explanation of the synaptic transmission model, they admitted that their ideas were sufficiently eccentric that educators might still question them:

> But is the model useful? It will be remembered that earlier theoretical positions have often been roundly criticized for their failure to suggest positive action. From the present position, the clinician is advised to alter ChE and ACh balance and level and to reduce anxiety before instituting reading therapy. Hormones, amphetamines, and tranquilizers have been suggested as likely agents, though much must still be learned about the complex action of such substances. Let us conclude that, if the effectiveness of such treatment can be demonstrated conclusively, the model will have proved useful (Smith & Carrigan, 1959, p. 88).

Frostig maintained that activities in global movement could promote achievement in academic learning (Frostig & Horne, 1964). Her motive for using movement-based training was that such movement integrated "the simultaneous experience of spatial and temporal dimensions, and is therefore a powerful tool in promoting the integrative processes of the brain" (Frostig & Maslow, 1973, p. 23). The use of movement and other nonacademic activities to solve reading problems seemed reasonable to her because "research emphasizes the multiplicity of connections and interdependence of feedback mechanisms among the various regions of the brain" (Frostig & Maslow, 1973, p. 24). Frostig judged that many traditional remedial learning activities were too restrictive, noting that "educators were no longer justified in modeling instructional procedures on a simple stimulus-response paradigm" (Frostig & Maslow, 1973, p. 24).

SUMMARY

The procedures for diagnostic testing that emerged during the early part of the 1900s complemented a model of scientific analysis in education that was developing during the same era. These scientific attitudes may have predisposed researchers and educators to search for a connection between physical factors and learning, a search illustrated by the investigation of readers' eye movements. Once they had noted that eye movements correlated with speed of reading, researchers suspected that the physical factors responsible for those movements might be critical to efficient reading.

Educators initially used this information to diagnose reading problems. But some went further, recommending regulated eye-movements to eliminate reading problems. Despite its controversial nature, this recommendation was readily adopted by many teachers who used specialized activities, materials, and devices to encourage optimal eye movements.

Some educators argued that the physical factors responsible for reading problems extended beyond eye movements to neurological organization. But the instructional activities that they prescribed were not markedly different from the skills-based activities being used by educators who were not sympathetic to such theories.

During the 1950s and 1960s a group of educators and researchers extended concepts about the physical basis for reading to new limits. Arguing that gross motor exercises or even the ingestion of vitamins and hormones could eliminate reading problems, this group recommended distinctive remedial activities.

Chapter 4

GOLDEN ERA OF REMEDIAL READING

The problem of remedial instruction in reading is to find a possible method of learning for those children who have not been able to learn to read by methods adapted to the group (Monroe, 1932).

During the 1930s a group of remedial reading specialists emerged. These specialists employed extensive diagnostic procedures and distinctive remedial activities. By the end of the decade many remedial programs had transformed into elaborate clinical approaches that were modeled after medical practices. Distressed at the increasing specialization within remedial reading, some educators devised lessons to be implemented by classroom teachers with groups of students.

*　　*　　*

During the 1920s and 1930s remedial reading developed an identity that became progressively distinct from general reading education. One sign of this identity was the inclusion of chapters on remedial reading in teacher training textbooks. This was apparent even among those educators who maintained quite amorphous philosophies of instruction. As an example, Wheat (1923) had explained in the preface to his book on reading methods that "the methods and devices of teaching a given subject are, in the main, purely personal" (p. v). Even with such a casual approach to education, he thought to include a chapter on "Special Help to Backward Pupils," in which he noted the types of errors that students might exhibit when reading orally or silently. Examples of specific oral reading errors were repetitions, insertions, omissions, substitutions, and the mispronunciations of words during oral reading. Illustrations of silent reading errors included inability to find essential ideas, omissions of parts of an idea, reading word for word rather than by thought groups, vocalization, and use of a finger to follow lines of print. Wheat was wary of instruction that required "assistance of 'special helpers,' 'trained supervisors,' or 'experts'" and judged that individualized reading lessons administered by

99

classroom teachers were the only antidotes required to cure reading problems. He carefully described individualized activities to promote eye training, oral reading, the search for specific information, differentiation of words with similar appearances, effective breathing, articulation, and oral expression. Citing case studies of "backwards pupils" who would benefit from remedial reading lessons, he identified the steps that instructors should follow when designing the lessons:

> (1) The abilities of the pupils should be measured; (2) their individual points of difficulty and of failure should be discovered and classified; (3) their various types of backwardness should be diagnosed; (4) special forms of remedial instruction should be planned for each type; (5) the pupils should be grouped into special classes and instructed according to the special needs of each group; and (6) their progress should be tested from time to time (Wheat, 1923, p. 333).

Wheat was an articulate advocate for individualized remedial instruction. Two distinct approaches to individualized instruction were popular in the early 1920s. Like Wheat, William Gray (1925) described instructors who custom-designed remedial reading programs to accommodate individual learners. He asserted confidently that "the importance and need of diagnostic and remedial work are widely recognized" and that "the possibility of doing effective work of this type in the public schools has been clearly demonstrated" (p. 208). In addition to individually administered instruction, Gray described approaches in which the learning problems of individual students were addressed through carefully arranged group activities. The group format for individualized remedial instruction was based on "the use of a specific device in all cases belonging to the same general class" (p. 208). Although Gray was sympathetic to individually administered reading instruction, he later questioned whether the limited access and exorbitant costs of highly individualized programs were in proportion to their benefits.

In contrast to Gray's cautious endorsement of individualized instruction, Uhl (1924) supported not only individualized instruction but also a specially trained class of teachers to administer the lessons. He predicted that a new era in education was approaching in which specialists would diagnose learners and then implement remedial reading instruction:

> The days of the untrained practitioner are numbered. Education is now conducted on too large a scale to permit children to loiter through the elementary school and later waste their adolescent years in inefficient reading of high-school textbooks. Public policy as well as individual interests require teachers to discover the reading ailments of pupils and then prescribe remedies for the curable causes. The teacher's formula is therefore, first, diagnose; second, prescribe and apply remedies (Uhl, 1924, p. 264).

Though he supported the training of specialists, Uhl thought that ordinary teachers could use diagnostic and remedial activities in the classroom as well. Not only did he judge that all teachers could benefit from training in remedial reading, but he was confident that remedial "work can profitably be pursued by all the pupils in a class" (p. 276). He was similarly confident about the benefits of tests that were to be administered by classroom teachers. He wrote optimistically that "diagnosis by means of standard tests scores is also a simple matter; the accurate giving and scoring of tests is so easy that no one should be deterred therefrom" (p. 276).

INITIAL IDENTITY FOR REMEDIAL READING

During the economically and socially tumultuous 1930s, politically liberal educators berated both administrators and conservative teachers for failing to implement the radical changes they thought were needed to end the country's plight. Remedial reading instructors were hardly disturbed by this ranting. Some protection may have been provided after remedial reading instructors had resolved to promote science rather than politics when making decisions about their programs. On the basis of this commitment, they were drawn to diagnostic techniques and remedial activities that were to be experimentally validated.

Not only did remedial reading teachers wish to keep liberal ideologues from influencing their approach, but they also wished to prevent the public from viewing their approach as a conservative, political reaction to liberal politics. After acknowledging the hundreds of articles critical of the politicized, progressive practices that had appeared during the beginning of the era of remedial reading, Hildreth (1936) insisted that the expansion of remedial reading was not a knee-jerk response to inadequate progressive educational programs:

> The inclusion of diagnostic work as part of the regular school program, closely integrated with classroom teaching, must be recognized not as a confession of failure, but as an indication of improved practice. A single teacher with a class of thirty or forty pupils is scarcely capable of doing an efficient job in skills without the accurate checks that diagnostic methods afford. Diagnosis may refer not only to the special intensive study of deficient learners, but to the constant checking of pupil progress that good teachers carry on regularly with all pupils (pp. 537-538).

Mort and Gates (1932) assured teachers that "standard tests are to-day quite generally looked upon as useful devices the limitations of which are so well known that they need not be feared" (p. iii). They argued that diagnostic testing should be implemented on a broad scale because this might reveal information essential to all students' curricula. As such, diagnosis, even when it had been selected to evaluate individual students, might also result in the assessment and improvement of programs. They recommended that students' strengths, weakness, and needs be evaluated on the basis of their attitudes and home environments as well as their aptitudes. Though they thought the remedial work for students with severe disabilities could be "individual for a time," they assured teachers that "pupils who reveal no conspicuous defects in intelligence, in vision, or in the more elementary techniques, though they may read very slowly or inaccurately or with inadequate comprehension, need not be taught separately, but may be grouped together for corrective work" (p. 32). The remedial reading procedures they advocated contained six steps:

1. Grouping the pupils according to individual needs.
2. Introducing the topic so as to stimulate interest.
3. Making adjustments and providing incentives to overcome special weakness.
4. Supervising the work of individual pupils so as to encourage improvement, and to detect and correct deficiencies.
5. Recording and using results for diagnostic and remedial purposes.
6. Encouraging certain follow-up activities to increase interest, provide further experience, and strengthen desirable habits (Mort & Gates, 1932, p. 34).

Estimating the Need for Remedial Reading Programs

When Storm and Nila Baton Smith (1930) wrote their textbook on elementary reading instruction, they concluded it with a comprehensive chapter about reme- dial reading. The activities reviewed in this section were intended for the students "found in every group" who "fail to make progress in the ability to read according to the objectives set up for their grade" (pp. 350-351). However, when Nila Baton Smith (1934) wrote her history of reading education four years later, her excite- ment had diminished. Although a section on remedial reading was still included in her book, it was less than three pages long. Not only was the section brief, but a portion of that limited material warned teachers that "when remedial work on the basis of individual diagnosis was first recommended, many teachers came to look upon every child who was slow in reading as a remedial case, in need of indi- vidualized instruction" but that the term "is now generally used to apply only to problem cases" (p. 227).

Three years later Monroe and Backus (1937) presented a counterpoint. They wrote that "remedial reading is needed by not just a few scattered and very special cases, but by a large proportion of the school population." They concluded that "from 12 to 15 percent of the school population are sufficiently retarded in read- ing to need remedial work" (p. 3). Though Gray (1925) had called for remedial reading in the schools more than a decade before Monroe and Backus, he calcu- lated that the demand for these services would be required by only the "thousands of boys and girls" who failed each year in reading.

A year before Monroe and Backus had published their estimate, Betts (1936) had noted that the incidence of reading disability was typically judged to be between 8 and 15 percent. However, in a footnote, he personally estimated that 10 to 25 per- cent of all children were "retarded in reading." Gates (1941) was extremely con- servative, indicating that "typical teachers can learn to handle at least 90 percent of the reading defect cases in our schools" and that "for the remaining 10 percent, which would represent about two percent of the entire elementary school population, more expert diagnosis and remediation are desirable" (p. 83).

Acknowledging the wide variability in several decades of published reports about the number of students that required remedial instruction, Austin (1953) summarized the results, noting that "numerous investigators have estimated that from 5 to 40 percent of the school population are retarded in reading and should receive corrective instruction" (p. 19).

Grouped Remedial Reading Instruction

Near the end of the 1940s Gates (1947) was skeptical about many of the specialized remedial reading programs that had been implemented in the schools. He argued that the format rather than the content of these programs might be a better explanation for their effectiveness:

> If reading could be taught by individual tutoring, failure or serious deficiencies would be relatively rare.... Indeed, individual tutors or remedial "teachers" are highly successful even when they employ positively wretched materials and methods. Many classroom teachers would be more successful than some of these freakish specialists if they had equal opportunity to work daily with a single child. The "magic" of some remedial teachers is nothing but the potency of individual instruction (Gates, 1947, p. 5).

Gates also worried that remedial reading lessons segregated learners from their peers. As a consequence, he supported grouped reading activities as the instructional alternative that should be implemented most often.

Like Gates, William Gray (1947) had supported classroom-based corrective reading rather than the specialized programs that had expanded so dramatically during the 1940s. He counseled teachers "to look to the future for anticipated developments in corrective reading" so that they might confirm that it was not "a 'fad or frill' which will disappear from American education" (p. 17). Even decades earlier Gray (1925) had called for "changes in regular classroom instruction in order to reduce remedial cases" and the use of diagnostic and remedial activities as "an integral part of each elementary school and high school" (p. 208).

Gray was a member of the Committee on Reading of the National Society for the Study of Education, a group also disposed toward instruction by classroom teachers to groups of students. Whipple (1924) wrote that the members of this committee encouraged each teacher to make "continuous studies of the needs of her pupils in order to determine which types of training should be emphasized most" (p. 61). After he had elaborated specific directions for implementing grouped corrective activities, he gave practical advice about how to conduct a class while implementing these suggestions. He wrote that "while the teacher is engaged in [diagnostic and remedial activities] with one or more pupils, the remainder of a class may devote themselves [sic] to a special assignment or they may read independently at their seats or at the library table books in which they are interested" (p. 62).

Although he pointed to the increasing number of articles about remedial reading that had been published during the 1930s, Traxler (1941) seemed to be aware of the skepticism with which this growth was viewed by some when he reassured his audience that "an especially significant and encouraging fact in the reports is that in a great proportion of the experiments the teaching has been done by classroom teachers rather than by specialists in reading" (p. 44). In a similar manner, Russell, Karp, and Kelley (1938) had advised worried colleagues that "good remedial programs" could be "either individual or group" (p. 6).

McCallister (1936) had highlighted the distinction between remedial and corrective reading techniques when he wrote that "*remedial* implies individual instruction based on thorough diagnosis" and in contrast "the term *corrective* implies group instruction based on the common needs of a number of individuals" (p. 83). He advocated a three-tiered approach to secondary reading intervention programs characterized by "individual remedial training for those pupils who are seriously retarded," "corrective group instruction for mild cases of retardation," and "guidance for pupils who, though not necessarily retarded, encounter reading difficulties in studying content subjects" (p. vii). Although he acknowledged that specialized training was desirable, he still believed that "any competent teacher who has a sympathetic attitude toward pupils and who carefully studies their weakness and problems can make some contribution to the remedial program of a school" (p. 405). Ten years later Blair (1946) addressed the same question and concluded that "remedial teaching is just good teaching" (pp. 405-406).

Durrell (1940) attempted to avoid this dispute by distinguishing two types of specialized classrooms, the "remedial-reading laboratory" and the "remedial-reading homeroom." These classrooms were designed to supplement the regular classrooms where corrective reading programs would be implemented. The remedial-reading laboratory was a school-based, clinical facility in which students who had been taken from their classrooms were instructed individually. Such clinical laboratories were prevalent in 1940. However, remedial reading homerooms were intended to be more cost effective. Durrell described them as programs in which "children with reading difficulty are placed under the guidance of a trained remedial teacher for all of their subjects" (p. 355).

Attempting to differentiate individuals who could benefit respectively from remedial and corrective reading programs, Austin (1953) observed that "reading retardation has been described in terms of a continuum, ranging from nonreaders with an extreme type of associative learning disability to relatively mild problems" (p. 24). Although acknowledging that readers with the most extreme problems should receive immediate attention, she advised that "the difficulties of the less severely handicapped be detected as early as possible so that carefully planned instruction may prevent a major problem from arising" (p. 24). As to the precise point at which learners should be shifted from corrective to remedial programs, she concluded that "there cannot be any one general answer to this problem" and advised that a decision be made expediently on the basis of each school's "individual philosophy, its personnel, the number of retarded readers, and the best judgment available at the time" (p. 24).

REMEDIAL READING EMERGES DECISIVELY

By the end of the 1930s reading education had been discussed and debated by educators and the public for more than a century. However, remedial reading had become a topic as popular as general reading education during the two decades prior to 1940. Betts (1936) wrote that "during the past ten years a tremendous and growing interest has been evidenced" in remedial reading and that "teachers everywhere are confronted with the problems of pupils who are retarded in reading" (p. vii).

Trying to summarize key investigations about reading from the preceding decade, Traxler (1941) noted that "so large a proportion of the research studies since 1930 has been concerned with the provision of remedial and corrective instruction in reading that is not feasible to attempt to summarize even the major conclusions in the present review" (p. 42). As proof that the interest of educators in remedial reading had eclipsed developmental reading, Traxler reported that "the section on remedial and corrective reading in this bibliography contains 124 titles while the number of articles and monographs in which developmental reading is emphasized is not large enough to make it worth-while to set up a separate section for these publications in the bibliography" (p. 46).

Grace Fernald

Although the general concept of remedial reading had become sufficiently popular during the 1920s to be of interest even to authors of general education textbooks, the distinctive identity of remedial reading was linked closely to the development of increasingly specialized approaches in assessment and instruction. For example, Grace Fernald's kinesthetic reading exercises helped both to define remedial reading and increase its popularity. In the foreword to one of Fernald's books, Terman (1943) acknowledged that her kinesthetic reading techniques had "been in use for more than twenty years." Fernald and Keller (1921) had described these techniques:

> The child was asked to tell some word he would like to learn. The word was written in large script on the blackboard or with crayola on cardboard. The child looked at the word, saying it over to himself and tracing it if he wished to do so. The tracing was done with the first two fingers of the right hand (or of the left hand if the child was left-handed) resting on the copy. It was never done in the air or with pencil. When the child was sure he knew the word, the copy

was erased and he attempted to write the word, saying the syllables to himself as he wrote them (p. 355).

Fernald did not develop a theoretical explanation to reconcile her exercises with generally accepted learning principles. Aware of this shortcoming, she and Keller apologized that "perhaps we can go no further in theory than to say that, in the specific cases studied, lip and hand kinaesthetic elements seem to be the essential link between the visual cue and the various associations which give it word meaning" (p. 376). Referring to Fernald's "seemingly miraculous cures of word-blindness," Terman (1943) chastised those who had criticized her for failing to establish an appropriate theoretical base. Challenging critics who doubted the effectiveness of her methods to "present documentary evidence of cure after cure by some radically different method," he announced pugnaciously that "until such evidence is forthcoming the theoretical basis of Dr. Fernald's approach will not require modification" (p. ix).

Many of the kinesthetic lessons that made such an impression on Terman were described by Fernald (1943) in her book on remedial techniques. Her techniques were similar to the instructional strategies that were advocated by proponents of the sentence method and the story method. This similarity was accentuated when she wrote that "words should always be written in context" (p. 39). The following passage illustrated the instructional practices that would follow-up Fernald's tracing activities:

> The word is written for the child with crayola on paper in plain blackboard-size script, or in print, if manuscript writing is used. The child traces the word with finger contact, saying each part of the word as he traces it.... He repeats this process as many times as necessary in order to write the word without looking at the copy. He writes the word once on scrap paper and then in this "story".... After a story has been written by the child...it is typed for him and he reads it in print. After the story is finished, the child files the words under the proper letters in his word file.... This takes some extra time at first, but children become quite skillful in identifying the first letter of the word with the same letter in the file.... In this way they learn the alphabet without rote learning of the letters.... This practice with the word file is excellent training for later use of the dictionary and the use of the alphabet in organizing and filing (Fernald, 1943, p. 35).

Although Fernald influenced the course of remedial teaching, she also made contributions to assessment. With regard to "partial disability," she noted three primary causes—difficulty in recognizing specific words, inability to read in a fashion other than word by word, and failure to comprehend content. She recommended that the remedial learning for such cases comprise a three-stage approach, the first stage of which was "the giving of diagnostic tests to determine the intelligence" (p. 70). In addition to intelligence tests, Fernald underscored the value of reading achievement tests and diagnostic reading measures. Although aware that the analysis of oral reading errors had been strongly endorsed by Marion Monroe, she was unconvinced about its value. She wrote acidly that "careful analysis of reading errors is more essential for the technique used by Miss Monroe than it is for our work" and that it was "not essential for our technique except as a means of obtaining scientific records" (pp. 72-73).

Marion Monroe

Grace Fernald had alluded to Marion Monroe, who had also investigated remedial reading during 1930s. Monroe's books on diagnosis and remedial reading (1932, 1935; Monroe & Backus, 1937) were practical, comprehensive, and influential. Her pragmatic philosophy of education was revealed in the concluding remarks to a chapter on diagnostic reading when she wrote that in all remedial learning, the teacher should strive to "fit the method to the child, not the child to the method" (1932, p. 227). Fernald may have felt annoyed at Monroe because she thought that Monroe had implicitly directed these remarks at her own, less individualized approach.

Among the many innovative diagnostic procedures that Monroe advanced were attention to "qualitative measurement" as well as "quantitative measurement" of reading. She also recommended that scores on standardized reading tests be analyzed with reference to supplementary information, such as the results of mathematics, spelling, and intelligence tests. These concerns were consistent with her belief that "a child may fail to learn to read and yet be of adequate intelligence" (1932, p. 1).

Some of Monroe's most insightful contributions involved the analysis of oral reading errors. This research was built on the pioneering efforts of William Gray. Prior to the 1920s Gray had developed a popular diagnostic procedure that could be employed by classroom teachers with any type of reading materials. Brueckner and Melby (1931) described this procedure, in which the frequency with which children made errors and the types of errors they made were compared to previous samples of their own oral reading:

> The Gray Oral Reading Check Tests...can be used with any reading material which the teacher uses in giving the test. The pupil must be tested alone. He is asked to read the paragraphs, and the teacher notes the nature and number of errors made. The record sheet makes provisions for repetitions of the test. Progress can thus be noted (p. 317).

Among the various types of oral reading irregularities to which Gray had suggested that teachers attend were errors from enunciation, incorrect accent, rearranged letters, substitution, insertion, omission, changes in word order, and repetition. The summary sheet for Gray's procedure is illustrated in Figure 4.1.

Like Gray, Monroe suggested that instructors analyze the errors made by children while they orally read their lessons. She believed that an analysis of these errors could help the teachers understand the reading strategies that the students were employing. As part of this analysis she directed instructors to tabulate the numbers of errors involving mispronunciation of vowels or consonants as well as

GRAY ORAL READING CHECK TESTS

No. of Set Used_____

INDIVIDUAL RECORD SHEET

PROGRESSIVE ANALYSIS OF ERRORS IN ORAL READING

Pupil's Name...............................Age.............Grade..........

TYPES OF ERRORS	No.1	Daily	No.2	Daily	No.3	Daily	No.4	Daily	No.5	Daily
I. INDIVIDUAL WORDS										
1. Non recognition										
2. Gross mispronunciation										
3. Partial mispronunciation										
a. Monosyllabic Words										
1. Consonant										
2. Vowel										
3. Consonant blends										
4. Vowel digraph										
5. Pronounce silent letters										
6. Insert letters										
7. Pronounce backwards										
8. Rearrange letters										
b. Polysyllabic Words										
1. Accent										
2. Syllabication										
3. Omit syllable										
4. Insert syllable										
5. Rearrange letters of syllables										
6. Incorrect pronunciation of a syllable										
4. Enunciation										
5. Substitutions										
6. Insertions										
7. Omissions										
8. Other types of error {										
II. GROUPS OF WORDS										
1. Change order										
2. Add words to complete meaning according to fancy										
3. Omit one or more lines										
4. Insert two or more words										
5. Omit two or more words										
6. Substitute two or more words										
7. Repeat two or more words										
8. Other types of error {										
Pupil's test record { Rate										
{ Errors										
Standard Scores for the Grade { Rate										
{ Errors										
Date of Each Test										

Figure 4.1. Record Sheet Developed by Gray in the 1920s to Assist Teachers in the Analysis of Errors During Oral Reading

those involving the insertion, omission, or reversal of sounds. She also advised instructors to be aware of substituted, repeated, added, or omitted words. The final category of oral reading error that she directed teachers to record were those words that readers had not attempted to pronounce after a lengthy delay (which Monroe judged to be 15 seconds) and for which the instructor would eventually provide aid. Monroe referred to the irregularities that teachers analyzed as *oral reading errors*. In 1936 Hildreth used the term "cues" to distinguish the different features of words to which students could attend when reading. She advised teachers to analyze oral reading errors using five categories: reversals, omissions, repetitions, separate words that the reader blended together, and words that the reader spelled out. In the 1960s the term *oral reading miscues* was used again by Kenneth Goodman (1965) when he repopularized these concepts for a new generation of teachers.

Monroe and Backus (1937) listed multiple examples of factors contributing to reading problems and the behaviors that correlated with them. For example, they noted "visual defects" that could be indicated by excessive reversals, excessive line skipping, word and letter omissions, repetitions, extremely slow reading rate, errors with words of similar configuration, eye strain, or unusual positions for holding a book. Potential auditory problems might be indicated by excessive errors in the vowel and consonant sounds of words, additions and omissions of sounds, speech defects in conversation and oral reading, confusion of words which sound alike, or the inability to use phonics as an aid to word recognition. Other problems for which Monroe and Backus provided checklists of indices included motor control, debilitating physical conditions, low intelligence, verbal disabilities, peculiar modes of thought, inappropriate attitudes, inadequate motivation, and inadequate reading readiness. They also included signs that might reveal inappropriate instructional methods, a nonsupportive home environment, a history of instruction with inappropriate reading materials, and even poor administration in the schools (e.g., "overcrowded classrooms" or "inappropriately regimented procedures").

Monroe and Backus provided another example of the discretion that they brought to remedial reading when they identified two general approaches to instruction. They noted that teachers could select "direct therapy in the field of weakness" or they could choose to build upon "the child's abilities rather than correcting his weakness" (pp. 44-45). They concluded that not only were both of these approaches desirable but that "it is usually a safe plan to combine other methods; providing the child with many reading experiences which will utilize his best abilities, and also win his interest and co-operation in attacking his specific weaknesses" (p. 45).

Monroe (1932) had identified the inappropriate selection of instructional strategies as a factor that could contribute to reading problems. For example, she warned that "overstress of speed of reading may develop habits which impede progress in reading" and that "overstress of some methods of word-recognition may develop habits which impede progress in reading" (p. 109). Although aware that remedial intervention might inadvertently contribute to learners' problems, she also warned teachers to be cautious before rejecting any prospective remedial methods because "the problem of remedial instruction in reading is to find a possible method of learning for those children who have not been able to learn to read by methods adapted to the group." She also cautioned that "the method found helpful for reading-defect cases may not be necessary or advisable in ordinary instruction." She concluded pragmatically that "although some of the methods which we have used stimulate at first a mechanical approach to reading, we have not discarded them on that basis if they brought measurable improvement in reading without sacrificing comprehension" (p. 113).

Not only did she and Backus endorse both whole word strategies and phonics strategies, but they (Monroe & Backus, 1937) later illustrated lessons in which these two types of strategies were combined:

> The teacher writes the following sentence on the board, leaving the last word blank. She says, "Who can guess what word belongs in this blank space?"
>
> The boy went to the s_____.
>
> The children now suggest school, store, etc..... She writes
>
> The boy went to the st_____.
>
> The teacher explains to the children how they may solve unknown words in this way. They will be able to read many unknown words accurately if they think of words which fit into the meaning of the sentence and then choose the ones which begin with the right initial sounds (p. 85).

The ideological balance for which Monroe and Backus provided evidence in the preceding passage was exemplified in their remarks that "a remedial reading program which leaves the child mechanically perfect in reading but with no interest or zeal for reading falls far short of its goal; just as does a remedial reading program which, on the other hand, arouses the child's desire to read but does not give him the mechanical ability to satisfy the desire created" (p. 85).

Harris's Remedial Reading Textbook

During the 1930s remedial reading was transformed from a topic of discussion into a specialized field with scientific aspirations. Books such as those by Fernald and Monroe were evidence of this emerging professional identity. Another indicator of this change in professional identity was the appearance of remedial reading textbooks that were patterned after those marketed in general reading education. Albert Harris's textbook (1940), *How to Increase Reading Ability: A Guide to Diagnostic and Remedial Methods*, exemplified a series of general books on remedial reading that appeared regularly during the 1940s and subsequent decades.

Recalling the difficulty he had locating a suitable book for the class he taught at his university, Harris wrote that "there were several good books available, but they were either accounts of research or expositions of the author's own ideas about how remedial work should be done" (p. ix). Unlike Gates, Fernald, and Monroe, Harris himself was not well known for his original contributions to the field. But he judged the professional literature that had been developed by others to be sufficiently rich that he would be able to write a comprehensive textbook. The dimensions of remedial reading that were apparent in the professional literature in 1940 were revealed in the titles of his 13 chapters: "The Significance of Reading Disabilities," "How the Normal Child Learns to Read," "Readiness for Reading," "Practical Applications of Reading Readiness," "How to Diagnose Silent Reading," "How to Diagnose Oral Reading," "Investigating the Causes of Reading Difficulties," "Basic Principles of Remedial Reading," "Materials for Remedial Reading," "How to Improve Word Recognition," "How to Improve Comprehension, Fluency, and Speed," "Teaching Reading to Specially Handicapped Children," "Organizing the School for Better Reading," and "Individualizing Reading in the Classroom" (pp. xi-xvi).

Harris (1940) believed that remedial reading, though diagnostic and individualized, was an approach to reading that was similar to general reading instruction because "most cases of reading disability are not caused by special types of deficient learning ability, but arise from relatively simple causes" and that "the task of the teacher is to find out which difficulties are present in each case, and then to apply common sense to the problem of overcoming the pupils' handicaps" (p. 19). Because many of the conclusions that he could have drawn in his 1940 textbook would have been controversial, he diplomatically phrased his remarks from the vantage of a reporter rather than an expert educator with vested interests. For example, he seemed wary of committing too strongly to phonics when he concluded that "systematic phonetic training is not helpful in the low first grade" (p. 32). But he was similarly noncommittal toward the whole word method, which he depicted as "a good method when combined with other procedures, but may lead to serious difficulties if used alone" (p. 33).

CLINICAL APPROACHES TO READING

Writing in his autobiography about his research from 1920 to 1935, Gates (1971) indicated that his goals had been inspired by the medical model of evaluation and treatment "in the hope that sooner or later schools would provide teachers and specialists who could rival in their field the expertness of a well-trained physician" (p. 206). In an article written when she was working in the experimental school at Teachers College, Hildreth (1928) recommended that "clinical study is necessary in the more serious cases of maladjustment" and that "such study should bring together all available data as to the child's heredity, family history, developmental history, home background, school record, present physical condition, mental and educational status, parents' and teachers' reports of the child's behavior, and the child's own story of his difficulties" (pp. 13-14). She added that "all pupils who appear to suffer primarily from physical disturbances should have more thorough medical examination" and that "neurological examinations will be necessary in several cases" while "the advice of nutrition experts should be sought in others" (p. 14). She adjured educators to use an approach that was "more scientific" as a result of "greater refinement of our tools for observation and with a growing fund of information furnished by genetic studies of school children" (p. 14).

Almost 15 years later Lazar (1942a) observed that an "intensive interest in reading" which had begun "over a decade ago in clinic and laboratory" had created an "impetus that has been felt at every level of the school structure" (p. 1). He recommended that educators search for the etiology of reading problems in learners' school histories, physical developments, intellectual abilities, emotional traits, social characteristics, family relationships, and environmental conditions. Reviewing sources of information that could be incorporated into a clinical diagnosis of reading problems, Lazar (1942b) identified report cards, samples of work by students, health records, parent interviews, records of direct observations by teachers, test data, observations made during home visits by teachers, and reports from psychologists, counselors, or social agency personnel.

In the preface to Robinson's 1946 book, William Gray also emphasized the link between medical services and education. Reviewing the history of research on "reading retardation," Gray noted that interest in this topic had originated among medical researchers in the late 1800s:

> Research in this field was begun in the eighties and nineties by surgeons and neurologists, who made detailed examinations of seriously retarded readers and of others who had "lost" ability to read. On the basis of objective evidence in some cases and through reasoning by analogy in other cases, they concluded that brain lesions of one form or another were largely responsible for failure to learn to read and for the loss of ability to read. Their findings influenced to a large extent the thinking of teachers and specialists in reading during the next two decades when the view prevailed that reading disability was due to a highly specialized deficiency in ability to learn (Gray, 1946, p. v).

Gray was convinced that the 1920s and the 1930s had been two of the most important eras for reading education. Similar to the developments during these earlier decades, distinctive types of research and remedial reading practices were developed during the 1940s, a period during which clinical models of reading were emphasized. Though Gray had characterized the 1920s as a time when remedial reading was moving away from the influence of medical researchers, this purported movement was temporary. Despite the return to a once popular model, the research of the 1940s was distinct from that conducted earlier because the range of factors to which reading problems became linked expanded beyond unitary neurological causes.

Writing in the book for which Gray had provided a preface, Robinson identified herself on the title page as the "director of reading clinics" at the University of Chicago. By itself, this was not unusual. Durrell (1940) had listed his credentials as "director of the educational clinic" at Boston University and Betts (1936) had identified himself on the title page of his book as "director of the reading clinic" at Penn State College. In fact, Betts had presented a model of public school administration in which the responsibility for referrals to reading clinics was shared jointly by school personnel, parents, and health department professionals. But the medical dimensions of the reading clinics from the 1930s were primitive compared to those that emerged during the subsequent decade.

In her book on the causes of "severe reading retardation," Robinson (1946) included information about the neurological basis of reading disability. This section contained chapters on factors that contributed to reading but that originated with hearing, speech, physical development, intelligence, emotions, personality, social circumstances, and environmental situations. The medical orientation to Robinson's remedial reading approach was apparent in her vocabulary and rhetoric as well as her content. For example, in a passage describing evaluation in her clinic, she used medical jargon to recount that "if it appeared that a further study might aid in diagnosis and in prescribing treatment, a case was accepted for preliminary examination" (p. 108). Tests were administered at Robinson's clinic by psychiatrists, pediatricians, neurologists, ophthalmologists, speech-language therapists, otolaryngologists, and endocrinologists. With regard to endocrinology, she explained that because "a number of references indicated the possibility of relationships between poor reading and thyroid deficiency, pituitary deficiency, or delayed sexual development, an endocrinologist...seemed very pertinent" (1946, p. 116).

The model of assessment and treatment that Robinson developed was an intimidating one. However, its expense limited its adoption by schools or even by other clinics. For this reason, proponents of the clinical approach often differentiated distinct techniques for achieving diagnostic and learning goals in clinical and nonclinical environments. As an example, the proceedings of an annual conference on reading held at the University of Chicago in the early 1950s (Robinson, 1953) contained separate reports about the implementation of diagnostic procedures and instructional strategies within clinical settings.

Also writing about clinical approaches to instruction, Stauffer (1947) recommended approaches for "disabled readers" incorporating special observational techniques, rating scales, and questionnaires with which to assess personality. He wrote that "since reading is one facet of language, which in turn is one aspect of personality representing the dynamic unity of an individual, it is the personality of the disabled reader that calls for rehabilitation" (p. 427). At a more practical level, he advised that "for correction to be adequate, it is necessary to find out whether the emotional tensions are antecedent to the reading difficulty; whether the reading disability evoked the emotional disturbance; or whether the reading disability and the emotional disturbance are related to some other factor" (p. 427).

In a report written that same year, Lund (1947) advised teachers to keep in mind that "the reaction systems (cerebro-spinal) involved in the establishment of mental and physical skills are influenced not merely from without but from within" and that "accordingly, they can be set in motion by given external stimuli only if they have been brought into appropriate readiness by internal conditions, by impulses arising from internal tissues, from conditions of the blood stream and the vital organs" (p. 416). Later in the report, he adjured instructors that "not only must the teacher learn to understand these inner forces but she must develop the techniques thorough which they may be mobilized in the interest of educational objectives" (p. 421).

The influence of reading clinicians continued to be discernible in the professional literature of the 1950s. In a guide for developing remedial reading programs in the junior high school, Lazar (1952) identified the "essential" provisions for remedial reading programs, one of which was a special reading room supported by a reading teacher, reading supervisor, and a reading administrator. Health care and child guidance services were also listed as essential provisions because these "supplement the work of the reading teacher in studying and ameliorating physical problems, emotional difficulties, and other factors which complicate the learning problems of the retarded reader" (p. 17). In the preface to a textbook on corrective reading written five years later, Bond and Tinker (1957) identified three audiences at which that book was directed— "the classroom teacher, the school remedial teacher, and the clinician" (p. v). They emphasized that the classroom teacher could not be expected to assume complete responsibility for children who required "more detailed diagnosis and highly individualized remedial training" (p. v).

The perceptions of reading clinicians about the distinctive nature of their services was evident in the remarks of Potter (1953) when he wrote that professionals should be careful to "decide whether a child's reading retardation is severe enough to warrant the individualized and expensive treatment provided by the clinic" (p. 43). Like Potter, Stauffer (1953) addressed the issue of selecting persons to be treated at reading clinics when he wrote that they should be "extreme cases who require intensive study and special differential instruction" (p. 120). Potter had identified the cost of treatment as a factor determining which clients would receive clinical reading services. High expenses within clinics were inevitable for a number of reasons, such as the elaborate preliminary diagnostic procedures that were typical. Lohmann (1953) described the breadth of these clinical screening procedures:

> Diagnosis includes case-history data in the form of school progress and attendance records, basal materials used, parental and school descriptions of difficulties, family history, developmental record, health information, a record of previous tests given and of previous clinical

help. Diagnosis also includes current evaluations of intelligence, vision, hearing, speech, interests, attitudes, adjustment, general personality, reading, other selective content areas, home
and school environment (p. 75).

In addition to expense, other factors influencing the limited impact of the clinical model on teachers may have been the model's lack of instructional implications and the esoteric format that many clinical reading approaches assumed.
Although such esoteric reading procedures may have had restricted application
outside of clinics, the 1940s and early 1950s were years during which remedial
reading programs continued to grow rapidly in the schools. Harris (1968)
described this growth in a passage about the decade that ended in 1955, which he
characterized as an era "marked by a general expansion of interest in remedial
reading." This expansion was obvious because "scores of colleges and universities organized reading clinics, and many started graduate training programs for
reading specialists," "the number of remedial teachers in public school systems
continued to grow," "remedial reading programs began to spread upward from
elementary schools to the secondary schools," and "commercial organizations,
offering everything from tutoring the nonreader to speed reading for executives
sprang up in the larger cities" (p. 30).

SUMMARY

Paralleling the 1920s developments in novel methods for diagnosis and individualized learning, remedial reading began to assume an identity separate from that
of general reading education. This was a period when estimates of the number of
persons who required remedial reading instruction escalated dramatically. As the
growth of remedial reading became apparent, some educators questioned the
expense and accessibility of these highly individualized programs, many of which
were being administered by specially trained teachers in isolated facilities. These
critics advocated corrective, group activities that were to be administered by
classroom teachers. The chasm dividing individualized remedial reading from
grouped instruction widened further as increasingly hermetic clinics became more
frequent during the 1940s.

Chapter 5

TENSION BETWEEN POLITICAL AND PRAGMATIC PHILOSOPHIES

Pedagogy should be the most pragmatic science in the world (Briggs, 1940).

Politicized rhetoric tore through the general field of education during the 1930s, the era of World War II, and the postwar years. Convinced that the economic depression signaled the end of capitalist society, political activists had adjured teachers to participate in a revolution they saw as inevitable. In stark contrast, conservative political initiatives during World War II prodded teachers to emphasize traditional values. This nationalist era, which extended into the 1950s, was fanned not only by the war but also by fears engendered by the subsequent cold war. Much of the reactionary rhetoric was directed at alleged abuses by progressive educators. Though this alternating pattern of assault and retreat by politically liberal and conservative educators was dramatically highlighted during the final decades of the progressive education movement, it remained apparent even after that movement's formal demise. Despite the intensity of these disagreements, remedial reading, because it was grounded in a characteristically pragmatic philosophy, was hardly perturbed.

* * *

Writing about social movements on a grander scale than one finds in reading education, Heberle (1951) maintained that "mere similarity of sentiments occurring independently do not constitute a movement" and that "a sense of group identity and solidarity is required, for only when the acting individuals have become aware of the fact that they have sentiments and goals in common—when they think of themselves as being united with each other in action through these sentiments and for these goals—do we acknowledge the existence of a social movement" (p. 7). Heberle judged that the first step in explaining the etiology of social movements was "an inquiry into the attitudes and motivations which are typical of participants in social movements, and which determine the socio-psychological

117

texture of various types of movements" (p. 13). After examining the socio-psychological textures of several movements, he concluded that "the chances of an idea's becoming part of the creed of a mass movement depend not so much upon its intrinsic value as upon its appeal to the interests, sentiments, and resentments of certain social strata and other groups" (p. 14).

Writing about mass movements a decade later, Smelser (1962) observed that "in all civilizations men have thrown themselves into episodes of dramatic behavior, such as the craze, the riot, and the revolution" and that "often we react emotionally to these episodes" (p. 1). Among the characteristics of collective behavior that Smelser pointed out were a "belief in the existence of extraordinary forces— threats, conspiracies, etc." and "an assessment of the extraordinary consequences which will follow if the collective attempt to reconstitute social actions is successful" (p. 8). Smelser than added a clarification of these characteristics, explaining that "the beliefs on which collective behavior is based...are thus akin to magical beliefs" (p. 8).

Also attempting to explain collective behavior, Hoffer (1966) noted that history was replete with the true believer—"the man of fanatical faith who is ready to sacrifice his life for a holy cause" (p. 10). Hoffer assumed that persons were transformed into true believers by frustration, which "without any proselytizing prompting from the outside, can generate most of the peculiar characteristics of the true believer." If persons did not become true believers by themselves, "an effective technique of conversion consists basically in the inculcation and fixation of proclivities and responses indigenous to the frustrated mind" (p. 10).

As with Heberle's and Smelser's speculations about the factors that were responsible for collective behavior, the connection that Hoffer discerned between frustration and fanaticism was a speculative concept that enabled him to rationalize and predict the rise and fall of social movements that otherwise seemed inexplicable. To the extent that Heberle's, Smelser's, and Hoffer's concepts clarified rather than clouded an understanding of social movements, one can speculate whether the relationships these theorists posited existed on a continuum that could have been applied not only to groups that were capable of massively destructive actions but to the less intense but quite pervasive discord that has characterized educators during the twentieth century.

If such generalizations about collective behavior were appropriate, at one end of the decision-making continuum would have been all those educators, conservatives and liberals alike, who were motivated by their intensely political commitments. At the antipode of the continuum would have been pragmatists who had attempted to choose alternatives on the basis of the consequences for those decisions. The movements of education along this continuum were apparent in the deliberations of educators throughout the century. But in a special way, the events surrounding World War II dramatized these movements.

LIBERAL POLITICAL APPROACHES PRIOR
TO WORLD WAR II

During the 1920s remedial reading had begun to emerge from developmental read-ing education as a scholarly field and as a separate area of educational practice. However, it was not until the 1930s, a decade of unprecedented economic and social commotion, that remedial reading developed a pragmatic identity that was independent of the political turmoil that was tearing through the general field of education. In a book about social changes in New York's Greenwich Village from 1920 to 1930, Ware (1935) wrote that this period "saw the serious disruption of the culture patterns of the nineteenth century" and conjectured that even had World War I not transpired, "this generation or the next might well have seen the complete collapse of the traditional American economic and social structure" (p. 5). Though the crisis to which Ware referred may have been influenced by the war and chang-ing values during the 1920s, the social, political, intellectual, and emotional dis-ruption of the 1930s was fueled largely by the financial depression.

Characterizing the 1930s as "the angry decade," Gurko (1947) observed that "from the crash of stock market prices in October, 1929, to the crash of bombs on Pearl Harbor in December, 1941, America endured twelve of the most turbu-lent years of her history" (p. 1). Only several years into that depression Walter Lippmann (1931) expressed the consensus of the nation's citizens about the depth of the crisis into which they had been plunged when he wrote that "it is now two years since hard times reached this country, and it is no longer open to serious question that we are in the midst, not of an ordinary trade depression, but of one of the great upheavals and readjustments of modern history" and that "in all the vast confusion which has resulted one thing at least is certain—the world, when the readjustments are made, can not and will not be organized as it was two years ago" (p. 4). Two years later Lippmann (1933) observed eloquently that "it has fallen to us to live in one of those conjunctures of human affairs which mark a crisis in the habits, the customs, the routine, the inherited method and the traditional ideas of mankind" (p. 7).

Butts and Cremin (1953) noted that "within the context of the depression, the 1930's saw greater and deeper changes in American life than in any other period in history" (p. 461). In a book about social reform movements, Greer (1949) antic-ipated these remarks when he wrote that the early 1930s were years of "deepening gloom" in which "the golden hopes of the 1920's lay shattered, and many pre-dicted the complete overthrow of capitalism." He added that "radical groups has-tened to spread the idea that only a revolution could lead the country out of its dilemma" (p. 241).

Numerous persons represented the "radical groups" to which Greer referred. After concluding that "we are living in an epoch of revolutionary change," Davis (1930) identified factors contributing to that revolution such as industrialization, geographical shifts in population, urbanization, a movement to increase the civil rights of African Americans, changes in home life, and altered class structure. Observing insightfully that "history teaches us that many a nation has been profoundly affected, sometimes almost revolutionized, by foreign movements," Davis called attention to "an epoch which has already seen two Labor governments in power in Great Britain and a Communistic state in Russia" (p. 3). In a pamphlet with the title *Out of the Depression,* Chase (1931) reported that even "dignified college professors have begun to produce strange, if not subversive, textbooks" (p. 3). A year later Thomas (1932) observed that the nation's problems were the "expression of a dying capitalism" and that "capitalism is doomed because of its well-nigh complete lack of standards and sanctions, intellectual or ethical" (p. 8). The Committee of the Progressive Education Association on Social and Economic Problems (1933) used precise examples to convey to teachers the reasons they thought were responsible for "the spirit of rebellion" which they judged to be everywhere:

> Factory wheels stop turning, locomotives stand idle, ships remain in port, workmen lose their jobs, banks and trust companies fail, the financial structure collapses, money passes out of circulation, barter comes into vogue, business houses go bankrupt, the total social income falls, the tax burden rises, strong men become dependent on charity, life is narrowed to a savage battle for bread, theft and robbery increase, the cultural services decline, starvation reaches into many homes, bitterness enters the hearts of men, and the spirit of rebellion broods over the land (p. 10).

Debates about the potential promise or threat from communism were discernible in the intellectualizing of that period. Even during the preceding decade, liberal theorists such as the historian Charles Beard had made controversial broadsides upon the traditional intellectual foundations of the American social and economic system. Beard had written in 1923 that "in reviewing the history of government in Western Europe, from the disintegration of the Roman Empire to the opening years of the nineteenth century, we discover that wherever the simple sword-won despotism of the war leader, prince or king, is supplemented or superseded by some from of representation, it is not the people, considered as abstract equal personalities, who are represented, but it is propertied estates" (pp. 46-47).

During the 1930s Beard's parries became more poignant. In a pamphlet with the title *The Myth of Rugged American Individualism,* he recited a litany of "leading economic activities of the Federal Government" during the 1920s all of which "may be justified to national interests" (1932, pp. 17-18). He viewed many of the socialist proposals that had been recommended as no more intrusive than already established instances of government intervention and decried "the anarchy celebrated in the name of individualism" (p. 27). In his later writings Beard (1934) was even more explicit in his call for social and financial restructuring. He insisted that "a wide distribution of property and its fruits is necessary to the perdurance of popular government, to the enjoyment of security, to life, liberty, and the pursuit of happiness" (1934, p. 14).

Even though Beard had launched academic salvos against the national political structure, his attacks seemed feeble compared to the rhetorical assaults made by partisan communists during the 1930s. After noting that "the early years of the Depression saw widespread non-Communist theorizing upon the use of the schools in the reconstruction of society," Iversen (1959) added that "it seemed natural to expect that the Communists, who were advocates of the total reconstruction of society, would have some view on the role that the schools should play in the process" (p. 60).

Bertrand Russell, the philosopher and mathematician, articulately expressed the views to which Iversen had referred. For even though he had demonstrated that he could criticize communism, Russell was unqualifiedly ruthless in his condemnation of capitalism. He generalized this condemnation to the system of education that prevailed in capitalist countries, writing of "the evils produced in education by the institution of private property and its connection with the patriarchal family" (1932, p. 173). Despite his reservations about the theoretical foundation supporting communism, Russell argued that communism "creates an economic system which appears to be the only practicable alternative to one of masters and slaves" (pp. 189-190). He wrote enthusiastically of the system of education in the Soviet Union, noting that since Russian education was still in a formative state, "it is more instructive, for our purpose, to consider what the Soviet Government hopes and intends than what it has already achieved" (p. 173). Emphasizing that education comprised socially useful work, Russell (1932) described two categories of socially useful work that were being inculcated among Soviet youth:

> Socially useful work in the school is divided into two main departments, the first consisting of agitation and propaganda, the second of practical work. Under the former heading children are to agitate on a great variety of topics, e.g. for rotation of crops, for the "most worthy" candidates in elections, against religion, malaria, bed bugs, smoking and drunkenness. Practical work shows a similar diversity. Children are to engage in disinfecting grain with formaline, in combating ravines by tree-planting, in putting electric light into the homes of peasants, in distributing election literature, in reading newspapers to illiterates, in exterminating parasites, and in aiding needy widows (pp. 179-180).

Like Russell, George Counts was an enthusiastic advocate for the educational changes transpiring in Russia. And like Russell, he admitted the problems that restricted Russia's ability to achieve its educational goals. For example, in his panegyric book, *The Soviet Challenge to America*, Counts (1931) still admitted that "perhaps the most insistent of all the cultural problems faced by the Soviet leaders in their effort to build a new society is the liquidation of illiteracy" and that "the Soviet Union can scarcely hope to overtake its rivals in technical and economic achievement until this severe handicap has been removed" (pp. 123-124).

Events in education during the late 1920s and the 1930s reflected the general social mayhem that was disrupting the country. Writing on the eve of the great depression, Finney (1928) had emphasized the need for educators to set priorities about which needs of children should be addressed initially. He warned his readers that "the individualistic psychology now so generally in vogue is one sided and misleading" (p. v). And he adjured teachers to set priorities by attending to the "telic function of education," which he equated with the "the appraisal of present trends in social evolution" (p. 119). He continually directed teachers to look to the future and not be restricted by current problems:

> There are, as in any age, certain trends that are not promising; and we should try to redirect them through our education program. It involves a deliberate, conscious comparison between the institutions of the future, as they are likely to become if present trends are left to themselves, and as they ought to become in the interest of human happiness and welfare. For if the educators of to-day can blue-print the institutions of to-morrow approximately as they ought to be, it is possible for them, within limits of course, to pour the developing minds of to-day into molds that will fit them into the mosaics of such worthy institutions (p. 119).

Two years later the depression was creating turmoil throughout the educational system. Describing disturbances in teacher education during the depression, Borrowman (1956) wrote that "there was a critical need for a time of stability to permit a careful resurvey of what had happened and a dispassionate analysis of existing thought and practice" because "the chaos that was teacher education became part of the chaos that was the great depression" (p. 181). Bode (1930) wrote in *The New Republic* that "the tremendous activity now going on in education [in the United States] is evidence of far-reaching social changes, but we do not seem to know what these changes signify or how they are to be directed" (p.62).

Three years later Bode (1933) presented a picture of education in Russia in which he wrote that the Russian teacher "is not merely a purveyor of information but a co-worker in a magnificent enterprise" and he added that "there is little cause for wonder that such a situation should appear attractive to the pedagogic mind" (p. 23). Not wishing to take the chance that his readers might fail to see a parallel between the dynamic program being implemented in Russia and the opportunities for a similar program in the United States, Bode pledged his hope that the Russians would not emulate the United States where "in a world of change, any significant departure from familiar principles, such as free competition and private profit, is apt to be regarded not only as incredible but as rank heresy" and where "loyalty and patriotism are identified with stand-pattism" (p. 24).

As the severity of the economic depression was gradually recognized, the confrontational rhetoric addressed at teachers increased proportionately. An article that appeared in a 1932 edition of *Education Worker* had the title "English Teachers, Awake." This article (Montgomery, 1932) began with a clear call to arms:

Fellow instructors in the English language and literature, are you aware that you are living in a revolutionary period? The classes and nations of Europe and Asia march forward to the day of military conflict. In the United States the representatives of the hungry millions present their demands and sing the International before the American Congress, unawed by machine guns and gas grenades. Capitalism is bankrupt, "democracy" is exposed, the League of Nations has shown its imperialist hypocrisy, the Soviet Union constructs its socialist industries with amazing rapidity, the capitalist states have no answer but desperate military preparation and intrigue. These are not obscure matters known to the elect; they are the commonplaces of the daily newspapers. Teachers cannot escape from the turmoil and danger of revolution into academic cloisters. Those who do not attempt to ignore the world about them and who wish to adapt themselves courageously to new situations are faced by the question: In a revolutionary period, why not revolutionary teaching? (p. 3).

Montgomery gave several examples of revolutionary teaching, suggesting that teachers "not hold up the great writers (Shakespeare, Keats, Hardy, and the like) as intellectual guides" but instead realize that "a mediocre contemporary radical writer may be of immeasurably more intellectual value to a student than one of the giants of a vanished age" (p. 3).

Equally militant, Redefer (1949) recounted the incidents surrounding the 1933 annual meeting of the Progressive Education Association at which "a short distance from the hotel in Chicago where the Board of Directors met prior to the annual meeting, men fought each other to obtain the scraps thrown out in garbage cans" (p. 188). He described a "stormy" session in which the board approved a manifesto titled *Dare the Schools Build a New Social Order?* The following passage is from that manifesto:

[Teachers] owe nothing to the present economic system except to improve it; they owe nothing to any privileged caste except to strip it of its privileges. They must emancipate themselves from the domination of the business interests of the nation, cease cultivating the manners and associations of bankers and promotion agents, repudiate utterly the ideal of material success as the goal of education, abandon the smug middle class tradition on which they have been nourished in the past, acquire a realistic understanding of the forces that actually rule the world and formulate a program of thought and action that will deal honestly and intelligently with the problems of industrial civilization. Progressive minded teachers of the country must unite in a powerful organization, militantly devoted to the building of a better social order (Board of Directors of the Progressive Education Association, quoted by Redefer, 1949, p. 188).

A 1933 report from a committee of the Progressive Education Association was titled *A Call to the Teachers of the Nation.* It began with the sentence "in an era of unlimited possibilities the American people pass from disaster to disaster" (Committee of the Progressive Education Association on Social and Economic Problems, 1933, p. 6). The members of the committee described the conditions that they though should persuade teachers to realize that "capitalism, with its extremes of poverty and riches and its moral degradation of millions, makes an empty farce of our democratic professions and dooms multitudes of children to lives of severe privation" (p. 18). Pointing to a connection between problems in society and a depression that had been caused by capitalists, they adjured teachers to enlist as political activists:

> Today [the citizens of the Untied Sates] find themselves near the close of the fourth year of the greatest depression in their history—a depression that has thrown millions out of work, consumed the savings of years of toil, brought malnutrition and severe privation to multitudes of children, generated a spirit of demoralization and despair among the youth, spread a feeling of fear and uncertainty throughout all classes, and made a hollow mockery of their most cherished ideals. In the face of these conditions teachers, the guardians of childhood, the bearers of culture, the avowed servants of the people, cannot remain silent (Committee of the Progressive Education Association on Social and Economic Problems, 1933, p. 6).

After noting that George Counts had been chairman of the committee that had drafted this report, Dilling (1935) indicated that it left "little doubt as to the actual pro-revolutionary character of the Progressive Education Association" (p. 216).

Many politically liberal educators wrote about the need for radical social changes in the United States. Langford (1936) was an articulate socialist who recounted the devastating effects of the depression on education:

> The effects of the depression have not been confined to school budgets. Large numbers of children (in New York City, for example) have been going to school without adequate food and clothing, so that the teachers have had to pay what has amounted to a tax on their salaries in the effort to make good the most serious deficiencies. Such conditions prevent the full realization of objectives which have become commonplaces in the thinking, if not always in the practice, of educators. A program intended to insure the full development of the child can mean little unless adequate provision is made for the satisfaction of his basic physical needs (p. 10).

Though many socialist and progressive educators who documented the impact of the depression on education expressed dismay, they still wrote with a self-righteous style of rhetoric that indicated a parallel satisfaction because the damage was an indication to them that capitalism had reached its eleventh hour. However, several progressive educators, such as Beiswanger (1936), genuinely rued the effect of the depression on the educational reforms they had sponsored:

> The courses in public and private schools which develop appreciations and tastes and which teach the use of leisure-time for creative activities have suffered widely in the slashing of school expenditures, and the programs of experimental and progressive education have been seriously jeopardized. Crowded classrooms are again the rule (and are being justified by the painstaking research of "bourgeois" science). Reduced budgets have told as heavily upon library orders, laboratory equipment, and the materials for teaching the so-called "frills," as upon faculty salaries (pp. 246-247).

Though a special 1939 edition of *Survey Graphic* focused on the turmoil within American education, the articles in that issue did not defer to the economic depression in order to explain problems. For during this period the prospects that the United States would emerge from it economic depression had increased. And educators were aware that participation in war might be the price for economic recovery. The changing political situation in the United States, from a nation that was in the throes of economic depression to one that was not only recovering but threatened by a war that could imperil its government and economy, lowered the threshold of tolerance to confrontational, political liberals. The initial article in this journal issue set the rhetorical tone for the pieces that followed:

> The dread fact of a world at war throws into relief the whole picture of education.... By what failure in the educational process are young people turned out, so insecure and so undiscriminating that they flock to rabble-rousers? What educational gap let in hate and prejudice? What quickens curiosity? Strengthens integrity? Distinguishes truth from propaganda? Encourages neighborliness and good will? Turns knowledge and training into the stuff of action? (Amidon, 1939, p. 569).

In another article from *Survey Graphic*, Lindeman (1939) emphasized the need for a new generation of progressive educators and socially liberal school administrators. At the same time, he noted regretfully that "our educators, especially school administrators, are becoming exceedingly timid; they are the victims of pressure organizations whose leaders have no competence in the field of education" (p. 570). A special section of in this magazine contained quotes ("Some Educators Define," 1939) from prominent educators who had expressed their convictions about a critical link between democratic government and excellence in education. Among the admonitions to ensure excellence in education were a wider adoption of preschool programs (Barnard, 1939), sponsorship of programs for out-of-school youth and adults (Chamberlain, 1939), elimination of incompetent teachers (Neilson, 1939), and support for more equitable educational expenditures among schools ("The Nation's Biggest Business," 1939).

Beale (1941) wrote in the introduction to his *History of Freedom of Teaching in the Schools* that he had been persuaded to commence this project in 1931 by George Counts, who had been a member of the American Historical Association's Commission on Social Studies in the Schools. Beale's confrontational, politically liberal attitudes were apparent when he remarked in the preface that he had discerned "striking parallels between the attitudes of slaveholders of yesteryear and big-business men of today toward the schools and toward teachers who question the virtues of the dominant economic systems of their respective periods" (pp. ix-x). He criticized not only slaveowners but the teachers who had worked under the "slavocracy" because they "were not of the stuff that made abolitionists" and because "the schools were looked upon as the people's agencies, whose duty it was to foster the business interest and the provincialism of the locality that supported them (p. 156). Beale completed this analogy by criticizing his contemporaries because "a majority feel it unsafe to approve communism, criticize the breaking up of a meeting of 'Reds' by local police, or suggest that revolution by force is necessary in order to establish justice" (p. 241).

Five years earlier Beale (1936) had published a companion volume about the freedom of teachers in which he argued that all instruction was a type of propaganda, and that "even reading lessons, through the selection of things suitable, inculcate a point of view" (p. 678). He continued that "if one limits 'propaganda' to advocacy of changes in the *status quo* or the beliefs of some minority group, then many teachers would oppose propaganda who would favor indoctrination with community beliefs" and that "the question resolves itself into a choice between propaganda for new ideas or group interests on the one hand, and indoctrination with accepted attitudes on the other" (p. 679). The following passage illustrated his exhortatory rhetoric:

> It cannot be too often reiterated that it is only unconventional, progressive, or radical teachers who are not free to "teach" children what to think. If indoctrination is accepted as the purpose of education, then the question of freedom is whether those who do not conform to the views of the crowd shall have a chance to indulge in it. Shall the schools bulwark the *status quo* or shall they help create a new social order? (Beale, 1936, p. 679).

Publication of *The Social Frontier*

The progressive education movement's reformers had spoken out in favor of educational reform. For example, Overstreet (1929) had written in *Progressive Education* that traditional "education has always concerned itself rather sedulously with the training of the mind" and it "perpetuates the medieval point of view that truth is something which has been revealed, rather than something which has to be arduously sought and found" and that consequently students have been trained to accept "academic 'scriptures'" (pp. 63-64).

A 1932 editorial in the same journal ("Must Teachers Sink," 1932/1933) adjured teachers that "the task before us is of somehow getting our industrial civilization under control lest it destroy us, lest we be smothered by the excess of our own wealth, lest we continue this ridiculous situation where hungry, ragged, shoeless men are walking the streets while the warehouses are bursting with food, clothing, and shoes, and the people who produce them are going bankrupt because they can't sell them, and the men in the streets are starving and wretched because they can't use them" (p. 5). But this article also consoled readers that "education is not more fairly to be indicted than is the church, the press, or any other important social organization" (p. 5). In 1933 George Counts was the primary author of a politically incendiary set of statements from the Progressive Education Association's Committee on Social and Economic Problems. A report ("Notes on the Convention," 1932) contained the following remarks about the attitudes of the Progressive Education's Association's delegates toward a speech made by Counts at their twelfth national convention:

> The point at issue was the responsibility of the schools for social reconstruction. The challenge of Dr. Counts was easily the high point for the program. Following the dinner meeting at which

he spoke, small groups gathered in lobbies and private rooms to discuss, until far into the night, the issues raised in Dr. Counts' sharp challenge. These discussions were marked by a general willingness to accept the viewpoint of Dr. Counts that the schools have a real responsibility for effecting social change. There was however, a considerable difference of opinion as to how this was to be accomplished. The method of indoctrination, advocated by Dr. Counts, was widely questioned (p. 288).

Although a group of educators within the progressive education movement had called for radical political solutions to educational problems, the majority of members were politically cautious. For example, Adams wrote in *Progressive Education* that the 1933 report from the Progressive Education Association's Committee on Social and Economic Problems was "filled with assumptions stated as truism or accepted fact, assumptions with which an honest intelligent, and 'progressive' person may or may not agree " (p. 310). In a widely discussed pamphlet, *Dare the School Build a New Social Order?*, George Counts (1932) dismissed progressive education as a weak, elitist reaction to the profound and pervasive problems with which the country was being confronted:

The weakness of Progressive Education thus lies in the fact that it has elaborated no theory of social welfare, unless it be that of anarchy or extreme individualism. In this, of course, it is but reflecting the viewpoint of the members of the liberal-minded upper middle class who send their children to the Progressive schools—persons who are fairly well-off, who have abandoned the faiths of their fathers, who assume an agnostic attitude towards all important questions, who pride themselves on their open-mindedness and tolerance, who favor in a mild sort of way fairly liberal programs of social reconstruction, who are full of good will and humane sentiment, who have vague aspirations for world peace and human brotherhood, who can be counted upon to respond moderately to any appeal made in the name of charity, who are genuinely distressed at the sight of *unwonted* forms of cruelty, misery, and suffering, and who perhaps serve to soften somewhat the bitter clashes of those real forces that govern the world; but who, in spite of all their good qualities, have no deep and abiding loyalties, possess no convictions for which they would sacrifice over-much, would find it hard to live without their customary material comforts, are rather insensitive to the accepted form of social injustice, are content to play the rôle of interested spectator in the drama of human history, refuse to see reality in its harsher and more disagreeable forms, rarely move outside the pleasant circles of the class to which they belong, and in the day of severe trial will follow the lead of the most powerful and respectable forces in society and at the same time find good reasons for so doing (pp. 7-8).

This denigrating view of progressive education by Counts was identical to the vantage from which other critics examined the progressive social and economic reforms of the 1930s. For example, Fairchild (1934) assessed the New Deal as "inspired by a truly humanitarian spirit, refreshingly experimental in its outlook, abounding in details that are in themselves admirable, it not only lacks any vital and original philosophy of social reorganization, but also for its main landmarks clings tenaciously to the dominant system—profits and capital accumulation" (p. 18). In a similar manner, Mitchell dismissed the New Deal because "it does not discard but attempts to buttress the price-and-profit system" (p. 15).

Counts (1932) had observed that "the fact that other groups refuse to deal boldly and realistically with the present situation does not justify the teachers of the country in their customary policy of hesitation and equivocation" and that "the times are literally crying for a new vision of American destiny" (pp. 53-54). The opportunity for sharing the vision to which Counts referred would be presented several years later by a new journal, *The Social Frontier*.

Twenty-four months after its initial publication, Brameld (1936) observed that "the *Social Frontier* exemplifies the most progressive trends in educational thought in the United States" and that "it has now achieved one of the largest circulations among American journals in the academic field" (pp. 1-3). The opening editorial ("Orientation," 1934) of the first issue alerted readers to the distinctive nature of this liberal journal. This editorial announced that "American society, along with world society, is passing through an age of profound transition" and that this shift was proclaimed by "changing forms of economy and government, in the increasing instability of the whole social structure, in the swelling armaments and the intensification of international rivalries, and in the wars, revolutions, and social calamities throughout the world" (p. 3). The author indicated that the journal was intended to amplify the "few voices [that] have been raised within the ranks of educational workers in acceptance of the challenge of social reconstruction" (p. 4).

The second editorial in the inaugural issue ("Educating for Tomorrow," 1934) began with advice that "an organized educational profession can play an important role" in an effort that would transform "the plane of social living from insecurity to security, from chaos to planning, from the private profit audit to that of collective utility, from the lurid contrast of vulgar luxury and dire want to the shared abundant life made possible by technological advance" (p. 5). Later in that same editorial, the authors adjured their readers that "we submit to the membership of the N.E.A. that its role in the life of the nation would be greatly enhanced if it identified itself with an ideal of social living which alone can bring the social crisis to a happy resolution—a collectivistic and classless society" (p. 7).

In the second issue of the journal the editors indicated that they accepted "the rise of a collectivist order as irrevocable" and that the journal would "throw all the strength it possesses on the side of those forces which are striving to fashion a form of collectivism that will make paramount the interests of the overwhelming majority of the population" ("Collectivism and Collectivism," 1934, p. 4). After two additional issues of the journal, the editors explained that the rationale for the publication ("The Position of the Social Frontier," 1935) was to align schools with "socially reconstructive forces" by proposing "to teachers of the country that they ally themselves with the conception of social welfare which may be expected to serve the many rather than the few—that they strive to substitute human for property rights, a democratic collectivism for an oligarchic individualism in economy, social, planning and security for anarchy and chaos" (p. 31).

Recounting the history of *The Social Frontier* from its first issue, Moreo (1996) indicated that the influential educators who published in this journal did not uniformly support the entreaties in the journal for teachers to create a revolution in the schools. Despite the fact that articles in this journal were cited by contemporary conservatives as an indication of the temerity of socialist educators, Moreo judged that such advice was "out of step with the politics of most Americans" who were looking for "*restoration*, not excursions into utopia" (p. 39).

As an example of the extremist excursions to which Moreo referred, Hicks (1935) had written that "since the World War, however, and especially since the beginning of the depression, it has been extremely difficult to convince anyone that capitalism is a success" (p. 10). Describing methods by which teachers should meet the "onslaught" of capitalism in the schools, Hicks (1935) recommended that the appropriate response "ought to include teachers from kindergarten to university, that it will have to use the methods of struggle employed by labor unions—the strike, picketing, the boycott, and so forth—and that it will be much more powerful if it is affiliated with labor unions" (p. 12).

In an article that appeared in the journal that same year the editors wrote that "it is not essential to make a detailed study of the history of American education to discover that the school has always aimed not only at the dissemination of neutral factual knowledge and the mastery of so-called tool subjects, but also a the inculcation of attitudes, values, beliefs, loyalties, and ideals" ("Introductory Remarks on Indoctrination," 1935, p. 8). They concluded that "many teachers now realize that unless educational practice flows from a vision of social life rendered necessary, feasible, and desirable by existing material conditions, from a theory helpful in devising methods and instruments adequate to the realization of a functional way of life, and from a hypothesis which throws light on the place of education in such a scheme, there can be no consistent and socially significant educative effort in this day of conflicting values and ideals" (p. 9).

Also writing in *The Social Frontier* during 1935, Browder had warned that teachers should not expect reform from within education because "bankers and their lawyers make up about 95 percent of all controlling boards in the educational system" (p. 23). Like Hicks, Browder pointed to the failure of capitalism as the pretext for revolution in the schools:

> Those of us whose analysis of the crisis of capitalism leads us to the revolutionary situation, and who see the institutions of learning as inextricably involved in this crisis, must therefore be pardoned for our skepticism toward any program of social change which relies upon the school system as an important instrument in bringing that change about. The school system must itself be revolutionized, before it can become an instrument of revolution—or of any serious social change (1935, p. 22).

One of the themes that recurred predictably in *The Social Frontier* was an appeal to teachers by virtue of their special role in the social restructuring to which the editors were committed. In an article noting that over a million persons were employed as teachers in 1930, the editorialists wrote that teachers' "strength is strategic and functional as well as numerical" because "they spread over the country in a fine network which embraces every hamlet and rural community" and that they come "into close and sympathetic relations with the rank and file of the people of the nation" ("1,105.921," 1935, p. 6). The writers of this editorial praised teachers because of their political power as one of the potentially strongest forces in American life, noting that "particularly might they aspire to such a position, if they should choose to identify themselves with the masses of the people and refuse longer to make obeisance to the badges of wealth and rank" (p. 6). Another editorial ("Teachers and the Class Struggle," 1935) pointed out that "since teachers are essentially workers," they should "align themselves with labor and...utilize the school in an attempt to bring about a decision which is favorable to the working population" (p. 39).

Attempts to Moderate the Liberal Rhetoric in *The Social Frontier*

In a book about the South that appeared in 1935, Kendrick and Arnett (1971) alluded to the "red hysteria that so agitated the North in the years that followed the Russian Revolution." They wrote that even though the South was not as preoccupied with detecting communists, "the fact that the South had been less perturbed about economic radicalism does not imply that she had been any more tolerant of it" and described how business leaders and reporters "were especially alarmed by the liberal teachings in the social science departments of some of the universities (p. 173).

The "hysteria" toward socialists that Kendrick and Arnett observed extended to radical educators as well as social scientists. And as was the case with their liberal colleagues in the South, many of the writers in *The Social Frontier* were singled out for their radical views. For example, in the same year that Kendrick and Arnett were writing, Browder (1935) wrote in *The Social Frontier* of his skepticism toward any program of social change which relied upon the schools because the school system had to be revolutionized. Insisting that "issues in the educational world must be linked up with the class issues upon which the social struggles are conducted," he acknowledged the "objections from the majority of progressive educators" when he paraphrased their argument: "we are not revolutionaries essentially what we want is to conserve the best of human culture, handed down through the ages, and now endangered by the fascist reaction bred by capitalist decline" (p. 23). But Browder was intolerant of timid educators, lecturing them that "the answer is, unfortunately, that the pace cannot be set by your choice in the matter" (p. 23).

Despite such uncompromising rhetoric by many persons associated with *The Social Frontier*, some moderate spokespersons, who may have been intimidated by an increasing antagonism within society to radical liberal attitudes, did attempt to persuade their colleagues to endorse less confrontational opportunities for social change. In an article with the bold title "Karl Marx and the American Teacher," Brameld (1935) assured readers that Marx's book *Das Kapital* was admired not only by radical reformers but had been "listed by such outstanding scholars as Professors Dewey and Beard as the most influential work of the past several decades" (p. 53). Brameld had written that Marx believed that social revolution could not be brought about by democratic methods and that he instead judged "that the problems of capitalism must be solved by the principle of 'class struggle'" (p. 54). Even though he respected Marx's convictions, Brameld did not insist that all teachers become revolutionaries who would be totally committed to resolving the class struggle:

> The teacher who wishes to conduct his activity—within the school and without—in behalf of the collectivist ideal must free himself from the fallacy that the choice before him is naught or all. The question is not whether he as citizen and as worker *can* or *cannot* direct his energies along the lines indicated by Marxian tactics. The question is rather *in what degree can he.* The answer would of course vary within the individual school and community, and it would include activities not always immediate in their results but broad in scope and future in aim.... Teachers first, should recognize that unless they choose to follow the older educational philosophy of neutrality they must accept a point of view consonant with the requirements of the new America. They must then influence their students, subtly if necessary, frankly if possible, toward acceptance of the same position (1935, p. 55).

Brameld indicated that a technique that teachers could employ to influence students would be informing them about "the magnitude of the forces aligned against the attempt to bring into being a collectivist society" and "the innumerable persecutions of Negroes, miners, textile workers, and the imprisonment in California of farm organizers who dare to rise up against abominable working conditions" (p. 56). A year after this editorial had appeared, Brameld (1936) wrote that "the thesis of the article was simply that liberal educators who look toward collectivism as a way out of our economic, political, and cultural morass must give more serious consideration than they have thus far to the methodology of Marx" (p. 2). But he predicted the conclusions that persons would draw after an examination of Marx like that for which he had called:

> In accordance with these remarks it is necessary to insist, I think, that methodologically the Marxian hypothesis of class struggle may, as hypothesis, ultimately turn out to be false. And it is necessary to insist also that, though such a choice is not inconsistent with the broader meaning of scientific method, it does not necessarily follow that this is the only choice possible, or even the best (Brameld, 1935, p. 16).

Harold Rugg (1936) assumed an even more moderate position, advising teachers that "a careful study of the American Marxian's data, which purport to apply Marx's theses to twentieth-century America, leaves grave doubt as to their validity" (p. 140). He argued instead that "a realistic analysis of government in

America shows that it is carried on, not through warfare of two great fighting 'classes,' but rather through the interplay of many small special interest-groups" (p. 139). Bode (1935) expressed his dismay that the genuine "purpose of *The Social Frontier* is to bring, not peace, but the sword" and concluded that "according to the view held by the Editors, our obvious duty is to insist, in season and out of season, on the reconstruction of our economic and industrial life as a preliminary to reconstruction in other areas" (p. 42). He chastised the editors because the journal "seems to be trying to make up in aggressiveness against the economic order for what it lacks in educational programs" (p. 43).

Childs (1936) wrote an angry rebuttal to an editorial in *The Social Frontier* in which Rugg had challenged the conceptual validity of class struggle as an explanation for political and educational change. Childs disagreed with the following remarks by Rugg:

> There are, today, two conspicuous ways of designing an educational strategy, and of appraising its probable effectiveness in helping to bring about social change in America. One is to base it on the historical study of such foreign crises as the French Revolution, or on famous social theories, such as that of Karl Marx. The other way is to build it directly from the study of American conditions and problems, both past and present and continually emphasizing the loyalties of the American people. While some of my colleagues sponsor the former, I, in company with others, follow and advocate the latter (Rugg, quoted by Childs, 1936, p. 219).

Writing from a similar perspective during the same year, Kilpatrick (1936) noted that "as for *The Social Frontier*, I think it too should make clear that, while it may allow others to advocate high-Marxism or Communism in its columns, it does not itself look to either as the way out of our American difficulty" (p. 274). Kilpatrick added parenthetically that "there are, so far as I know, very, very few Communists within the ranks of American professors and no Communist or even high-Marxian teaching with the immediate institution in which I myself work [i.e., Columbia University]" (p. 274).

In a 1928 issue of *The New Republic* John Dewey had chastised his contemporaries because "while an American visitor may feel a certain patriotic pride in noting in how many respects an initial impulse came from some progressive school in our own country, he is at once humiliated and stimulated to new endeavor to see how much more organically that idea is incorporated in the Russian system than in our own" (1928b, p. 94). Although Dewey had written about his admiration for the Russian economy, government, and educational system, he later disagreed with the extreme Marxist rhetoric that characterized many of the articles in *The Social Frontier*. In the very first issue of that journal Dewey (1934) responded directly to Counts's controversial question, *Dare the School Build a New Social Order?* (Counts, 1932) with his terse opinion that, though the school would inevitably "share" in this task, "I do not think...that the schools can in any literal sense be the builders of a new social order" (p. 12).

Wirth (1972) observed that though Dewey believed that "human experience was being changed by the advent of science, technology, corporate-industrialism, and urbanism, and that these developments contained potentials for debasing and dehumanizing life and for undermining the ideals of the democratic dream," he was distinguished from his liberal contemporaries by virtue of "his conviction that cultural renewal could be engendered from within the very system of science and technology which threatened men" (p. 220). As an example, Dewey admitted that he was "rather confused by the articles that have appeared in *The Social Frontier* urging that educators adopt the class concept as their intellectual guide and practical dynamic." Dewey (1936) paraphrased the arguments with which he disagreed:

> A radical reconstruction of the existing social order is demanded. The needed reconstruction is opposed by the powerful class now in control of social affairs, whose property, power, and prestige are threatened by the reconstruction that is required. On the other side are the workers who suffer in countless ways from the present social order and who will be the gainers in security, freedom, and opportunity, by basic change. Teachers are workers and their own class interest is with fellow-workers. Moreover, social consciousness and social conscience should lead them to side with the workers; they belong on that side of the struggle that is going on (p. 241).

Dewey dismissed such rhetoric, noting that "I do not see how the terms of a social problem are identical with the method of its solution" and that "I do not see how they constitute the leading ideas that will give direction to the efforts of educators" (p. 241). Dewey added emphasis to these objections when he observed that "I have difficulty in imagining any educator taking this point of view unless he has abandoned in advance all faith in education" (p. 242).

The Social Frontier had been published from 1934 until 1939 when its organizers approached the Progressive Education Association and asked it to sponsor the journal. The June 1939 issue of the journal contained the following announcement from the president of the Progressive Education Association:

> When THE SOCIAL FRONTIER was independently launched, the Progressive Education Association was on the verge of publishing a journal that would do for the educational world what THE SOCIAL FRONTIER has so ably done in the last half decade. During this period, THE SOCIAL FRONTIER has gone far ahead in professional pioneering and adventure, and it has had the good will and support of many members of the Progressive Education Association.... Beginning next fall, the Progressive Education Association will continue the journalistic enterprise so ably initiated by the original Social Frontier group (Ryan, 1939, pp. 259-260).

When making this announcement, Ryan added that "it may be that readers will wish to rebaptize THE SOCIAL FRONTIER" and that "suggestions are invited as to what better name could be borne by this publication" (p. 260). The Progressive

Education Association's Board of Directors decided to change the name to *Frontiers of Democracy* and to publish it as a companion journal to *Progressive Education*. However, Redefer (1949) acknowledged that "the issue of whether the Progressive Education Association should publish 'Frontiers of Democracy' was never a settled matter." Although the following passage from a 1941 issue of the *Frontiers of Democracy* was intended to chastise progressive educators who had not declared their political commitment to the movement, it also revealed their lack of unity because of fear about the social stigma that might be attached to such a declaration:

> There are some who believe oh! so wholeheartedly in progressive education...if they can call it by another name. There are others, more shy ones, who refuse to name at all what they are doing in their schools, although with vigor surprising, they deny in public that it is progressive education. And there are bolder ones, too, who courageously affirm that maybe it is progressive education, but horrors no! not with a capital "P"! There are the subtle strategists who sneak in their new practices with their left hand while their right hand denies all connection with that "new" progressive education. There are others who in their writing do not want to be too closely linked with the Progressive Education Association, even though their work is only possible because of this organization. And there are the home-bodies who in the privacy of their living rooms, with shades drawn, will concede their acceptance of the philosophy but shun like a plague any forthright public acceptance of it in the bold clear light of day ("A Rose is not a Rose," 1941, p. 100).

In an article in the *Frontiers of Democracy* Barnes (1940) wrote that though "MARX is usually interpreted as contending that revolution is the only road to the better social order of the future," that "more recent students have pretty successfully demonstrated that MARX was an eclectic in the matter" (p. 108). Despite such reconciliatory rhetoric by Barnes as well as prominent progressive educators such as Dewey, Kilpatrick, and Rugg, *The Social Frontier* and the *Frontiers of Democracy* became lightening rods that attracted criticism from enraged conservative educators. Writing in an article that appeared in *The American Legion Magazine*, Armstrong (1940) noted that "mouthpieces of this Fifth Column attacking Americanism in the schools is the magazine called *Social Frontier*, edited by Dr. George S. Counts" (p. 51). Observing that "in educational circles Dr. Counts, Prof. Rugg and their fellow comrades are know as 'Frontier Thinkers,'" Armstrong provided citations from Rugg's textbooks and teachers' manuals to indicate Rugg's anti-Americanism. He provided a list of subversive textbooks that included 17 books by the prolific Rugg as well as a high school weekly reader for which Rugg was the social studies editor. Additionally, Armstrong adjured parents to patrol schools to search for signs of sedition, such as copies of *The Social Frontier*.

WORLD WAR II AND CONSERVATIVE POLITICAL APPROACHES

In a 1902 book titled *The Making of Citizens* Hughes observed that "the school is a political institution maintained by the State for the cultivation and propagation of national ideas" and that "in democratic states future rulers must be trained, in military states future soldiers" (1902, p. 4). Attempting to answer a question about which country maintained the optimal system of education, Hughes argued that the best system was different for each country, based on the political goals that had been established within those countries:

> The question is, "Which of all these various systems of national training makes the best citizens?" and when the question is put thus one sees that its answer depends entirely upon what the phrase "best citizen" may connote. The phrase in France or Germany does certainly not connote the same attributes as in England or America, so that it is immediately evident how difficult, if not impossible, it is to answer such a question as "Which is the better educational system—that of Germany or of England?" (1902, p. 4).

Hughes endorsed a national system of education in which reading occupied a central position because "by reading, the individual obtains the experience of the race" and "national culture is impossible without books" (p. 393).

Though the connection between education and democracy had been emphasized prior to World War II, the expansion of communism during and after that war caused many persons to question the danger of the socialist initiatives, some of which had been associated with progressive education. Many of the threats about communism before World War II had been dismissed as unfounded and even paranoid. Beale (1941), an ardent socialist, complained that the war "gave new life to a particularly blatant sort of patriotism and fathered a brood of patriotic societies organized to force chauvinism upon the people." He added that "apparent prosperity and huge profits, which great masses of the people were making on paper, at least, in an orgy of speculation, rendered exceedingly unpopular the criticism of the *status quo* and the warnings of disaster that were voiced by intellectual leaders who did keep their heads." Beale wrote with approval of progressive educators who had "attempted to make the schools play a more vital rôle in American Life" and rued the opposition to this initiative by a public which had "wished to be left in peace to make money" (p. 236).

In a book with the sensational title, *Our Children Are Cheated*, Fine (1947) recapitulated material from a series of 12 articles that he had written for *The New York Times*. Confronting charges by conservatives that "teachers are communistic or engage in subversive activities," Fine protested that his "evidence indicates that the overwhelming majority of teachers are patriotic, conscientious American citizens" (p. 9). He did admit that "public confidence in the schools has dropped sharply" but judged that this "school break down" originated primarily with "the physical disintegration of the school plants and the deterioration of teacher morale" (p. 11). He wrote that "schools have deteriorated alarmingly since Pearl Harbor" and gave examples such as school buildings requiring repair, shortages of school supplies, and overcrowded classrooms. Convinced that the liberal initiatives espoused by progressive educators were still viable, he suggested steps to end the educational crisis, including increased financial support, increased teachers' salaries, increased federal aid to education, better working conditions for teachers, more protective tenure laws, expanded use of progressive teaching methods, and greater decision making by teachers.

Though numerous twentieth-century educators had highlighted a link between free government and education, this connection became increasingly apparent when specific educational practices were emphasized as critical to the survival of democratic government. And though this conviction was tied to science, mathematics, social studies, and many of the subjects of the curriculum, literacy received special attention, particularly during times of war, because it was seen as indispensable to freedom of the press. In his book on citizenship, Hughes (1902) had represented the views of the majority of nineteenth- and early twentieth-century educators who fervently supported literacy education because they thought it was indispensable to a democratic society. Hughes's view was certainly prevalent until the economic depression of the 1930s. And even though it was challenged by a strident group of politically liberal educators during the depression, Hughes's fundamental assumptions were accepted by most Americans throughout the first half of the 1900s.

Sentiments about a critical connection between literacy and democracy grew stronger during the Second World War. The National Education Association established a commission in 1935 that "made the improvement of education for democratic citizenship the central point of its work" (Educational Policies Commission, 1940, Foreword). Though the members of this commission wrote that "the development of an active and intelligent loyalty to democracy is clearly the nation's supreme problem in education and in defense," the editors added a caveat that "the reporting of specific projects in this volume does not involve an endorsement" (Educational Policies Commission, 1940, Foreword). In response to an earlier publication from this same commission, the National Education Association had also placed a qualification in the "Foreword" section by stipulating that "even if you do not agree with us, our publication will succeed if it helps you to think seriously about the great cause of education" (Educational Policies Commission, 1938, p. ix).

The rhetoric in the National Education Association's proclamations became noticeably more nationalistic after the United States entered the war. For example, a report titled "American Education and the War in Europe," published in November of 1939, had advised that those persons who aspired to rebuild the world after the war "can approach their task best if their hands are unstained by blood, their spirits uncorroded by hatred, and their minds uncrippled by months or years of wartime regimentation" (p. 225). The preceding remarks were adopted by the Educational Policies Commission, as was another statement that was published less than a year later ("Education and the Defense," 1940). In this second statement the commission's members acknowledged their earlier remarks but then stipulated that intervening events had "created a new situation" and that "there are many factors in the national and world scenes of today which were not present, or even predictable, nine months ago" (p. 161). As evidence of these changes, the later statement contained sections with titles such as "Military Preparation Is Needed for National Defense," "Occupational Training Is Needed for National Defense," and "Moral Defense Requires the Maintenance of Conditions Conductive to National Unity."

Even the editors of the liberal journal *Frontiers of Democracy* published a declaration about the war ("This War and American Education," 1942) in which they made pleas for the defeat of totalitarianism. But the editors were less reconciliatory than the editors of the *National Education Association Journal*, reminding their readers that "the liberal elements in our present able political leadership should be supported and strengthened" and that "we must not let the crucial necessities of the military situation become the occasion for the introduction of the fascist pattern into our own way of thought and action" (p. 1). In a passage about the war written before the entry of the United States ("This War and America," 1941), the editors of *Frontiers of Democracy* had warned that "we call on both Britain and the United States to renounce publicly all thought of national aggrandizement in this struggle" because "Anglo-American imperialism would be no more acceptable than any other" (p. 10). In a statement about the attitudes of the editors of *Frontiers of Democracy* that was written several years later, Rugg (1943) reported that winning the war abroad had "long been a foregone conclusion because of our unchallenged economic supremacy" but that the editors were still concerned because two wars were actually being fought, "The War Abroad over military fascism and The War at home over property and work, over security and social control" (p. 4).

Some educators argued that the type of curriculum needed to preserve liberty and education should be reinforced through nationalized planning and standardized textbook selection. Referring to himself as an "essentialist," Bagley (1938) spoke out against progressive educational practices that had emphasized "interest, freedom, immediate needs, personal experience, psychological organization, and pupil-initiative" and in favor of programs that prioritized "effort, discipline, remote goals, race-experience, logical sequence, and teacher initiative" (p. 245). The Board of Editors of the liberal journal *Frontiers of Democracy* ("The Mission of Education," 1942) retorted that "pre-preparation for war" curricula were based on assumptions that "a proper physical education can help give the needed bodily 'toughening'; suitable mathematics and physics can shorten the actual study of these subjects in the training camp; pre-flight aeronautics is a further possibility" and that "all such must fit specific army or navy planning"

(p. 69). The editors chastised proponents of such curricula for forgetting that "the prospective soldier needs to know not only how to fight, but as truly why he fights and for what" and that "these pre-preparations are in fact preparations for war, not for peace."

In sympathy with the Board of Editors for *Frontiers of Democracy*, Kilpatrick (1942a) warned that the progressive education program should not be dismantled because "it is so new in our history that it is not yet acclimated in the minds of our people." Kilpatrick blasted the opponents of progressive educational reforms whom he thought were motivated by "selfish and vested interest" and who were "taking advantage of the war" to "demand that the schools cease 'pampering,' stress 'discipline' and begin once more to 'harden' youth by the 'good old-time methods' of useless tasks, formal discipline and authoritarian management" (p. 199).

The conservative Bagley (1938) anticipated such criticism, insisting that his advice should not be seen as wartime opportunism because he had "publicly called attention for more than thirty years to manifestation of this influence [from progressive education], and to its weakening tendencies" (p. 245). As an indication of the longevity of his concerns about the erosion of the "essentialist" curriculum many years before the war, Bagley (1929) had berated progressive educators for undermining the moral authority of the family. He predicted that a reactionary effort would develop to redress the damage when he wrote that "there are signs that a more virile and less elusive educational theory is even now in the offing" (p. 573).

Writing during World War II, Bagley (1938) observed progressive education's continued damage to the elementary schools. He regretted that "American education should be unnecessarily weak at a time when the situation both at home and abroad is critical in the last degree" (p. 250). He argued that a literate electorate was "absolutely indispensable" to the survival of the United States. More than this, he advised that the country required a "community of Culture" comprising a "common core of ideas, meanings, understanding, and ideals" (p. 252). These essential pieces of information would be learned through a common curriculum, which Bagley thought was justified because "a specific program of studies including these essentials should be the heart of a democratic system of education" and because "there is no valid reason for the extreme localism that has come to characterize American education" (p. 253).

An editorial in a 1939 issue of *Forbes* magazine had described the "shocking discoveries" in a textbook "reputedly used in over 4,000 schools" and written by "a professor in a college devoted to turning out school teachers" ("Treacherous Teaching," 1939, p. 8). The editorialist observed that the book was "viciously un-American" and that "its author is in love with the way things are done in Russia, that he distorts facts to convince the oncoming generation that America's private enterprise system is wholly inferior and nefarious" (p. 8).

The unnamed author to which this editorialist alluded was undoubtedly Harold Rugg at Columbia's Teachers College. A report in *Time* magazine ("Book Burnings," 1940) recounted bannings by local school districts of Rugg's books because of his expressed sympathy for the Soviet Union during the 1930s. However, in an article that had appeared in the radical journal, *The Social Frontier*, Rugg had expressed his opposition to a Marxist explanation for political change, noting that "the American way of controlled social change follows the democratic method of building consent among the people" and that "this can be done only by educating the people to an understanding of and participation in their collective affairs (1936, p. 142).

Rugg's reputation among conservatives was hardly enhanced when, several issues after Rugg had made remarks in support of democratic governance, Childs (1936) praised Rugg in *The Social Frontier* as a "liberal educator" who realized that changes in society necessitated "the reconstruction of many fundamental modes of American life and thought" and as the creator of curriculum adaptations that had "a real influence in stimulating the elementary and secondary schools to a more realistic treatment of modern social conditions" (p. 219). A 1940 *Time* magazine report had indicated that "his critics object to the Rugg texts for picturing the U.S. as a land of unequal opportunity, and giving a class conscious account of the framing of the U.S. Constitution" ("Book Burnings," 1940). Rugg (1941) wrote a lengthy defense of himself and his textbooks in which he lamented that "a year and a half ago I returned from a six months' nationwide survey of creative work and public opinion" but that in 1940 "eight to ten million Americans talked about [Rugg's books] over the breakfast, luncheon or dinner table, heard about them over the radio, read about them in the newspapers" and that "hundreds of editorials took sides pro and con" (pp. 5-6). Rugg indicated that he had written responses to the "absurd charges" that had appeared in *Forbes* magazine but that his responses had not been printed. However, such protestations of innocence had little influence on Rugg's political adversaries. A decade after Rudd had argued in his own defense, Hughes (1950) wrote bitterly that "Mr. Rugg had the opportunity to indoctrinate at public expense one-fifth of the school children of the nation with his 'great ideas'" (1950, pp. 272-273).

A special 1942 issue of *The Elementary English Review* was devoted to a symposium about the response of reading educators to a literacy crisis that was threatening the armed forces. Betts indicated the basis for the alarm when he wrote that "and now it is reported that the Army has found it necessary to teach *some* of the draftees how to read" and "because of this situation, both outright accusations and subtle inferences are made about the educational program in these United States" ("What Shall We Do," p. 225). In an introduction to the symposium, the president of the National Council of Teachers of English expressed his disappointment with a commissioner of the National Institute of Education who had observed that the "essential organization of the elementary school curriculum...requires no far-reaching revision as a result of the war" (DeBoer, 1942, p. 224). But several reading educators agreed with that commissioner. For example, Dolch responded to the question about the schools' responsibility for "the poor reading on the part of our young men, as shown by the tests given draftees," with the remark that "the school should keep on doing just what they are doing and do it more widely and energetically" ("What Shall We Do," 1942, p. 229). No consensus was developed even among those educators who thought changes were appropriate. For example, Betts warned teachers to avoid remedial reading, which he referred to as the "fad of the 1930s," while Witty noted that "convincing evidence again demonstrates the need for remedial reading" ("What Shall We Do," 1942, p. 251). In his analysis of wartime reading problems, William Gray objected to "recent editorials which maintain that current deficiencies in reading are the product of 'pseudo-scientific bungling' and the innovation of so-called progressive methods of teaching." Gray observed that "the implication of these vague criticisms is that recent innovations in teaching reading have been adopted without due consideration of essentials and of methods of achieving desired ends" ("What Shall We Do," 1942, p. 235). Though Gray thought such attacks were "unsound and merit no more consideration than a purely defensive attitude," the volume and intensity of the precise sort of criticism he feared did increase.

Childs (1942) warned that though "there is no more patriotic group in this country than the teachers" nonetheless "we find certain school boards who seem to think that the teachers of the public schools are members of the armed forces of the nation, and that they are to be ordered into any kind of community defense work which the members of the school board outline" (p. 166). In a book published originally in 1949, Kandel (1974) suggested that World War II's impact on education was more pervasive than that of World War I:

> Because of the large numbers of mothers who entered war industries, provision had to be made for the care of their children. Because of the disruption of home life, a result of this as well as other causes, the care of children in general and the increase in juvenile delinquency gave rise to another set of problems. Finally, a serious and growing crisis was caused by the withdrawal of teachers from schools for war service or for war industries (p. 4).

Kandel also recounted that "the war imposed new demands upon educational institutions" and that "the normal programs of secondary schools had to give way to a large extent, if not wholly, to programs of 'Education for Victory' and to vocational preparation" (p. 4). Referring to wartime reading programs, Kilpatrick (1942b) had cautioned teachers that "merely to have children do 'leg work' which their elders have planned is but exploitation" (p. 167). However, Bert Smith (1943) had a different reaction to the scholastic regimentation associated with the war and judged that standardization of the curriculum had resulted in "improvement of instruction in the wartime emergency." He gave an example in which standardization had been introduced into a school district and that, as a result, "many significant improvements were made in the social sciences, industrial arts, home economics, agriculture, music, sciences, reading, language, and all other areas to meet the needs found in the community analysis" (p. 224).

In the Wake of the War

In an article that appeared in the *Saturday Review* 10 years after the launching of Russia's *Sputnik*, Jennings (1967) argued that contemporary problems in education did not begin with the appearance of that satellite. Although this was a period when many Americans were startled by the apparent educational advances that had enabled Soviet scientists to surpass American researchers, Jennings indicated that the initial recognition of a decline in American education had transpired during the 1940s and early 1950s when "the intellectuals and the scholars, the academicians who had divorced themselves from the concerns of the schoolmarms when education turned professional, now turned vehemently upon progressive education as the primary cause of all our classroom ills" (1967, p. 95). Jennings judged that shock at the high number of illiterates inducted into the armed services during the Second World War rather than the launching of *Sputnik* had been far more responsible for causing disillusionment with progressive education. He vented his frustration at the U.S. Office of Education, which had convened a 1955 conference to explore the crisis in education but which Jennings characterized as a "valedictory for progressive education" that had devolved into "swan songs, pious hopes, expressions of conventional wisdom, demands for 'reality orientation,' and bold new looks at ancient and stubborn facts" (p. 78).

Even while under attack, progressive educators were lobbying for changes in the schools that would reduce the emphasis on academic skills and promote learner-centered experiences to prepare students to solve practical problems. Hofstadter (1963) wrote that the intellectual basis for the "life-adjustment movement" was difficult to establish since its primary records were "repetitive bulletins on the subject compiled by the Office of Education in Washington" (p. 345). Hofstadter attributed the origin of the movement to a threefold confidence in the concepts of John Dewey, psychology, and "piety for the findings of 'science.'" However, Hofstadter did add sarcastically that "life-adjustment educators would do anything in the name of science except encourage children to study it" (p. 345).

A 1947 article in *Newsweek* magazine ("High-School Overhaul," 1947) reported the distress expressed by U.S. Office of Education personnel who had concluded that problems in education could be explained by the fact that most students in American high schools were being educated in college preparatory curricula while only 20 percent of these individuals actually went on to college. The report indicated that Office of Education spokespersons had characterized these curricula as "rigid, dull, and inadequate." As an alternative, the Office of Education had established a Commission on Life Adjustment Education for Youth to develop techniques for "relaxing curricula to include more 'real' subjects for those who do not go to college" (p. 86). A report in *Time* magazine ("Get

Adjusted," 1947) about the attitudes of John Studebaker, the U.S. Commissioner of Education, cited the identical statistics about the low number of high school students who went on to college. The report stated that "Studebaker believes that educational reverence for the 'white-collar myth' produces frustrated and maladjusted citizens" and quoted him as asking "why not frankly admit that most girls would be housekeepers and most men mechanics, farmers, and trades-people— and train them accordingly?" (p. 64).

In a report about government initiatives to develop curricula, Basler (1947), a former officer in the U.S. Office of Education, described a national conference to help implement life adjustment curricula. He wrote that "the committee in charge of arrangements was guided by the fact that the developments to that date revealed that there was one inevitable and compelling purpose to be achieved by the National Conference, namely, *to devise an effective plan of action for developing a program of universal secondary education*" (p. 5). This universal plan of education about which the Office of Education felt "great eagerness" was intended to aid "the schools of the nation to move more rapidly toward the provision of appropriate educational opportunities for those youth of secondary school age whose interests and abilities are such that they are neither candidates for college and the professions nor for training in the skilled occupations" (pp. 3-4).

Providing leadership at the national conference on life adjustment curricula, the government-appointed Commission of Life Adjustment for Youth had included members from prominent professional organizations such as the National Education Association, the American Vocational Association, and the National Association of Secondary School Principals. Presenting a report about life adjustment curricula to the members of the National Association of Secondary School Principals, Nickell (1949) described a life adjustment curriculum "built around 55 real-life problems of high-school youth" with categories such as "'Earning a Living,' 'Developing an Effective Personality,' 'Living Healthfully and Safely,' 'Managing Personal Finances Wisely,' 'Spending Leisure Time Wholesomely and Enjoyably,' 'Taking an Effective Part in Civic Affairs,' 'Preparing for Marriage, Home-Making, and Parenthood,' and 'Making Effective Use of Educational Opportunities'" (p. 154).

An earlier report (Division of Secondary Education/Division of Vocational Education, 1947) defined life adjustment education as "that which better equips all American youth to live democratically with satisfaction to themselves and profit to society as home members, workers, and citizens" (p. 4). The report went on to provide a detailed clarification of this statement:

It is concerned with ethical and moral living and with physical, mental, and emotional health. It recognizes the importance of fundamental skills since citizens in a democracy must be able to compute, to read, to write, to listen, and to speak effectively. It emphasizes skills as tools for further achievements. It is concerned with the development of wholesome recreational interests of both an individual and social nature. It is concerned with the present problems of youth as well as with their preparation for future living. It is for all American youth and offers them learning experiences appropriate to their capacities. It recognizes the importance of personal satisfactions and achievement for each individual within the limits of his abilities. It respects the dignity of work and recognizes the educational values of responsible work experience in the life of the community. It provides both general and specialized education but, even in the former, common goals are to be attained through differentiation both as to subject matter and experience. It has many patterns.... It emphasizes deferred as well as immediate values.... It recognizes that many events of importance happened a long time ago but holds that the real significance of these events is in their bearing upon life of today. It emphasizes active and creative achievements as well as adjustment to existing conditions.... It is education fashioned to achieve desired outcomes in terms of character and behavior.... Above all, it recognizes the inherent dignity of the human personality (Division of Secondary Education/Division of Vocational Education, 1947, pp. 4-5).

During the same year that government officials were expressing their unrestrained support for progressive curricular initiatives, Kandel (1947) pointed out that some of the suggested changes were hardly novel. He wrote that the "adjustment to life curriculum" had been amply discussed during former periods using terms such as *specificity of learning, functionalism,* and *education through deferred values.* Indicating that elements within the adjustment to life movement had been extracted from progressive educational programs used before the war, he concluded that "education as adjustment is not new in American education literature, but it was discarded on the ground that would result in a static society" (p. 372).

In a scathing attack that appeared in *The Scientific Monthly,* Fuller (1951) criticized progressive educators who supported adjustment to life curricula for their "debasement of liberal education and of sound scholarship." Fuller labeled as "rubbish" a belief that "education is a process of fulfilling needs...and therefore only those things needed for adjustment in society should be taught" (p. 34). He called for curricula that accentuated "the study of the dignity and uniqueness of man and of his creations, as they are made evident in the pursuit of knowledge of literature, of languages, of philosophy, of the arts, of the sciences" (pp. 32-33). Writing a year later Kahrhoff (1952) criticized progressive practices because "this system of education overemphasizes the 'active' life and neglects the 'contemplative' life." He wrote that the contemplative life was that exemplified by philosophers and that it had produced "the theories that are the bases, or the reasons, for the actions in the life of the 'active' person" (p. 21).

Bestor (1951) had written that any person who made negative remarks about the schools was "automatically branded an enemy of the schools by those who have a vested interest in the educational status quo" (p. 11). Despite this risk, he indicated that he did not judge "qualitative educational achievement" in the public schools to be commensurate with the money invested in them. He insisted that "the school exists to provide intellectual training, in every field of activity where systematic thinking is an important component of success" (p. 11). Bestor argued that such thinking was directly connected to the stability of the country's government and that "to build our defense of freedom firm and deep, we need to eradicate, before it is too late, the anti-intellectual tendencies that have crept into our public education system" (p. 13). Bestor was praised by the conservative Kirk (1954) as an accurate reporter of the "pedantic tyranny," "follies," and "humbuggeries" that had been perpetrated by "stubborn doctrinaires who, in any age, make up too large a part of the body of teachers (true conservatives of stupidity, for they make the sentences of Dewey, Kilpatrick and Counts into unalterable secular dogmas) [and who] have obtained, by virtue of the dogged and dreary lust of 'administrative positions' which characterizes them, a mortal clutch upon our poor educational institutions" (Kirk, 1954, pp. 62-63).

In a book about the intrusion of communism into American society, Budenz (1954) pointed out that the nation was being weakened by the communist infiltration of education and the subversive pragmatic philosophy represented by progressive education. Budenz noted that both of these influences were evident in the work of George Counts, whom he described as "an outstanding figure in the Progressive Education Association" as well as an author of several books that were "laudatory of the Soviet dictatorship" (p. 217). In addition to Counts, Budenz accused other prominent educational professors such as John Dewey, William Kilpatrick, and Harold Rugg of subverting the nation through their politicized, progressive approaches to education.

In an issue of *The American Legion Magazine*, Kuhn (1952) presented a report about subversive communist activities in the schools in which he displayed pictures of Kilpatrick, Rugg, and other professors from "the Teachers College Brain Trust." Warning of "3500 professors who are members of Communist fronts or in allied activities," Budenz identified those universities with the heaviest concentrations of subversive personnel. In an earlier article that had appeared in *The American Legion Magazine*, Budenz (1951) named scores of university professors whom he judged to be communists. He complained nonetheless because "uncover a Red on a college faculty and a hue and cry is raised over 'academic freedom,' as though these people had a God-given right to infect our children with their made-in-Moscow virus" (1951, p. 168).

Not all critics of progressive education adopted preeminently political arguments. Some conservative educators highlighted academic reasons for dismantling progressive programs. For example, McCracken (1952) deplored the poor performance of youth on standardized tests. He observed that "in a college class where most of the students came from the upper 50% of their high school classes, 20% needed remedial reading," and judged such statistics to be "conclusive evidence" of the country's reading problems. McCracken thought that a single pedagogical development had been responsible for these reading problems. While applauding progressive innovations such as an emphasis on materials that were appealing and relevant to children's interests, he spoke out against the insistence by progressive educators that children delay reading instruction during the initial elementary school years to develop "reading readiness" instead. He wrote bitterly that "because we have failed to provide reading programs with which we can teach nearly every child to read, we have tried to justify our predicament by over-emphasizing the readiness needs of the pupils" (p. 272).

Rudolph Flesch (1955) focused on the holistic approach to reading that had been supported by progressive educators when he published his best-selling book, *Why Johnny Can't Read*. Mayer (1961) evaluated Flesch's volume as "possibly the most influential book about education published in the last decade" (p. 184). Though he was one of the many persons who were convinced of a connection between democracy and education, Flesch insisted that this connection not only required reading but also was routed through phonics instruction. Consequently, he viewed whole word reading approaches as an explicit threat to the literacy on which democracy had been established. Though the rhetoric about failure in reading had been passionate during the initial half of the twentieth century, it escalated to unprecedented levels with the publication of Flesch's popular book. Addressing whole word approaches in a sequel, Flesch (1981) wrote that "the results of this mass miseducation have been disastrous" (p. 1). Flesch praised the "Phonic Five," sets of reading textbooks that emphasized word attack skills, and excoriated the "Dismal Dozen," materials that incorporated holistic learning strategies. He adjured parents to "go to your child's school tomorrow morning and find out what system it uses to teach reading" and that "if the school uses one of the Phonic Five series, Johnny or Mary will be all right" (pp. 9-10). In the first edition of his book he had described the whole word method as an "inhuman, mean, stupid" approach that would train "children as if they were dogs" (1955, p. 126). His comments were no less emotional in the 1981 version of his book.

A year after Flesch's 1955 book had been published, Jones and Oliver (1956) made an even more strident attack on whole word approaches to instruction. Just the title of their book, *Progressive Education is REDucation*, indicated the bond the authors attempted to establish between nontraditional teaching techniques and communist subversion. Jones and Oliver warned that "the 'research' angle fools a lot of busy teachers" because "it is such a high-sounding word to parrot," in spite of the fact that educational research was actually a set of "commercials" that had a "tendency to fraud." They indicated that teachers should be especially wary of the massive and frequently cited research of Arthur Gates in support of whole word methods because "not only are his data of questionable scientific method and therefore of questionable value, but they have been used and reused by all subsequent authors who think children can learn to read 'silently' or by osmosis" (p. 35). In similarly caustic manner they dismissed Anderson and Dearborn's book on the psychology of reading as "reminiscent of the hoax of the patent medicine man in grandma's day" (p. 34).

In 1959 James Bryant Conant published an extremely influential report on the state of American high schools. Conant was a chemist who eventually became president of Harvard University. Among his impressive credentials was service as chairperson of the national committee that had developed the atomic bomb during World War II. When Conant (1959) published his powerful report on high schools, he maintained that curriculum developers had made too many concessions to the demands of progressive educators. Because he was "convinced that American secondary education can be made satisfactory without any radical changes in the basic pattern," he recommended that curricula be implemented by individual schools in cooperation with the citizens in the communities where those schools were located rather than through federal or state directives. After advising that "it is impossible to draw a blueprint of an ideal high school," he counseled his readers to "avoid generalizations, recognize the necessity of diversity, get the facts about your local situation, elect a good school board, and support the efforts of the board to improve the schools" (Conant, 1959, p. 96).

In a chapter titled "The Whole-Word and Word-Guessing Fallacy," Lowe (1961) warned that "reading is no longer presented to the beginning reader as a matter of learning how to get from the printed page as exactly as possibly the ideas committed to the text by the writer" and that "it has become a process in which the reader projects his imagination, his preferences, his conjectures, his limitations, his inexperience, and his ignorance" (p. 90). In the same volume as that in which Lowe was writing, Walcutt (1961) expressed his disregard for research supporting the use of context strategies and other techniques recommended by proponents of whole word methods because "the look-and-say system was worked out in purest theory; it has never been objectively tested by the educationists; and a significant portion of the thousands upon thousands of books and articles on reading that have poured from the schools of education during the past forty years have demonstrated the superiority of proper phonic instruction to look-and-say" (Walcutt, 1961, p. 141).

Much of the educational literature written in the period that followed the 1940s and 1950s echoed warnings from prior decades of crises in general education and reading education. Koerner contributed several books to this dialogue, two of which he portentously titled *The Miseducation of American Teachers* (1963) and *Who Controls American Education: A Guide for Laymen* (1968). After noting that "the central government has apparently decided that formal education is to be one of the chief instruments for solving all sorts of social and economic problems— poverty, hate, discrimination, unemployment, maladjustment, inequality," Koerner (1968) reassured his readers that he would "neither endorse nor deprecate this redistribution of power" (p. 4). However, he relaxed this self-imposed restraint when he commented that "a cynic might say that there has been a kind of closed shop in reading, a collusion between publishers and reading experts to exploit and protect a big textbook market" (p. 74).

Packard (1974) referred to surveys that indicated "a worrisome trend: the general low state of literacy and ability to write clearly among younger and older people alike" (p. 82). He recommended that teachers respond to the literacy crisis by turning away from the whole word approaches which were "the predominant way reading has been taught for many years in U.S. schools" and instead support phonics programs that would enable children to "learn visually to recognize key elements used to build almost all words" (p. 84).

In a similar fashion, Copperman (1978) synthesized the many surveys that had indicated declining scores by youth on standardized reading tests, attempting to document that "since the 1960's, academic performance and standards have shown a sharp and widespread decline" (p. 15). Urging his audience to recognize a reading crisis that was "tragic in its consequences for the individuals it affects, and for our society," he advised educators to "take control of their classes, assign meaningful tasks in a meaningful curriculum, and positively motivate their students" (p. 215).

Disputing the Literacy Crisis

Though the public and many teachers were alarmed by the allegations from conservative educators about increased reading failure, some late twentieth-century supporters of liberal programs argued that the crisis was largely a rhetorical fabrication devised to promote conservative political objectives. In an article titled "The Decline in Literacy Is a Fiction, if Not a Hoax," Ohmann (1976) remonstrated that "when people set out to find the *causes* of an event that may or may not have happened, and whose nature is unknown, you can expect a certain amount of floundering" (p. 32). Television was only one of a "cast of villains" that Ohmann thought had been unfairly credited with causing this alleged crisis:

> [Factors responsible for the alleged literacy crisis include] the "creative school" among English teachers, structural linguistics, Webster's *Third*, less teaching of grammar, English teachers who themselves can't write, the fact that kids no longer read the Bible, educationists' jargon, the "new sentimentality," "the mono-syllabic speech habits of the young," open-admissions programs, the increase of mass education, the Free-Speech-Movement, Vietnam, Watergate, children's books, replacement of writings by telephone conversations, non-verbal parents, advertisements, popular songs, worship of the machine, the "complexity and illogic of the English language," students with tin ears, Kurt Vonnegut, Hermann Hess, Abbie Hoffman, Zen Buddhism, the new primitivism, drugs, permissiveness, and the federal government (Ohmann, 1976, p. 32).

Almost 15 years later Purves (1990) also argued that the literacy crisis might be contrived. He noted that the drive for universal literacy was a relatively recent occurrence and that failure to achieve it had been primarily the result of the increasingly sophisticated reading skills required by an "urbanized global market economy." Though he conceded that an actual decline in literacy had transpired, Purves thought this decline was restricted to the middle third of the twentieth century and discernible only among the most sophisticated readers. He attributed the decline to two somewhat amorphous factors: a pervasive materialism that had persuaded persons to devalue critical reading and a stifling proliferation of specialized printed materials that had indirectly reduced the general public's access to information.

After noting the dramatic increases in literacy during the twentieth century, Graff (1991) questioned why so many educators had declared a literacy crisis. Although he acknowledged "problems with popular levels of skills and learning," he pointed to similarities between past and contemporary discussions about literacy declines and observed that "'crises' and 'declines,' in literacy, as in other aspects of society, are recurrent throughout modern history" (p. 390). He explained that "at times of large-scale, rapid change and confusion about the condition of civilization and morality, literacy has seemed to suffer a 'decline' almost generationally across the span of recorded history" (p. 373). Graff worried that educational problems were being politically exaggerated because "the contemporary context heightens the seriousness of perceptions and exacerbates fears" (p. 390).

In a book with the title *The Manufactured Crisis*, Berliner and Biddle (1997) dismissed the view that schools were failing to teach literacy and other fundamental skills as a "fraud" perpetuated during the 1980s when "reactionary voices were given more credence in America." They analyzed these reactionary voices as a composite of conservatives, neoconservatives, and religious political activists. Acknowledging that allegations of an educational crisis had continued even after the conservative presidents of the 1980s had been replaced by a politically liberal administration, they admitted that "many Americans (including leaders in the Clinton Administration) have embraced some ideas from these [conservative] rhetorics" and that therefore "educators may have to contend with the debris of reactionary educational thought for some time to come" (p. 138).

POST-WORLD WAR II LIBERAL POLITICAL APPROACHES

During the post-World War II era, politically liberal educators directly confronted challenges from conservative educators. Mortimer Smith (1954) documented these confrontations when he identified books written by liberal educators who were distressed that their progressive recommendations had not been adequately implemented. One of the books Smith listed was a 1950 textbook on curriculum development by Smith, Stanley, and Shores. In the 1957 edition of this book the authors noted that Americans had become "socially callous and insensitive to gross violations of their professional ideals" (p. 81). They recommended that the curriculum should focus less on the development of academic skills and to a greater degree on "the moral content of the culture."

Mortimer Smith also identified other liberal textbooks that he hoped prospective teachers "would have the good sense to repudiate," such as a book on educational philosophy by Brameld (1950). Similar to the adjurations made by liberal critics in the 1920s and 1930s, Brameld warned that "the schools are now dominated by pressure groups, vested interests, and obsolete practices, that often paralyze them" (p. 8). Noting that "liberalism more than any other single outlook has implemented as well as verbalized the meanings and intentions of American culture" (p. 186), Brameld recommended adoption of a reconstructionist philosophy that "seeks, above all, to develop an education that can powerfully contribute to rebuilding, not merely to perpetuating, hitherto dominant, structures, habits, attitudes" (p. 524). The need for federal authority to aid in the restructuring of education was a key provision in Brameld's plan. In an article that appeared in a popular magazine, Brameld (1951) insisted that "the battle for free schools" would be won only if four measures were implemented, one of which was that financial support for American schools should be doubled or tripled.

In a book about the connection between curriculum change and "human engineering," Benne and Muntyan (1951) warned that "the approach to social change which these readings incorporate is not the approach of an observer who stands apart from on on-going change" (p. ix). Although they endorsed democratic approaches, they also insisted that "the current necessity for change in our school program is dictated primarily, not by the whims and vagaries of educational leadership, but by inherent maladjustments between the school and our unevenly and drastically changing society" (p. 295). If professionals did not step forward and exercise democratic ownership of education they would "sell out control of required changes to non-democratic leadership" (p. 295).

In an earlier article in which Benne (1949) had referred to himself as an engineer employing education to create "deliberately planned social change," an editorial sidebar noted that even though "the term 'engineer' when used in connection with social and educational change is often associated with the 'manipulation' of people and is hence deemed to be a bad word" that "nevertheless all persons engaged in educational work are trying to foster changes in the persons with whom they work" (p. 201). This logic was a shift from the arguments of progressive educators such as Dewey who had maintained that the progressive approach was more effective in responding to individual needs than a regimented instructional approach.

Other liberal educators began to advocate for a philosophic shift from Dewey's convictions. For example, Evans (1949) observed that "we have been culturally conditioned by a distorted notion of privacy which is related, perhaps basically, to our deep seated notions concerning individual rights and freedoms, and to the privateness and sacredness of property" (p. 163). He concluded that the traditional concept of *individualism*, a concept with which the emerging variations on progressive philosophy were incompatible, had actually not been *individualism* at all, but a distinct concept—*specialization*, which was "motivated largely by the needs of scientific and technological advance and by the grafting of excessive individualism on the democratic way of life" (p. 161). As an alternative to this misrepresented type of individualism, Evans counseled that "many individuals may benefit from social therapy resulting from experiences with group problem solving" and that "full participation on the part of an individual in a group problem solution involves reconstruction and this reconstruction can be oriented toward greater individual satisfaction and security which in turn will contribute to the common welfare" (p. 164).

An editorial in *Progressive Education* a year earlier ("A New Policy," 1948) had advised that "teachers who have convictions of their own—convictions which they do no not foist *upon* students but which at appropriate age levels they share *with* students" should ensure that classroom learning included "extensive educational practice in building detailed social designs which come to grips with problems arising in, for example, economic planning" (p. 46). Only six years later, Childs (1954) declared simply that "we misconceive the nature of this controversy about the ends and means of education if we assume that it is primarily an affair of individuals" and that educators could not "escape the impact of this controversy by making appeals to the general public to condemn these 'interest groups' as mere pressure groups who have permitted narrow selfish interests to override their devotion to the common good" (p. 91).

Revolutionary calls to restructure schools were in opposition to the advice of conservative educators such as Kandel (1957) who wrote confidently that "American education continues to be rooted in a deep faith in its importance and value for a democratic society" and that "citizens throughout the country recognize...[that] the American school is not used as an instrument to propagate the policy of government or to preserve the privileges of a social class" (p. 19).

Attacked mercilessly by conservative educators and scrutinized by a skeptical public, progressive education had fallen into disrepute by the 1960s. Even as early as 1945, DeBoer, a staunch advocate of progressive education, admitted that "the intellectual climate of our time has been so inhospitable to progressive social ideas that many educators have taken pains to absolve themselves of any imputation of progressivism" (p. 225).

However, politically liberal intellectuals, such as Paul Goodman, remained committed to the progressive philosophy. Though he acknowledged that progressive, student-centered education had been a failure, Goodman (1960) remained an avid and eloquent advocate for its essential premises. He defiantly challenged critics of progressive education to demonstrate that any of the alternative approaches they had championed were better. He was convinced that critics of progressive education would not be able to respond successfully to his challenge because "there cannot be a 'perfect' education system" and because the effectiveness of each educational system should be judged on the basis of the degree to which it could "meet its social situation" (p. 82). However, no sooner had Goodman indicated the inadequacy of progressive education and all competing systems than he qualified his remarks by writing in highlighted italics that "*no lesser program is seriously conservative of human resources*" (p. 82). Goodman concluded that public educators who were genuinely concerned about human resources should therefore continue to adopt progressive educational practices. He complemented this affirmation of faith in progressive education with a denunciation of those who had criticized it for being "weak in curriculum." He retorted that "there *is* only one curriculum, no matter what the method of education: what is basic and universal in human experience and practice, the underlying structure and culture" (p. 82). Goodman then unpredictably rebuked those who had argued that geometry and science were too difficult to be made universal components of all curricula.

In a later work, Goodman (1970) emphasized the political implications of education. He wrote that "progressive education is always a political movement, for the exclusion of a human power or style of life is the effect of a social injustice, and progressive education emerges when the social problem is breaking out" (p. 81). He referred to the inherent social inequities that marred American education when "the tendency of contemporary society, collectivized, technocratic, managerial, is to impose a culture on its members, to train them to carry it and perform" (p. 338).

Goodman's view was similar to that of Edwards and Richey. In a later edition of a history book that they had published originally in 1947, Edwards and Richey (1963) wrote that "the purpose of education institutions is to prepare the learner to participate intelligently and helpfully in the social order" and that within that order "the prevailing ideology is modified or supplanted by one essentially new; political power passes from one dominant element in society to another; the role of government is modified; the whole pattern of economic life may be greatly changed by technological progress; and the whole society may be transformed from one that is essentially religious or ecclesiastical to one that is essentially lay or secular" (p. xi). They indicated that "much more space is devoted to the treatment of recent than of earlier periods" in their textbook because teachers "need to cultivate a comprehensive and realistic view of the society into which they are helping to induct youth" (p. xii).

Though political proselytizing by the historians of the preceding eras had been noticeable, their rhetoric seemed innocuous when compared to the hurricane of caustic publications produced by the revisionist educational historians of the 1970s. These historians depicted the schools as reactionary political agencies concerned with economic progress at the expense of children's welfare. For example, Katz (1971) described schools as "fortresses in function as well as form, protected outposts of the city's educational establishment and the prosperous citizens who sustain it" and wrote that "their main purpose is to make these children orderly, industrious, law-abiding, and respectful of authority" (pp. xvii-xviii).

Katz's revisionist views were shared by Greer (1972) who warned of "a pernicious legend" in which the public schools were depicted as the foundation for American democracy. He estimated that this fantasy "justifies the exclusion of millions who will never share in America's greatness as long as the legend persists" (p. 3). Greer's bitterness was obvious when he argued that the disenfranchisement of children from the schools was a calculated component in a willful conspiracy. He wrote, "America is a very conservative society which likes to claim that it is devoted to equality and social change" but that "the public school stands as an instrument of the conservative strategy for defusing movements for social change which seriously challenge the established order and it typifies social reform in the United States" (p. 59).

In his book, *Education and the Rise of the Corporate State*, Spring (1972) attempted to document that persons who adopted "as an image of the good society a highly organized and smoothly working corporate structure" played "an influential role in shaping the form and direction of American public education in the twentieth century" (pp. xi-xii). He discerned a cause-effect connection between industry and education, maintaining that "the corporate image of society turned American schools into a central social institution for the production of men and women who conformed to the needs and expectations of a corporate and technocratic world" (p. 1).

Karier, Violas, and Spring (1973) also detected a link between education and industry when they described the school as an "instrument of social and economic power for the most influential elite groups" (p. 6). They characterized the era after World War II as "a world of burgeoning government bureaucracies effectively allied with corporate wealth, which fashioned a mass system of schooling to maintain corporate security at home and abroad" (p. 4). These authors were convinced that learners were suffering because educators who were themselves dominated by a racist, conservative, industrialized society had failed to adopt progressive, student-centered practices in the schools.

In his book, *Education as Cultural Imperialism*, Carnoy (1974) argued that capitalism was not an efficient economic and social system unless "the primary function of society is to produce more material goods" and that schooling could be viewed as a constructive component of society only in a capitalist system "when it contributes to individual and collective increases in material output" (p. 5). As a consequence of this logic, he concluded that "it is not necessary to make the dichotomy between the schools and economic hierarchies, since both are part and parcel of the same system" (p. 362). Explaining that an optimal system of education would not "set knowledge apart from the context in which it is transmitted" Carnoy cited the approach to literacy espoused by Paulo Freire as "an example of learning in the context of reality" (p. 366).

Freire, an Arch Politician

Freire was a politically liberal educator who wrote specifically about the role of literacy education in social and economic change. Discussing the political struggles of workers in Brazil, he used a Marxist paradigm to explain the dynamics of repression and exploitation that he thought were connected to literacy. In a preface to one of Freire's works, Chonchol (1973) described Freire's writing as "difficult to follow" though profound and penetrating. The following passage, from a section titled *Education as a Gnostical State*, illustrated the sometimes impenetrable style of Freire's work:

> The condition of the human being is to be in constant relationship to the world. In this relationship subjectivity, which takes its form in objectivity, combines with the latter to form a dialectal unity from which emerges knowledge closely linked with action. This is why unilaterally subjective and objective explanations which sever this dialectic are unable to comprehend reality. If an erroneous solipsism claims that only the Ego exists and that its consciousness embraces everything (since it is an absurdity to think of a reality external to it), the a-critical, mechanistic, grossly materialistic objectivism, according to which reality transforms itself, without any action on the part of men and women (who are mere objects of transformation) is equally in error (Freire, 1973, p. 146).

In the introduction to the book in which the preceding passage appeared, Goulet (1973) summarized the "basic components" of Freire's approach to literacy. Although Goulet used jargon throughout this summary, the essential elements of Freire's approach were apparent:

- participant observation of educators "tuning in" to the vocabulary universe of the people;
- their arduous search for generative words at two levels: syllabic richness and a high charge of experimental involvement;
- a first codification of these words into visual images which stimulate people "submerged" in the culture of silence to "emerge" as conscious makers of their own "culture";
- the decodification by a "culture circle" under the self-effacing stimulus of a coordinator who is not "teacher" in the conventional sense, but who has become and educator-educatee—in dialogue with educatee-educators too often treated by formal educators as passive recipients of knowledge;
- a creative new codification, this one explicitly critical and aimed at action, wherein those who were formerly illiterate now begin to reject their role as mere "objects" in nature and social history and undertake to become "subjects" of their own destiny (Goulet, 1973, p. viii).

In a book to which Freire had contributed the foreword, Shor (1986) noted that Freire had restated and updated Dewey's turn-of-the-century theory of "imposed silence." With regard to imposed silence, Dewey had written that when "language taught is unnatural, not growing out of the real desire to communicate vital impressions and convictions, the freedom of children in its use gradually disappears" (Dewey quoted by Shor, 1986, pp. 75-76). Shor explained that Freire had relabeled "imposed silence" as "the culture of silence" and then portrayed reading, writing, and speaking as "political moments of alienation or animation, disempowerment or empowerment" (p. 76). Shor used a mixed metaphor drawn partially from banking to explain Freire's belief that traditional programs were driving students into "silence or angry resistance" by encouraged teachers to make "information-deposits into the empty accounts of their students' brains" (p. 184).

The preceding metaphor by Shor referred to Freire's differentiation of active from passive education. As with the concept of "the culture of silence," the distinction of active and passive education was anticipated by Dewey in a book he published originally in 1900:

> Another thing that is suggested by these school-rooms, with their set desks, is that everything is arranged for handling as large numbers of children as possible; for dealing with children *en masse*, as an aggregate of units; involving, again, that they be treated passively. The moment children act they individualize themselves; they cease to be a mass, and become the intensely distinctive beings that we are acquainted with out of school, in the home, the family, on the playground, and in the neighborhood (Dewey, 1907, p. 49).

As a young man, Dewey had been influenced by the German philosopher Hegel, whose theory of dialectics had provided the basis for Marxist philosophy. Writing about the connection between pragmatism and Marxism, Novack (1975) outlined similarities between the two paradigms, one of the most striking of which was the emphasis that both Dewey and Marx placed on the reform of capitalist society. However, unlike Freire, Dewey turned away from Marx's philosophy because Dewey's "final verdict was that Marx's theory was incurably tainted with Hegelian idealism and lead to the absolutism proper to theology" (Novack, 1975, p. 271).

In an influential book that he titled *Pedagogy of the Oppressed*, Freire (1970b) had explained that the type of instruction that he espoused was the "pedagogy of men engaged in the fight for their own liberation" (p. 39). He warned that "the oppressed want to resemble the oppressor" and this trait was particularly evident among the "middle-class oppressed, who yearn to be equal to the 'eminent' men of the upper class" (p. 49). Instead of accepting education that would entrap learners in this dehumanizing scheme, Freire counseled his readers to "reclaim their primordial right to speak their word" and to "prevent the continuation of this dehumanizing aggression" (pp. 76-77).

In a publisher's introduction to one of Freire's essays, an editor indicated that "Freire writes from a Third World perspective, but with obvious implications for education in general" and that Freire "rejects mechanistic conceptions of the adult literacy process" (1970a, p. 5). Freire's approach was both political and holistic. His holistic view was obvious when he specified that the educator's role was "to enter into dialogue with the illiterate about concrete situations and simply to offer him the instruments with which he can teach himself to read and write" (Freire, 1973, p. 48). Freire (1985) castigated reading primers for having been "developed mechanistically" and for being "instruments for 'depositing' the educator's words into the learners." He described reading textbooks as "domesticating instruments" that would occlude workers' views of their oppressive situation by instructing them "with sweetness" as they learned phrases that symbolized a seductively attractive but artificial world. He disapproved of textbook-centered reading programs because "this kind of literacy can never be an instrument for transforming the real world" (p. 9).

Other Political Theorists

The tradition of liberal, political theorizing about education continued beyond the 1970s. For example, Apple (1986) depicted the government's continuing attempts to exploit females and underprivileged classes as driving, dynamic forces of the educational system. Though he conceded that "not all teaching can be unpacked by examining it as a labor process or as a class phenomenon" nor by depicting it as "totally related to patriarchy" he added that class and gender "intertwine, work off, and codetermine the terrain on which each operates" and that "at the intersection of these two dynamics that one can begin to unravel some of the reasons why procedures for rationalization the work of teachers have evolved" (p. 34).

Possibly worried that they would be criticized for having politicized educational issues, some liberal educators alleged that ulterior values had motivated their academic adversaries as well. For example, Frank Smith (1986) characterized Flesch's phonic approach as a political rather than educational initiative, because "in recent years more parents and teachers have been trying to teach children the Flesch way than in any other period of history, urged and supported by the federal government, abetted by the regional research and development laboratories, encouraged by the publishers of elaborate commercial tests and programs, and browbeaten by politicians and administrators" (pp. 108-109). Frank Smith also warned that commercial publishing houses, which he referred to as the "nonsense industry," had supported phonic approaches solely to increase their profits. Shanon (1992) emphasized that reading education "in its current form" was a repressive effort "to provide unjust services that benefit social groups so unequally" (p. 10). Kenneth Goodman (1993) maintained that phonic programs had been espoused by conservative politicians to expedite their self-interests and consequently dismissed the research purporting to support these programs. Responding to the "common assumption" that children learned to read as a result of the way they were taught, Bartoli (1995) argued instead that most children learned with materials that were produced by "powerful, profit-focused companies, many of whom have been exposed as fraudulent" and that "those who do learn to read successfully more often learn in *spite* of the system by which they are taught" (pp. 15-16).

Though the progressive tradition of liberal political theorizing remained strong in the 1980s and 1990s, the retorts from conservative critics also continued to be as forceful and nonreconciliatory as they had been during the progressive era. Bracey (1991, 1992, 1993, 1994) challenged those critics who had been speaking out against the educational reforms championed by political liberals. Nonetheless, he did acknowledge the frequency of such criticism. Beginning one of his educational reports by admitting that "virtually everyone" had gone on record attesting that contemporary schools were ineffective, he incorrectly predicted a change in national attitudes as a result of which "the days of school-bashing [in which liberal educators are vilified] are over" (1991, p. 106).

ATTEMPTS TO RESTRAIN POLITICAL APPROACHES

Among the educators who attempted to explain change in education, some argued that theories of political predetermination had been overstated. Ravitch (1978) rebuked the revisionists of the 1970s for portraying the schools as "oppressive institutions which regiment, indoctrinate, and sort children, either brutally or subtly crushing their individuality and processing them to take their place in an unjust social order" (p. 3). Ravitch wrote that "the trouble with this line of analysis is that it treats both schools and minority groups in stereotypical fashion: schools are oppressive; minority groups are oppressed" and that "so simplistic an approach cannot provide the intellectual groundwork for serious history" (p. 58).

From a similar perspective, Quantz (1985) challenged historians of education who had used "predetermined categories" to create a "top-down history" that reduced study of the past to "the charting of structural features" (p. 457). He thought such political approaches to history had been particularly unfair to female teachers, who he judged had been "portrayed as objects rather than subjects, as either the unknowing tools of the social elite or as the exploited minority whose labor is bought cheaply" (p. 439). Quantz analyzed interviews with female teachers during the 1930s to illustrate the inaccuracy of such politicized depictions.

Ginsburg and his colleagues wrote extensively about the overgeneralizations that resulted from highly politicized models of instruction. Not confining themselves to the politics of teaching reading, Ginsburg, Kamat, Raghu, and Weaver (1995) indicated that all education was political because it either reinforced or challenged existing power relations. Referring to themselves as "scholar activists" Lindsay and Ginsburg (1995) explained that their analysis had focused on "political conditions and structural conditions that maintain the status quo" (p. 266). Ginsburg, Kamat, Raghu, and Weaver (1995) gave examples of educational activities for which the political dimensions might not be readily apparent to some observers. Their examples included delivering instruction in a particular language, interacting in fashions that differentially reinforced select cultures, or implementing instruction that did not attend uniformly to different types of learners.

In a paper published in 1980 Dearden had anticipated the argument that Ginsburg and his colleagues later elaborated. He had written that "concerning any activity within a State, we may say that it is either permitted (perhaps even enforced) or not permitted, and in that trivial sense the State cannot be neutral towards it" (p. 150). Dearden extended the implications of this insight to education as well as the other ubiquitous activities in which governments had been involved. He wrote that politics, which was not found exclusively in government activities, was "concerned with ruling decisions on such matters as the allocation of resources, the regulation of competing interests, the establishment or reform of certain institutions, the determination of priorities in such contexts and the ends of such activities" (p. 150).

Like Dearden, Ginsburg and his colleagues concluded that the intersection of education and politics was unavoidable. However, Ginsburg emphasized that the inescapable, political dimensions of education did not restrict the ability of teachers to be effective because those political dimensions did not force teachers to designate a particular pedagogical paradigm. Instead, he adjured teachers to assess the political implications of the decisions they made while discharging their responsibilities as instructors. These decisions were made on a daily basis by teachers through actions that were individual or collective, active or passive, conservative or change-oriented. Decisions were made by teachers in the context of instructional techniques and curriculum as well as through assessment, research, and professional association. Ginsburg and his colleagues provided a list of sample questions that reflected the political character of these decisions:

> What ideas and perspectives should I include in school...curriculum? What form of pedagogy and classroom social relations should I seek to institute in the classroom? What kind of system should I adopt or encourage for evaluating the performance of students? What topics should I research, from what perspective, gathering data from what sources, and for whom should I report the findings of my own and others' research? How should I operate in relation to colleagues and others in my workplace? Should I belong to and be active in unions and associations, and what goals and strategies should I encourage such groups to pursue? How would I behave in relation to spouse/companions, children, grandchildren, parents, grandparents, and so on? Should I be active or passive in my role as a citizen of local, national, and global communities; on what issues should I focus attention; with what other people should I ally; and what end and means should I emphasize? (Ginsburg, Kamat, Raghu, & Weaver, 1995, pp. 33-34).

In a foreword to a book on radical school reform published in 1973, the philosopher Sydney Hook had considered the identical arguments upon which Ginsburg and his colleagues later deliberated. Like Ginsburg, he concluded that just because education involved political indoctrination, teachers were not restricted from being effective instructors. Rather than employing a political analysis to reach this conclusion, Hook (1973a) used a set of logical syllogisms to draw an analogy between the indoctrination involved in learning about democracy and that in mathematics:

> If all teaching entails indoctrination, what would the opposite of indoctrination be? Nonteaching? Ordinary English usage requires a distinction between teaching that indoctrinates and teaching, however rare, that does not. Even if all teachers indoctrinated, it would still be necessary to differentiate conceptually between indoctrination and its absence. Otherwise we could not even identify indoctrination.... To deny that teaching without indoctrination is possible is like denying that objectivity is possible. It would be like obliterating the distinction between truth and falsity, history and fiction. Indoctrination is the mode of teaching that induces the acceptance of beliefs by rational or nonrational means or both.... Democratic values are taught to children by nonrational means and methods, and so are being taught by indoctrination. Does this not confirm the radical school reformer's claim that *all* teaching is and should be by its very nature indoctrination? Not at all.... Children must be taught the

multiplication tables when they're quite young and not yet able to read or understand *Principia Mathematica* by Russell and Whitehead, which offers a proof that $2 + 2 = 4$. Learning cannot be postponed until they understand the proof. They therefore acquire knowledge of these tables by rote memory, through song and verse, i.e., by nonrational methods. Children may be conditioned by nonrational methods to learn many other things. But this indoctrination is educationally permissible only, and only if, at the same time we are developing within the child his powers of intelligence to their fullest measure. When the child has reached his full maturity as a youth, he will then have the critical grasp, skills, and knowledge to test and check the validity of the multiplication tables himself (pp. ix-x).

Unlike the liberal, educational historians of the 1970s or the Marxist theoreticians who bifurcated society into persons who either supported or opposed rigorously defined political premises, the scholars who attempted to restrain some of the political rhetoric associated with educational and social issues had advanced arguments in which change was seen as the response to complex, interdependent factors. In his history of counterculture movements during the 1960s and 1970s, Frank (1997) depicted those movements as maintaining a veneer of irreconcilable opposition to the economic establishment while actually being entwined with business, consumerism, and advertising:

Our standard binary understanding of the 1960s revolt as the negation of the "conformity" of the 1950s is but the historical rendering of this nonstop pageant of rebellion against order.... We believe in the rebel sixties, in the uprising against the humorless "establishment," like we believe in World War II as "the good war." Yet, through it all, capital remained firmly in the national saddle, its economic and cultural projects unimpeded even though the years of conformity that had given way to those of cultural radicalism. What changed during the sixties, it now seems, were the strategies of consumerism, the ideology by which business explained its domination of the national life. Now products existed to facilitate our rebellion against the soul-deadening world of products, to put us in touch with our authentic selves, to distinguish us from the mass-produced herd, to express our outrage at the stifling world of economic necessity (pp. 228-229).

Frank wrote that the counterculture's "symbols, music, and lingo were transformed safely into mass culture" (p. 229). In a comparable manner, much of the opposition to established education was incorporated safely into academic discussions among professors, administrators, teachers, and vested academicians within mainstream institutions.

Attempts at Reconciliation in Reading Education

Just as some educators in the general field of education attempted to reduce the ideological polarization created by extremist political rhetoric, some reading educators attempted to reconcile the factions that were at war about literacy. Documenting the impassioned antagonism between proponents of holistic approaches and proponents of skills-based approaches, Chall (1967) underestimated the chasm separating the groups when she expressed confidence that "by now the debate has lost much of its bitterness, and each side is willing to concede points to the other" (p. 2). Mathews (1966) also documented the animosity between educational partisans in his history of reading education. Like Chall, he incorrectly predicted that the antagonism between the disputants was subsiding. Writing more than a decade later, Balmuth (1982) was more realistic than Mathews or Chall in her estimation of the prospects for cooperation among reading educators. With regard to the fate of phonics, she used the past to gauge the future, predicting that "while phonics finds a fair degree of acceptance in the present climate of eclecticism in reading methodology...it has also been peculiarly vulnerable to the general societal moods of each era...and more chapters will no doubt be added to its venerable history" (p. 2).

Bettelheim and Zelan (1982) agreed with those educators who had pointed to a crisis that had resulted from children's reading failure. They were genuinely distressed by whole word approaches that "introduce the child in the first year of instruction to some seventy uninteresting simple words" at a developmental period "when his functional vocabulary is some fifty times as large" (p. 32). But they were equally distressed by phonics programs that could foster the impression "that skills such as decoding are what reading is all about" (p. 22). Recommending that teachers focus neither on academic nor functional skills, they adjured teachers to adopt reading programs that would develop within the child "a fervent belief that being able to read will open to him a world of wonderful experiences, permit him to shed his ignorance, understand the world, and become master of his fate" (p. 49). They were confident that the critical pedagogical decision in producing this inspiration was the selection of materials that corresponded to the fears and goals of individual learners.

Aware of the chasm separating advocates of skills-based and language-based approaches, Adams (1990) acknowledged the instructional value of both approaches. She attempted to bridge the chasm between the political groups advocating and opposing phonics when she wrote that orthographic, semantic, and phonological processes "cannot be invoked independently of one another" and that "reading reflects the coordinated, interactive knowledge and behavior of all three" (p. 94). Despite such reconciliatory overtures, Adams challenged educators who categorically opposed phonics instruction because she believed that "the single immutable and nonoptional fact about skillful reading is that it involves relatively complete processing of the individual letters of print" (p. 105). In an afterword to Adams's book, Strickland and Cullinan (1990) agreed with Adams's reconciliatory rhetoric, remarking that though Adams's argument had shortcomings, "the evidence supports a whole language and integrated language arts approach with some direct instruction, in context, on spelling-to-sound correspondences" (p. 433).

Speaking about literacy in a broad, historical context, Graff (1991) disagreed with those who thought a single, optimal route to literacy could be designated and was convinced that "the history of literacy shows clearly that there is no *one* route to universal mass literacy" (p. 12). He noted that informal, voluntary, and private approaches to literacy education had been as effective as public, formal, and compulsory approaches. As an example of an atypical but highly effective approach, Graff described events in eighteenth-century Sweden during which reading was required by law. In response to an edict sponsored by the Lutheran church and the government, a system was developed that did not rely on formal schooling or instruction in writing but which instead was based on home schooling. This mandatory home schooling was restricted exclusively to reading and was monitored by the clergy. Graff judged that the citizens of Sweden were "perhaps the most literate in the West before the eighteenth century" as a result of an educational system that was not connected to "urbanization, commercialization, and industrialization" and "without any concomitant development of formal schooling or economic or cultural development that demanded functional or practical employment of literacy" (p. 13). While politically oriented educators such as Freire had assumed a direct connection between literacy and social progress, Graff questioned whether literacy was truly a cause of social change. He observed that historically "literacy is only one of the factors linked to change and action" and challenged the type of political activism built on the assumption that progress in literacy caused revolutionary social change:

> The hopes of radical political use of literacy and schooling for an organized, educated, independent and self-conscious working class became a minor if persisting, legacy of literacy, embraced by those seeking changes from below in many parts of the world. That has not proved to be a major impact of literacy. Education seldom served to fulfill such hopes; they depended on more than the kind of schooling that was developed for the majority of working-class children and their parents (Graff, 1991, p. 333).

PRAGMATIC PHILOSOPHY

Resilient to political arguments and committed to an experimental method for confirming the effectiveness of learning activities, remedial reading reflected the essential characteristics of pragmatism. For pragmatism had developed as a philosophical approach for resolving questions that otherwise might invite an infinite amount of metaphysical analysis. It was an attempt to resolve issues in light of their logical consequences. This philosophy was popularized by William James (1907b) in a classic book, *Pragmatism: A New Name for Some Old Ways of Thinking*. This book more than any book in the early twentieth century distilled and defined a new philosophy that was regarded as distinctively American.

As one reviews the arguments that have shaped the attitudes of teachers and the public toward reading education, disparate approaches based on political commitment can be distinguished. Not restricted to diatribes about the optimal approach to instruction, these passionate arguments have attempted to establish monolithic, political foundations for instruction. In contrast, pragmatism incorporated an approach to learning in which judgments about instruction were made only after experimentation. As such, it was attractive as a philosophical foundation for remedial reading. For most remedial and corrective reading programs were intended as instructional alternatives to politically prescriptive models of instruction. Proponents of remedial reading questioned not only the merits of specific programs with which readers had failed but also whether zealous political commitment provided an effective base for learning in the schools.

Origins of Pragmatism

Butler (1951) traced the historical origins of pragmatism from Heraclitus and the Sophists in the sixth-century BC, through prominent European scholars such as Francis Bacon and Auguste Comte, and eventually to influential American philosophers. Brameld (1950) credited Plato and Aristotle with providing some of the critical elements of pragmatism and pointed to Bacon, Locke, and Rousseau for helping to generate the "liberalism" associated with it. Brameld also credited Kant with "attempts to ground a liberal glorification of the individual in the unassailable dignity of human personality" as well as Hegel for his insistence "upon the dynamic, ever-readjusting processes of nature and society" (p. 102).

Ulich (1968) concluded that "trends of thought similar to the pragmatic had existed since the days of the Greek Sophists and had been revived in modern form (under different names) in all the more advanced countries since the eighteenth century" (p. 316). James explicitly discussed his own debt to English philosophers for the concepts of pragmatism that he and Peirce had employed:

> I am happy to say that it is the English-speaking philosophers who first introduced the custom of interpreting the meaning of conceptions by asking what difference they make for life. Mr. Peirce has only expressed in the form of explicit maxim what their sense for reality led them instinctively to do. The great English way of investigating a conception is to ask yourself right off, "what is it *known as*? In what fact does it result? What is its *cash-value* in terms of particular experience? And what special difference would come to the world according as it were true or false?" (James, quoted by Childs, 1931, p. 13).

Childs had documented that Dewey was influenced by the ideas of the German philosophers Kant and Hegel. Dewey himself admitted that his approach to pragmatism had developed from "a critique of knowledge and of logic which has resulted from the theory proposed by neo-Kantian idealism" (Dewey, quoted by Childs, 1931, p. 14).

Despite its inspiration in the works of European thinkers, pragmatism developed a popular reputation as a distinctively American philosophic movement. Childs wrote in 1931 that "there is to-day rather general recognition, both here and in foreign countries, that...an indigenous American philosophy has emerged" (p. 4). Childs was able to remark confidently that "while many have contributed to its development, there would be common agreement that the most fundamental and original contributions have come from the works of Charles Sanders Peirce, William James, and John Dewey" (p. 4). Using five propositions, Butler (1951) synthesized salient points about the philosophies that had been developed by Peirce, James, and Dewey: "all things flow; nothing remains the same," "it is impossible to gain knowledge of ultimate reality," "hypotheses tested by experience constitute the nearest approach to knowledge which we have," "science should become a social pursuit by being applied cooperatively to the study of all of the problems of man," and "in order to determine the meaning of an idea, it must be put into practice" (p. 421).

This last proposition was originally expressed by Peirce, with whom both James and Dewey had studied. Though she did not challenge the stature of an intellectual whom she described as one of America's greatest philosophers, Misak (1994) recounted that Peirce had been unable to secure a permanent position at a university and that he was a "difficult and not altogether pleasant character" who had been criticized for "moral lapses." Even James had described Peirce as "a queer being." In contrast, Pierce had referred to James as "so concrete, so living" and himself as "a mere table of contents, so abstract, a very snarl of twine" (Peirce, quoted by Thayer, 1981, p. 71). Peirce had expressed the essential feature of pragmatism in the maxim that "we must look to the upshot of our concepts in order rightly to apprehend them" (Peirce quoted by Misak, 1994, p. 358).

Peirce's pragmatic maxim became widely understood as a result of James (1907a), who referred to it as the *pragmatic principle*. Annoyed at the popularization of his thoughts about pragmatics by the charismatic James, Peirce changed the name of his own philosophy to *pragmaticism*. (James himself, searching for a name with which to christen pragmatism in 1898, had originally suggested "practicalism" [Tiles, 1994].) Despite the contributions of Peirce to James's concepts of pragmatism, Peirce's prolific writing was not published until after his death in 1914. By this time James, although he gave credit to Peirce, had already become indelibly identified with pragmatism:

> This is the principle of Peirce, the principle of pragmatism. It lay entirely unnoticed by any one for twenty years, until I...brought it forward again.... The word "pragmatism" spread, and at present it fairly spots the pages of the philosophic journals.... It is evident that the term applies itself conveniently to a number of tendencies that hitherto have lacked a collective name, and that it has "come to stay" (James, 1907a, p. 47).

James was an immensely popular scholar. As late as 1950 Brameld described James's influence on twentieth-century thought as "gigantic" and evaluated his *Principles of Psychology* as "the single greatest achievement in this field by any American scholar-scientist" (p. 103). Although he had begun his career teaching anatomy at Harvard in 1873, James changed his scholarly pursuits to philosophy in 1879. Emphasizing an approach to philosophy that reflected his broad scholarship and eclectic interests, James extended the pragmatic principle to education in his *Talks to Teachers*. Clifton (1933) estimated that *Talks to Teachers* had been read by more teachers and students than any other popular educational text and that James was the authority on education "cited in current books on education more than any other writer, living or dead" (p. 230). Curti (1935) agreed about the influence of this book on teachers, observing that it was "James more than anyone else who brought modern psychology into the classroom by applying it to the everyday problems of instruction" (p. 429). The book to which Clifton and Curti referred was based on a set of lectures that James had delivered more than 50 years earlier. The following passage is from *Talks to Teachers*:

> An "uneducated" person is one who is nonplused by all but the most habitual situations. On the contrary, one who is educated is able practically to extricate himself, by means of the examples with which his memory is stored from circumstances in which he never was placed before. Education, in short, cannot be better described than by calling it the organization of acquired habits of conducts and tendencies to behavior (James, 1925, p. 269).

James's stances on educational issues were distinct from the more political positions assumed by the progressive educators. Woodring (1958) characterized James's concept of pragmatism as "too flexible, tentative, and experimental ever to become a new dogma" (p. 11). Miller (1946), a former student of James who had attended his lectures during the 1890s, agreed that "the one thing apparently impossible to him was to speak *ex cathedra* from heights of scientific erudition and attainment" (p. 233). Instead of using his impressive credentials in psychology to persuade teachers to adopt his views about the degree to which learning should be child-centered or skills-centered, James admitted that his own views were merely opinions. In his engaging, self-deprecating style he warned his readers that "the worst thing that can happen to a good teacher is to get a bad conscience about her profession because she feels herself hopeless as a psychologist" (1958, p. 27). Because teachers' opinions could not be validated by psychology, he encouraged them to trust their intuitions in the same way that he had learned to rely upon his personal intuition:

> To know psychology, therefore, is absolutely no guarantee that we shall be good teachers. To advance to that result, we must have an additional endowment altogether, a happy tact and ingenuity to tell us what definite things to say and do when the pupil is before us. That ingenuity in meeting and pursuing the pupil, that tact for the concrete situation, though they are the alpha and omega of the teacher's art, are things to which psychology cannot help us in the least (James, 1958, p. 24).

James vacillated between pragmatism and a genre of philosophic subjectivism that bordered on mysticism. In his later years he became convinced that mysticism represented an opportunity for intellectual growth that was as legitimate a path to knowledge as philosophy or psychology. In his biographies of eight influential pragmatists, Conkin (1976) wrote that James maintained religious beliefs to which "mysticism was only an extension, or a deepening of more normal types of religious experience" (p. 341). In his biography of James, Clifton (1933) acknowledged that the proclivity toward mysticism, to which James gave progressively more attention as he aged, was a distraction that "in the minds of scientific observers added nothing to his prestige as a scientist and thinker" (p. 223). Conkin wrote that though James had intense and unusual experiences, James doubted that they were genuinely mystical.

Lamenting that he lacked a natural disposition for mysticism, James attempted to induce mystic insights with nitrous oxide, a chemical that could precipitate psychic experiences. Tymocozko (1996) gave examples of passages that James had written while under the spell of nitrous oxide and that exhibited a disorientation not apparent in his philosophic discourses. But other passages that James had written without the aid of drugs repudiated James's belief that he lacked the proclivity for mysticism. Even within *Talks to Teachers* are sections that are certainly poetic and which some might judge to be mystical:

> Those philosophers are right who contend that the world is a standing thing, with no progress, no real history. The changing conditions of history touch only the surface show. The altered equilibriums and redistributions only diversify our opportunities and open chances to us for new ideals. But, with each new ideal that comes into life, the chance for a life based on some old ideal will vanish; and he would need be a presumptuous calculator who should with confidence say that the total sum of significance is positively and absolutely greater at any one epoch than any other of the world (James, 1925, p. 190).

The preceding passage indicated subtlety of insights as well as undisputed eloquence as a writer. This eloquence was evident in the final paragraph of his book, when James counseled teachers that "no outward condition in life can keep the nightingale of its eternal meaning from singing in all sorts of different men's hearts" (p. 191).

EXAMPLES OF PROGRESSIVE, NONPRAGMATIC EDUCATORS

Though James flirted with mysticism, he embraced logic and the experimental method. In contrast, his contemporaries, as well as twentieth-century progressive educators, relied on their political convictions when making decisions about appropriate educational practices. As one example, Rudolph Steiner was an advocate for mysticism who used his insights to design educational programs. In his autobiography, Steiner (1928) described one inspiration for his ideas as the formation of a European society committed to spiritual insight, mystical learning, and the "preservation of the ancient symbolism and cultural ceremonies that embody the 'ancient wisdom'" (p. 325). Steiner counseled his followers that "one must not merely learn theoretically, but must take everything to dwell in the innermost emotions of the soul's life, in order to view everything from the most manifold points of view" (pp. 200-201).

Steiner dismissed the various schools of philosophy which "lose all interest for one who knows the supersensible" (p. 201). He identified himself as a *theosophist* and then later an *anthroposophist* rather than a philosopher. This distinction by itself should have warned readers that Steiner's ideas had been developed in a manner that philosophers would find unorthodox. In the introduction to the twentieth edition of his most popular book, *An Outline of Occult Science*, Steiner (1972b) admitted that this book presumed "the goodwill of the reader in coping with a difficult style of writing" (p. xiii). In fairness to Steiner it should be mentioned that this book was translated from German. Still the book did presume the patience of readers who would have to accommodate to an unusual style of thought as well as rhetoric.

In a set of lectures delivered in Germany after World War I, Steiner (1969) made the point that "natural science together with the machine threatens civilized humanity with threefold destruction" (p. 10). This destruction would consist of "mechanization of the spirits," "vegetizing of the soul," and "animalization of the body" (p. 10). Convinced that education constituted a defense from these threats, Steiner started a school for children of workers at the Waldorf-Astoria factory in Germany. Originally established in 1920, similar schools were developed in Switzerland and England before Steiner died in 1925. These school employed a curriculum based on holistic learning, development of intuition, and the validation of mystical knowledge.

Steiner (1972a) continually advised teachers about the need to educate the whole person. For example he warned that "if reading is taught first, and not after writing, the child is prematurely involved in a process of developing exclusively concerned with his head instead of with the forces of his whole being" (p. 138). He advised against the teaching of skills before children were nine and one half years old, counseling that teaching of younger learners be based on "pictures, rhythms, measure—these qualities must pervade all our teaching" (p. 138). Like many proponents of holistic education, he thought that sensitivity to children's feeling was the structural basis for teaching. But he provided a distinctive twist to this concept, recommending that "we must begin with the child's feeling life and from feeling in connection with the world, develop thinking through a comprehension of the kingdom of the plants" (pp. 150-151). The following passage, from a set of 1923 lectures, was written in a conspiratorial fashion about one of the learning strands within the curriculum Steiner advocated:

It is indeed a fact that just as the sun draws the coloured blossom out of the plant, so is it the forces of the moon which develop the again contracting seed-vessels. Seed-vessels are brought forth by the forces of the moon. In this way we place the plant as a living thing into the working of the sun, moon and earth. True, one cannot enter yet into this working of the moon forces, for if the children were to say at home that they had been taught about the connection between seed-vessels and the moon, their parents might easily be prevailed upon by scientific friends to remove them from such a school—even if the parents themselves were willing to accept such things! We shall have to be somewhat reticent on this subject and on many others too, in these materialistic days (Steiner, 1972a, p. 142).

In a memoir about the influence of Steiner's philosophy on his own father's ideas, Tompkins (1997) explained the precise function of the seeds to which Steiner had referred in the preceding passage. To communicate this information to his disciples, Steiner had relied on mystical visions of the vanished world of Atlantis. Tompkins paraphrased Steiner's teaching about Atlantis:

In Atlantean times...the air was denser than it is now. The water, meanwhile, was thinner, and as a result the Atlanteans, who received their knowledge about the world clairvoyantly from spiritual sources, were able to move about the earth and exploit its secret forces in ways very different from those that are known today. The Atlanteans understood the forces of nature so well that they formed a kind of partnership with them. The airships that glided through the thick Atlantean air were powered by life-energy extracted from plant seeds; the Atlantean cities resembled huge, growing gardens, with houses built from the interwoven branches of trees. It was only when the Atlanteans grew indulgent and started misusing the formidable energies that had been bequeathed to them that things started to go wrong. Ultimately, Atlantis sank, and the clairvoyant and magically energized world they had known hardened into the stubborn and unyielding one we know today—a world where machines run on gasoline and the air is disappointingly thin and objects do not yield easily and instantly to human desires (Tompkins, 1997, p. 83).

In a lecture delivered in 1921 Steiner (1986) referred to "soul economy," a key feature of his instructional approach. He explained that this concept would help instructors "arrange the entire teaching in such a way that within the shortest time the maximum amount of content can be given to the pupils with the simplest means possible" (p. 123). In a lecture delivered just four days earlier, Steiner had included a drawing of a facial profile staring at a wall. On the other side of that wall was a sphere. Steiner indicated that the wall was the sensory world and the sphere was a domain of higher-order knowledge. Through this drawing Steiner attempted to convey his belief that the world about us was actually a hindrance rather than a channel to wisdom. In one of the rare passages where he precisely described instructional procedures in the Waldorf schools, he spoke about the need for spontaneous instruction and learning:

What matters most during actual teaching is an ability to meet the ever-changing classroom situations, which result from the immediate response of the pupils. But who in this wide world trains teachers to do that? Are they not trained to decide beforehand what they are going to teach? This often gives me the impression that the child is not considered at all during educational deliberations. Such an attitude would be tantamount to making papier-mâché masks of each pupil as he enters school in order to deal with these masks rather than with the actual children (Steiner, 1986, p. 129).

In 1921, the year after Steiner had opened his school, A. S. Neill founded the Summerhill school in England. Summerhill was intended for children from five to

15 years of age who were placed into programs that were based on psychology rather than traditional principles of education. Neill (1960) indicated with pride that he "was never influenced by the big educators" and that he "never read Dewey or anyone else" (1960, p. 13). Although the school he developed had many similarities to the laboratory school at the University of Chicago which Dewey directed between 1896 and 1903, Neill insisted that he "came to education through psychology—through Freud and Reich" (p. 13). Neill was a social iconoclast who decried structure in learning. Like the progressive educators in the United States, he espoused investigative learning, claiming that "children should find things out for themselves" and that "they shouldn't be told that Beethoven is better than Ellington" (p. 9).

Having personally engaged in a "long analysis" with a therapist who had changed his life for the better, he was convinced that instructors needed to "let children be free so that they won't need analysis" (p. 13). Neill (1972) wrote acerbically that "I hate centralization of any kind" (p. 100). This animosity was revealed in his aversion to the structured organization and authority represented by Roman Catholicism:

> My greatest aversion is the Roman Catholic Church. I hate—as violently as H. G. Wells did, an authority that gives five hundred million a guilt about sex—a guilt that makes them all underlings. To me, this church is anti-life, paternalism writ large. How comic, were it not tragic, that a pope, who has never had a sex life, orders millions of women not to use the Pill.... The savage beatings that go on in Catholic schools in Eire must be expressions of bottled-up sex coming out as sadism (Neill, 1972, p. 252).

Because of Neill's resistance to structure, he hesitated to write in detail about the educational practices at his school. He philosophically assured teachers that "the Summerhill theory is that when a child has played enough he will start to work and face difficulties, and I claim that this theory has been vindicated in our old pupils' ability to do a good job even when it involves a lot of unpleasant work" (1967, p. 14). Truswell (1975), who identified himself as a workshop instructor at Summerhill, assembled a book of projects from Summerhill. Among the projects he described were plaster eggs, chopping boards, sundials, and trash can decorations. Though Truswell provided precise drawings of these projects, he "deliberately left out detailed information about dimensions" because in his "experience a mass of detail, while it may indeed be relevant, may not seem so to the child whose aim is to make a skate board or a machine gun" (p. vii).

Much of Neill's advice about classroom practices was communicated through disapproval. For example, he wrote that "no teacher has the right to cure a child of making noise on a drum" and that "the only curing that should be practiced is the curing of unhappiness" (1960, p. xxiii). He wrote about his disregard for the conventions of style in communication:

Does style matter very much? A Cockney looking at Niagara Falls might exclaim: "Ain't that pretty?" yet he would possibly have the same emotion as that of a scholar who called them magnificent or awe-inspiring. It isn't words that matter; it is what is behind them (Neill, 1967, p. 70).

Neill did impose some limits on the freedom of learners as well as their teachers. As an example, he wrote with scorn of children's fascination with American comic books:

If we had these horror comics from America, I think I would chuck them out. I wouldn't have such things here. I don't think it's fair for a small child to be faced with all that perversity and sickness that we call humor, made by sick men—mind you—perverted men. I'd kick them out, just as I wouldn't have one of the Gestapo on my staff. There are certain things you protect yourself against (Neill, quoted by Snitzer, 1968, p. 10).

Neill (1960) also indicated his disapproval of educators who assigned grades as a means for rewarding students and encouraging them to be competitive. However, the physical education curriculum at Summerhill was based on a competitive model in which trophies were awarded to motivate participants and reward those who excelled. Neill responded curtly to critics that "the game of tennis is naturally competitive and consists in beating the other fellow" while "the study of geography is not" (p. 74). Possibly insecure about the logic of these two statements, Neill added emphatically that "I know that children *want* prizes for games, and they don't want them for school subjects—at least not in Summerhill" (p. 74).

DEWEY'S RESOLUTION OF THE POLITICAL–PRAGMATIC CONTROVERSY

In the foreword to Neill's most widely read book, Eric Fromm (1960) had written that "the beginning of progressive education" was marked by the "replacement of authority by freedom, to teach the child *without the use of force* by appealing to his curiosity and spontaneous needs" (p. ix). John Dewy was by far the most visible spokesperson for the progressive educational movement from which Neill had attempted to disassociate himself but to which Fromm wished to connect Neill. In a book about experimentalism and progressive education, Childs (1931) noted that Dewey "stands to-day as the most eminent leader in this new approach both to philosophy and to education" (p. 4). Dewey's influence was sustained by a continual flow of influential publications. Hickman (1990) calculated that Dewey's publications comprised more than 13,000 pages. Dewey's influence as a writer was complemented by extensive public speaking not only throughout the United States but also in China, Turkey, Mexico, Russia, and Japan. In addition to his prolific writing and lecturing, Dewey was recognized for his extensive liberal political activities. With regard to Dewey's political credentials, Jones and Oliver

(1956) reported that he had been president of the League for Industrial Democracy, a founder of the American Association of University Professors, a contributing editor to the New Republic, a member of the American Civil Liberties Union's Committee on Labor Injunctions, a member of the National Committee of the American Civil Liberties Union, and a participant in a sufficient number of additional organizations that it required five pages for them to be listed.

Dewey's dynamic ideas about education were developed during the decade beginning in 1894 when he was chairperson of the department of philosophy at the University of Chicago. He remained there until 1904, when he had a bitter feud with the university's president and left for Columbia University. However, before he departed he had collaborated with George Mead, a close friend and a fellow member of the philosophy department who Dewey had brought with him from Michigan. Like Dewey, Mead was a political activists as well as scholar. In his book about political anarchy Schaack (1889) referred to Chicago during this era as "the Mecca to which [socialist] exiles came" (p. 44). Feffer (1993) documented Dewey and Mead's political activities as liberal spokespersons in the progressive movement when for about a decade "Chicago philosophers allied with the most militant advocates of labor's educational cause" (p. 193).

Although aspects of Dewey's philosophy were apparent in the ethereal approach of Steiner as well as the passionately political approach of Neill, Dewey's view of education was closer to the practical approach of James. Dewey (1916) had defined education simply as the "reconstruction or reorganization of experience which adds to the meaning of experience, and which increases ability to direct the course of subsequent experience" (pp. 89-90). Viewing philosophy as inextricably connected to education, he wrote that "if we are willing to conceive of education as the process of forming fundamental dispositions, intellectual and emotional, toward nature and fellow men, philosophy may even be defined as the general theory of education" (p. 328). In a similar fashion, Dewey had posited a unity between educational psychology and general psychology in papers that he had published earlier and in which he had argued that educational psychology was distinguished from general psychology only by its emphasis upon two factors, student development and social interaction.

Much of the uproar in twentieth-century education was caused by clashes among zealots with distinct political views about the schools. These zealots included conservatives who saw schools as an opportunity for the equitable advancement of all persons and liberal educators who viewed schools as partisan institutions committed to the advancement of special financial interests. In contrast, a third group of educators recommended that initiatives in the schools be evaluated pragmatically, based on children's demonstrated success. Dewey stood out from his contemporaries because of his unassailable credentials as both an individual who had been politically committed as well as pragmatic.

The Political Transformation of Progressive Education

Pragmatism was the attempt to assess solutions to problems by weighing the practical consequences of potential responses. In his analysis of pragmatism and education, Childs (1956) concluded that James, Dewey, Mead, and Peirce believed that "experimental inquiry defined the pattern of all significant thought" because "for the pragmatist, a significant idea of any kind is essentially an hypothesis, and an hypothesis is a plan for an act, or an experiment, to be performed, and an expectation of a result that will follow when the projected act is performed" (p. 17). In a chapter about philosophy of education Dewey had written with Childs (1933) that "all education is an affair of action" and that the experimental method which complemented this viewpoint was "opposed to dogmatism, to empiricism as the rule of custom, to authoritarianism, to personal egoism" (p. 308). Thayer (1981) wrote that "from its inception, pragmatism was never intended as a philosophy, or as a school or a new orthodoxy" but rather that "it was conceived as a way of philosophizing, a method for dealing with problems" (p. 348).

Though unorthodox, pragmatism was not spurious. Its consistency resided within its methodology rather than within a body of residual knowledge assembled by experts who had applied that methodology to educational issues. Brameld (1950) wrote that the progressive philosophy of education that developed out of pragmatism "is peculiarly pendulum-like in that it is more concerned to keep the *process* of interaction between self and society continuous, than it is to determine the normative and descriptive *products* of that interaction" (p. 206). Brameld noted that for proponents of this philosophy "the one thing that should be avoided is rigidity in static requirements, absolute boundaries, mechanical standards, preconceived solutions" (p. 149). In the introduction to Briggs's book on pragmatism and pedagogy, Hall-Quest (1940) wrote that pragmatism "shows that the value of education lies in the amount and quality of the difference that the education process makes in any one individual" (p. x).

Despite bold assurances by progressive educators about the unbiased vantage from which they were examining educational problems, Lasch (1965) observed insightfully that a necessary assumption of Dewey's philosophy was a belief that social evils could be eliminated through education. These assumptions were apparent in the *Charter for Progressive Education* that Dix (1939) had published. In addition to being a professor of education at Columbia University, Dix was principal of the progressive experimental school affiliated with Teachers College when he wrote that democratic government assumed a faith that the informed and motivated individual would "cooperate effectively in a social solution of his problems and the attainment of his desires" (p. 36). He adjured educators to recognize "the primacy of human personality as the center of all our social arrangements, including the school" (p. 15). Lasch (1965) noted that defining the purpose of education in such terms forced Dewey and his colleagues back into a conception of education as indoctrination, which was the precise conception they wished to avoid. He wrote that Dewey's social agenda was "simply substituting one set of values for another, progressive values for conservative ones." He concluded that because "the social evils that were 'obvious' to Dewey were not obvious to all of his followers," that "in the hands of educators of narrow social sympathies and thoroughly conventional opinions, progressive education could become an instrument not of reform but of conformity" (p. 160).

In spite of their calls for unobstructed pragmatism, progressive educators had inadvertently replicated behaviors as political as those of their adversaries. After noting the confidence that proponents of the progressive movement placed in a belief that the environment could be modified to achieve a better world, Burnham (1960) observed that "the most elusive element in the basic social thinking of the Progressives was—who should tamper with the environment and so foreordain the fates of his fellow men." Burnham added that "it turned out, inevitably, that the progressives themselves were to be the self appointed arbiters of man's destiny" (p. 458). Even in his early book on pragmatism in education, Briggs (1940) had censored teachers who failed to take "the trouble to insure that the content of the printed page assuredly and continuously contributes to attitudes and to actions that make the individual a happier and more effective member of society" (p. 5). Discussing the political stances of educators in the progressive education movement, Graham (1967) observed that this political posturing was incompatible with the experimental attitudes that progressive educators had originally adopted.

In an early book about progressive education, Mirick (1923) had written about those original attitudes, values, and assumptions when he had described the progressive educational approach as an essentially scientific one that "employs the art of the systematic investigator," "recognizes only relative values," "is inductive," "is pragmatic," and "is interested it setting to work the new" (p. 14). Mirick compared the attitudes of a progressive educator to a "savage" who "chanced upon a gun, a keg of powder, and a box of bullets" and then attempted to divine their connections. Hall (1940) had expressed attitudes similar to those of Mirick when she wrote that progressive programs were based on procedures in which "nothing is used, either in method or materials, merely because it has been used before, but the working out of methods and choice of materials are both truly experimental in that they are constantly studied for evidence of success or failure" (p. 4).

The daring attitude described by Mirick and Hall inevitably changed as the approach that was once synonymous with experimental teaching methods was transformed into a politically orthodox avenue along which to construct educational programs. Bestor (1985) wrote that when he had received his high school training from 1922 to 1926 at the progressive Lincoln School of Teachers College, progressive education had been "definitely on the right track" (p. 45). However, even during this early period, he had noted indications of a political transformation:

Progressive education ceased to an effort to accomplish more effectively the purposes which citizens, scholars, and scientists had agreed were fundamental. Progressive education began to imply the substitution of new purposes. Experts in pedagogy were feeling their oats, were abandoning their proper task of improving instruction, and were brazenly undertaking to redefine the aims of education itself. By disregarding or flatly rejecting the considered educational views of the scholarly, scientific, and professional world, these new educationists succeeded in converting the division between secondary and higher education from a mere organizational fact into a momentous intellectual schism. Progressive education became regressive education, because, instead of advancing, it began to undermine the great traditions of liberal education and to substitute for them lesser aims, confused aims, or no aims at all (Bestor 1985, p. 47).

The transformation of progressive education from a revolutionary to a reactionary movement was apparent in the writing of progressive educators during the 1930s. For example, Cobb (1934) noted that "the social quality of progressive schools is strongly formative of character" and then assured readers that "there are certain factors in progressive education which definitely make for the building of character" (pp. 51-52). Cobb warned teachers that "the unsupervised recreation and social life of large public schools produce a certain type of character, that of aggressive independence" (p. 52). In contrast, Cobb observed that "the supervised, skillfully guided recreational and social life of children in progressive schools forms a character independent, it is true, but not aggressively so" and that "added qualities of kindliness, courtesy, cooperativeness and harmony are achieved in progressive schools" (p. 52).

Another articulate spokesperson for progressive education, Bode (1938) wrote that "education must be based on a philosophy of social organization if it is to be a worthy occupation for grownups," and that "if progressive education is to fulfill its promise, it must become consciously representative of a distinctive way of life" (pp. 4-5). Describing progressive education as "the strongest and most evangelistic movement in American education at the present time," Bode characterized the progressive school as "a place where children go, not primarily to learn, but to carry on a way of life" (p. 9).

Proponents of progressive education were aware that they were being accused of having replaced the orthodox educational practices against which they had railed. Washburne (1932) wrote that "our desire to share with others the results of our research and practical experience in the form of definite suggestions may cause our critics to consider us doctrinaire" (p. viii). Demiashkevich (1935b) was one of the obdurate critics to whom Washburne referred. He charged that progressive education "seems to be characterized, fundamentally, by its opposition to the general education method aiming at the direct and controlled mastery of systematic consecutive, and continuous curricula" and that "a measure of consecutive and continuous study may enter the educative process under the activity method only in so far as it is invoked by and is compatible with the joyful interest of the learner motivated by a tangible, immediate purpose" (1935b, p. 170).

By the end of the 1940s progressive educators could not misinterpret the multiple attacks by adversaries who had labeled them as a newly emerged class of reactionaries. Bell (1949) spoke out angrily against progressive educators because "John Dewey and his disciples, whatever be their wisdom or lack of it, do not come to their conclusions a result of experimentation one whit more than do for example, the Jesuits, who are at the opposite pole in method" (p. 8).

Redefer (1949), who had been a director of the Progressive Education Association, reminisced about the political agitation in the association when its members tried to agree on a modernized definition of progressive education more than 20 years after Dewey (1928) had proposed a pedagogical definition. Redefer described the disagreements in detail:

> The progressive educators split whenever social issues were injected into the educational picture. They resisted the acceptance of any clear statement of position. Even in the field of education there was resistance to a definition of progressive education. Critics within the Association repeatedly asked for a statement of the philosophy of those grouped under its banner. Finally, stung by repeated challenges, the Board of Directors appointed a well qualified committee to prepare a statement of the philosophy of progressive education. The committee labored long and brought forth a report which was presented to the members in annual conference in Detroit. But even the committee did not agree in open meeting. Communication and semantics proved to be major obstacles with one committee member confessing publicly that although he had a hand in phrasing the statement, he did not know what it meant. The document was accepted for study, but no one seriously considered adopting this or any other statement as the educational viewpoint of the Association (Redefer, 1949, p. 190).

Graham (1967) cited remarks from former leaders in the progressive education association to illustrate its transformation into a political organization. Describing in detail how the professional association identified with this movement had been attacked during its waning years, she reported that former leaders conceded that the progressive education had come to be viewed as a "fixed mode of education rather than a continuing experimental search" (p. 22). So prevalent was this negative perception that the leaders judged that the continued inclusion of the term *progressive education* in the name of the association had limited its opportunities to attract and retain members. Graham noted insightfully that another major factor leading to the decline of the progressive education movement had been the inability of its leaders to reconcile the warring elements within the organization. Fearing that any philosophical commitment might restrict its activities, the progressive educational community rationalized this failure as a conscious choice.

Prevalence of Progressive Instructional Innovations

Estimating the prevalence of the instructional innovations associated with progressive education has been complicated. Zilversmit (1976) judged that progressive education "had not significantly altered the broad pattern of American education" (p. 260). One of the factors complicating an accurate assessment of the impact of progressive education was the inconsistency of the terminology linked to the movement. Confusion about the terms with which to accurately describe progressive instruction was apparent throughout the 1900s and, in response to this confusion, progressive educators decided to create new terms rather than parse the existing ones.

This burgeoning vocabulary may have actually inhibited understanding of the philosophy that progressive educators endorsed. In an article with the witty title, "Pedagogues and Pedagese," Gibson (1943) observed that the growth of unnecessary academic language was "deplorable" and that "the worst offender" was "education as it is exemplified and taught in American colleges of education" where "the paraphernalia of pseudo science is rankest and the subject itself so overladen with false sophistications of technique and terminology that the only remedy would appear to be extirpation root and branch" (p. 96).

After reviewing jargon associated with curricular changes recommended during the 1930s and 1940s, Knight (1952) remarked that he would be "reckless" to appraise reform efforts since he was "uninitiated in the mysterious ritual of making, remaking, coring, and perhaps also 'yo-yoing' the curriculum" (p. 74). To illustrate his confusion, Knight provided an alphabetized list of curricula that would be encountered by "even the casual student of proposals for change" (p. 74). The following passage identifies the curricula he identified:

> [Recently proposed curricula include the] activity curriculum; areas-of-living curriculum; Batavia curriculum; challenging curriculum; broad-fields curriculum; cooperative curriculum; core-curriculum; developmental curriculum; cycle curriculum; Dalton curriculum; dynamic curriculum; dynamics-of-behavior curriculum; emerging curriculum; energizing curriculum; experiencing curriculum; formal curriculum; functional curriculum; fusion-curriculum; Gary curriculum; guidance-curriculum; individual-differences curriculum; multiple-track curriculum; opportunistic curriculum; orientation-curriculum; personal-problems-of-living curriculum; planless curriculum; project-curriculum; problem-curriculum; shared-experiences curriculum; subject-centered curriculum; teacher curriculum; unit curriculum; Winnetka curriculum; world-wide curriculum (Knight, 1952, p. 74).

Knight waggishly pointed out that "enthusiasm for constructing or reconstructing the curriculum may tend to cause the teachers to spend so much time in that endeavor that they will have little time to do anything with it after it has been constructed or reconstructed" (p. 74).

Estimating the prevalence of progressive educational innovations was complicated not only by inconsistent terminology but because reports about the implementation of those innovations were made by persons with strong personal convictions about the merits or risks of these strategies. For example, a critical *Time* magazine report ("Progressives' Progress," 1938) indicated that "twenty years ago Progressive Education was a tiny and, in many eyes, a crack-pot movement quarantined in a handful of private schools" (p. 31). Yet, the report continued that "now predominantly a public-school affair, Progressive Education has strongholds in the suburbs of greater New York, Chicago and Los Angeles, is transforming such major public school systems as those of Denver, San Francisco, Los Angeles, New York City, Detroit" and that "no U.S. school has completely escaped its influence" (p. 31). In contrast, Stearns (1939) estimated that the adoptions of progressive curricula by schools were still "isolated exceptions."

Writing a year later Crockett (1940) disagreed with Stearns about the extent to which the progressive education movement had been implemented in the schools. Borrowing Bode's 1938 vocabulary to describe progressivism as "the strongest and most evangelistic movement in American education," she pointed out that "the official membership in the Progressive Education Association numbers 10,000'" and that "a national conference in New York City in 1938 attracted 5000 educators, and sixteen regional conferences throughout the country were attended by more than 20,000" (p. 29). Crockett's own attitudes toward progressive education were quite obvious in her article's title, "Lollipops vs. Learning."

Numerous educators had singled out progressive education for causing a general degeneration in educational excellence. Aware of such criticism, Jersild, Goldman, Jersild, and Loftus (1941) reviewed data indicating that elementary school students in progressive education programs were indeed advancing less rapidly than those in skills-based curricula. However, their partisan attitudes were evident when they rationalized this delay by observing that the students were still "advancing at practically a normal rate in their subject-matter skills" while having the "opportunity of obtaining such benefits as accrue from giving a considerably greater amount of time than the non-activity pupils to other enterprises, including arts, independent study, work in the crafts, dramatics, oral composition, and the like" (p. 302).

After Krause (1941) visited 217 intermediate classrooms to observe the extent to which "principles of modern and progressive education are practiced," he concluded that "the practice of modern and progressive principles are well established in from 5 to 7 per cent of the public classrooms; moderately established in 15 to 20 per cent of the classrooms; and in 70 to 80 per cent of the classrooms they are rarely practiced" (p. 262). The most frequently exhibited characteristics of progressive education that Krause observed included teacher pleasantness, moveable furniture, and homelike learning environments. The least frequently exhibited characteristics were learning activities of a physical nature, social learning, and the practical application of skills.

Another study that corroborated the limited impact of progressive education was the exhaustive "Middletown" chronicle (Lynd & Lynd, 1937). A follow-up to the original documentary about the incidents in a typical, medium-sized American town from 1885–1924, this second report included information about educational changes during the decade that ended in 1935. As an example of these changes, the school board of this city had adopted a 10-year reorganization plan based on a philosophy that recognized the centrality of individual children. Lynd and Lynd

(1937) employed turgid, academic prose to describe the ensuing conflict in Middletown that prevented this plan from being implemented:

> There is conflict over the question of whose purpose the schools are supposedly fulfilling: Are these purposes those of the parent who wants education for *his* child in order that, through the acquisition of certain skills and knowledge or, more important, certain symbolic labels of an "educated person," he may achieve a larger measure of success than the parent himself has known? Or are they those of the citizen who wants, on the one hand, to have the fundamentals of community life, including it politico-economic mores, transmitted unchanged, and, on the other, to use the schools as an instrument of change sufficiently to bring any alien or backward children in the community up to these familiar standards? Or those of the teacher, with ideas derived from outside Middletown, loyal to a code of his own and obeying its philosophy? Or those of the taxpayers, businessmen, and school board members, whose chief emphasis is on "successful" and "progressive" schools, to be sure, but within the limits of a practical, sound, unextravagant, budget? Or are they the purposes of any one of the pressure groups who want to teach the children patriotism, health, thrift, character building, religion,—or any of the other values more or less accepted by the community as a whole but become an emotionally weighted "cause" with one special group? (p. 232).

Though concluding that Middletown had "been emotionally ready for change of a 'conservatively progressive' sort in its schools," the Lynds insightfully noted that emotional receptivity to school change was only one of several critical factors that were required before substantive changes would transpire. The other factors essential for change were the community's wealth, the urgency of other problems being confronted, the strength of traditions, the commitment of strong local leaders to change, and the rate of educational change in the larger culture surrounding the community.

In one of the few articles from this period where the objectivity of the author was unlikely to have been an issue, Bennett (1940) documented trends in the sales of school furniture. He may have validated the hypothesis that the superficial aspects of progressive education were those that had been most readily implemented when he presented data that "the outstanding accomplishment in school equipment [during the preceding half century] is the transition from stationary to moveable types of regular classroom seating" (p. 43). Bennett noted that sales on moveable classroom furniture had increased from an insignificant fraction to 80 percent of all purchases during the 25-year period that ended in 1940. Fifteen years earlier, Caldwell and Courtis (1925), both progressive educators, had described a "good schoolroom" as one that "includes plenty of blackboard and bulletin space, pictures, and moveable seatings" (p. 35).

Demise of Progressive, Politicized Education

Despite the valiant defense of progressive education by its proponents, no approach would have survived the unrelenting criticism to which progressive education was subjected after World War II. Knight (1952) observed that "public education in the United States at mid-twentieth century was under heavier attacks than it had been subjected to in all its long history" (p. 458). Personally committed to progressive education, Butts and Cremin (1953) warned readers that acquiescence to the massive critical literature that had been assembled "would be a hasty judgment." Nonetheless, they did observe that "one who reads many of the books and articles written during the last thirty-five years might have the impression that few people were satisfied with the educational program of the public schools" (p. 538). They judged that "one great cluster of criticisms that marked the recent period had to do with the nature of the curriculum and the methods of learning" (p. 541). Describing two groups of adversaries who respectively supported "traditional" or "modern" programs, they defined the former group as supporting "older and well-established subject matters" and the latter group as committed to enriched activities characterized "by means of creative, expressive, physical, handcraft, and social activities" (p. 541).

Even though they felt sympathy for the progressive educators who had attempted to repel the increasing attacks upon them, Butts and Cremin conceded that a genuine problem existed because "whether the profession could convince the public of the superiority of modern methods remained a question" (1953, p. 542). Scott and Hill (1954) noted that a new heading, *Public Schools—Criticism*, had been introduced into the *Education Index* in 1942 and that "criticism of education has recently established new records for volume, breadth of coverage, and intensity" (p. 3). They identified four aspects of the schools on which this criticism had centered: purpose of education, instructional methods, academic achievement, and teacher education. Though only 29 articles under the heading of *Public Schools—Criticism* had been referenced in the *Education Index* from 1942 to 1946, the number of references increased to 77 during the succeeding five years. Forty-nine references were listed in 1952 alone.

Kandel (1957) observed that "since the end of World War II the lay public has launched an avalanche of attacks on the public schools in all parts of the country" (p. 5). Although he admitted that "there were many well-intentioned and sincere citizens and professional educators who were critical," Kandel still charged that "the sincere and honest critics were not infrequently used by individuals and groups whose motives were not above suspicion" (p. 5). Among the ulterior motives that had attracted Kandel's suspicion were "unwarranted alarm at the rising cost of education, charges of responsibility for the rise in juvenile delinquency, the alleged defeat of 'Progressive' education as subversive, [and] suspicion of indoctrination in favor of an international outlook or of a supergovernment" (p. 5).

Although Kandel had referred to dissatisfaction with progressive education as only one of several elements contributing to the public censure of education, much of the criticism was directed exclusively at progressive practices. Writing in an issue of the journal *Progressive Education*, the editor characterized this precisely focused criticism as "unwarranted," "unjustified," and "savage"

(Anderson, 1952). Acknowledging that many of the attacks on progressive educational practices had been made at distinct levels, Anderson accused national and local tormentors of conspiring with each other. He wrote of "three elements which are present in the usual pattern of an organized attack: the local malcontents and critics, the local self-constituted organization which spearheads the attack and seeks to unify the opposition to public education, and the national organizations which supply the local organizations with their ammunition and strategy" (p. 68).

Like Anderson, Ernst (1953) was a proponent of progressive education who acknowledged the frequency with which progressive education had been assaulted. Overwhelmed by the sustained intensity of the assault, Ernst also speculated that "in part at least, these criticisms are a concerted, planned attack" (p. 59). Hulburd (1951) had confirmed Ernst's speculation by providing a "blow-by-blow" account of the dismissal of the progressive superintendent of the Pasadena school system. He characterized the superintendent's opponents as "viscous, well organized, and coldly calculating" and wrote that the Pasadena school district had fallen "prey to pressures within the city limits and infiltrating influences originating thousands of miles away" (p. ix). Selecting the incendiary title *This Happened in Pasadena*, it was not necessary for Hulburd to include a warning in the preface that similar events could "happen in towns and cities throughout all our forty-eight states" (p. x).

An issue of the *Saturday Review of Literature* published that same year contained six reports (e.g., Martin, 1951) on the "public school crisis." Setting the context for this series, the editors explained that they wished to call attention to communities where educational systems had been attacked. However, they expressed their personal convictions that the greatest crisis in these communities resulted not as much from inadequacies within those systems as the attacks against them. They viewed the educational challenges within those districts as assaults on progressive education by misinformed persons.

An article in *McCall's* (Morse, 1951) that was also sympathetic to progressive education attempted to startle readers with a warning that the magazine contained the "shocking facts that every parent should know" (p. 26). Articles supporting progressive education warned of a conservative political organization called the National Council for American Education. An article from the *Saturday Review of Literature* described the activities of Allen Zoll, who had been associated with this council:

> Mr. Zoll's newly hewn cudgels were being wielded in defense, so he said, of the American public school against enemies who wished to convert it into an agency of Socialism and Communism. He prepared a number of pamphlets under such apprehensive titles as "The Commies Are After Your Kids" and others appropriate to that general idea. The texts implied, or stated flatly, that progressive education is a device of subversion (Martin, 1951, p. 10).

Though persons preoccupied with fears of communism were among the opponents of progressive education, these were not the only opponents. Anticipating that supporters of progressive education would misrepresent and then dismiss their opponents, Woodring (1953) advised readers to be on guard against this strategy because many educators "have been reluctant to interpret it as a ground swell running against the new education" and "they have preferred to believe that *all* these attacks are motivated by malice, by a desire to reduce taxes, or by ignorance of what is actually going on in the schools" (p. 1). Woodring suggested two primary explanations for the criticisms of progressive schools. One explanation stemmed from the pragmatic basis for progressive education, which Woodring judged many citizens to find "disquieting." The other explanation concerned the disenfranchisement of parents and members of the public by professional educators who had "progressively pre-empted the responsibility for policy making to such an extent that interested citizens, even members of elected boards of education, feel that they no longer have an adequate part in the establishment of basic educational policies" (p. 2). In an article that appeared in *Life* magazine, Woodring (1957) lamented that "because its adherents were uncritically tolerant of their movement's lunatic fringes, progressivism came to be identified in the public mind solely with the excesses of those fringes" (p. 124).

Lynd (1953) wrote a book with the abrasive title *Quackery in the Public Schools* in which he, like Woodring, assailed educators who had been trying to dismiss their critics as religious zealots or political eccentrics. He wrote that "there would be less quackery in the public schools today if the Educationists had devoted to the correction of the shoddy pseudo-intellectual pretensions within their craft a fraction of the energy they have used in fabricating straw men to represent their critics" (p. 9). Lynd also raised concerns about the questionable value of progressive education and the alienation of the public from decision making in education. He challenged educators who supported progressive education to "convert most of the parents and the citizens to whom the schools belong, before they presume to impose their philosophy upon children" (p. 280). Lynd also remonstrated against "dedicated Educationists" who exhibited "an occupational contempt for parental opinion" (p. 17). Maintaining that education was only "in part a technical enterprise," he insisted that "everyone with some degree of personal education has a right critically to appraise its program for his children" (p. 11).

Extensively citing Lynd in her book about problems in education, Allen (1955) filled the initial chapter with comments indicating alarm by "businessmen, university professors, ministers, judges, politicians, commentators, doctors, writers, parents, and many others" (p. 9). On the basis of these comments, Allen asked readers whether changes in education "may easily result in a rising generation who will have a concept of American freedom completely foreign to that of their parents" (p. 26). She saw a connection between the degeneration of schools and a reliance by liberal educators on Dewey's philosophy, which she characterized as "materialistic, recognizing no permanent truths or values" (p. 28).

Critics of progressive education generally depicted themselves as representatives of a community that was frustrated by elitist educators who had fallen out of step with public values. In the preface to *The Diminished Mind*, Mortimer Smith (1954) listed his credentials, one of which was that he had read "vast quantities of what is euphemistically called educational literature" (p. 1). However, five years earlier Smith (1949) had begun a diatribe against progressive education with a rhetorical assurance that he was a "layman and amateur" in education and a "non-professional with a limited knowledge of the subject." Smith indicated that he had become interested only when "by chance" he had been elected as a member of a board of education. In the preface to *Crisis in Education*, Bell (1949) advised his readers that not only had he "read widely in the field of education" but that he had been "the president of a small college and a professor of a great university, a research student of education here and in Europe" (p. vii). But both Smith and Bell assured their audiences that they had formed their opinions only after conversations with many individuals from the general public as well as the educational community. Bell claimed that he had "corresponded with hundreds of parents, teachers, administrators, and professors of education; and in trips undertaken for the express purpose, I have talked with them in their native habitats, from the eastern seaboard to the western" (p. 1). In such conversations, he had asked whether the United States was "today a nation composed chiefly of people who have not grown up, who think and act for the most part...with the immaturity and emotional impulsiveness of adolescents (p. 1). He answered this question by advising his readers that "many shrewd observers of the American scene, both abroad and here at home, are saying that...it is our education system, defective in its understanding of man, which is largely responsible for our dangerous juvenility" (p. 1).

"Colonel" Rudd (1957) explained that his book about problems in the schools "grew out of the anguished concern of a typical American parent over the disturbing trends of American contemporary public education" (p. 3). Rudd included an entire chapter in which he recounted multiple failures in the schools that could be attributed to the progressive educational practices that he referred to as the "New Education." He wrote emotionally that "brave and patriotic teachers in scores of our communities, who have had the stamina to stand up against them, have suffered loss of job or loss of promotion as the price" and that "parents and laymen who have challenged the New Education also have been smeared and misrepresented" (p. 8). Rudd's book went through numerous printings and was frequently cited by other critics. In a 1970s supplement, Rafferty (1972) stated that it was "nothing short of remarkable" that Rudd's book had continued to be popular for so long. To underscore this point he recited a litany of current educational incidents about which the public was concerned and which still exemplified the problems that Rudd had popularized in 1957.

Persons sympathetic to Rudd invariably referred to him as *Colonel* Rudd, enabling him to use his former military rank to bolster the credibility of his opinions. Vice Admiral Rickover was another person whose credibility was buttressed by his military commission. He was a naval engineer who had led the team that developed the nuclear powered submarine launched in 1954. Rickover (1957a) drew comparisons between Russia and the United States, alerting his readers that "the more disturbing fact which emerges from the Russian satellite program is her success in building in record time an education system which produces exactly the sort of trained men and women her rulers need to achieve technological supremacy the day after tomorrow" (p. 86). Rickover (1957b) evaluated the United States as "severely handicapped because the American education system is defective, both in quantity and quality," creating "a crisis in education which must be dealt with promptly and effectively or the machinery which sustains our material prosperity will begin to slow down, endangering not only our standard of living but also our position in the world" (p. 19). He warned readers that "only massive upgrading of the scholastic standards of our schools will guarantee the future and freedom of the republic" (1959, p. 15). While training Navy recruits about nuclear energy, Rickover had developed a conviction that fundamental skills would be promoted through a sound liberal arts curriculum. Convinced that the education required to support technological progress was "our first line of defense," he warned his readers that "in my work I have had a glimpse of the future" which "belongs to the best-educated nation." To prevent his audience from misunderstanding his advice about which nation should brandish the banner for the best educated youth, Rickover urged his readers to "let it be ours" (1959, p. 38).

Trace (1961) wrote an article with the provocative title, "Can Ivan Read Better than Johnny?" In the byline to that article the editors pointed out that "when American grade-school children are reading something akin to baby talk, Russian kids of the same age are mastering difficult textbooks" (p. 30). Trace highlighted the rigor and sophistication of Russian reading education materials, which he claimed required the mastery of 2,500 new words each year. He compared these to the 300 or 400 words that were being introduced annually into American textbooks. In addition to superior reading, Trace alleged that the typical Russian youngster "is running a good two years ahead of our boy in learning mathematics" and that he "graduated from a ten-year school having studied a foreign language for six years" (p. 30).

Trace's article had appeared in *The Saturday Evening Post*. Three years earlier Wilson (1958) had written an editorial for *Life* magazine that was equally critical of an educational crisis created because "a surprisingly small percentage of high school students is studying what used to be considered basic subjects" (p. 36). In a section of this article with the subtitle, "Falling behind Russia," he explained that the United Sates had slipped in the educational race when "instead of trying to find students to fit a rigid curriculum, the schools decided to try to hand-tailor a course of instruction for each child" (p. 36).

Writing in the popular *Saturday Review* toward the end of the 1960s, Jennings (1967) declared that progressive education had died as a movement. Even though Jennings thought the deceased movement had left a "modest but most precious legacy" in which educators cherished children for their "biological and social rights," he cautioned that this "legacy must be invested in a more tough-minded enterprise than the progressives could ever devise" (p. 97).

Eight years later Gold (1975) attributed America's educational crisis to the "child-centered syndrome and the relevance retreat" which he characterized as "two monsters which joined to form a hydra-headed dragon guarding our schools" (p. 12). He disapproved of progressive education for pandering to students who almost invariably came from an "intellectually privileged" home and which was successful only when the fortunate students were "*already educated*." He concluded that though such privileged children would excel in any classroom, they were still at a decided advantage "in a system without clearly stated subject-goals, without intensive individual instruction, and without strong teacher leadership" (p. 12).

Dewey Embraces Pragmatism

Writing about the practical changes that had transpired within progressive education, Iversen (1959) criticized those developments while simultaneously exonerating Dewey. He wrote that "the progressive teachings of John Dewey have found their way into most of the country's schools, and have, in fact, been world-wide in their influence" but that "reduced to platitudes and administered by overzealous and underbright disciples, progressive education often became characterized by classroom anarchy" (p. 63).

Mayer (1961) concluded that "Dewey is always being blamed for things he did not do." However, he did concede that Dewey inadvertently "lent the weight of his intelligence to the fearfully wasteful cut-and-parse procedures which have dominated sociology, social psychology, anthropology and education" (p. 69). Kurtz (1966) wrote in defense of Dewey that "the name of Dewey is synonymous with the liberating movement in progressive education—though Dewey cannot be identified with all of its supporters, as his many critics attempt to do" (p. 161). Drawing conclusions from a similar perspective, Kliebard (1986) wrote that Dewey both "personified and transcended what was to become American education in the twentieth century" and that "Dewey's own position in critical matters of theory and doctrine actually represented a considerable departure from the main line of any of the established movements" (p. 30).

Dewey himself had upbraided the attendants at the 1928 Progressive Education Association for behaving as though "orderly organization of subject matter [was] hostile to the needs of students" (Dewey, quoted by Bowers, 1969, p. 11). Bode (1930) had written in *The New Republic* that "according to Dewey, freedom is achieved through the exercise of intelligence, whereas the least discriminating of his disciples understand him to mean that intelligence is achieved through the exercise of freedom" (p. 63). After employing a prefatory remark that "it is an open question whether Dewey's educational philosophy has been more flagrantly distorted in the accounts given of it by some of his latter-day disciples than by the criticisms of his vociferous detractors," the philosopher Sydney Hook (1973) wrote that "the first misconception of John Dewey's philosophy stems from the notion that because he stressed the importance of freedom, he was therefore opposed to authority" (p. 58). Hook cited passages from Dewey's writings in order to substantiate his commitment to the place of authority in education.

Addressing the issue of freedom by learners, Spring (1986) concluded that "Dewey wanted to free individual action, not submerge it in the mediocre standard of group consensus" because he "believed that motives and choices grow out of social situations, and not as many other educators were to argue, that individual motives and goals should conform to the wishes of the group" (p. 175). Power (1996) noted that "together with progressive schoolmasters, most pragmatists embraced the child-centered school to allow the interests (critics said the whim) of children to infiltrate the curriculum and dilute or, sometimes, suppress respectable subject matter" and that these pragmatists "demonstrated disdain for the content of the learning experience" (p. 138). But Power (1996) observed that Dewey did not agree with progressive educators on this point:

> [Dewey] admitted to lack of inherent worth in many of the data that appeared from somewhere in the school's curriculum, but declared, nevertheless, that experience cannot be had in a vacuum. Experience must be of something. Some kinds of experience are more formative than others—a discovery that comes not from edict but from experience itself—and these are the experiences that should be put into the curriculum (p. 138).

Addressing the issue of freedom by educators, Graham (1967) had written that Dewey "strenuously opposed unlimited freedom" in the building of curricula and that "to Dewey, intelligence entailed order, and he never countenanced the anti-intellectualism that passed, at certain extremes of the progressive education movement, for authentic interest in the child" (p. 15).

In his history of four influential pragmatists, Scheffler (1974) wrote insightfully that he could not encapsulate the content of pragmatic scholars' thoughts because "it would be contrary to the spirit of pragmatism to attempt a final summation" (p. 257). Scheffler explained the basis for these remarks by paraphrasing a premise from *Human Nature and Conduct*, a book that Dewey had published in 1922:

> For pragmatism, there are no final summations, no essential meanings, no ultimate reckonings. A movement of thought is not a jewel in a casket, enclosed for contemplation. It is part of a continuous process. Where it is significant, it provokes new problems, sets new paths (Scheffler, 1974, p. 257).

The categorical rejection of skills-based pedagogy by some educators was as pragmatically inappropriate as the categorical dismissal of language-based strategies by many of the proponents of skills-based approaches. Since remedial reading programs were designed to help specific learners with precise problems, a pragmatic philosophy represented the only defensible base for instruction. However, the use of a pragmatic philosophy was not restricted to remedial reading education. For a majority of teachers may have been preeminently pragmatic during the past century in their approaches to instruction. Writing about the history of classroom practices, Spring (1986) advised readers to differentiate the rhetoric of scholars from the activities of practitioners, cautioning that "one must be careful that statements about what would be are not confused with reality." Although he acknowledged that the theories of instruction that had been popular in the late 1800s and early 1900s had an impact on classroom practices, he still concluded that "there is no evidence that this impact occurred in any consistent or organized pattern" and suggested instead, "after closing their classroom doors, teachers tended to teach using a variety of personal and instructional methods" (p. 169).

Spring's cautionary words were similar to those of the psychologist Jerome Bruner (1973), who, when addressing the interrelationship of culture, politics, and pedagogy, proposed four reasons why a theory of instruction might have had only a restricted effect on classroom practice. For example, a theory might simply have been wrong. Or it might have been irrelevant to the problems that practitioners were confronting. Just as a theory might not have addressed the needs of teachers, it could also have failed to address the "urgencies of a society." Finally, the instructional implications of a theory might simply have been unmanageable. To the extent that the four reasons suggested by Bruner were relevant to those progressive ideas about reading instruction that were not widely implemented or that were implemented for only a limited time, pragmatism was an antidote that remedial reading teachers administered in order to diagnose and remedy unhealthy instructional procedures.

SEVERAL PRAGMATIC EDUCATORS

Well before the educational arguments of the late twentieth century, educators had debated the extent to which reading education should be politicized. In fact, the political stances assumed by some late twentieth-century educators were hardly distinguishable from the viewpoints of progressive educators during the first half of the twentieth century. Indicating that progressivism had been a movement that had well-defined political as well as educational dimensions, Welter (1962) wrote that "the progressive movement in education and the progressive movement in politics were not simply parallel phenomena but variant forms of the same middle-class impulse" (p. 258). Prominent among the early twentieth-century opponents to the politicization of education were those pragmatic educators who endorsed remedial reading. For example, Hollingworth (1923) had exhibited emotional restraint and pragmatic logic when she observed the need for flexibly when designating reading methods. She chastised her overzealous contemporaries who had urged that a single instructional method be used with all learners because "no investigator has established his or her method as the only method of successful approach to particular cases " (p. 90).

Like Hollingworth, Monroe (1935) was a preeminently pragmatic educator who advised teachers that "remedial methods should at all times be flexible and adapted to the peculiar needs of the individual" (p. 227). Though most of her contemporaries were zealously committed to exclusive programs, she counseled teachers to refrain from selecting an approach because they admired the characteristics of the approach itself. Instead, she recommended that "in all remedial work the teacher should start first with the child and then find the appropriate method" (p. 227).

Hildreth (1936) may have been the educator that exhibited the most consistently pragmatic approach to remedial reading instruction during the 1930s. She wrote that teachers should "realize that reading is not one thing but a manifold activity employed in a variety of situations" and that they should therefore demonstrate "less adherence to a single method, and more tendency toward flexibility in methods and varied instructional techniques" (p. 114). Although Hildreth supported language-based techniques, she advised teachers who used them exclusively that this type of instruction "carried to an extreme is as conductive to bad habits of reading as a highly formal, analytical, or mechanical method" (p. 131). Reacting to a question about the best method for corrective reading instruction, she delivered a preeminently pragmatic response:

> None of these so-called methods represents a complete program either for normal teaching of reading or for remedial work. Attack on individual problems requires variation in emphasis depending on the nature of the child's problem. With a deaf child, a visual perception method obviously would be the correct approach. The dull child will require more analysis and repetition than the bright child, and even the slow process of writing or spelling out his reading material may have a legitimate place in his program. A child who does nothing but guess, "look and say" as a result of prolonged use of the whole method, gains from having his attack systematized by phonetic drill. A child with considerable language difficulty would benefit from sound-discrimination, ear-training, and language drills. To follow any one method slavishly because it has been highly recommended is to repeat the error that has caused reading problems in the first place (Hildreth, 1936, p. 671).

Schonell (1945) had reviewed three popular approaches to reading—phonics, whole word, and experience-based approaches. He concluded that research did not indicate the superiority of any of these methods over the others "in every aspect of reading." Using italics for emphasis, he clarified this remark in the fourth edition of his book, stating that "*each method or major aspect of reading instruction that has been developed over the decades makes its own contribution to the teaching of reading*" (1961, p. 92). He wrote that a "dumb as ditchwater" phonics method that used uninteresting materials would certainly be ineffective. But he immediately rejoined that a holistic approach that overwhelmed students with an unregulated stream of novel vocabulary would be equally ineffective. After noting that knowledge of phonics did not preclude children from recognizing words holistically, he countered that neither did mastery of holistic learning strategies prevent children from using phonics. He therefore resolved that teachers should use eclectic approaches that incorporated the best of the respective instructional techniques.

Schonell's pragmatic attitude was similar to that of Barzun. Also writing in 1945, Barzun (1988) had chided his readers that "if you send your child to a 'modern' school, you will be spanked for showing him the alphabet" (p. 86). Though he did not oppose holistic instruction, Barzun noted that analytical strategies such as phonics "did not prevent the acquiring of the one-glance reading habits" (p. 86). Unlike Schonell who concluded that teachers should be eclectic, Barzun recommended that initial reading begin with phonics and then progress to holistic strategies.

In a textbook intended for "college courses in the teaching of elementary school reading and for the practical use of the in-service teacher," Adams, Lillian Gray, and Reese (1949) wrote that the information in their book was focused on practical teaching methods and techniques. However, they qualified the presentation of this information with their personal convictions that "method will do no good unless it is well grounded in philosophy; [and] a technique is valueless unless it is based upon sound educational psychology" (p. vi). They warned their readers that authors who made such stipulations usually did so as "justification for the idea that there is one best method." Disapproving of such a bias, they insisted that "instruction must vary with the child" and that "there is no comprehensive method" (p. vi).

Anderson and Dearborn (1952) had observed that "all conventional methods of teaching reading have their strengths and weaknesses." But instead of concluding that it did not matter which approach instructors used, Anderson and Dearborn recommended that "reading might best be taught by a combination of methods" (p. 293). They advised teachers to employ an eclectic approach that included every major technique of instruction that had been developed, hoping that the strengths of any method would compensate for the weaknesses of the others:

> The experience method serves the functions of the story or sentence method. These functions include (1) transmitting the idea of reading, (2) developing a thought-getting attitude as a first step to reading, and (3) arousing an interest in reading. The pupils are next introduced to their preprimers. The vocabulary of the preprimers is usually taught by the word method. The use of the word method at this point will serve to check the habit of memory reading which is associated with experience reading, and to launch the children on the road to real reading. The alphabet and phonetic methods are next called into action to promote skills in word analysis. These methods will serve to counteract the inaccuracy which characterizes learning to read by the word method, and they will also help the children gain independence in word recognition. Quick recognition drills are often useful at this point to keep the pupils from becoming too analytical in their word recognition. Many of the children will now be reading word by word. The phrase method is brought into play at this juncture to combat that problem (Anderson & Dearborn, 1952, p. 294).

In their 1957 book on remedial reading, Bond and Tinker established basic principles for effective instruction, one of which was that "treatment must be based on an understanding of the child's instructional needs" (p. 206). To ensure that this principle was embodied in instruction, they advised teachers to clearly formulate a remedial program, modify it as needed, and use a variety of remedial techniques. The authors explained their view about the need for employing a variety of strategies:

> There is an unfortunate tendency, once a form of remedial instruction has been prescribed, to stick to the use of that specific type of exercise to overcome a known deficiency. Basing a remedial program upon a diagnosis does not imply that a given exercise can be used until the child's reading disability is corrected. There are many ways to develop each of the skills and abilities in reading. An effective remedial program will use a variety of teaching techniques and instructional procedures (Bond & Tinker, 1957, p. 206).

Identifying principles for developing pragmatic curricula, Bayles (1966) highlighted "relationalism," which he judged to be an "essential tenet of pragmatism" that discouraged the delineation of "long lists of itemized specifics." He defined relationalism as the educational "search for a single, unifying principle or generalization, from which by logical deduction the multifarious details of particular cases can be derived" (p. 95). Although Bayles did not discuss reading curricula, he did provide details about pragmatic approaches to instruction in several related areas, including spelling. He wrote that "the present theory implies a return to grouping words according to phonetic relationships, and the use of rules," but that these rules "are to be formulated by the class instead of by the writer of the textbook, and are to grown out of reflective studies of list of words grouped phonetically" (p. 112). Acknowledging that much of English spelling was nonphonetic, Bayles illustrated that nonphonetic words could be pragmatically incorporated into instruction without disrupting teachers' learning plans:

> During this time, the teacher needs to manage so that all words placed on the blackboard and studied by the class are strictly phonetic.... Now comes a surprise—an incompatibility. With something up her sleeve, teacher will somehow get a few *ite, ate, ute*, and other silent-e words on the blackboard.... With teacher's help, a new *kind* of conclusion will be reached—that certain rules which the class has previously adopted have to be changed somewhat so as to take care of exceptions (Bayles, 1966, p. 114).

The approach to teaching phonetic patterns and irregularities that was illustrated by Bayles reflected a fundamental objective of pragmatic education. This principle was to "provide the learner experience in effective experiencing," which Butler (1951) had clarified as "practice in coping with the indeterminacies of experience" (pp. 462-463).

SUMMARY

Corrective and remedial reading approaches were responses to the problems encountered by children in their general reading programs. Some educators had recommended that only the schedule of instruction or the degree of individualization be altered when children were failing in a specific literacy program. In contrast, most remedial and corrective reading programs, which identified instructional interventions that went beyond the simple intensification of the current approaches used by those learners, did not attempt to maintain loyalty to the specific approach with which learners had encountered reading problems in the first place.

Pragmatism, the educational philosophy popularized by Dewey, incorporated an approach to learning in which instructional strategies, materials, and learning activities were evaluated only after experimentation by instructors and students. Pragmatism was an alternative to the political approaches that attempted to categorically direct instructors' behaviors. Though multiple examples illustrated the influence of political approaches to education throughout the twentieth century, this influence was especially evident during the great depression and World War II, two eras when the popularity of politically liberal and conservative values respectively peaked. However, even during such periods of sustained political activism in education, pragmatism and restrained political approaches characterized remedial reading.

Chapter 6

SKILLS-BASED APPROACHES

Without a good curriculum there is bound to be great waste (McMurry, 1913).

Skills-based reading programs dominated instruction in the schools throughout the twentieth century. These programs structured learning through materials that were arranged sequentially and linked to a hierarchy of skills. This regulation, for which an explicit well-organized curriculum became the most evident sign, was part of a broad initiative to promote standardization in the general field of education.

*   *   *

Despite the emergence of competing programs, skills-based approaches dominated reading education throughout the twentieth century. Impressed by the overwhelming support he still detected for skills-based programs in the middle 1980s, Kenneth Goodman (1986) concluded that whole language instruction was "not yet a popular movement" and that "only a limited number of curriculum workers, administrators, and teacher educators actively support it" (p. 62). On the many occasions when proponents of the different approaches to instruction testified about the popularity of the approach they personally supported, conflict of interest may have influenced their perceptions. However, when educators such as Goodman admitted the popularity of an approach that they were criticizing, the credibility of their estimates was enhanced precisely because they disapproved of that approach.

Concessions about the popularity of skills-based programs by critics of those programs were a frequently occurring motif. Despite her personal opposition to skills-based programs, Greene (1978) wrote of her frustration because "schools' advertised failures strike [parents] as threats to their children's survival in this world" and consequently "they support demands that the schools move 'back'— 'back to basics'" (p. 76). Equally outspoken in their disaffection for skills-based reading materials, the members of the Commission on Reading of the National

Council of Teachers of English (1989) conceded that the reading textbooks on which they frowned were employed "in roughly 90 percent of the elementary classrooms in the United States" (p. 896). Though Luke (1991) acknowledged his distaste for the reading textbooks developed in the 1940s by the Scotts Foresman Publishers, he admitted that those textbooks were "a model for the basal readers that to this day dominate beginning reading instruction" (p. 166). In the preface to a critical report published by the Council for Basic Education, Down (1988) warned that though textbooks were "Trojan horses—glossily covered blocks of paper whose words emerge to deaden the minds of our nation's youth," they still "dominate what students learn" (p. vii). In the report for which Down had written the preface, Tyson-Bernstein (1988) regretted that teachers had been "seduced by textbook programs that offer to take much of the work out of teaching" (p. 12). But like Down she admitted that textbooks were not only popular but "will remain a fixture in American education" (p. 12). Altbach (1991) was another critic who admitted the ascendant popularity of the instructional materials with which he was displeased. Distressed at the political disadvantages created when prosperous, industrialized nations published textbooks for international markets, he nonetheless conceded that "textbooks, despite the recent criticism of them in the United States, are virtual icons of education" (p. 242). Allington and his colleagues (Allington, Guice, Michelson, Baker, & Li, 1996) argued in favor of literature-based reading programs, observing a "recent rapid shift" away from the skills-based instruction. Though they were optimistic about a change from the skills-based reading approaches of which they disapproved, they also conceded that skills-based programs had reigned for "nearly a quarter of a century as the dominant curriculum model" (p. 73).

Although some of the reasons for the uncontested prevalence of skills-based instructional strategies were straightforward, others were less obvious. A link to direct teaching would be an example of an obvious reason that skills-based programs remained attractive to educators and the public. The term *direct teaching* had been used by Farnham (1895) who referred to the "direct teaching of reading, spelling, and writing" (p. iv). But Farnham conceived of direct teaching as an antidote to the popular phonics-based lessons that he opposed. Because he thought that "the unit of expression is a sentence," Farnham deduced that the sentence should be the basis for initial reading instruction. Used more recently to describe a type of instruction with different connotations from those proposed by Farnham, the term *direct reading instruction* has been focused upon the specific skills required by learners to be successful readers (Carnine, Silbert, & Kameenui, 1990).

As an example of the longevity of the connection between the term *direct instruction* and skills-based reading, Betts (1946) had referred to "directed" reading activities in the textbook that he wrote after World War II. Even though connected to such references, the popularization of the term *direct instruction* may be better explained as a consequence of the bitter debates between academic antagonists. For opponents of skills-based programs assigned negative connotations to those programs by depicting the teachers using them as pedagogic mechanics who were insensitive to the communicative needs of students. A 1950s report (National Education Association, 1959) contrasted knowledge-centered, student-centered, and skill-centered learning. Whereas the instruction synchronized to the initial two types of learning respectively developed critical thinkers and "fully functioning people," the report insisted that a less glamorous rationale explained skill-centered instruction:

> Some education is specific and direct. Many of the learning tasks for military personnel are of this order. Information is needed for the proper use of equipment, the characteristics of a new weapon, techniques of map reading, and a host of similar problems. Telephone repairmen attending a maintenance school go to learn how to correct specific difficulties. Shop foremen learning how to service a recent model automobile need specific information. And salesmen may desire to learn about new items in the line (National Education Association, 1959, p. 27).

Several decades later the opposition between supporters and opponents of skills-based instruction had not subsided. The acrimony of opponents was even discernible in the derisive titles of books such as Kenneth Goodman's (1993) *Phonic Phacts* and Frank Smith's (1986) *Insult to Intelligence: The Bureaucratic Invasion of Our Classrooms*. Goodman (1993) depicted advocates of phonetically oriented, skills-based programs as bullies who badgered teachers and parents. He dedicated his book to "the pursuit of truth and to the liberation of teachers and learners from the shackles of imposed ignorance" (p. iii). Smith portrayed the publishers of skills-based materials as avaricious and unprincipled, exhorting that the "invasion of education by instructional programmers must be turned back now" (p. xii).

Because the term *skills-based* has sometimes carried a connotation that the programs to which it referred employed isolated drills and ignored the overall needs of learners, some individuals preferred the term *direct instruction*. The use of the latter term placed opponents in the uncomfortable rhetorical position of having to develop a rationale and demonstration of accountability for the alternatives to direct instruction that they had proposed.

A key feature of direct instruction has been the identification of precise skills for which instructors were responsible. For this reason, these approaches were regarded as easier to implement than those that assumed that teachers possessed advanced prerequisite training. Making an observation about the progressive education movement, which had been an alternative to the skills-based model for instruction, Cremin (1969) had noted that "from the beginning, progressivism cast the teacher in an almost impossible role: he was to be an artist of consummate skill, properly knowledgeable in his field, meticulously trained in the science of pedagogy, and thoroughly imbued with a burning zeal for social improvement" (p. 168). This same point had been made by Schwab (1959) who observed that persons committed to progressive education were required to be effective teachers but also to use the "classroom as the occasion and the means to reflect upon education as a whole (ends as well as means), as the laboratory in which to translate reflections into actions and thus to test reflections, actions, and outcomes against many criteria" (p. 159).

Cremin's and Schwab's remarks can be extended to other reactionary educational movements that emerged after progressive education had subsided but which had many of the same characteristics. In contrast to these movements, direct instruction was depicted as an opportunity to reduce the demands upon teachers who were to be supported by an organized plan of instruction and comprehensive support materials. Gunter, Estes, and Schwab (1995) wrote that direct instruction was "most useful in teaching skills that can be broken into small, discrete segments, with each segment building on the prior one" (p. 79). Direct instruction assumed that the fundamental knowledge for learning to read could be identified, segmented, and organized so that it would be available as a system to benefit both teachers and students. (Despite the possible rhetorical advantages of the term *direct instruction*, the phrase *skills-based instruction* clearly conveys the distinctive characteristics of the identical program to which both terms refer.)

SYSTEMIZATION IN EDUCATION

Current approaches to skills-based instruction have been portrayed as attempts to systematize learning through activities that were sequenced and that embodied precisely defined skills. However, systemization in reading education was not novel. As early as 1886, G. Stanley Hall had written that "some method there must be, or there is great waste" (1897, p. 11). Hall called attention to the care that reading educators had demonstrated when selecting and arranging the words that would appear in initial reading texts:

> Most [primers] give precedence to nouns, while several proceed to adjectives, verbs, and a few to prepositions and adverbs, while one uses as normal material the forms of the verb *to be*. Some prefer monosyllables, some words of two or three letters, and one, with great pains, takes the name of each child as its first normal word. Most prefer Anglo-Saxon, or at least those words that carry their etymologies with them, that are of familiar meaning and about equally hard to read and write. Most of the rigorous script-methods begin with a noun containing the vowel, which is reached by analysis, and perhaps permanently painted on the board with slant of the due number of angles, and transition is made to *u, m, n,* and in German scrip *e*. Sometimes a bias toward science, art, industry, etc., is freely indulged in the selection of those words and the object-teaching on which they focus. Sometimes the form-elements of letters and sometimes the vocal elements of speech, minutely analyzed and graded on some real or arbitrary genetic principle, or according to the least change in transition, are the main determinants in the choice of normal words. The finer the analysis, and the more fully one set of conditions in the choice of normal words is fulfilled, the less perfectly are the other desiderata met. All advantages cannot be combined in any single series of words, or even of meaningless noises, so that several sets of normal words may have about equal merit, the best thing being, of course, those that realize, though but partially, most of the conditions of excellence (1897, pp. 11-12).

Proponents of Systematized Reading Instruction—After 1900

Boyer (1908) was an early spokesperson for systemization in reading education who advised teachers that reading lessons should be carefully organized, and that "the habit of reading good books developed into love" (p. 114). Believing that the application of systemization was not limited to the development of students' behaviors in their reading lessons, he argued for a "natural precedence of ideas, thoughts, sciences" that would in turn determine "the order in which topics, lessons, and fields of work should be taken up" (p. 42). He explained that this approach to learning was foolproof because "when this progressive correlation is perfect the pupil is prepared for every new mental conquest by the most appropriate preparatory conquests" (pp. 42-43). In order to illustrate the optimal scope and sequence for learning, Boyer carefully elaborated categories of terms, such as ideas, names, and signs, as well as categories embedded within these terms. He concluded that the "royal road" to instruction and learning was based on a succession of lessons that "related known to the new, and from the simple to the complex" (p. 45).

An indication of the popularity of this type of systemization in reading education was discernible when educators chastised publishers for not fulfilling their marketing promises to thoroughly regulate reading textbooks. If systemization had not been such a popular feature of reading textbooks, this criticism would have seemed inane. As an example, Jones (1915) reported a study in which he had analyzed the vocabulary from 10 popular basal reading series and compiled a list of words that students were expected to learn holistically. He also composed a separate list of words that conformed to phonetic principles. The 10 most frequently occurring words in the phonetic list ranged from a frequency of 704 occurrences (*and*) to 206 occurrences (*ball*). The 10 most frequently occurring words in the nonphonetic list ranged from 1,733 occurrences (*the*) to 334 (*do*). Jones worried that the heterogeneity evident in the reading materials showed a disregard for systematized instruction.

Also critical of the failure of publishers to systematize instruction, Selke and Selke (1922) complained that "although writers of textbooks have stated that their books are characterized by a 'constant reappearing of old words' or that 'supplemental primers use largely the same vocabulary of fundamental words though their stories differ,' even a cursory examination shows that there is wide variance in introductory readers along these lines" (p. 745). To demonstrate this point the authors analyzed the vocabulary of 10 popular reading series, concluding that "a large number of words appear only once in each book" (p. 749). In a similar manner, Hosic (1920) had compiled an index of the content in 22 reading series and concluded with disappointment that "the most striking fact which this index presents is the lack of a consensus of opinion as to what American children should read in school" (p. 180). A year earlier Dunn (1921) had analyzed 1,029 selections from 29 reading books, concluding that "there is as yet no agreement as to minimum essentials in reading matter for the primary grades" (p. 10).

G. Stanley Hall (1924) wrote in his autobiography about the continued prevalence of phonics in reading education during the early 1920s. Estimating that the popularity of holistic approaches had begun to decline because of a perception that they were ineffective, he recounted that "where and when this method was at its height I have been told by librarians that children in the eighth or ninth grade could not repeat the alphabet and were helpless in finding what they wanted in card catalogues or the dictionaries" (p. 481). Although a prediction by Hall that holistic programs would disappear proved inaccurate, his observations did indicate that skills-based instruction was still robust during this period. The popularity of skills-based instruction was also apparent in the writing of authors who supported holistic instructional strategies but who insisted that systematized activities be integrated with them.

In a detailed bibliography of children's literature, Pennell and Cusack (1924) recommended that students be instructed not only with children's literature but also with newspapers, content area texts, and reference books. However, they cautioned teachers against abandoning their basal readers because "the use of some uniform materials is necessary to develop and check standards and habits of good reading" (pp. 250-251). Acknowledging the abuses of oral reading and recitation in the schools, they still advised teachers to maintain recitation as a fundamental component of reading instruction because it provided opportunities to share information publicly, to aid in recalling difficult words, to aesthetically appreciate certain types of passages, and to develop the human voice as an "instrument in life."

Thayer (1928) had written an entire book about the recitation lessons to which Pennell and Cusack had referred. Convinced that recitation and drill-based learning were moribund, he noted that "traditional procedures, as embodied in what is generally termed the recitation method, are found to be out of harmony with the objectives of modern education" (p. iii). But Thayer had characterized learning through recitation in a narrow fashion. In a chapter titled "Educational Principles Taken for Granted by the Recitation Method," he wrote that this method assumed that the minds of learners were merely wax tablets and that drills and recitations based on the content of textbooks were thought to be the only method for making impressions on those mental tablets. Such assumptions would not have been endorsed by most of the proponents of skills-based instruction. Additionally, many proponents of progressive programs continued to view drilling and recitation as effective.

As one example of how broadly recitation activities were defined, Cohen (1919) had described the "socialized recitation" which was designed "to make any subject function in the classroom under much the same circumstances under which it will have to function when the student leaves school" and which "aims to train students to initiate thought processes without continual stimulating and prodding from the teacher, and to conduct their proceedings on a democratic basis" (p. 240). Cohen gave an exhaustive list of benefits that she attributed to the socialized recitation lesson. Many of these benefits resulted from the systemization inherent in recitation lessons, such as "the use of the assignment to suggest the lesson plan for the following day," "the training of students to look for and follow a valid aim in their work," "drill through mutual correction and group consciousness," and "the students realizing what the goal is and achieving it as independently as possible, and thus finding in the schoolroom the ideal at once of intellectual independence and rational self control" (p. 240). Though they recommended that reading be reinforced through dramatization and constructive projects, Anderson and Davidson (1925) still advocated drilling as an important component of a comprehensive program.

Even Flora Cooke (1926), who had been mentored by Colonel Francis Parker himself and who became principal at the University of Chicago's laboratory school, was not prepared to disavow the usefulness of drilling. But Cooke did temper her recommendation with the observation that "since children differ greatly in power to grasp and retain, the amount of *drill* which individuals receive must always vary greatly in any group" (p. 306). Cooke consequently advised that "each child should have enough drill to give him adequate control of the tools of learning which he needs and no more" (p. 306).

After noting the value of skills-based instruction, Thorndike and Gates (1929) observed that the drilling associated with it could be valuable because it was "the most economical method of learning yet invented" (p. 258). Based on Thorndike's pioneering work in educational psychology, he and Gates developed five principles that defined the "optimum placement of a fact or skill" in the educational curriculum. The principles respectively concerned *need*, *felt need*, *difficulty*, *temperamental compatibility*, and *facilitation*. The principle of *difficulty* advised educators to "introduce a fact or skill when it is most suited in difficulty to the ability of the learner" (p. 209). The principle of *facilitation* advised teachers to "introduce a fact or skill when it is most fully facilitated by immediately preceding learnings and when it will most fully facilitate learnings which are to follow shortly" (pp. 209-210). Both of these principles reflected the organizational basis for skills-based reading approaches. Thorndike and Gates used the learning of the alphabet to illustrate the need for appropriate sequencing of skills within a curriculum. Discouraging the rote learning of the alphabet because "there is little real demand for this stunt even in the lower grades," they wrote that learners needed "to be able, in a general way, to think where a given letter such as K is in the series and in which direction and about how far off it is from another letter which he has come upon, such as N" (p. 114).

Proponents of SystematizedReading Instruction—After 1930

Witty and Kopel (1939) looked back on the 1920s as a period that was "memorable chiefly for the improvement in the techniques for the presentation of highly organized units of subject matter and for the widespread emphasis upon the so-called scientific method" (p. 3). Even though they disdained the experimental method, they did acknowledge the prevalence of a belief that "isolated facts and elements may be learned by the process of drill" and that the skills that would be mastered could then "be employed when they are needed in meaningful situations" (p. 5).

The beliefs that Witty and Kopel observed among educators of the 1920s continued to be popular during the 1930s. Endorsing the role of drill learning in his textbook on curriculum, Harap (1934) advised teachers of an "important psychological principle" that required them to introduce "sufficient repetition to assure permanence of learning" (p. 211). A year earlier Bloomfield (1933) had recommended that teachers employ a sequenced outline of skills to assist them during reading instruction. He scolded progressive educators whom he thought had appealed to "a metaphysical doctrine which sets out to connect the graphic symbols directly with 'thoughts'" (p. 500). The metaphysical doctrine to which Bloomfield was referring was the wholeness principle that had been championed by educators such as George Farnham and Francis Parker. Bloomfield also criticized Farnham's and Parker's adversaries because they had advocated the "so-called 'phonic' methods, which confuse learning to read and write with learning to speak" (p. 500). Bloomfield gave an example of a scope and sequence of skills that was based on words grouped according to phonetic patterns. Though he approved of this scope and sequence, he cautioned that "methods of procedure, the order of presentation, and the various minor devices can be determined only by experiment." And even though he endorsed experimentation, he still reminded teachers that "from the outset, however, one must know what one is doing" (p. 501). Bloomfield's firm conviction that teaching methods should be validated through scientific research would remain a hallmark of skills-based instruction during subsequent decades.

At the end of the 1930s systematized reading instruction still prevailed in most schools. In a report to the regents of New York, Gray and Leary (1939) indicated that they had conducted an extensive investigation to "discover the kinds of instruction given in the field of reading" and "to determine the extent to which such instruction represents modern trends in educational thought and practice" (p. 282). After examining 310 classrooms in New York, they judged that the programs in more than 60 percent of these classrooms comprised traditional learning strategies rather than progressive approaches. They did not conceal their annoyance when they editorialized that the methods, even though they were used in the majority of classrooms, "represented a narrow, formal type of instruction which was provided during the reading period two and three decades ago, and which gave major emphasis to mastery of the mechanics of reading rather than to the broader ends which reading may serve in child life" (p. 285).

Proponents of Systematized Reading Instruction—After World War II

Support for skills-based curricula became particularly noticeable during World War II. In a publication of a commission (Wartime Commission of the U.S. Office of Education, 1942) that was concerned with the schooling of young children, the members stated that the "war does not alter the fundamental principles of childhood education" but rather that it "does call for a statement of aims in terms of the present crisis" and that "the Wartime Commission looks to the schools of America to interpret and implement this policy" (p. 198). However, most wartime publications were assertive about the course toward which education should be directed.

For example, the National Education Association published the *Wartime Handbook for Education* (National Educational Association, 1942) in which the authors emphasized the need for schools to comply with its recommendations. The initial item from a list of nine recommendations encouraged teachers to lead students to obey expert authority. The subsequent three recommendations encouraged the teachers to emphasize the fundamentals, instruct students to read, and ensure accuracy in arithmetic.

In a 1943 joint publication of the National Education Association and the American Association of School Administrators (Educational Policies Commission, 1943), the authors wrote that "the teaching profession in the United States understands clearly that the nation is engaged in a desperate struggle for its very survival" and that every teacher, like every other citizen, must go 'all-out' for victory" (p. 1). The members of the commission outlined the responsibilities of the elementary school, the first of which was to "lay a sound foundation of skills and habits of accuracy in reading, spelling, writing, and arithmetic" (p. 4). They recommended that "the major types of skilled work in the armed forces should be subjected to job analysis to insure that all necessary knowledge and skills, and not unnecessary ones, are taught" and that "the curriculum should be developed from the resulting job specifications" (p. 10).

Proponents of Systematized Reading Instruction—After 1950

Duncan (1953) was an outspoken opponent of skills-based instruction who warned that the "use of unsuitable approaches and methods is the greatest single cause of real backwardness" (p. 18). He disdained materials that lacked purpose, that were overly analytical, and that involved "unwise drilling." Even though he thought that "the brightest young children learn to read without any teaching of phonics," he still conceded that "older backward readers, who are not so bright, usually benefit from doing some phonic work if it is introduced at a stage after they have acquired a small reading vocabulary" (p. 38). Despite his negative attitudes toward skills-based approaches, Duncan saw the value of exposing learners to reading materials with a structured plan, recommending that materials be arranged in lists based on graded vocabulary. He wrote that "the decisive factor in the ability of these pupils to read a book is the verbal difficulty of the book" and that therefore "it is important that at initial stages they should not face books which are for them too difficult verbally" (p. 79).

Writing in that same year, Kearney (1953) recapitulated the content of a report that had been supported by the U.S. Office of Education and the National Education Association and which contained a litany of the specific skills that should be part of a scope and sequence of reading skills:

> The child should be able to recognize at once the words that are part of his basic reading sight-vocabulary, and to define many common words that he uses orally, including common abstract terms. He knows how to read the period at the end of sentences (and some children will read quotation marks around direct quotations, question marks, and exclamation marks). He should be building a proper acquaintance with children's literature. He should understand that many words "pair off" as opposites. He should be able to distinguish between the names of persons and things and the action words. Basic to his understanding of communication is his growing recognition that words and sentences are useful only as they have meaning for him. He should be able to name and recognize all the letters of the alphabet in random order and to repeat the alphabet. He should be able to spell from dictation 7 out of 10 unfamiliar one-syllable words if they are completely phonetic. He should be able to spell from 500 to 700 of the most commonly used words. Children should know the common sounds (in words) that go with the letters that represent them. They should recognize simple phonetic clues in spelling and use simple word-analysis techniques as an aid in spelling. They should know the standards for letter formation, spacing and alignment, in manuscript or cursive form (p. 102).

In a classic book published during this same period, Vernon (1957) identified "one fairly universal characteristic of [reading] disability, namely, the child's general state of doubt and confusion as to the relationship between the printed shapes of words, their sound and their meanings" (pp. 186-187). She specified four precise areas of understanding about reading, which, if absent, led to problems:

1. Printed words consist of units, the letters, each of which has a characteristic shape.... Each word has also a characteristic and invariable structure which is determined by the letters in it.
2. The enunciation of words in speech is not merely a simple motor activity; but these words have definite connotational significances which correspond with their sound patterns. Each sound pattern, however, consists of a combination of phonetic units possessing certain permanent residual characteristics.... The same phonetic units can be combined in various ways to constitute different word patterns.
3. When the printed letter units and the spoken phonetic units have been analyzed out from the word wholes in which they are combined, they can be associated together in such a manner that visual perception of the letters calls forth certain speech patterns, and hence the corresponding auditory sensations. But the associations, although invariable and consistent for any particular word, are often arbitrary and unsystematic as between words....
4. When the separate phonetic units have been enunciated, they must be combined or blended together in the correct order to produce the total word sound, and hence to indicate its meaning. But frequently the correct enunciation and blending of the phonetic units can be determined only when the total word sound has been achieved, and this may have to be modified in accordance with the meaning of the word (Vernon, 1957, pp. 187-188).

Vernon compared the disabled reader to a young child beginning to read. Convinced that successful readers understood the principles she had enunciated, she advised teachers in remedial reading programs to help learners develop these insights as well. This advice proceeded from a conviction that "the child with reading disability has broken down at some point, and has failed to learn one or more of the essential processes...[and] remains fixed at a particular point and is unable to proceed further" (p. 189). The solution to this problem consisted of systematic instruction that would lead students through the essential steps of learning to read.

Like Vernon, Bond and Tinker (1957) saw a connection between skills-based instruction and successful remedial reading lessons. They recommended that the workbooks accompanying skills-based reading series be made components of diagnosis and remedial teaching. With regard to diagnosis, they recommended that samples of children's classroom work be maintained in portfolios that were to be indexed to the scope and sequence of skills. Because the learning exercises that were included in workbooks or described in teachers' manuals were synchronized to the scope and sequence of reading skills in the basal reading programs, they concluded that such "exercises are not only excellent for remedial work, but they can also be used as models for exercises that the remedial teacher can develop for correcting specific types of comprehension abilities" (p. 326). Since they espoused a comprehension-based approach to instruction, comprehension skills dominated the initial activities as well as the majority of the other activities that they illustrated. Despite this emphasis, they still included a section on *word-recognition techniques* in which they illustrated root words, prefixes, suffixes, syllabification, compound words, variant endings, contractions, vowels, consonants, blends, digraphs, diphthongs, diacritical markings, pronunciation aids, accents, and use of the dictionary.

Proponents of Systematized Reading Instruction—After 1960

The dominance of skills-based instruction was evident in the changing attitudes of William Gray, whom Mathews (1966) had characterized in his history of reading education as "the greatest of the reading experts of his time." Despite Gray's undisputed prominence as an authority on reading, Mathews recounted how Gray was pressured to modify the whole word-centered approach that he had championed for several decades "on the basis of what he knew was being felt by schoolmen and parents" (p. 149). Mayer (1961) made a similar observation when he noted that "even William S. Gray, in the post-Flesch edition of his Scott-Foresman 'basic readers,' told the second-grade teacher that 'phonetic analysis enables the child at this level to derive the pronunciation of many printed words the first time he encounters them'" (p. 185).

One gains an understanding of the degree to which Gray (1960) modified his whole word approach by examining the terms with which he preceded the initial chapter of his book's 1948 revision. The skills-based modifications of Gray's approach were indicated by the items he selected for this prefatory list of key terms: accent, affix, compound, consonant, consonant blend, derived form, diphthong, ending, homograph, homonym, inflected form, inflectional ending, meaning unit, morpheme, phoneme, phonetic analysis, prefix, primary accent, root word, schwa, secondary accent, stress, structural analysis, suffix, syllable, voice, vowel, and word.

Like Gray, Helen Robinson (1961) was an influential professor from the University of Chicago. Although best known for her elaborate diagnostic procedures, she advised teachers that the types of material that they used for reading instruction should include not only basal readers but workbooks, textbooks, specially designed remedial reading materials, tradebooks, magazines, newspapers, pamphlets, and teacher-constructed resources. To help teachers sift through the wealth of potential materials, Robinson suggested that they assess whether instructional materials were interesting, variable in length, and suited to the purposes for which they had been selected. However, she proposed additional criteria that indicated her commitment to systematized, skills-based instruction when she advised that reading materials be designated at appropriate levels of difficulty, increase progressively in complexity, and promote sequential development of skills.

Also writing in the early 1960s, Carroll (1964) provided a theoretical base for skills-based systems of instruction. He characterized learning as the arrangement of tasks to facilitate progress "from ignorance of some specified fact or concept to knowledge or understanding of it, or of proceeding from incapability of performing some specified act to capability of performing it" (p. 723). Carroll thought reading instruction was simply teaching children "to perform certain acts in response to written or printed language" (p. 723). He assumed a behaviorist perspective from which to predict success in reading as well, assuring instructors that "the learner will succeed in learning a given task to the extent that he spends the amount of time that he *needs* to learn that task" (p. 725). He pointed to three features of the learners themselves that influenced the amount of time that they would need to spend on a task: aptitude, ability, and perseverance. Another two features that influenced the amount of time that students should spend on successful learning pertained to external conditions: adequate opportunity to learn and quality of instruction. The development of a scope and sequence of skills that was responsive to the abilities of learners and the demands of learning tasks became a critical calculation when implementing Carroll's suggestions.

Later Proponents of Systematized Reading Instruction

Testimonials in support of systematized approaches to instruction were especially apparent during the 1970s. Otto, McMenemy, and Smith (1973) outlined a set of basic reading skills that included learning about sight words, phonics, and structural analysis at the first-grade level. These skills were to be reinforced and expanded at progressive grade levels throughout the early elementary school.

Two years later Bloom (1976) published a book that was frequently cited by proponents of systematized instruction. Writing about himself in the third person, he acknowledged that his theory developed "a style of explanation which may not be as widely accepted as the author might desire" (p. 203). Having understated some of the negative responses that his proposals would elicit, he seemed to still anticipate vitriolic reactions when he lectured potential opponents that "the critical test of a causal system in education should be the extent to which it can be used to produce change in the learning of students" (p. 203). He cited examples of such change across a wide sample of research studies in order to establish a "causative" model of education. Maintaining that his system was based on "evidence readily obtainable in most of the classrooms of the world," Bloom had the foresight to qualify this last remark by noting parenthetically that any evidence not readily observed in classrooms could be found "in educational research laboratories" (p. x). He explained that the model he had elaborated was built on a demonstration that "learners' previous characteristics and the quality of instruction determine the outcomes of the learning process" (pp. 202-203).

Writing at the end of the 1970s, Downing (1979) acknowledged an intellectual debt to Vernon. Using her 1957 book as the text in a *Psychology of Reading* class that he was teaching, he established the "cognitive clarity theory" of reading. Similar to Vernon, he thought that "the critical factor in developing reading skill may be the child's clarity of thought in the reasoning and problem-solving tasks involved in learning how to read" (p. 5). This clarity of thought extended from phonic generalizations to the abstract concepts that were the basis for comprehension.

Downing outlined a developmental model in which children initially approached reading in a state of "cognitive confusion" but then progressed to stages of increasing clarity that could be expedited through skills-based instruction. But he emphasized that learning would not transpire unless students "*understand* the communication functions of written or printed language" and "understand the technical concepts we use in talking about speech and writing" (p. 44). Identifying holistic approaches that promoted the former type of understanding and skills-based approaches that fostered the second, he thought that the types of understanding developed in these two disparate instructional approaches could be fostered simultaneously. In eclectic programs where both types of concepts would be nurtured, "every reading and writing activity in the classroom should have a genuine communicative function" and "all instruction in sub-skills such as letter-sound associations should be organized so that it appears to arise quite naturally from the pupil's desire to learn the easiest and most efficient ways of getting meaning from print" (p. 152).

Two years earlier Roswell and Natchez (1977) had attempted to develop a comparably eclectic approach. Observing that in "a developmental program, there are a large number of skills that are presented according to a systematic plan," they contrasted this with an exclusively skills-based program in which "the number of skills are cut to a bare minimum to make it easier for children with reading disability who have already been exposed to them unsuccessfully" (p. 83). Not only did they think a scope and sequence was appropriate for general reading education but they suggested that it be used even in remedial reading, provided that the instruction begin with holistic recognition of common sight words and be followed by phonics instruction, etymological analysis, knowledge of compound words, use of context, and dictionary skills.

SUMMARY

Although they were the most popular approach to reading education for more than two centuries, skills-based programs continually shifted their emphases to distinct patterns of skills and strategies. The convictions that the skills prerequisite to efficient reading could be identified and then arranged hierarchically were two characteristics of these programs that remained constant. The precise skills reinforced within skills-based programs included word recognition and comprehension as well as the use of illustrations, resource materials, and the organizational structure within books. Although not restricted to word recognition, skills-based programs were nonetheless associated with a belief that the systematic and thorough teaching of word recognition skills was an avenue to independent reading. This assumption may have contributed significantly to the enduring popularity of skills-based approaches.

Chapter 7

TEXTBOOKS, ARCHETYPES OF SYSTEMIZATION

Textbooks usually determine the success or failure of any educational method (Horn, 1922b).

Indicted for their inadequacies as well as the proclivity of teachers to rely excessively on them, textbooks were defended with comparable passion by their proponents. Recognizing that the faults attributed to textbooks might originate in those reading programs where students relied uncritically on them, some pragmatic educators attempted to subdue this dispute when they recommended that basal readers be used in an adapted fashion that could compensate for any weaknesses. Although synchronized to precision teaching as well as to textbooks, skills-based programs and the general movement to increase systemization in the schools became distinctively associated with textbooks. The interdependence of textbooks and the movement to expand systematization became particularly evident as educators searched for mathematical readability formulas that could reveal textual patterns on the basis of which to design and select books.

* * *

Although admitting that textbooks were often disparaged, Daniel Boorstin (1981) evaluated them as the "foundation of much of our intellectual life" (p. ix). More pragmatic, Ravitch (1995) pointed out that the textbooks had maintained their critical position in the schools because they were viewed as the primary means for implementing standards in American education. Even authors who did not concede the value of textbooks still admitted their popularity and influence. For example, Apple (1986), an irreconcilable opponent of textbooks, advised that "whether we like it or not, in the United States and an increasing range of other countries, the curriculum in most schools is defined by the standardized, grade-level-specific textbook in reading, mathematics, social studies, science, and so forth" (p. 12). In a similar manner, Woodward, Elliott, and Nagel (1988) observed the influence of textbooks to be so great that "local curriculum development has been largely replaced by the work of authors, publishers, and textbook

203

selection committees" (p. 1). Ciborowski (1992), another opponent of textbooks, also conceded that they "dominate the elementary, middle and secondary curriculum as the major instructional tool" (p. vii).

EARLY CRITICISM OF TEXTBOOKS

Just as early skills-based instruction engendered debate, so did the textbooks that were linked to this instructional approach. Much of the criticism in the late 1800s and early 1900s was aimed at the biases of authors who selectively, casually, or sometimes inaccurately assembled materials. Stuart (1910) wrote about the tendency of authors and publishers to use a "scissors and paste" method to appropriate materials from their competitors in order to quickly create products for the "deluge of text books which floods the educational world every year" (p. 428). Writing a year later about errors in high school biology textbooks, Cockerell (1911) advised his colleagues that "vigilance is the price of accurate text-books" (p. 562).

Almost two decades later Bogardus (1928) warned that "textbooks skillfully written often depict the favorable traits of the given nation and its people without mentioning the worst practices" and that "concomitantly, they may emphasize the less worthy features of other races to the neglect of the best traits" (pp. 245-246). He gave an example in which "the emphasis upon the greatness of the United States and upon 'her glorious past' often gives children exaggerated impressions of their own country and an inadequate background against which to measure other nations" (p. 247).

Although critics had been directing their barbs at textbooks since the middle of the 1800s, they also attacked those teachers who relied excessively on them. The investigators of an 1845 survey concluded that "the text-books are made quite too much [teachers'] guides" (quoted by Caldwell & Courtis, 1925, p. 56). Wyer (1914) chastised educators because "too much school teaching is done with, from, in or by text-books only" (p. 427). Discussing progressive educational practices in the schools of up-state New York during the 1890s, Maddox (1924) wrote admiringly about a curriculum in which the teacher rather than the textbook was the "active agent." As with enduring reproaches about the content of textbooks, these early warnings about the proclivity of teachers for abusing their textbooks would be restated throughout the twentieth century.

Criticism of the teachers who relied on textbooks became particularly noticeable after World War I. Cast (1919) had written that "in most European countries the text-book, if used at all, is merely a more or less unimportant aid to the teacher, and serves primarily as a compendium or compilation of the materials with which the teacher and the pupils must work" (p. 468). Judging that this tradition had been implemented because of the professional training that European teachers had received, he contrasted this practice with the American practice, where the textbook had been used "practically as a substitute for the teacher" (p. 468). Like Cast, Hall-Quest (1920) noted the different degrees to with which teachers in Europe and the United States depended upon textbooks. However, he conjectured that the reason teachers in Great Britain discouraged the use of textbooks was simply that the printed learning materials to which British students had access were "meager or even obsolete" (p. 3).

DEFENSE OF TEXTBOOKS

Just as many educators had rallied in defense of systematic, skills-based approaches to learning when these were attacked, significant numbers came forward to defend textbooks as well. In a book written originally in 1907, Bagley (1916) was convinced that the "text-book, indeed, is the easiest solution of the problem of educating children in the mass" and that the need to help students at different levels of ability in the same classroom had been the most likely condition that had influenced the wide adoption of textbooks. However, Bagley did consider the implicit weaknesses as well as the strengths of textbooks:

> [The textbook] makes possible the systematic assignment of seat work by providing each pupil with the same task. It relieves the teacher very largely of the task of mapping out his own courses, and keeps instruction to a definite line. On the other hand, it introduces a dangerous element in that it makes for lower standards of scholarship in the teaching profession than would be possible if every teacher were responsible for direct instruction. The system is also defective in that the text-book frequently "tells" too much and leaves very little latitude for the discovery of truth by the pupil. On the whole, however, the textbook system possesses virtues which probably counterbalance its defects, providing, of course, that an adequate technique of using text-books is developed (1916, pp. 189-190).

A year later Dutton and Snedden (1908) observed that "much capital and business enterprise go into the making of text-books; many are made by the ablest of teachers; they are large, splendidly illustrated, and usually well executed mechanically" (p. 208). They identified two factors which they thought explained the extensive popularity of textbooks, "widespread prevalence of rural schools, with many classes, where the teacher could give each pupil or each class but little time, and where it was of utmost importance that the pupil, during the time that he was not reciting, should have abundance of well-organized material to study" and "the large proportion of teachers who are immature and lacking in experience and funds of information as well as in control of method apart from the text" (p. 208).

Writing in 1912, Thorndike (1973) opposed the textbook criticism and technology bashing that was being perpetrated by progressive educators. He noted that "a human being should not be wasted in doing what forty sheets of paper or two phonographs can do" and concluded that "the best teacher uses books and appliances as well as his own insight, sympathy, and magnetism" (1973, p. 167). Thorndike differentiated the misuse of textbooks as an issue that was separate from the evils of textbooks:

> Many of the evils attributed to the over-use of textbooks are really due to misunderstanding and misuse of them. In the case of a good text-book there is a reason for every item and for its position in the whole. Too few teachers know the exact purpose of the text-books they use. Too often a teacher uses a section of a book much as a savage might use a coat to cover his legs; or a child uses a saw to cut string, scissors to cut a board, and a padlock as a bracelet (1973, p. 166).

Like Thorndike, Harris (1914) was confident about the value of textbook instruction because "in the hands of a trained teacher the good of the method is obtained and the evil avoided" (p. 317). Acknowledging the expanding dissatisfaction with textbooks, he did suggest strategies to ensure that they were being used appropriately. As a key component of such strategies, he advised teachers to instruct students "to assume a critical attitude towards the statements of the book and to test and verify them, or else disprove them by appeal to other authorities or to actual experiments" (p. 317).

Unlike Harris, some contemporary educators highlighted only the positive features of textbooks. In a report about the "vitality and virility" of textbooks, Winship (1915a) asserted that "if the school books cost as much as teachers' salaries, we should still have them" because "a school is a teacher and text-books" (p. 285). In a separate report printed that same year, Winship (1915b) amplified this chauvinistic rhetoric, maintaining that not only were textbooks essential but that "the American school book is the most perfect [sic] feature of American education" (p. 255). An editorial in a 1915 edition of *The Journal of Education* ("Quality and Cost of Text-books," 1915) began with the strident affirmation that "conspicuous among the things in which the United States holds the undisputed first place among nations are our text-books" (p. 681).

In a pioneering report Hall-Quest (1920) indicated that his goal was to write a simple but comprehensive account that would explain the prominence of the textbook in American education. Characterizing the textbook and the teacher as the two pillars for instruction, he noted that "each without the other is inadequate" (p. 1). He advanced several student-centered explanations for the popularity of textbooks, including opportunities for the textbook to be a type of reference material, a tool facilitating appropriate study habits, and a compendium of applied learning. He also pointed to administrative benefits when textbooks became a path to uniform education, a template for curriculum, an aid to assessing the progress of students, and a mechanism for making appropriate placements within a school system.

A year earlier Maxwell (1919) had written that the well-publicized problems about textbooks were not the result of the books themselves but had "been caused by the pernicious activity of unscrupulous representatives of book companies and petty politicians who represent the people on the school board" (p. 45). Although he noted a growth in the business ethics of publishers during the initial two decades of the twentieth century, he admitted that "the unsavory business methods which were formerly used to influence school authorities to select inferior text-books are still remembered by the public" (p. 45). After acknowledging the general disdain in which book representatives were held, Chancellor (1914) had responded defensively that "there are many bookmen really far abler and far better men than most of the school superintendents in their territory" (p. 163).

An editor with the Macmillan Publishing Company, Brown (1922a, 1922b) was aware of the attacks on textbooks. He thought this criticism was "unfortunate" because "the teacher through a strong personality, broad scholarship, and professional enthusiasm for his work ought to have more influence upon his pupils than any other factor" (1922a, p. 380). He judged that those concerns about textbooks that could be justified were actually the result of abuses that should have been blamed on teachers because "the average teacher follows the textbook more or less blindly, and it is the book rather than the teacher that determines what the pupil will get of fact or inspiration" (1922b, p. 383). Confronting the criticism that publishers might be motivated by "material gain," Brown responded with a romantic characterization of the publisher as "an idealist, a constructive worker in the field of education, ambitious to do his share in putting into the schools of the nation the ideas and ideals which express the nation's best thought now and which should later be wrought into the national life through the influence of schools" (1922b, p. 388).

Though an advocate of textbooks, Butcher (1919) acknowledged the recurring accusations about the extent of textbook dependency by teachers in American schools. Citing a National Education Association report indicating that one half of the 600,000 teachers in the United States had no special preparation for teaching, he concluded that "under such teachers the textbook becomes all-important" and is in effect the "subject-matter and teacher" (p. 501). However, Butcher was so impressed with the quality of textbooks that he was not distressed by teachers' reliance on them. He wrote confidently that "textbook-making in recent years has kept pace with the rapid progress in education in general" (p. 504).

Noting that the "textbook method" was still popular in the 1920s, Curtis (1922) also agreed that textbooks clearly had multiple positive features, and he speculated that these attractive features might even be responsible for encouraging an over-reliance on the books. He highlighted the complexity of resolving this issue because a weak teacher's "path is smoothed somewhat by the use of the textbook method," while a competent teacher received "little or no stimulus toward improving her preparation when she is obliged to read up the day's recitation material in only one book" (pp. 771-772).

Unlike those critics who relied on personalized reminiscences about textbooks or anecdotes from teachers, Robinson (1930) formed his opinions only after he had examined 212 reading textbooks that had been published between 1915 and 1926. Other than an attempt to develop books that would sustain the interest of children, he concluded that the primary concern of the authors and publishers had been "the proper classification [of reading passages] as to age and grade of the children" (p. 68).

A year later Schorling and Edmonson (1931) also attempted to bolster their opinions about textbooks with data. They cited contemporary educators whom they respected because those educators had attempted to validate procedures in which "research and classroom experimentation are presumably superior as a basis for textbook construction, individual opinion, present practice, or even a composite of expert opinion" (p. 55). They noted approvingly that textbook authors conducted research studies and consulted "other textbooks, children's literature, expert opinions, research investigations, and the principles of psychology" (p. 55).

Writing in that same year, Bagley (1931) cited surveys indicating that textbooks dominated classroom instruction in American schools. This dominance was maintained "in spite of the wide and increasing vogue of an educational theory which lays a minimum of emphasis upon the systematic mastery of knowledge" (p. 7). In the introduction to the yearbook in which Bagley's report was published, Edmonson (1931) corroborated a general recognition of "the significant position" of textbooks in American education.

Although testimonials from individual educators and surveys of groups indicated the popularity of textbooks, sales records provided incontrovertible evidence. In his 70-year history of the Ginn textbook publishing company, Lawler (1938) characterized elementary school reading books as "the most important single unit from the point of view of the number of copies issued and the financial return" (p. 187). After documenting reading textbooks that had earned unprecedented profits, Lawler certainly expressed the attitudes of other publishers as well when he pronounced that "the reading program of an educational house is a matter of great moment" (p. 187).

STATE-PUBLISHED TEXTBOOKS

Writing about the era prior to the Civil War, Beale (1941) reported that "the Southern press deplored the dependence of the South upon Northern textbooks and publishers" but that "since the South produced very few good texts, it was necessary not only to banish Northern books but to subsidize Southern authors and publishers to produce others" (pp. 155-156). Beale recounted that reading, speech, and spelling textbooks published in the North were seen as particularly offensive because "the selections in the orations were mostly Northern, often anti-slavery eloquence" (p. 163). He identified many textbooks, including Noah Webster's spellers, that were "denounced as abolitionist propaganda" (p. 163). Noting that multiple resolutions to create state-subsidized textbooks had been passed at conventions throughout the South and that some Southern textbooks were actually published, Beale still concluded that "little resulted, however, except resolutions" (p. 158).

Although state-subsidized publishing did not flourish prior to the Civil War, such efforts were more successful at the beginning of the twentieth century. After observing that "there is no influence in American schools which does more to determine what is taught to pupils than does the text-book," Judd (1918a) wrote approvingly of efforts in California, Kansas, and Canada in which public printing houses had been established as an alternative to materials "published by a commercial concern which is organized for profit" (p. 143). Four years earlier Chancellor (1914) had written that the cities of Chicago and New Orleans were preparing to publish their own series of spelling books.

Not all educators greeted state-supported publishing with enthusiasm. Winship (1915a) did not conceal his emotions toward them when he observed hyperbolically that "there is no greater educational tragedy, no greater wrong perpetrated upon youth, no greater handicap to the next generation, than for a state to permit somebody, or a group of somebodies, to make a school book without a great evolutionary process, and then put it tyrannically upon the teachers, superintendents, and school officers" (p. 286). As early as 1909 an editorial ("The California Text-book Plan," 1909) had criticized California's state-subsidized publishing plan for having been undertaken "for the sole purpose of economy" and concluded that "after more than twenty years of costly experiments, the result has shown no economy, and hence has failed in its prime purpose" (p. 173). This editorial highlighted the style, content, organization, printing, production, and delivery of these "most unsatisfactory" books. Because the most competent authors in the state had already signed profitable contracts with commercial publishers, the persons who were available to write the California textbooks were represented as less than "desirable" writers. The editorial alleged that California's parochial textbooks had not only disrupted education in the schools but also resulted in a major financial loss.

Five years later Evans (1914) advised the citizens of Georgia that they should not emulate California's model for producing textbooks because the American textbook was "the best made book in the world" and was "sold for as small a price as it can be sold for" (p. 8). Evans warned that the development of state-produced textbooks had resulted in problems that were different but no less severe than the problems the schools had suffered when textbooks had been purchased from private companies. He concluded that the primary consequence of state-produced textbooks had been a reduction in quality. In a similarly caustic manner, Hall-Quest (1920) articulated reasons why state publication of textbooks should be discouraged, some of which were based on his conservative philosophy of government, such as his belief that "the state should engage in no business enterprise which can safely be left to private effort" (pp. 63-64). Ten years later Branham (1930) examined the initiatives to publish state-sponsored textbooks in California and Kansas, concluding that both had been financial failures.

EVALUATION OF TEXTBOOKS

A late nineteenth-century edition of the *Atlantic Monthly* contained "candid confessions" from six teachers about politics in the schools. In an introductory note an editor ("Confessions of Public School Teachers," 1896) observed that readers would be surprised at the "matter-of-fact way in which these teachers write about the influence of the publishers of textbooks in the selection and the retention of school officers" (p. 7). One of these anonymous teachers, who wrote that "for obvious reasons names are withheld," reported his frustration at those portions of his job that he "could not directly control." The initial example he provided was textbook selection, for which "the influence of certain publishing houses" was not only greater than that of the teachers and principals but in fact "was always stronger than the recommendations of the superintendent" (p. 99).

Thirteen years later Brown (1909) noted that "in most schools the selection of the text-book is an important part of the work of the teaching staff." He then added that "unfortunately the selection of these books is sometimes made by members of the school board on the basis of ignorant prejudice or personal advantage, the result of the agent's enthusiastic, persuasive efforts" (pp. 165-166). Brown emphasized the importance of selecting books in a professional manner when he pointed out that even though "a superior teacher will do well with any text-book," a teacher having difficulty "will have his efficiency appreciably increased by the use of a good book" (p. 166).

Dutton and Snedden (1908) had cited laws from Pennsylvania and New York which mandated the procedures by which school textbooks would be selected. They examined the regulations in other states as well and concluded that though "compulsory uniformity of textbooks has come to be the rule in all states" that "the areas over which uniformity must prevail, differ widely, as do also the agencies designated to select books" (p. 211). They noted that in the New England states textbooks were usually designated by local school districts, while in the South county boards made the selections. Statewide adoption commissions had been created in many western states, with the exception of California, which had begun to publish its own textbooks. Observing that greater degrees of uniformity had been progressively imposed on the textbook selection process, Dutton and Snedden judged that this movement had been in response to factors such as the difficulty of educating itinerant groups of students and "the acknowledged failure of purely local boards in dealing with the problem of selection" (p. 212).

Though Judd (1918a) had endorsed the state-subsidized publication of textbooks, he conceded that "there seems little probability that public production of books will spread in the United State" (1918a, p. 144). Because he was concerned that teachers were still "showing so little wisdom" in their selection of textbooks, he endorsed checklists that could assist them. He gave an example of six items that had been developed by Mean in 1918 and that were designed to help school personnel evaluate spelling textbooks. This early textbook "score card" was the prototype for those that would follow during the 1920s. The initial two items on it were that "the words listed should be those which investigations have shown pupils will need most in their written work at school" and that "provision should be made for frequent review of words commonly misspelled" (Mean, quoted by Judd, 1918a, p. 149).

Whereas Judd gave an example of a score card for spelling textbooks, Horn (1920b) illustrated a checklist for books intended to promote silent reading. The set of questions in this list considered whether books contained passages with ample factual information, appropriate length, adequate details, problems to guide readers, tests of comprehension, suitable printing, and textual features such as an index, table of contents, or marginal headings.

Three years later Otis (1923) indicated that he had examined textbook score cards for particular academic areas, but neither he nor the students in his college classes could find one that was sufficiently general to be applied to textbooks from diverse academic areas. Therefore, he developed a general textbook score card that contained the features that would later be incorporated into other checklists such as those that Donovan (1924) and Johnson (1925) published. For example, Otis advised teachers to attend to organization, instructional aids, mechanical features, and subject matter. But he also included a section for "local adaptability" with items such as supervision, teaching, children, class, and equipment. The elements in Otis's list contained differential weightings that had been devised by the students in his college classes. In a checklist with a total value of 1,000 points, *selection and balance*, *project method*, and *usableness* had a combined value of 270 points. In contrast, *attractiveness*, *illustrations*, and *print* had a combined value of only 100 points.

Donovan (1924) presented a score card that contained general factors that could be tabulated to evaluate textbooks in any of the academic areas. The factors on his score card included interest, comprehension, method of study, permanent value of the content, mechanical construction of the book, organization of the material, and teaching aids. A year later Johnson (1925) proposed a textbook score card with similar categories: general considerations, subject matter, aids to instruction, and mechanical make-up. Under each of these headings were detailed questions to assist the persons using the textbook score card.

Weber (1926) identified eight prevalent methods for analyzing textbooks. These approaches ranged from those that were extremely casual to highly structured:

1. A cursory, rather superficial personal analysis with reference to a few general rules, admonitions and reminders, or to a list of desirable qualities to be sought in any text-book.
2. A ranking and averaging of personal judgments based on specific qualities to be sought in text-books on some particular subject.
3. Arriving at the score of individual personal judgments by fixing weights or values to certain specific features of text-books.

4. Making a careful impersonal analysis of text-books in order to arrive at comparative data to be used in determining the worth of any book for classroom instruction.
5. Checking a careful impersonal analysis against the clearly practical demands of life as shown by a survey of human activities.
6. Scoring a careful impersonal analysis on the basis of a previously accepted standard of curricular content.
7. Actual class use.
8. Arriving at a summation of ranks based, on the one hand, (1) on expert opinion of the worth of the content of the text-book as shown by a careful impersonal analysis, and, on the other hand, (2) on personal judgments based largely on class use (Weber, 1926, p. 678).

Woellner and Lyman (1930) indicated that many of the techniques for assessing textbooks that had been documented by Weber four years earlier were still being employed in 1930. They spoke favorably about the score card method as well a method that "exposes the books to children at various grade levels and attempts to ascertain the reactions of the children both as to their understanding of the books and as to their enjoyment and appreciation of the books" (p. 192). With regard to this second method, they did admit "considerable skepticism" among other researchers about the "questionable statistical treatment that has been applied to the rough data in determining the ultimate conclusions" (p. 192).

This continuing controversy about procedures for adopting textbooks was an indication of the important role attributed to textbooks. The same year that Woellner and Lyman made their recommendations, Branham (1930) identified only 18 states in which textbooks were still being adopted by district authorities without any types of restriction from state or county boards. He pointed out that "in 25 states the selection of textbooks for elementary public schools is made by the state board of education, or by an especially created textbook commission; in 5 states selection is made by the county board of education, or by an especially created county textbook commission" (p. 60).

ENDURING POPULARITY OF TEXTBOOKS

Despite early predictions about their demise, textbooks preserved their pivotal position in the schools. Although worried that textbooks were reducing teachers' creativity and their sensitivity to community needs, Andree (1948) was one of many critics who still conceded that teachers' reliance on textbooks had actually increased during the years when they were being attacked most aggressively by progressive educators. At a more practical level, he was also concerned about the physical hazards of textbooks for girls who "carry these things for miles on their hips" as well as boys "who sling a green bag over their shoulders and stoop their ways to school" (p. 54). Another spokesperson for progressive education, Zirbes (1949) also admitted that a majority of educators "conceive of curriculum resources and materials as texts" (p. 187).

After observing that "reading is taught with an extremely high degree of competence in current textbooks," Knowlton (1948) concluded that the teachers who had adopted them were providing the highest quality instruction to the greatest number of learners. He predicted that "unless radically new and unpredictable patterns of teaching are devised...further improvements may be expected to be subtle, not radical" (p. 96). This prediction proved accurate, for neither the popularity nor the format of skills-based materials changed appreciably after 1948.

William Gray developed one of the most popular sets of skills-based materials for the Scott Foresman Company. The initial reader in the series was titled *Fun with Dick and Jane* and the entire series was often informally referred to as the *Dick and Jane Readers*. As an indication of the popularity of this series, Chall (1967) estimated that Gray's reading materials and the next most frequently adopted basal reading series, that published by Houghton Mifflin, accounted for 80 percent of the total reading sales during the late 1950s and early 1960s. Although Luke (1991) did not view Gray's reading materials positively, he showed his respect for their influence when he wrote that "a generation of inter- and postwar American and Canadian children was introduced to literacy through the Dick and Jane readers, which have been among the most widely selling textbooks in the twentieth century" (p. 166).

The approach to instruction that motivated Gray was evident in the following passage about word analysis skills. The passage appeared in the 1960 edition of his textbook on reading education. He began this chapter by assuring teachers that he would answer questions about the sequence in which skills should be developed and the reasons why careful sequencing was necessary:

> An effective program in word analysis should be carefully planned to develop in sequence the skills and understanding that enable a child to attack independently unfamiliar printed words that are in his oral vocabulary. Obviously the program should progress from simple to the complex.... The skills and understanding taught at any level should be basic to those that follow and should keep pace with the kinds of words that a child meets in his reading (Gray, 1960, p. 33).

Basal readers and the skills-based programs with which these were associated systematically arranged learning strategies into comprehensive arrays that indicated the skills for which students were accountable as well as the order in which those skills were to be learned.

As an example of the sustained popularity of such textbooks, the Joint Committee of the National Education Association and the American Textbook Institute (1963) reported details of a 1962 survey in which 1,442 elementary and secondary school principals were questioned about the materials and resources they viewed as most helpful. Defying intimidating odds, the principals answered with a unanimous response—textbooks. A report from the National Education Association published that same year (Redding, 1963) also noted the dominance of reading textbooks. Writing two years before the publication of these reports, Herrick, Anderson, and Pierstorff (1961) had compared a 1931 survey of reading practices with one they conducted 30 years later, concluding that "the thirty years which have intervened between these two groups of surveys have not changed appreciably the use of a single reading text as the major basis upon which children in America's elementary schools are taught to read" (p. 183).

One of the reasons for the protracted popularity of reading textbooks was the assurance that they provided to administrators, teachers, and parents that fundamental skills were being systematically taught to students. After examining most of the popular basal reading series, O'Brien (1973) identified common, standardized categories of skills within them. The categories included silent reading, oral reading, comprehension, critical thinking, vocabulary, word recognition, and extension of reading beyond the textbook. She noted that authors of basal reading series during the 1970s had also incorporated linguistic skills into their programs. She recapitulated advantages of skills-based reading programs such as the orderly sequencing of skills, organization of instruction, synchronizing the reading program with grade levels, and the use of materials that reflected a balanced content of fiction, nonfiction, and poetry. She also identified disadvantages that included passages with unnaturally controlled vocabulary, cultural biases, irrelevant content, and insensitivity to the individual needs of learners.

Rather than offer her own opinion about whether teachers should use basal readers, O'Brien (1973) posed a set of eight questions, highlighting the positive and the negative features of the readers, so that teachers themselves could determine the value of specific basal reading series:

1. Is it possible that the basal program offers a foundational support in sequential skill building that may otherwise become a hodgepodge of fragmentary activities?
2. Does the basal program serve to alleviate some of the time pressures in an already overcrowded curriculum?
3. Is it possible that creative teachers can overcome the lack of relevancy to the student's environment by creative discussion and intelligent use of the materials?
4. Is it possible that many of the criticisms of basal readers are inherent in abuses of basal reader programs?
5. Is selectivity the key to the problem; i.e., *which basal program for which group of students, for how long, and under what conditions?*
6. Is it true that some basal programs are totally irrelevant to a particular socio-ethnic group and should not be used?
7. Does the vocabulary control of some readers so stultify the content that it turns off children's interest?
8. Do basal reader programs fail to provide for the wide range of abilities, interests and social backgrounds among a student group? (pp. 141-142).

Acknowledging that skills-based approaches had been criticized, O'Brien advised educators to use their creativity to neutralize the negative features they might discern instead of categorically rejecting the approaches.

Writing 11 years later, Kirst (1984) referred to two national surveys when he calculated that teachers used textbooks for more than 70 percent of their instructional activities and that this percentage escalated to more than 90 percent when all commercially developed instructional materials were considered. That same year Beck (1984) differentiated the current style of textbooks from those that had been popular during previous decades, noting that "the kind of vocabulary control found in the older basals is not in evidence in current programs." She added that "newer basals are virtual anthologies" and that "authors of the selections are professional writers using the best words available from the general vocabulary to communicate their ideas" (p. 9). Convinced that even basal readers with weaknesses were critically important to teachers, she recommended that the faults of basal readers be reduced by refining the instructional strategies synchronized to them. She and her colleagues (Beck, McCaslin, & McKeown, 1981) concluded that the indisputably widespread adoptions of basal readers by teachers actually constituted a validation of the value of those materials.

Schuster (1985) defended textbooks against charges that they contained inadequate content. Employing recollections from his career as a textbook author, he contrasted older editions of textbooks with more recent editions in order to dispute the allegations that textbooks had been "dumbed down." He also disputed a 1984 resolution from the National Council of Teachers of English that had equated the adaptation of materials in literary anthologies with censorship. Presenting examples of reputable writings that would not have been included within unedited school textbooks, he argued that failure to edit controversial selections, because it would have resulted in the *de facto* suppression of those pieces, resulted in greater censorship than the decision to make adaptations.

Although he did not address the subtle points made by Schuster, Gagnon (1987) indicated that even censored textbooks could be rationalized because they directed both teachers and students to relevant information. Although he conceded that "what is not printed is assumed to be not worth knowing," he recognized that the textbook "is taken as the final authority on most matters, if only because teachers lack the time and resources to offer alternative materials and counterarguments" (p. 33).

Based on observations comparable to those made by Gagnon, Wesbury (1990) asserted that "in all modern systems the textbook has long served not only to support instruction but also to symbolize that instruction—in other words, the textbook defines the curriculum" (p. 2). Viewing the textbook industry as a "faithful reflection" of the schools, Westbury depicted publishers as "totally intertwined with both the structures and the cultures of the school systems" (p. 18). Writing during that same year, Woodward and Elliott (1990b) represented a generally held opinion when they characterized textbooks as "virtual national curricula in the basic subjects" (p. 146). They noted that "many present-day teachers would be hard pressed to maintain basic instructional programs in the basic subject areas without elaborate multigrade textbook programs" (1990a, p. 223).

Five years later Ravitch (1995) agreed that textbooks had been important not only in shaping instruction but also in helping to secure educational standards. After drawing connections between educational practices and the standards embodied in high school graduation requirements, standardized tests, common curricular prerequisites, and mandatory teacher licensing, she noted a similar connection between educational practices and textbooks.

ENDURING CRITICISM OF TEXTBOOKS

During the early part of the twentieth century many critics had fiercely criticized textbooks and predicted that they would become less popular. After it became clear that their popularity was not waning during the second half of the century, this criticism of textbooks became even more strident. Though declining scores on college entrance exams had been attributed to the watered-down content in textbooks during the 1970s, Chall and Conard (1991) observed that this somewhat focused criticism expanded during the 1980s when "all attributes of textbooks have come under attack" (p. 5). In addition to continuing concern about the lack of adequate difficulty in the content of books, other features such as social content, curricular format, literary style, and the textbook adoption process itself were editorialized and widely discussed.

Five years after Chall and Conard had made these remarks, Apple (1996) rephrased the critical argument about textbooks' inadequate content when he argued that even those publishers who had not been directly pressured by conservative political groups to adapt textbooks had engaged in "self-censorship" in order to raise the probability of lucrative adoptions in well-populated states. Apple cited legislation that directed schools in Texas to purchase books that emphasized conservative values as an example of a situation that might persuade publishers to censor their own materials to bolster profits.

DelFattore (1992) had also discussed the influence of state sales markets as well as legislation on the types of materials that publishers produced. However, she was less parochial than Apple when she admitted the influence of liberal as well as conservative pressure groups. She concluded that "it would be misleading to suggest that all textbook activism—conservative or liberal—is censorship, since decisions about what to teach and what not to teach are a necessary part of every educational system" (p. 6).

During the initial half of the 1900s many critics had spoken out against textbooks not only because they disapproved of their content but also because of their seductive lure as a substitute for more creative forms of teaching. This criticism continued throughout the entire twentieth century. For example, Shanon (1989) warned teachers that any progress they had observed while employing skills-based materials had been achieved at the expense of their own creativity.

From a similar perspective, De Castell and Luke (1989) warned that "what occurs in many modern classrooms is a mechanistic reduction of literacy into a hierarchy of constituent skills" (p. 85). They judged it "profoundly unsatisfactory" that "both teachers and students are thus 'deskilled' and 'reskilled' by [curricular] technology, as previously acquired knowledge and competence are replaced by externally defined, transmitted and tested skills" (p. 85). De Castell and Luke argued that political rather than pedagogical factors were responsible for the popularity of skills-based reading textbooks, which were an attempt to divert public attention from the "structural deficiency inherent in the public system itself" (p. 79).

The Commission on Reading of the National Council of Teachers of English (1989) published "A Call for Action" in response to the common use of basal readers. The commission's members thought that basal readers could restrict the creativity of teachers because the "series are often viewed as complete systems for teaching reading." They also disapproved of the textbooks' sequenced skills, which they thought had been developed "not because this is how children learn to read but simply because of the logistics of developing a series of lessons that can be taught sequentially" (p. 896).

Although the content of textbooks and the dangers posed to instructional creativity of teachers who relied excessively on them remained issues throughout the twentieth century, many of the most enduring allegations were directed at publishers who were portrayed as consumed by greed and unconcerned about students' best interest. The revenue from textbook sales had been estimated at only 12 to 15 million dollars a year prior to the First World War (Chancellor, 1913; "Quality and the Cost of Text-books," 1915). As an indication of what a modest amount this was, annual sales from chewing gum reached 25 million dollars during this same period ("Quality and the Cost of Text-books," 1915). Williamson (1981), who was president of a major textbook publishing company, figured that annual textbook sales had climbed to 700 million dollars by 1981. And sales increased to over a billion dollars a year by the late 1980s (Britton, 1986; Chall & Conard, 1991; Davis, 1985). Squire and Morgan (1990) estimated that the total amount spent by public and private schools on textbooks and all published instructional materials was two billion dollars in 1987 alone. As the amount of money at stake in school textbook sales escalated, suspicions by the public about potential conflicts of interest by publishers increased correspondingly.

Such misgivings were not new. For example, Rugg (1926) had warned that "publication of the materials of the school curriculum is founded upon profit" and that "the business of publishing textbooks has become one of first commercial magnitude" (p. 31). Though he was a zealous proponent of progressive education, Rugg was still reassured that "under the leadership of a few large publishing houses, the quality, workmanship, and content of our school books have put the American textbook in the world lead" (p. 31). He concluded loyally that "in my comments, therefore, there is no suggestion that curricular materials should be made available to schools except through the agency of established commercial houses" (1926, p. 32).

Though less reconciliatory than Rugg, later textbook critics employed arguments that were otherwise similar. For example, Doyle (1984) wrote bitterly that inexorable "market forces" had pressured publishers to reduce the quality of textbooks in the hope that bland textbooks would have a greater likelihood of adoption. After calling attention to national reports demanding an emphasis on phonics and precise comprehension skills, Venezky (1987) was similarly cynical when he predicted that reading textbook publishers would "probably" relabel their existing inventories rather than develop new materials.

SUPPLEMENTARY MATERIALS

Although their primary feature may have been their sequenced organization, skills-based reading textbooks were traditionally assembled into packages that included supplementary materials. In a chapter on the history of reading, Briggs and Coffman (1911) reported about reading series from the 1820s that were coordinated with spelling books. Klapper (1926) described the "auxiliary equipment" that accompanied reading series from a century later. With reference to the popular *Story Hour Readers*, he identified "elaborate materials" for "tracing, cutting, and mounting pictures" as well as "freehand drawing, imaginary drawing, matching words on small cards with forms on the blackboard" and "perception cards, objects, pictures, outline forms of animals and people, [and] charts" (pp. 99-100).

Six years later Washburne (1932) listed materials with which teachers could develop elementary reading skills, admitting that "it sounds as though the method described involves a good deal of paraphernalia" (p. 74). But he indicated that this should not discourage teachers because "every good primary teacher" employed "many charts, devices, and games, either furnished with her books or made by herself" (p. 74). He expressed his doubt "whether the materials used in the technique described here are as elaborate as the combined homemade and bought materials used by most primary teachers" (p. 74).

Because skills were taught precisely and comprehensively, and because supplementary aids were integrated into instruction, Knowlton (1948) judged that skills-based programs required teachers to develop less instructional sophistication than language-based programs. Observing that the goal of skills-based programs was to escalate the performance of teachers rather than compromise their independence and creativity, he questioned the relative effectiveness of materials created by teachers when these were compared to the published materials that had been devised by experts with "vast expenditures" of labor and money. To defend the workbooks that accompanied basal readers, Knowlton differentiated their "use versus abuse." Like other proponents of skills-based programs, he admitted that such workbooks were abused when teachers relied upon them excessively. He also acknowledged the difficulty of appeasing special interest groups within reading education which demanded that skills-based materials incorporate the specific procedures that they espoused. He lamented that the inclusion of such additional information had caused "the rapid approach to the teacher-saturation point in teachers' manuals" (p. 96).

Lazar (1952) gave multiple examples of the materials that were available to support remedial reading programs in junior high schools. In addition to reading textbooks, workbooks, and tests, she included word cards, games, charts, materials based on children's experiences, supplementary books, specialized workbooks connected to specific skills, reference books, newspapers, periodicals, and content-area books. Believing that a varied inventory of materials would simultaneously reinforce "the development of the basic skills" and "extensive independent reading," she advised that "teacher-made materials should be used to supplement published materials" (p. 115).

Herrick, Anderson, and Pierstorff (1961) assumed a more restricted focus when they identified the "commonly considered" supplementary materials as readers specially designed to enrich materials in a specific basal reader series, readers designed to supplement any basal reading program, and collections of stories. But they also identified music, prose, poetry, and trade books as common supplementary materials.

ADAPTATION OF SKILLS-BASED MATERIALS

A 1935 research bulletin of the National Education Association illustrated the degree to which teachers were adapting skills-based materials. The bulletin contained a report about a survey that had been administered to over 1,500 elementary school teachers. The teachers were asked whether they used the materials in their textbooks in the order in which selections were arranged by the publisher or whether they adapted the organization of the materials to meet students' needs. Less than 50 percent of first-grade teachers and only 25 percent of second-grade teachers followed the publishers' sequence within the materials. Less than 25 percent of the teachers in grades three through six followed the organization within their reading textbooks.

At the end of the 1940s Cottrell (1948) described procedures for using skills-based materials in a manner that addressed the concerns of those critics who had deplored the use of a common textbook:

> The child's needs for reading are taken care of in a basic program that provides for an orderly, systematic development of skills and abilities. At the heart of such a program is the manual, through which the philosophy underlying the series is interpreted to the teacher. The manual contains daily lesson plans and suggestions for follow-up work. Methods for adapting the materials to individual needs and for combining basic and experience approach are included. There are correlated activities to extend and enrich reading experiences. While the teacher follows the manual, she goes beyond it as her group, her resources, her enthusiasm, and her purpose demand. She adjusts the materials to the abilities, needs, maturity, and rate of learning of the groups (p. 105).

Like Cottrell, Gates (1947) had emphasized that the adaptation of skills-based materials was a critical step in effective instruction. In fact, he concluded that the chief problems associated with reading disability resulted "from failures to identify all possible handicaps and to arrange instruction in such a way that they are directly or indirectly surmounted" (p. 15). He identified four goals for remedial reading teachers, advising them to study the reading process, learn about diagnosis, become familiar with instructional methods, and "know how to adapt the materials and methods of instruction to meet precisely the individual needs, the strengths and weaknesses, of each child" (p. 15).

Focusing on young readers rather than students in remedial reading programs, Anderson and Dearborn (1952) emphasized that basal reading materials should be used in an adapted fashion "because first-grade children vary widely in their readiness for reading" (p. 269). If children in the same classroom inquired about their variable learning schedules and different materials, Anderson and Dearborn counseled teachers to reassure them that they "already know that some of their classmates are taller and heavier than others, and that some have lost their first teeth while others have not" and therefore "the slow starter should be told that it is the same with reading" (p. 271). As an illustration of the adaptation of basal reading materials for "slow learners," they suggested that teachers use "big book" activities with groups in which the mature readers would learn advanced literacy skills while less mature learners developed global concepts about print. Anderson and Dearborn (1952) also suggested the adapted use of basal reading materials to stimulate language-based instruction:

> A few of the children may still not be ready for the simplest kind of word recognition, but they feel discriminated against because everyone else has a book, while they do not have one yet. These children can make up their own stories about the characters in the preprimer, preferably using the names the book has given the children and animals in the story. The teacher covers the print with a blank piece of paper. She discusses the characters in the story with the children, who then make up their own stories, which the teacher writes down for them (p. 271).

Anderson and Dearborn reviewed a survey in which "successful" teachers of early reading were asked to specify the "units" with which they introduced pupils to reading. The survey revealed the popularity of supplement basal reading instruction with language-based activities. They reported that roughly 95 percent of the teachers introduced reading with sentences and short paragraphs and that only "a few" began instruction with phrases and "still fewer" with isolated words. Though they admitted the popularity of the "experience-reading approach," they did not unqualifiedly endorse it because "experience stories obviously cannot match the controlled vocabularies of basal reader materials as a means of teaching word recognition" (pp. 265-266).

Like Anderson and Dearborn, Cronbach (1955) recommended that teachers use skills-based materials in an adapted fashion. Although he acknowledged that the preorganization of skills could actually dissuade teachers from attempting adaptations, he responded that "many leading texts have loosened their sequence of ideas sufficiently to allow such freedom" (p. 204). Also convinced that the effective use of textbooks involved teacher discretion, Spalding (1955) recommended that individual teachers be educated about the factors that contributed to useful textbooks and that they subsequently use these factors to designate the actual textbooks that they would use in their classrooms. Convinced that this information should be incorporated into teacher preparation programs, Spalding advocated that "college courses in teaching methods should teach the best current thought about the selection and use of texts" (p. 186).

While citing criticisms of educational textbooks, McMurray and Cronbach (1955) reported allegations that texts presented oversimplified subject matter, disassociated the content of their passages from the personal problems of students, discouraged critical thinking, and failed to help learners develop the skills they required to select the textual materials needed for solving problems. But they concluded that "each of the criticisms, no matter what its origin, points toward modifications of the text and its use, not to its abolition" (p. 27). They noted that "only the program originally espoused by Dewey, in which learning was to rise from the daily experience of the child, is incompatible with major reliance on the preorganized textbook" (p. 27).

McMurray and Cronbach's criticism of Dewey should have been directed to some of Dewey's extremist supporters rather than to Dewey himself. For it is true that Dewey (1938) had spoken out against traditional teachers who depended on textbooks to the exclusion of experience-based activities, even chastising those who viewed textbooks as "the chief representatives of the lore and wisdom of the past" (p. 3). But Dewey also warned proponents of progressive education that "there is always the danger in a new movement that in rejecting the aims and methods of that which it would supplant, it may develop the principles negatively rather than positively and constructively" (p. 6). Speaking even more assertively to overly zealous progressive educators, Dewey pointed out that "an educational philosophy which professes to be based on the idea of freedom may become as dogmatic as ever as the traditional education which is reacted against" (p. 10). Addressing the "organized subject-matter" that was represented in textbooks, he posed several questions to progressive educators two of which were "Is there anything inherent in experience which tends towards progressive organization of its contents?" and "What results follow when the materials of experience are not progressively organized?" (p. 7). Having posed these questions, Dewey restated his warning that "a philosophy which proceeds on the basis of rejection, of sheer opposition, will neglect these questions" (p. 7).

Scott (1964) was a British educator who recommended that teachers use skills-based programs in an adapted fashion. He had developed remedial, skills-based materials by following "principles akin to those which in America later came to be known as programmed learning" (p. 7). He wrote that he was "forced" to admit a connection between his own ideas about learning and the

American model of mechanistic learning. His approach to reading education contained several adaptive features that were associated with holistic programs, which may have explained his initial reluctance to admit a connection to a behaviorist model of learning. One of the adaptive features was an encouragement to learners to take risks while experimenting with reading. He wrote that "we did not aim at protecting [students] from error" because "errors—provided they can be corrected as made—have learning value" (p. 8). Other adaptive traits of reading instruction that Scott advocated and that later became part of whole language instruction included peer teaching, heterogeneous grouping, and peer correction (to which he referred as *mutual correction*). Scott maintained that "mutual correction" was the "distinctive characteristic" of his technique and suggested that the approach be called "group programmed learning."

Though Scott was an ardent advocate of phonics, he was concerned that children would encounter words that did not conform to the phonetic principles that they were learning. In order to ensure that these encounters would not upset "the child's maturing phonic knowledge," Scott acknowledged that basal readers with limited, controlled vocabulary could be effective antidotes. But since he questioned the practicality of creating suitable materials with strictly controlled vocabulary, he instead endorsed an approach that "introduced the basic phonic facts and inculcates the habits for their use independently of actual reading materials in the first place" (p. 47).

Scott thought his approach was a novel alternative based on valid psychological assumptions. He contrasted it with the holistic approaches that had become "standard infant practice" in the British schools and which he thought were based on a faulty understanding of perceptual psychology. For even though persons normally viewed things as wholes, he pointed out that "unless we (unconsciously for the most part) take account of the distinguishing features we cannot perform the act of matching up or recognition" (pp. 96-97). He also disapproved of holistic approaches because they required learners to remember unlimited and separate mnemonic templates, a mental effort that he thought was greater than that required to make generalizations from a finite set of phonic principles.

ANALYZING SKILLS-BASED MATERIALS

Because they developed skills in an orderly progression, it was inevitable that skills-based instructors would investigate whether reading materials could not be devised in a parallel fashion. After the sequencing of materials was determined to be practicable, publishers' success in achieving this goal was viewed increasingly as one of the primary factors with which to evaluate books for adoption in school districts. Summarizing the factors from the 1920s that were the basis for textbook adoption decisions, Patty and Painter (1931) listed the academic credentials of the authors, accuracy of content, illustrations, writing style, interest, printing, format, cost, and psychological suitability for certain grades. However, they also identified skills such as the organization of materials, degree of emphasis placed on selective topics, and the selection of vocabulary. Although Patty and Painter had called attention to vocabulary, it was only one of many items that they thought should be used to determine the suitability of books.

Writing the same year as Patty and Painter, Brown (1931) focused exclusively on the differences in the vocabulary used in history textbooks and in reading textbooks, concluding that social studies textbooks had been assigned to grades for which the vocabulary in them was too difficult. He advised that the books be rewritten, designated for higher grades, or supplemented with vocabulary drills to help learners understand the inappropriate vocabulary. Three years later Dale and Tyler (1934) were also concerned about matching reading materials with learners when they noted that "this situation can be improved through the development of methods by which the easier reading materials can be identified and which would serve to guide writers in preparing materials" (p. 384).

Writing a year later Lewerenz (1935) identified the best factors with which to judge the suitability of textbooks as cost, authorship, method of presentation, organization, illustrations, indexing, format, and vocabulary. Lewerenz advised that though these multiple factors were appropriate for assessing the suitability of materials, information about vocabulary should always be included. However, he warned that information about vocabulary should be incorporated into decision making without an "undue emphasis" and advised teachers to specifically examine the vocabulary's difficulty, diversity, and potential interest during their evaluations of books.

In contrast to their colleagues who were searching for quantitative measures of textbook readability, Bryson (1937) recommended that instructors examine the "internal logical construction of the writing, the kind of logical clarity which is the product of logical thought" (p. 401). He also thought educators should look at "lucidity" which "often depends more on [the reader] than on the writer's essential logical structure" and the "appeal" of a passage's content to the reader.

During the late 1930s and 1940s several educators discussed the objectives guiding the search for readability. For example, Washburne and Morphett (1938) were concerned that "children cannot be expected to learn from books which are so written that the mechanical difficulty of reading occupies the center of the children's attention." They published data about "readability" that would make it "possible for writers and publishers to check the difficulty of their manuscripts" and "for schools to evaluate the difficulty of books" (p. 364). Dale and Chall (1949) had concluded that the initial interest in readability of texts had developed from a need to select materials for adult literacy programs. However, Lorge (1948) observed that the readability movement had "originated in the desire to grade textbooks and other materials for use in the elementary grades" (p. 404). Referring to the work of scholars such as Dale and Tyler, Lorge noted that "subsequently, the research activities were extended not only to demonstrate the lack of adequate reading materials for adults, but also to suggest how more adequate materials might be prepared" (p. 404).

Early Readability Analyses—1920s

One of the most influential efforts at establishing readability was a series of research studies by Thorndike (1921) in which he sampled the frequency with which 10,000 words had occurred in 41 texts. The materials from which the samples were taken included "about 625,000 words from literature for children; about 3,000,000 words from the Bible and English classics; about 300,000 words from elementary-school text books; about 50,000 words from books about cooking, sewing, farming, the trades, and the like; about 90,000 words from the daily newspapers; and about 500,000 words from correspondence" (p. iii).

Teachers could consult Thorndike's list to scientifically confirm their intuitions about the importance of words that they intended to use in their lessons. Thorndike noted that "the conscientious and thoughtful teacher now spends much time and thought in deciding what pedagogical treatment to use" and suggested instead that his book could "help the teacher decide quickly which treatment is appropriate by telling her just how important any word is" (p. iv). After teachers had organized the words in the books that they intended to use with students, the high-frequency words that were present could subsequently be reinforced when they recurred in other materials.

Having used Thorndike's 1921 word list to estimate the "vocabulary burden" of textbooks, Lively and Pressey (1923) described Thorndike's materials. They wrote that "each word is followed by an index number indicative of its commonness" and they gave the example that "a common word as 'and' has an index number of 210; a relatively uncommon word like 'atom' has an index number of 4; still more rare words such as 'neolithic' do not appear in the word book at all" (p. 390).

The approach that Thorndike had proposed was limited because it required teachers to ignore the contexts in which words occurred. In addition, his list was extremely cumbersome. Lively and Pressey (1923) described the elaborate procedures they used after extracting 1,000 word samples from books and then looking up the values of those words on Thorndike's list. (A value of zero was assigned to words that were not listed.) Lively and Pressey then computed the median value of the words in the sample, concluding that "the higher the median index number the easier the vocabulary" (p. 391). For each passage they reviewed, they also reported the range of vocabulary and the total occurrences of words not listed on Thorndike's list. Though this procedure was awkward, Lively and Pressey's computation of readability scores on the basis of the difficulty of vocabulary was the harbinger of other readability formulas that would follow during the 1920s and the ensuing decades. As for Thorndike's word list itself, it remained popular enough that Thorndike (1932) expanded it to 20,000 words and still later to 30,000 words (Thorndike & Lorge, 1944).

Uhl (1924) recommended that "standards" be employed to organize or select materials for reading instruction. Examples of standards included "the grading of the material," "provisions of the vocabulary needs of pupils," and "the physical make-up of the book or books under consideration" (p. 357). To illustrate this procedure he made a detailed outline of the reading program objectives for a school district in New York, identifying silent reading skills (comprehension and rate) and oral reading skills (fluency, vocabulary development, phonetic analysis, pronunciation, and enunciation). Aware of the complexity of the procedure he was recommending, Uhl advised educators to both judge the degree to which each of his standards was being met and assign books to grades by simply examining the vocabulary within them.

Other educators with the identical insight would search for readability formulas that did not contain all of the factors responsible for the complexity of materials but which isolated a correlate of complex material. For example, Keboch (1927) acknowledged that "there are other factors than word difficulty which must be considered in determining the difficulty of reading material" while at the same time admitting that his study was concerned with only a single element "word difficulty."

In contrast to those educators who were searching for a single correlate, Vogel and Washburne (1928) were intent on devising a multivariate formula that would be an "objective method of determining grade placement of children's reading material" (p. 373). Surveying learners and teachers to discover the factors contributing to the difficulty of texts, they not only examined vocabulary but syntactic information, such as the number of prepositions, verbs, and adverbial clauses that were contained in passages. They also considered the frequency with which simple sentences occurred and the length of paragraphs.

The final set of four factors that they determined to be most useful were the frequency with which different words occurred, the number of prepositions, the frequency of occurrence for words not included on Thorndike's list, and the number of simple sentences that appeared within passages. They were sure that "by making a count of these elements, any teacher can determine the grade placement of any book" (p. 377). However, the 15 steps for examining and tabulating these four features of a text were complex and time consuming. As an example, the penultimate stage in the procedure was the calculation of regression equation with four predictor variables. Even with this calculation, Vogel and Washburne were still not satisfied that the procedure they had developed was sufficiently accurate. For they cautioned readers that their report, which had been limited to an analysis of the structure within passages, would be followed by "a similar study dealing with content."

Readability Analyses—1930s

Johnson (1930) recommended that the difficulty of reading materials be estimated by the frequency with which polysyllabic words occurred in passages. Writing in that same year, Dolch (1930) highlighted the limitations of such simple readability formulas. Worried about the expedient techniques for sampling the vocabulary to be used within readability formulas, he warned that the samples were often flawed because "the words in some books are repeated much more than in others" (p. 214). He judged this to be a problem because repetition of troublesome words, though sometimes an indication of difficult-to-read passages, could also be a feature designed to simplify texts. McClusky (1934) also criticized readability formulas that relied on vocabulary, pointing out that the correlation between vocabulary and the difficulty of materials was not the result of cause and effect. He therefore examined the "number of ideas" in different types of material to determine if this would be better than vocabulary for predicting difficulty. Contrary to the intuitions of many educators, he found the number of ideas to be a poor predictor of difficulty and concluded that simpler reading materials were "characterized by the short simple sentence structure and easy familiar vocabulary; while the difficult materials is characterized by a technical, unfamiliar vocabulary and a complex sentence structure" (p. 282).

Dale and Tyler (1934) concluded that most readability studies had sampled only a limited set from the factors responsible for effective reading. Additional factors that could have been included were "the reader's interest in the topic treated in the reading matter, his ability to read, the kind of comprehension appropriate to the purposes of the reading matter, and the difficulty of the ideas developed in the reading matter" (p. 384). They explained that comprehension could be defined in three ways—emotional reaction, ability to recall details, or ability to form general conclusions. After choosing the third definition, they isolated 25 variables to predict whether learners would exhibit this type of comprehension. They eventually concluded that the three variables with the greatest predictability were "the *number of different words in the selection*, the *number of different hard non-technical words*, and the *number of indeterminate clauses*" (p. 401). Though Dale and Tyler's analysis was more extensive than most of the studies that had preceded it, their research seemed casual when compared to the exhaustive efforts of Gray and Leary (1935). Gray and Leary noted that two general categories of factors influenced readability. The first category comprised those factors pertaining to the readers themselves. Though acknowledging the importance of these elements, they restricted their investigation to the second category, which contained the characteristics of reading materials. Even after setting this limitation, they still proposed 289 readability factors, which they subsumed beneath four general headings: format, organization, style, and content. Arranged under these four organizational headings were another 24 categories into which the 289 primary factors were sorted. Aware that a 289-factor formula would be unwieldy, they performed exhaustive statistical analysis to determine if a single variable could be isolated that correlated with the difficulty of materials. But even though the simplicity of a single-factor formula was tantalizing, they recommended that the most reliable estimates of readability should use several predictors:

> For instance, counting the number of different words in a selection gives a fairly good measure of its difficulty. Counting other elements—prepositional phrases, simple sentences, and personal pronouns—gives a much better indication of difficulty...[but] the best estimate of the difficulty of a selection involves the use of eight elements: number of different hard words, number of easy words, percentage of monosyllables, number of personal pronouns, average sentence-length in words, percentage of different words, number of prepositional phrases, and percentage of simple sentences (Gray & Leary, 1935, p. 16).

Despite their extensive analyses, Gray and Leary still conceded pragmatically that, in the final analysis, "the basic consideration in determining readability of a particular book is whether a particular reader finds that book easy and pleasant to read" (p. 38).

While reviewing the studies on readability that had been conducted during the 1930s, Lorge (1948) noted the simplicity of the research paradigm in which the "readability of the text is assigned the average reading ability score" for a "sample of persons whose reading ability is known" (p. 404). He also acknowledged that "in assigning the average reading ability score as an estimate of the readability of a text, one must assume, of course, that the variations in people's interests and purposes in reading are balanced" (p. 404). A decade earlier Lorge (1939) had reviewed the studies of readability that had followed that of Lively and Pressey in 1923. He noted that vocabulary, though it had been measured with diverse techniques, continued to be a correlate of readability in every research study and was "the most important concomitant of difficulty" (p. 229).

Later Readability Analyses

In 1939 Lorge had maintained that every study of readability had included some measure of vocabulary. In 1948 he made the identical observation. However, he did add that the more recent studies had included syntactic measures as well as vocabulary. Examples of syntactic measures included average sentence length, number of prepositional phrases, frequency of simple sentences, or frequency of dependent clauses. Lorge also noted that readability had been assessed on the basis of human interest, calculated by measures such as the frequency of personal pronouns, words expressing human interest, colorful words, or words expressing life experiences. Similar to Lorge, Hildreth (1949) noted that the range of readability factors was expanding and gave examples such as the number of ideas that passages contained, vocabulary, sentence structure, writing style, illustrations, the familiarity of ideas, typography, and editorial format.

When readability measures were based on correlates of difficulty rather than all the features of reading that might be responsible for that difficulty, they were criticized by some educators as lacking *face validity*, a term used to distinguish the degree to which measures resembled the traits they were designed to assess. After he had developed a readability measure that would be calculated through vocabulary (as estimated by the average number of syllables in words) and syntax (estimated by the average number of words within sentences), Flesch (1951) dismissed a question about face validity by noting that this concept was not applicable to his formula because all his formula did was "predict the *probable* readability (ease and interest for reading) for an *average* reader" (p. 37). He was confident that his readability formula did not require face validity since it was only intended to predict simple or difficult passages and not to explain the basis for those predictions.

Despite Flesch's distinction, the criticism persisted that vocabulary-centered readability formulas lacked face validity. Because of this dissatisfaction, it was inevitable that an alternative procedure for computing readability would be advanced. Taylor (1953) thought he had discovered such a measure with the *cloze* procedure, which he viewed as a "new psychological tool for measuring the effectiveness of communication" (p. 415). After remarking that the term *cloze* was "pronounced like the verb 'close' and is derived from 'closure,'" he expressed his gratification after he learned that the results of his procedure correlated positively with the Flesch formula, which was one of the two most popular formulas in the early 1950s. As an indication of the Flesch formula's popularity, Kingston and Weaver (1967) reported in the late 1960s that the Flesch formula was at that time still one of the three most commonly used formulas.

Taylor defined the cloze procedure as "any successful attempt to reproduce accurately a part deleted from a 'message' (any language product) by deciding from the context that remains, what the missing part should be" (p. 416). Although the procedure correlated with the Flesch Formula, Taylor emphasized that "the cloze method is not a formula at all" because it "takes a measure of the likeness between the patterns a writer has used and the patterns the reader is anticipating while he is reading" (pp. 416-417). However, just as vocabulary-correlated readability formulas were criticized for a lack of face validity, Kingston and Weaver (1967) eventually argued that students' performance on cloze tests was a correlate of passage redundancy and not truly a demonstration of reading comprehension.

Practical Readability Formulas

Since their incipience, readability formulas had been questioned not only for their validity but also for their practicality. Spache (1953a) noted that most of the interest in readability could be traced to the relatively simple formulas proposed by Flesch, Dale, and Chall. However, he advanced a more complex formula that he thought would still be adopted because it was purportedly more accurate:

Multiply the average sentence length in a sample of 100 words by .141. Then multiply the per cent of words outside the Dale "Easy Word List" of 769 words by .086. To these two figures, add a constant, .839. The sum represents the estimated reading difficulty of the book (Spache, 1953a, p. 412).

This formula was qualified with seven footnotes. Despite his personal predictions, Spache's readability formula never became as popular as the less complex procedures. Five years later Chall (1958) detected a consensus among experts that the factors contributing to readability included content, format, organization, and style. But she thought that only the stylistic elements had been "amenable to reliable quantitative measurement and verification" (p. 156). Furthermore, she discerned only four stylistic elements that were significant predictors of reading difficulty—"vocabulary load, sentence structure, idea density, and human interest" (p. 157). Despite the opportunity to use additional factors, she concluded that vocabulary was the most effective correlate on which to base readability.

A decade later Fang (1967) was quite aware that simplicity could influence whether a formula became popular when he noted wittily that "the trouble with most readability formulas is that they are as long-winded and difficult to understand as the worst sentences they measure" (p. 63). Attempting to ensure that persons would evaluate his own procedure as simple, he called it the "easy listening formula." Singer (1975) made observations similar to Fang's when he indicated that readability formulas had developed in two diametrically opposed directions. Whereas many of the formulas devised in the 1940s and 1950s had increased the complexity of making estimates as part of a search for face validity, the more recent formulas, such as that developed by Fry, had tended toward simplicity.

Fry (1968) had realized that formulas needed to be simple before they would be valued when he remarked that "perhaps the sheer time it takes to apply these formulas causes them mostly to languish in term papers and occasional magazine articles" (p. 513). Fry proposed a readability graph that could be depicted and explained on two pages of text. He contrasted this graph with the Dale-Chall formula, which he estimated required 18 printed pages of directions. In addition to the formula proposed by Fry, Singer identified the procedure of McLaughlin (1969) as an example of a simplified formula. In fact, McLaughlin thought his own formula was decisively simpler than that of Fry. Observing that Fry had titled the article about his formula "A Readability Formula that Saves Time," McLaughlin advised readers to use his procedure instead of Fry's because it would save even more time.

After educators resolved that they should not search for the causes of difficulty but instead identify those features of a text that could predict reading difficulty, the importance of vocabulary and simplified measures of grammatical complexity were apparent. But this expedient decision led to continued misunderstandings by critics, who thought that the vocabulary and simplified measures of grammar loaded into the formulas had been inappropriately adduced as the causes of difficult-to-read text.

SUMMARY

By the beginning of the twentieth century textbooks had become associated with systematized, skills-based instruction. This connection was especially evident when researchers sympathetic to the skills-based model attempted to devise formulas to assist them in creating and selecting materials that were suitable for the learners in different grades. Pointing to author biases, textbook errors, and formats for textbooks that restricted teacher creativity, early twentieth-century critics railed against these materials.

In response to the sustained criticism, skills-based educators retorted that many of the alleged faults were actually abuses that resulted only in the cases of teachers who used the materials in a nonadapted fashion. The inconsistent quality of textbooks was one of the few issues about which advocates of textbooks agreed with their opponents. As a result, both proponents and opponents attempted to devise procedures with which to differentiate high-quality from marginal materials. Predictably, the methods to which they were attracted were based on distinct philosophical paradigms.

Although some early twentieth-century educators had endorsed government-produced textbooks to reduce costs and eliminate the conflict of interest inherent in commercial publishing, the profits of commercial textbook publishers were never threatened. Because the majority of educators and the public continued to view privately published textbooks as the primary means for assuring that essential skills were being reinforced in the schools, basal readers and the supplementary materials synchronized to them were purchased continually and extensively.

Chapter 8

LANGUAGE-BASED APPROACHES

A reader does not think the thought of an author, he simply thinks his own thought (Francis Parker, 1891 [1937]).

Early twentieth-century, language-based approaches were supported by progressive educators who wished to build education on the experiences and functional language of children. At distinct periods of the century these language-based activities exhibited different degrees of compatibility with skills-based programs. For example, language-based activities were regularly supplemented with skills-based exercises during the 1960s. However, this interdependence decreased as language experience evolved into the more philosophical and political whole language programs. Unwilling to supplement language-based programs with learning activities from alternative reading programs, some educators developed remedial whole language procedures to help those readers who were failing within whole language programs.

*   *   *

Writing in the late 1890s Todd and Powell (1899) had recommended that initial reading instruction be centered about the oral language that children had already developed:

The vocabulary which the child has acquired during the years preceding his school life, and the vocabulary which may be acquired in a course of systematic talking lessons, must be the verbal material of his early reading lessons. These words were his ready instrument, which he uses when he desires to make others understand him. They are the symbols of things which he knows and loves and with which he plays; symbols of his desires; symbols of his emotions and of his will. The words which he learns before using a book and those learned in connection with the first book should form a community, a symmetrical vocabulary in which the different parts of speech are found in proportion to their use in ordinary speech. This vocabulary should consist of the words and idioms which he uses or may be trained to use in the study of plants, animals, minerals, rain, snow, frost and wind; in conversation about children's toys and other objects; in descriptions of familiar objects and simple pictures; in narrations suggested by pictures; in comparing and in contrasting simple objects; in reproducing myth, fable and folk-lore, and stories of child life (p. 47).

In a chapter about using blackboard transcriptions of oral language as the materials for introductory reading lessons, Todd and Powell summarized the spirit of the approach by advising that "as he has learned to talk, so he should learn to read" (p. 48). They recommended that educators initiate reading instruction with personally relevant and detailed information and then progress to the abstract, academic information that was beyond the experience of learners. Their assumptions about the educational benefits of proceeding from direct experiences to more abstract types of information became a truism for proponents of language-based instruction throughout the next century.

LANGUAGE-BASED ACTIVITIES FROM THE 1920s THROUGH THE 1950s

Though language-based activities had been used during the nineteenth and early twentieth centuries in American schools, their popularity increased during the 1920s when they were considered a key component of progressive instruction. Gans (1941) described the popularity of activities from the 1920s that were very much like the language experience exercises that flourished 40 years later. In an educational yearbook that focused on learning materials, Whipple (1920) noted that "primary teachers have long recognized the necessity of supplementing the reading material of the printed primers by exercises made up directly from the experiences of the pupils" (p. 20). In the foreword to Watkins' 1921 book on initial reading instruction, Horn (1922a) endorsed language-based exercises because they "add greatly to the interest of the children in first grade work, since they are based on facts and experiences common to the child" (p. 7). Watkins (1922) herself described a simple, language-based method of instruction in several sentences:

> A name-card containing the word to be taught is prepared. The child is told what the word in question is. The card is then withdrawn and replaced with other cards, and the child is told to watch for it when it reappears. Cards are shown one by one, and when this particular word reappears, the children will indicate their recognition of it in a prescribed manner (by actions of various kinds) (p. 20).

Watkins estimated that the variations on this exercise were "infinite" and she described lessons organized about functional topics such as "come to class," "children's names," "personal history," " salutation," "morning duties," "things in the room," and "street signs."

Six years later Harris, Donovan, and Alexander (1927) gave examples of creative activities that were precisely like the language-experience lessons that would become popular during the 1950s and 1960s:

Kodak pictures were taken of children engaged in different activities. Copies of the pictures and printed slips containing explanatory phrases were given to the children. They then matched slips and pictures. A key or guide set was accessible when needed. The children understood that as soon as they were able to match all the printed slips with the correct pictures they might paste the pictures and slips on sheets, tie them together, and take the completed booklet home to read to their parents (pp. 246-247).

In the foreword to Watkins's book on introductory reading education, Horn (1922a) had counseled that the method developed by Watkins was not intended to supplant phonics. Despite such assurances, language-based instruction had begun a movement away from structured learning. This movement would be repeatedly reversed and then reestablished during the following decades. Not only was a cyclical pattern discernible in the United States as well as in England (Gordon & Lawton, 1978), but Goodson and Marsh (1996) described a predictable pattern of instruction in Australia where "developmental or child-centered orientations occurred in cyclical fashion, as revealed by peaks in the 1890s, 1920s, 1930s and 1960s" (p. 36). This movement away from structure was apparent to Rugg and Shumaker (1928) when they established "articles of faith" that were to guide advocates of "the child-centered school." In a section of their book titled "Freedom vs. Control," they spoke confidently about "the new freedom" that had resulted in decreasing systemization. In fact they stipulated that "freedom to develop naturally, to be spontaneous, unaffected, and unselfconscious, is, therefore, the first article of faith" (p. 56).

During the 1920s Mearns published several influential books illustrating lessons to develop the verbal creativity of children. In the most popular of these books, *Creative Power* (1958), he exhorted teachers and parents to be aware that only a portion of children's abilities could be measured by their successful mastery of academic skills. He argued for a charismatic style of teaching that required an instructor with "ability to transform others by the contagion of his own peculiar creative powers" and concluded that good teaching was not systematic implementation of an organized curriculum but instead was "uncovering and enlarging native gifts of insight, feeling, and thinking" (p. 267). Referring to the "great ferment in education" during the 1920s, Hildreth (1965) corroborated Mearns's views about a drive to make fundamental changes in the schools. Having been a teacher during this era, she characterized the period as one in which "learning through purposeful activity, learning through direct experience were the slogans of the day" (p. 281). She identified 10 criteria that distinguished the experiential approaches to reading that were employed during the 1920s:

- Children's experiences were prioritized over academic learning.
- Reading was integrated with speaking, listening, writing and the other language arts.
- Basal readers and commercial materials were delayed until children had made progress with experiential materials.
- Vocabulary was not controlled.

- Experiential approaches were not viewed as pre-reading activities but as the most appropriate type of instruction for learning to read.
- The instruction was informal and spontaneous.
- Manuscript styles of lettering were used to prepare experience materials.
- Instruction was supplemented by the extensive use of trade books.
- Initial instruction involved comprehensive reinforcement of word recognition, comprehension, and pictorial illustration skills.
- The link between reading and writing was reinforced. (Hildreth, 1965, p. 281-282).

Numerous accounts during this period documented the implementation of experimental programs similar to those described by Hildreth. DeLima (1942) included an appendix to her 1926 book in which she identified 41 "experimental and progressive schools." But she acknowledged that even this list was not accurate because some of the more recently developed progressive schools had been omitted. DeLima's observations were validated in Storm and Smith's 1930 textbook on reading in the primary grades. For they included an entire chapter that was focused on the "psychological reasons why an effort should be made to provide children with purposeful reading experiences, and to suggest some practical measures to use toward achieving this goal " (p. 54). In the introduction William Gray emphasized that Storm and Smith's book was based on current research and that it comprised "a practical discussion of valid principles and progressive practices in teaching reading" (p. vii). Meriam (1930) wrote about a holistic program in reading that had been implemented between 1912 and 1916 and another that had been implemented between 1917 and 1921. These programs were based on the two philosophical principles that "the best way to teach reading is not to teach reading, but to provide the occasion...in which certain reading functions" and to "let pupils read to learn" so that "incidentally they will learn to read" (p. 414). Other corollary assumptions were that "people enjoy reading about their own activities" and "initial steps in reading are most effective when they relate to behaviors most active" (p. 415). Writing four years later Mossman (1934) described a district in North Carolina where "activity programs" had been used for 10 years. That same year Woody (1934) apologized to his readers that the number of "activity schools" founded in the previous 30 years was so large that he could not develop an account of all of them.

Language-Based Instruction—After the 1930s

Although activity curricula can be documented for the initial 30 years of the twentieth century, the meanings of the terms *activity curriculum* and *activity program* were not always clear. An Office of Education-sponsored bulletin titled *The Activity Program and the Teaching of Reading* (California Curriculum Commission, 1931) defined a procedure in which "the reading of any word involves its interpretation in terms of previous experiences, and the interpretation is clear in proportion to the reality of these experiences." The members of the commission explained that "this is the simple reason why children must see, touch, taste, smell, and otherwise experience the characteristics of many things before words can mean anything to them" (p. 1). However, this bulletin also included advice about employing techniques that many proponents of the activity approach would have viewed as incompatible, such as remedial reading strategies and the supplementary use of primers. Gray and Ayer (1934) pointed to the confusion entailed by the term when they wrote that "at one extreme are those who use the term 'activity curriculum' broadly and loosely" and that "to them it is synonymous with 'progressive education' and with the 'child-centered school.'" However, they added that "at the other extreme are those who use the term in a restricted sense" and that "to them it connotes such equivalents as units of work based on interest, interactions with environment, problems to solve, projects, and physical or mental activities, or both" (pp. 167-168).

The rhetoric in support of activity curricula and the holistic, language-based reading programs that were associated with them was apparent during the 1930s as well the 1920s. Betts (1936) reported that "of recent date much discussion has taken place regarding the value of experience type reading" (p. 27). Citing advice from teachers about the desirable format for this type of lesson, he recommended that stories should be based on class interests or experiences, short one-line simple sentences should be employed, vocabulary should be emphasized by teachers so as to prepare children for the vocabulary of pre-primers, and that writing in large letters should be done on blackboards or oversized chart-papers.

Two years earlier Martens (1934) had written about the "abundant literature on the subject of the activity program" and even spoke in favor of extending the holistic, activity curriculum to special education because "the basic principles of curriculum construction for the mentally retarded child are not different from those which should characterize its development for average or even gifted children" (pp. 1-2). At the end of the 1930s Zirbes (1940) listed characteristics of a "modern program" in reading that could be an alternative to "outworn ways." The holistic, language-based program that she described used varied reading materials and was sensitive to children's total language development, their purposes for reading, functional situations, and individual personalities. Additionally, the "modern program" emphasized learning to read by actual reading rather than by the acquisition of prerequisite skills.

Language-Based Instruction—After the 1940s

Referring to three historical approaches to reading, Lamoreaux and Lee (1943) correctly identified the alphabetical approach as a method that was used "long ago" and that was followed by the phonic and the whole word approaches. Without giving dates, they identified the fourth stage in this pedagogical progression:

A radical departure came when children read word groups or phrases, and even sentences, before they knew all the individual words in them. The present discussion of beginning reading takes one more step and begins with the background experiences and ideas of the child. The child expresses these experiences and ideas for the teacher to write down. He then reads them back, first as a whole and then in sentences, phrases, and finally in words (p. v).

During the same period in which Lamoreaux and Lee were writing, British scholars also documented the emergence of language-based programs. In her classic study of children who had been taught with language-based and skills-based approaches in Great Britain, Gardner (1942) referred to language-based instruction that had been based on "the principle of educating young children through their spontaneous activity or play" (p. 7). Remarking that language-based approaches were not new, she cited proponents and sympathetic intellectual allies from Plato through twentieth-century British educators. She substantiated the popularity of language-based approaches in England during the early 1930s by quoting a comment from a 1933 report which stated that "the play way [to instruction] is the best way" (Educational Report, 1933, quoted by Gardner, 1942, p. 8). Although she questioned the actual prevalence of the "play way," she did acknowledge that "I have myself witnessed, in the last twenty years, a steady growth in the acceptance by Infant School teachers of [holistic learning] principles which, whilst not indeed new, were far from widely applied in the Elementary Schools of twenty or even ten years ago" (pp. 6-7).

Also writing in Great Britain during the 1940s, Schonell (1945) published an influential textbook on the psychology of reading in which he identified three major approaches to reading instruction—phonics, whole word, and language-based. Using the term *sentence method* to refer to language-based instruction, he wrote in the 1961 edition of his book that the sentence method was "the complete opposite" of skills-based instruction. During the period between the publications of the 1945 and the later editions of his book, Schonell (1961) maintained a conviction that reading instruction should begin with sentences and then "much later" progress to the study of phonics. He wrote that "what the child does and says, what he has himself seen and experienced through play, projects and stories, is so vitalized for him that when he meets these ideas embodied in the printed words he has an excellent chance of understanding what they mean" (p. 95). Since he viewed analytical word recognition strategies as compatible with holistic learning, he recommended eclectic approaches to instruction because of "the particular contribution that different approaches to the teaching of reading can make for particular groups of children" (p. 92). Schonell noted that, in the 1940s, most British instructors who were employing experiential methods of instruction recommended that the methods employ "an organized, preparatory reading period involving all kinds of discussions and verbal activities and usually including group studies or centres of interest in which some of the common words occur" (p. 94).

At the end of the decade Hildreth (1949) reported that "reading, in the experience curriculum continues to be an integral phase of life in the school" (p. 97). She compiled a list of 10 improvements in reading materials that had, in turn, "contributed appreciably to the improvement of primary reading instruction." First on this list was "the use of manuscript-written context derived from the pupils' current experiences for introductory reading lessons" (p. 56). Several years earlier Betts (1946) had identified the three major categories of reading practices as basal reading programs, approaches based on the experience method, and approaches that integrated strategies from skills-based programs with experiential methods. The fact that Betts singled out language-based programs as one of three major categories of instruction is an indication of the popularity of this approach during the 1940s.

Language-Based Instruction—After the 1950s

Relying heavily on Betts's 1946 book, Wrightstone (1951) wrote an unusually insightful review of the literature related to language-based and skills-based approaches. Detailing the benefits of language-based instruction, he noted that abstract words were associated with the learners' experiences, students' interests were enhanced, opportunities were presented for teachers to informally assess readiness, reading was built on learners' oral language strengths, reading was represented as one of several linguistic avenues to communication, opportunities for using large print were made available, and opportunities for social learning were increased.

In addition to identifying strengths, Wrightstone summarized the limitations of language-based approaches. For example, language-based approaches could foster memorization instead of reading, the vocabulary that students exhibited could be insufficient for generating the most appropriate learning materials, and the quality of the self-generated prose the students read could be inferior to other materials that were available. Additionally, language-based approaches could lead to poor attitudes, encourage an over-dependence on context clues, restrict opportunities for creative reading, be unsuitable for the needs of some learners, make unrealistic demands on the teacher, and over-emphasize oral reading. With refreshing pragmatism, Wrightstone critiqued skills-based reading programs in a similarly dispassionate manner, not only differentiating their weaknesses but also distinguishing these from other types of problems that were the result of misuse. He concluded by observing that "both methods of instruction contribute to the development of basic understandings and skills in reading" and advised teachers to "make use of the advantages in both methods" (p. 7).

Writing in the same issue of the journal in which the article by Wrightstone had appeared, Zirbes (1952) attempted to be similarly pragmatic when she warned her readers that "any attempt to discuss the two approaches controversially, emphasizing the pros and cons of each and setting them off against each other sharply as disparate, would do more harm than good" (p. 1). However, no sooner had she given this warning than she proceeded to ignore it while writing two of the longest sentences in the educational literature:

Whereas pre primers pride themselves on the high frequency of a limited number of words that are also in the primer of the same series, the experience approach prides itself on its direct relation to the child's speaking vocabulary and on its use of his own experiences and his own statements and phrase patterns to initiate and foster reading for meaning from the very start. Whereas the procedures advocated in connection with most pre primers emphasize the acquisition of a visual vocabulary as a major objective and select it in terms of the vocabulary demands of the next book in the series, the experience approach recognizes the ways in which language usage provides for the functional natural repetition of certain very common useful words in varying contexts, while the experience itself contributes the associations that bring the content words to mind as contextual cues lead up to them (p. 2).

PROGRESSIVE EDUCATION AND LANGUAGE-BASED INSTRUCTION

In her history of the kindergarten, Vandewalker (1908) linked progressive educational changes in the elementary school curriculum to the influence of the kindergartens that were being developed in the United States. Such controversial allegations about the origin of progressive education continued throughout the twentieth century. Indicating that this origin was difficult to determine because of disagreements about fundamental issues such as the duration and extent of the progressive movement, Graham (1967) searched for pedagogical roots among scholars such as Plato, Rousseau, Froebel, and Pestalozzi. In contrast, Cohen (1964) and Cremin (1969) searched for the precedents of twentieth-century progressive education in the social and political events of the 1800s. The years that circumscribed the progressive era in the history of the United Sates are more readily defined than the years that were the boundaries for the progressive educational movement. Though Gould (1974) identified the "Progressive Era" as the years between the end of the depression of the 1890s and the end of World War I, the years of the progressive education era did not coincide with this political era. Highlighting the founding of the Progressive Education Association in 1919 as the pivotal event in the twentieth-century era of progressive education, Cremin viewed that era as spanning the years from 1917 through 1957.

Identifying a conceptual element critical to the progressive education movement, Dewey had remarked in 1897 that "the only true education comes through the stimulation of the child's powers by the demands of the social situations in which he finds himself" (Dewey, quoted by Archambault, 1974, p. 427). Student power in the formation of curriculum was exemplified by the project method, which became the most widely recognized indicator of a progressive classroom. Defining the project method as a problematic act carried to completion in its natural setting, Stevenson (1921) gave a detailed example of a socially arranged instructional project in reading:

When some pupils in a grade school asked their teacher if they might give an entertainment just before Thanksgiving, they were told that if they would write their own play and present it their request would be granted.... By the time the play was completed, the class had decided on the members who should impersonate the different characters. A little girl, a favorite with the class, was chosen for Priscilla; several Mexican boys wished to be the Indians; John Alden was impersonated by a tall slender boy. Then came the choosing of the costumes, which led to some more reading and to the study of pictures. Visits to the forestry supervisor were made to cut down some small pine trees for the stage. Thanksgiving songs were studied in the music period; the play was memorized in the language study period and practiced in the reading period. A few days before Thanksgiving, written invitations were sent out by the pupils to the children of an upper grade asking them to be present at the entertainment. This project cut across the subjects of reading, language, and construction work. The motive to carry out this project arose with the members of the class. It was carried to completion in its natural setting. The play was originated and was given for reasons not essentially different from those which would have prompted the giving of a similar play outside the school (pp. 200-202).

Although instructional techniques like these were distinguishable as progressive educational activities, progressive educators attempted to precisely define their approach even more thoroughly through a clear set of principles. A decade after Stevenson had provided the preceding illustration of the project method, a 1931 issue of *Progressive Education* apprised teachers about the principles that supported progressive education. The first of these principles was that teachers should be guides. As guides, they were to help the learner in "observing, experimenting and forming judgments that he may learn how to use various sources of information including life activities as well as books, and how to reason about the information thus acquired, and how to express logically and effectively the conclusion reached" (Brown & Finn, 1988, p. 41). Also attempting to define the philosophy that should guide progressive schools, Collins (1933) listed a key principle as "boys and girls learn, develop, grow in and through the pursuit of their own activities" (p. 309).

McKee (1934) wrote a textbook in which he indicated that reading was a fundamental skill needed "for the improvement of the present social order" (p. 578). He dismissed skills-based approaches, which he labeled *mechanical methods*, and advocated language-based approaches, which he called *thought methods*. McKee's book contained no chapter on word identification skills and its only concession to skills-based instruction was a section in which he supported the "work type" of oral reading:

The right sort of oral reading should be taught because it has values in its own right. In the first place, a study of the reading situations of life and the results of actual survey show that people do read orally at times, and that, although the frequency of its occurrences is not great, it is often crucial. Obviously, this means that oral reading must be taught in order to prepare children to engage successfully in the oral-reading activity of life. It must, however, be the kind of oral reading that people actually need. There is no room for the artificial sort of thing (pp. 566-567).

LANGUAGE EXPERIENCE APPROACHES

Although he preferred the popular terms "current-experience method" and "integrated activity program" to depict language-based instruction, Stone (1935) credited Nila Banton Smith (1934) with designating the phrase *experience method*. Stone described the theory buttressing this method as one in which "learning to read takes place largely in a natural, incidental way as reading is needed in relation to project activities which furnish enjoyable and profitable experiences and pleasant and interesting associations" (p. 105). In his 1936 textbook on elementary reading, Stone referred to this approach by still another term, the "natural experience method."

Forty years later Allen (1976) alleged that the first use of the term *language experience* to identify language-based instruction had been in his 1958 research report. In actuality, the practices connoted by this term preceded Allen's report by more than a century, and even the term *language experience* preceded Allen's project by several decades. For example, Lamoreaux and Lee (1943) referred to a 1940 book by Lee and Lee because "the chapter dealing with language experiences is particularly pertinent" (p. 198). In that 1940 book Lee and Lee used the terms *language experience* to describe an integrated language arts curriculum that was focused on communication and in which the learning was reinforced though social activities. They distinguished this approach from programs that did not adequately plan for language growth, warning that "one fallacy in the practices of many 'activity teachers' has been to substitute haphazard and fortuitous contacts for a planned sequence of development" (p. 344). They continued to use the term *language experience* in this fashion through subsequent editions of their book.

Stauffer (1970) indicated that he had begun to use the language experience approach as a clinical intervention as early as 1950. He explained that he judged *language experience* to be the optimal term with which to describe the approach because most children "have oral-language facility sufficient to provide the foundation for reading instruction" and because "they have had enough experience to provide the meaning, or concept, base for reading-instruction purposes" (p. 2). Ashton-Warner (1963) was another influential educator who supported language-experience but who referred to it as *organic reading*. Citing examples of the application of language-based reading principles throughout the nineteenth century, she concluded that the organic approach to reading was not new, but rather "it's our rejection of it that's new" (p. 31). Using the expressions *key vocabulary* and *first words* to describe words that "had an intense meaning" and that were "part of the dynamic life" for learners, she counseled that key vocabulary provided an especially rich opportunity to begin reading instruction.

By the 1970s language-based approaches had generally become known as *language experience*. Although Hall (1972) chose the term "whole experience," she defined it in a fashion that complemented the use of terminology such as *the sentence method* and *the story method* during the nineteenth century, *the language experience approach* at the time she was writing, and *the whole language approach* that would emerge during the subsequent decade:

> The "whole-experience" approach to reading denotes a method of teaching reading in which, during the early phases, reading materials are developed by recording children's spoken language. The content of pupil-created reading materials represents the experiences and language patterns of the reader. Listening, speaking, reading, and writing are integrated in language arts and reading instruction (p. 6).

By the time that the 1976 edition of her book appeared, the connection between language-based instruction, to which she then referred as language experience, and the emerging whole language approaches had become explicit:

> *The language experience approach is a personal way of learning and teaching.* Language experience reading starts with and values the reader—his thoughts, his experiences, his language, his products, his uniqueness. The language experience rationale and the application of the approach can be appropriate for many, but in each case the person makes the language experience materials unique. Language experience reading is free and unstandardized. The learner in the language experience approach is actively involved in the reading process as he creates and shares his reading. In the language experience approach it is possible to have material of high personal interest to each child. Group writing experiences are encouraged, but since the content of group stories will be related to common experiences and group interests, these materials will also be personal to the group (Hall, 1976, p. 4).

More philosophical and less focused on pedagogy, this 1976 definition already contained the political features with which language-based instruction would continue to become invested. As an example of this ideological continuity, Hall included the identical description of language experience in the 1981 edition of her book, but followed it with a section about whole language, concluding that these characteristics had been "implied in the preceding definition" (p. 3).

Goddard (1974) was a British educator who tried to maintain "the point of view of a practical teacher" because she was aware that "references to the history of educational ideas are often found tedious by teachers who are concerned with the pressing and practical matters of day-to-day life in the classroom" (p. 3). Despite this practical orientation, she was convinced that an understanding of current educational issues assumed familiarity with the ideas of pioneering educators such as Rousseau, Froebel, and Dewey. All of these educators had emphasized unique attributes of the developing child, the value of play in learning, and the advantages of natural, holistic formats for learning. She cited research reports from the early 1930s in which educators had viewed reading and writing as extensions of oral speech, views that became essential components of language experience approaches. Goddard also cited Schonell's 1945 textbook on the psychology of reading and the research of Piaget during the 1940s to prove that readiness, another concept essential to language experience, had preceded its popularization as part of language experience.

Another essential component of language experience was the "approach through wholes" which Goddard paraphrased as the development of literacy through "active and usually first-hand experience" and in which the teacher "places emphasis on meaning" (p. 17). She reassured her readers that "the approach through wholes is not of very recent origin" and added parenthetically that "it was to be found in infant schools in England in the 1930s" (p. 17). Having separated herself from colleagues who were drawn to the language experience approach because it was novel, Goddard confirmed that she herself was indeed "an exponent of the language experience way of learning to read" (p. 38). However, she attributed her commitment to an intellectual search during which she had taken inventory of her own practical experiences as well as representative research about child development, concluding that "language-experience approaches to literacy are, in general, compatible with modern understanding of child development" (p. 35). As an indication of her pragmatism, she acknowledged that the temperaments and attitudes of instructors should be taken into account before language experience approaches were implemented because teachers with complementary attitudes would be more successful than teachers with contrary attitudes.

Link Between Language Experience and Skills-Based Instruction

DeLima (1942) described a language experience program that had been implemented at a laboratory school in New York City during the 1920s and 1930s. This approach integrated expressive language with the reinforcement of precise skills:

> We make the approach to reading as natural as possible. A child may take a picture of a boat or a train and he or the teacher may say, "It is a big long train." The picture then may be hung on the wall and under it the teacher may write on a strip of paper level with the children's eyes, "This is a big boat." The teacher reads the words aloud. The children read them too. Next, the other picture may be put up with a strip which says, "This is a big long train." The teacher reads this also, and so do the children. Then the teacher asks the children if they can pick out the parts on the two strips of writing which are alike. Sheets of paper bearing these same words may be distributed and the children asked to match them to the charts on the walls and to read them after they have matched them. Besides matching words or sentences, we may match words and pictures, sentences and pictures, or we may complete a sentence by choosing one word from a group of words phonetically related. Or again we may find works which have the same beginning or the same endings; we might find small words in larger ones (pp. 137-138).

Writing at the end of the 1930s, Lee and Lee (1940) endorsed language experience as well as teachers' reliance on diagnosis, corrective reading, and remedial reading. They supported the continued use of word-analysis skills, remarking specifically that "some children seem to need almost no help from [phonics], whereas others find it a great aid" (p. 342). They also distinguished themselves from some of the more zealous advocates of progressive education when they recommended distinct stages for instruction with differing emphasis on skills:

Learning to read and reading to learn must of a necessity overlap. They are in a large part coexistent. *As soon as the child starts to read, he does it to find out something.* In a sense that is reading to learn. At the other extreme a person should always be improving his efficiency in these techniques, his appreciations, and his interests. That is really learning to read. However, a great deal of the emphasis is on the learning to read in the early years, and as a certain degree of facility is acquired, the emphasis shifts to reading to learn (p. 347).

Thirty years later Roach Van Allen (1969) also emphasized the advantages of language experience. He adjured teachers to avoid ineffective classroom practices such as the use of basal readers, a predetermined scope of skills, and workbooks. Disapproving of teacher-selected materials, he advocated that students themselves decide which materials would be used. He spoke out against self-contained classrooms and encouraged teachers to creatively group students into clusters to facilitate their learning. Despite such progressive adjurations, Allen was still convinced that the language experience approach involved skills that should be sequenced to enhance learning. He wrote candidly that "in an individualized skill development program such as is required of a language experience approach, children must get to know how to use the reading skill materials" (1976, p. 438). He listed phonetics, structural analysis, and associational analysis as types of word recognition skills that complemented language experience. As examples of associational analysis he identified the use of verbal context clues, alphabetical order, and the ability to predict while reading silently.

Writing at the beginning of the 1970s, Stauffer (1970) was convinced that word recognition skills could and should complement language experience activities. He agreed with many proponents of language-based activities that "children learn to read much as they learned to talk." But he made a distinction that had instructional implications when he observed that "learning to read differs from learning to talk, though, in that it is planned and directed and aimed at acquiring skills that are to be used deliberately and purposely to acquire knowledge" (p. 157).

As a result of this conviction, he recommended that "as soon as children have advanced a certain distance in learning to read, they need to be taught how their new skills can be used, refined, and extended for high utility" (p. 157). He advised instructors that reading skills should never be learned out of context nor assigned a higher priority than reading for meaning. But he went on to assure his readers about the critical relationship of word recognition skills and the language experience approach when he affirmed that "skills must be taught from the beginning of reading instruction and be maintained throughout" and gave the example that "at no time should the teaching of word-attack skills, including dictionary usage, be ignored" (1970, p. 177).

Stauffer judged that phonics skills were useful to beginning readers, especially when they could be generalized to the words in children's functional vocabularies. Grouping words to be learned into phonetic groups (e.g., *hill, bill, pill,* and *will*) to illustrate traditional phonics activities that could support language experience, he wrote that "the old game of building word families is just as captivating and beneficial today as it was a century and more ago" (p. 188).

Although Stauffer recommended that skills-based activities be sequenced, he referred to this as the "spreading of skills activities." Admitting that the "spreading skill activities could imply a discreteness that does not exist in actual language use," he still supported it because the simultaneous learning of multiple strategies was not practical. Less adversarial than some of his contemporaries who were also endorsing language-based activities, he viewed children's active involvement in learning rather than their avoidance of structured skills as the critical determinant of successful reading.

Dixon (1976) published a report about teaching reading to Mexican-American children in which she identified the language experience approach as the solution to many of the practical problems associated with bilingual learning. She applauded the approach because it built on the language and experiences of the students and represented a middle ground between two disputing groups of educators. Dixon thought that if skills were taught systematically with words that had been extracted from communicative language experience charts, "the language experience approach may be viewed as a way of combining the strengths of these two apparently antagonistic positions" (p. 144).

Writing about minority learners several years before Dixon, O'Brien (1973) chose the term "language-different" instead of the then frequently used term "culturally deprived" because "many students labeled as culturally deprived may simply have experiences in homes and neighborhoods which do not transmit the cultural pattern necessary for the types of learning characteristic of the school" (p. 9). Like Dixon, O'Brien had judged that language experience activities could be integrated with basic word recognition skills. In fact, she used italics to emphasize this relationship when she defined language experience as "a highly personal, individualized approach that can serve as a bridge between the child's out-of-school experience and his in-school learning experience *if it is modified to meet particular situations* and *extended to include other strategies*" (p. 104). She identified five basic skills that characterized the child who was successfully developing reading vocabulary, two of which were that "he is developing skill in coding speech sounds to written symbols" and that "he is becoming proficient in using phonological clues to unlock new words" (p. 131).

Donahue (1975) identified a modified form of language experience that used patterned sentences to help students who were learning to speak English as a second language. These oral language drills would then be recorded onto charts that would in turn be the basis for reading instruction. A single sentence pattern was employed repetitively in the following example:

There are 18 boys in our room.

There are 14 girls in our room.

There are 10 goldfish in our room.

There are 2 teachers in our room.

As learners developed proficiency reading in English, the activities would become less structured. For example, instructors could use activities in which the sentences in the experience charts preserved the same grammatical form, possibly exhibiting a subject followed by a verb and object. But the words in these grammatical categories could be varied. In the following illustration the words comprised by the verb and the object were varied:

We saluted the flag.

We sang songs.

We heard speakers.

Another variation on this modified approach to language experience included situations exhibiting dialogue. Teachers and students dramatized events that were recorded and later used as the basis for reading instruction:

Teacher: Good morning, class.

Class: Good morning, Ms. Johnson.

Teacher: How are you today?

Class: Fine, thank you. How are you?

Teacher: I'm fine too, thank you.

Donahue also recommended that teachers select words and grammatical structures from the language experience charts that the students had learned to read successfully and create new materials by recombining the selected items. Eventually, totally unfamiliar items would be introduced into passages that had been composed initially from recombined items. Depending on the frustration or success that students exhibited while learning to read the materials, the frequency with which unfamiliar items were to be introduced would be expanded or restricted.

Among other structured exercises that Donahue recommended were supplementary language experience activities to ensure that students produced sufficiently rich language samples and to help with the creation of a common bank of experiences that would be shared by the students and the instructors. Examples of structured activities that could precede the development of language experience charts included stimulating events arranged by the instructor, interpretation of pictures, dramatic play, pantomiming, puppetry, puzzle solving, listening to stories, music, or audio tapes, and the viewing of television or films.

A year earlier Goddard (1974) had also recommended that language experience be supplemented with skills-based activities. She was convinced that "to approach the language skills primarily through children's interests and experiences and to put into their hands the tool of phonics are not contradictory practices" (p. 74). Aware that opposition to phonics had persuaded many teachers to turn to language experience approaches in the first place, she counseled them to divert their attacks away from phonics and direct them toward instructional abuses, such as those cases where children had been drilled in phonics before they had developed the ability to benefit from that drilling. She concluded that all learners used phonics, including those who "appear to manage with no phonic teaching" and advised that "decisions have to be taken about when and how to help children acquire those skills" (p. 75). Goddard also advocated the use of a scope and sequence of skills, which she referred to as a "published reading scheme." Assuring her readers that language experience teachers should not be unsystematic, she wrote that "a measure of planning is not only desirable but necessary" (p. 81).

Goddard's book was published in the wake of an influential British report, *A Breakthrough to Literacy* (1970). In the foreword to a later edition of the teacher's manual accompanying this report, Halliday (1979) described the project as "a move towards structure in language education" that was an alternative to "the unstructured climate of the sixties" (p. 3). However, he did add defensively that "if teachers in the previous decade rejected the commitment to traditional notions of structure, they had reasons for doing so" (p. 3). Like Goddard, he cited abuses of skills-based instruction as the impetus for teachers to embrace holistic approaches. In the foreword to the 1970 edition of his book, a commitment to language-based instruction was evident when he wrote that "unless what they are doing in school relates to the uses of language with which they are familiar, and makes sense in terms of what they need language for, it will not carry them far" (Halliday, 1970, pp. vi-vii).

The authors of *A Breakthrough to Literacy* recommended that children learn phonics, but qualified this advice with a note that they should integrate it with communicative language. They also described materials to help teachers organize instructional activities. The core of these activities was a set of cards with words and phrases that students combined into sentences. The materials and activities were similar to those that had become popular in the United States as part of language experience. Among the specific skills that were emphasized in their curriculum were retelling of stories, asking questions, answering questions, dramatization, role playing, communicating through sentences, completion of unfinished stories, and description of characters in stories. In a brochure accompanying the 1970 edition of their commercial materials (Bowmar Publishers, 1970), the authors answered a question about the specific reading skills that were to be learned in their program when they stipulated a scope of 14 skills. However, they were reluctant to sequence those skills, maintaining that "*the crucial difference between* Breakthrough to Literacy *and traditional reading schemes is the way in which* Breakthrough to Literacy *places the learner himself in continuous control of the language he is developing*" (p. 5). In a brochure for commercial materials synchronized to their program (Bowmar, 1970), the authors indicated the program's basic assumptions: reading materials should include writing samples devised by the learners and they should be linked to children's language, interests, and experiences. But the authors emphasized that the most important assumption of their program was simply a recognition that the "child is an individual with personal needs" (p. 8).

Hall (1978) indicated that the materials used in language experience activities provided an adequate vocabulary for teaching common phonic generalizations and orthographic regularities. However, she acknowledged that "there is some concern that word analysis may be slighted in language experience programs" (p. 28). Hall herself included chapters on word recognition strategies and vocabulary development within the 1981 edition of her book and advised instructors to use word banks to group the words that students had learned from transcriptions of their oral language. She gave examples of categories into which words from these banks could be clustered, such as semantic (e.g., *colors, animals,* or *people*), syntactic (e.g., *actions, descriptions,* or *things*), academic (e.g., *science, social studies,* or *physical education*), or items that could be related to word recognition skills (e.g., words indicating generalizations about *phonics, word structure,* or *syllabification*). Hall also included motivational categories that could comprise words that were *silly* or *interesting*.

Writing at the end of the 1970s, Veatch, Sawaki, Elliot, Flake, and Blakey (1979) were articulate advocates for holistic instruction. In a section on teaching reading mechanics, they restated the nineteenth-century wholeness principle, adjuring their readers that "the direction of all learning goes from large to small." However, they were convinced that language experience activities could be supplemented with exercises that focused on *key words*. They described a six-step procedure in which an instructor would elicit key words, write them on cards, help the children trace them, apply the words in an activity (e.g., copying them on a chalkboard), review them, and then store them.

The authors listed numerous examples of activities into which the key words could be incorporated. Some of these activities included categorizing words, retrieving word cards scattered on the floor, exchanging words between learners, acting out words, arranging words alphabetically, making sentences from word cards, illustrating words, typing words, using word stencils, baking cookie-words, forming words with finger-paint, and tracing words made of tape, felt, or sand. Veatch and her colleagues recommended not only that word recognition be taught but that it be taught through skills arranged in a specific sequence. For example, they identified learning about the alphabet, consonant blends, and digraphs as initial skills while learning about syllables, prefixes, and suffixes were more advanced skills.

DEFINING THE WHOLE LANGUAGE APPROACH

Defining the whole language movement that developed in the 1970s was challenging even for proponents of whole language. Stewig and Buege (1994) concluded that the problem was compounded by the failure of whole language advocates to use a consistent term when referring to their approach. For this precise reason, Stahl and Miller (1989) recommended that all language-based approaches be treated as comparable, as long as they emphasized children's own language, child-centered lessons, trade books, and the teaching of decoding skills in context. Other proponents of whole language disagreed not only about whole language's definition but even about how to create a definition. Anderson (1984) had attempted an early definition of the whole language reading approach by pointing to its distinctive emphases on comprehension, communication, and learners' functional experiences. Two years later Newman (1985) identified whole language instruction as social, context-specific, and promoting a "risk of trying" by learners. Additionally, she thought that whole language involved choice, integration of the language arts, and a nondirective style of teaching. In 1986 Kenneth Goodman identified the characteristics of whole programs indirectly, by specifying the features of the reading approaches that did not complement whole language. These noncomplementary programs were artificial, segmented, dull, nonsensical, irrelevant, noncontextual, and inaccessible. Additionally, Goodman wrote that alternative programs belonged to someone other than the learners, were imposed on them, and rendered them powerless.

Watson and Crowley (1988) assumed a different tact, identifying a selective set of characteristics that they thought differentiated "all" teachers who employed whole language approaches. As an example of these characteristics, whole language teachers geared instruction to students' interests, abilities, and needs. Other characteristics were that teachers read or told daily stories to learners, taught communication-based writing, and ensured that students read literature. Whole language teachers also discussed the processes of reading and writing with children and promoted literacy development through social activities. Though Cambourne (1989) identified 10 principles of whole language, he acknowledged that they had been around "in various guises for a long time" but had regained momentum by their association with the whole language movement. Defining the principles as goals that needed to be achieved by learners within programs, he suggested that readers needed immersion in suitable texts, appropriate demonstrations of reading and writing tasks, and time to engage in reading and writing. Other principles alluded to learner empowerment, establishment of high expectations, and the positive effect of feedback.

Watson (1989) wrote that whole language was difficult to define because the adherents of the movement were passionate individuals who "reject a dictionary-type definition that can be looked up and memorized" (p. 131). She saw an additional complication in that the existing definitions had been developed by professors and scholars rather than teachers, who were the true experts in this populist movement. Despite these difficulties, she admitted that "whole language must be defined not only for those outside the movement but for whole-language educators as well" (p. 130). After reviewing the divergent definitions, she concluded that whole language could be considered a philosophy, a spirit, a movement, and a sense of professionalism by teachers. She explained that "the definitions are diverse because the personal and professional histories of the authors are different" but then added cryptically that "this variety frees those who have studied and practiced whole language to generate their own definitions, then to revise their definitions again and again" (p. 132).

Like Watson, other educators advised professors to defer to teachers in order to distinguish the essential features of the whole language approach. Cecil (1989) judged that the ability of teachers to model a love for language was the key feature of whole language instruction. In the preface to a book that she and Kenneth Goodman edited, Hood (1991) also listed several characteristics that she thought all whole language teachers shared. One of these was a philosophy that helped teachers persevere. Hood did not specifically elaborate this philosophy, but it was reflected in the other characteristics of whole language teachers that she identified: individual resolution of classroom problems, personalization of their classrooms, commitment to constant professional growth, and enjoyment of their work. Other authors in that same volume attempted to define the essential characteristics of whole language after discerning characteristics that all holistic teachers exhibited, such as, an understanding of learning and language development, ability to make skillful observations, vision of instruction's purpose, and continual reflection about self and learners.

Weaver (1990) identified characteristics of whole language that had been promoted frequently by other whole language educators—learning naturally without "a great deal of direct instruction," learning the language arts in an integrated fashion, writing with a communicative purpose for a real audience, an emphasis on the learners rather than on instructors, and a conviction that "there is no division between first 'learning to read' and later 'reading to learn'" (p. 6). Like Weaver, Shapiro (1991) was interested in the views of other educators; but he examined the professional literature in an effort to discern the characteristics of whole language instruction that were linked to research. The characteristics that he identified included convictions by practitioners that reading and writing were mutually reinforcing, that children should be active participants in learning, and that learning should be both child-centered and meaningful. Froese (1991) explained that the difficulty of developing a definition originated with proponents who themselves could not agree whether whole language was a philosophy, a set of instructional methods, a political movement, or a combination of these alternatives. But he was convinced that a consensus had developed on three compound characteristics that blended philosophic assumptions with instructional practices: "language is a *naturally developing human activity*," "language learning and teaching must be *personalized*," and "language is learned *holistically in context*" (p. 2). Among additional attributes that Froese thought should be included were recommendations that whole language teachers be responsible for curricular decisions and that they serve as model learners.

During the 1990s other educators continued the quest for a consensual definition of whole language. The Freemans (1992) advanced seven principles that they thought defined the basis for whole language instruction: "learning proceeds from whole to part," "lessons should be learner centered because learning is the active construction of knowledge by the student," "lessons should have meaning for students now," "learning takes place as groups engage in meaningful social interaction," "learning potential is expanded through faith in the learner," "in a second language, oral and written language are acquired simultaneously," and "learning should take place in the first language to build concepts and facilitate the acquisition of English" (p. 7).

Robb (1994) detailed 11 premises of whole language instruction that she was convinced were distinct from the assumptions supporting alternative models of instruction. Included in her list of premises were democratic decision making, promotion of independent problem solving, use of a curriculum geared to developmental needs, heterogeneous grouping of students, and support for collaborative learning.

Taking a different route from that which most educators had pursued, Delgado, Hilley, Bowie, and Allen (1995) described an incident in which classroom teachers implemented whole language instruction while guided by definitions that the teachers themselves had devised. Though they acknowledged that the definitions were "complex and varied," the authors identified shared perceptions about the need for instructors to integrate reading and writing, frequently use children's books in academic areas, thematically organize instructional units, and encourage students to read daily. They thought whole language teachers also encouraged their students to enjoy reading, gain knowledge, make choices, and express their feelings. Finally, they thought that whole language teachers encouraged collaborative learning, elicited a commitment from students about their personal responsibility for learning, and acknowledged that both teachers and students were learners.

Church (1996) observed with concern that "whole language means so many things to so many different people that it is in real danger of coming to mean nothing at all" (p. xx). Despite her apprehension, she thought that the multiple definitions should remain circumspect because "central to my theory of whole language is the understanding that it is complex and open-ended" (p. xxii). A component of whole language that she highlighted was its "political agenda," which she warned should not be hidden or else "we diminish the likelihood that whole language will reach its potential as a force for social change" (p. xxiii). She proposed that teachers explore "productive areas of inquiry" into whole language by attempting to answer political questions such as "Why and how has whole language been subverted with hierarchical institutions?" and "How should my theories and practices change to become more reflective of my commitment to democratic ideals of equity and social justice?" (p. xxiii). She acknowledged that a "backlash" had developed against whole language programs during the 1990s, after an acute decline in standardized reading test scores in California had followed the state's mandated implementation of whole language.

Church's remarks about a political reaction against whole language were similar to those made by Routman. Because Routman (1996) was convinced that the California instructional mandate and the subsequent decline in reading scores were related only indirectly, she encouraged educators to approach their colleagues, administrators, and the public to explain that the genuine reason for California's declined scores had been a lack of teacher training. She also encouraged her colleagues to define whole language, or "otherwise, we are at the mercy of noneducators and the media who make public statements that can set our teaching back" (p. 41). Although she did suggest a definition of whole language, she explained that definition by advising readers that the distinguishing features she listed were "not intended as dogma" but were instead "prompts to get you to think about, reflect, and solidify your own thinking about whole language beliefs, misconceptions, principles, and practices" (p. 41).

Remedial Whole Language

From their inception in the late 1800s, language-based reading activities had been advocated as an alternative to skills-based programs. For example, educators associated with the progressive education movement had been convinced that all children could have avoided learning problems had they only been instructed exclusively with language-based approaches. This type of general advocacy was distinct from the rationale adopted by remedial reading teachers who employed language-based activities as the antidote for specific learning problems. Despite a tradition in which language-based instruction had been employed as the remedy for children who had failed in skills-based programs, some whole language instructors began to distrust skills-based instruction as well as remedial reading. This distrust was based on their assumption that skills-based instruction and remedial reading were tied indivisibly together.

Convinced that the diagnostic procedures that were critical to remedial programs were flawed, some educators concluded that diagnoses should no longer be made and that all remedial reading programs should be eliminated. For example, Cole and Griffen (1986) recommended that children should not be diagnosed as problem readers and that all remedial programs should be eradicated. After identifying educators with views similar to those of Cole and Griffen, Walmsley and Allington (1995) reassured readers that it was wrong to insist that children did not benefit in any way from remedial or special education programs. However, they qualified this reconciliatory remark with the skeptical observation that those children who did benefit were "seldom in the majority."

Before they could dismiss remedial reading as unnecessary, some proponents of whole language realized that they needed to demonstrate that their own programs were remarkably successful. Otherwise, parents would demand some type of remedial recourse for those children who were failing. Since significant numbers of students had not learned to read within their respective educational programs, whole language teachers could have recommended that students with problems be shifted to distinct instructional paradigms, such as those supporting skills-based or literature-based programs. Whole language teachers might also have suggested a change in the pace of the whole language programs when the students in those programs were failing. Several proponents of whole language (Clay, 1993; Lyons & Beaver, 1995; Lyons, Pinnell, & Deford, 1993; Taylor, Short, Shearer, & Frye, 1995) chose the second alternative and developed remedial variations on the whole language approach. *Reading recovery* was an example of this second alternative.

Clay had used the term *reading recovery* to describe individualized instruction from a specialist to children who had been delayed in their reading after one year of school. Walp and Walmsley (1995) succinctly described this remedial program as one that "views its mission as taking in the lowest 20 percent of first graders, accelerating them up to grade level, and returning them as soon as possible to their regular classroom" (p. 179). Gaffney and Anderson (1991) described reading recovery as "a 'teacher dependent' program where success of the instruction appears to hinge upon the teacher's ability to make and execute the most 'powerful decisions' throughout each lessons" (p. 186). Henry (1991) also emphasized the central role of the instructor in a program that involved "a year-long in-service for teachers." Lyons, Pinnell, and Deford employed a philosophical description of reading recovery as "a system-wide intervention that involves a network of education, communication, and collegiality designed to create a culture of learning that promotes literacy for high-risk children" (p. 2). From a more practical perspective, Pikulski (1994) identified reading recovery as a pedagogical procedure in which tutors met individual learners for 30 minutes each day to observe reading, maintain annotated records of oral reading, implement activities in letter recognition, transcribe the child's oral language, and conduct follow-up activities with transcribed passages.

Even though they were intended as an exclusively language-based intervention for children who were not progressing on schedule in whole language programs, reading recovery activities were capable of integration with skills-based activities. Iversen and Tunmer (1993) demonstrated that such integration was not only possible but that reading recovery programs supplemented with skills-based activities could be even more effective than those programs that had not been integrated. Farkas (1996) employed skills-based intervention to supplement whole language instruction, arguing that an integrated program was not only effective but dramatically more cost effective than reading recovery. Farkas was not the first critic to point to the disproportionate cost of reading recovery programs. Although they were enthusiastic about a holistic remedial reading approach, Wilson and Daviss (1994) admitted that "like any tutoring effort, Reading Recovery is costly compared with other programs" because a "teacher works with only one child at a time, and usually no more than four children in half a day" and that "districts with teachers training as teacher-leaders may need to keep them on the payroll during the year they're studying" (pp. 69-70).

Reason and Boote (1994) thought that the reading recovery approach should be integrated with skills-based instruction because some children, even those who were from culturally and linguistically diverse backgrounds, would "need to learn about phonology and word recognition in a more systematic way." Instead of maintaining or abandoning an ineffective whole language program, they advised teachers to find "the most suitable combination of methods required by the individual" (p. 14). Although a strong proponent of whole language instruction, Church (1996) also questioned the value of reading recovery. Depicting it as one of many "quick fixes" to complex problems, she warned that proponents of reading recovery had relied on standardized tests to define literacy too narrowly. As a consequence, she judged that they had incorrectly labeled many healthy learners as children who required "recovery."

SUMMARY

Tension between proponents of language-based and skills-based instruction was discernible even in the early 1800s. Though this tension had helped to define it, language-based instruction did not develop a precise identity until the end of the 1800s, when it was viewed as functional, individualized, connected to the experiences of specific learners, and integrated with the language arts. Though it continued to be used throughout the first half of the 1900s, language-based instruction enjoyed a Renaissance among professors, teachers, and parents in the 1960s, when it was referred to as *language experience*. As was the case with earlier versions of language-based instruction, such as those that had preceded the progressive education movement, language experience lessons began with structured activities in which teachers and students were to cooperate. These learning sessions typically ended with the explicit reinforcement of skills.

As language experience evolved into whole language, the approach continued to accentuate integrated language arts and holistic principles of education. The lessons continued to be functional, individualized, and connected to the experiences and language of specific learners. However, the connections to structured experiences and systematically reinforced reading skills were replaced by an amorphous set of attributes about which even whole language advocates could not agree. Some of the proposed attributes included commitments to student empowerment, teacher professionalism, specific procedures for grouping students, symmetrical acquisition of oral language and literacy, and the reinforcement of reading through writing. Frustrated by the failure to develop consensus about these traits, some advocates of whole language attempted to define their movement through their opposition to scholastic publishers, skills-based activities, conservative political movements, and the experimental research paradigm. Because whole language assumed that children could extend the natural adaptability that they exhibited in their oral language to reading, some whole language educators recommended that those children who had not exhibited that adaptability be tutored with remedial programs that were still language-based.

Chapter 9

LITERATURE-BASED APPROACHES

Reading materials should be close to life and grow out of children's living (the staff of the Maury School, 1941).

Literature-based programs originated with concerns about the effects of reading on character development. These concerns evolved into a belief that the content of reading materials could influence learning. Educators began to search for books that were responsive to students' personal needs because they thought such materials could help eliminate personal problems and also because they hoped that the quality of the learning that relied on these meaningful materials would be elevated. Employing analytical procedures patterned after psychological therapy, some educators attempted to locate books for individuals who had already developed emotional problems. Other educators thought that carefully selected reading materials should be components of mental hygiene programs that were designed to help emotionally healthy readers when they eventually encountered problems. A philosophy comparable to that associated with the bibliotherapy movement reemerged in the late twentieth century as a rationale for storybook-centered programs.

*   *   *

Programs in remedial reading can be viewed as complex equations into which multiple factors have been loaded. One of these factors has been reading materials themselves. Attempting to define "vital factors" responsible for successfully learning to read, Anderson and Davidson (1925) specified seven factors, the last of which was "reading materials and equipment." Four years earlier O'Brien (1921) had identified 15 factors that influenced the rate of silent reading. Although the majority of the factors referred to the learners, one factor mentioned explicitly was the content of passages.

Although most educators who were attempting to develop effective reading programs singled out critical learning factors by directly naming them, others alluded to the undesirable consequences that resulted when certain learning factors were absent. For example, Brooks (1926) called attention to the importance of reading materials by listing the factors that caused poor reading, two of which were "not having enough suitable reading material" and "influences outside the school which draw away pupils' interest and effort" (p. 24). Brooks wrote that teachers should not "overlook the importance of leading children to appreciate good books and magazines" because "the connection between a given stimulus or situation and a given response is strengthened if the response is accompanied or followed by satisfaction and is weakened if accompanied or followed by an unsatisfactory or annoying state of affairs" (p. 7). He described the preceding statement as "a fundamental law of learning" that was nonetheless "commonly violated in teaching reading" (p. 7).

Even after a consensus had begun to develop among educators about the identity of the variables that characterized effective reading programs, they still disagreed about the emphasis that teachers should place on these variables when actual programs were implemented. Instructors who employed skills-based approaches predictably assigned a heavy weighting to *curriculum* as a critical learning factors. Because they were attempting to build success in reading on a foundation of oral language proficiency, the proponents of language-based approaches gave a higher priority to *communication* as a critical learning factor than they did to *curriculum*.

Just as advocates of skills-based approaches were not unconcerned with communication, advocates of language-based approaches did not disregard the organization of academic skills. But a difference was apparent in the emphases the two groups placed on these respective variables. Because language-based approaches placed a special emphasis on communication, they were faulted for not attending adequately to organized skills. And just as inevitably, skills-based programs were criticized for emphasizing acquisition of skills at the expense of meaningful communication. Literature-based programs focused intently on the *content* of reading materials as a critical learning factor. And comparable to the situations with language-based and skills-based approaches, they were criticized for being too attentive to *content* and for failing to attend adequately to the other essential characteristics of reading.

Psychoeducational and *bibliotherapeutic* programs were examples of literature-based programs. Though not inherently inattentive to basic reading skills nor to communication, these and the other literature-based approaches did concentrate on the content of materials. This emphasis proceeded from a belief that learning to read would be facilitated if it were presented as a response to personal problems. This conviction was especially apparent among the proponents of literature-based approaches who referred to themselves as bibliotherapists.

BIBLIOTHERAPY AS SCIENCE

In his history of reading, Manguel (1996) recorded that Diderot cured his wife of depression in 1781 by reading "raunchy" novels to her. Manguel judged this to be the initial incident in the new science that would eventually be referred to as bibliotherapy. Though other instances in which books were used to alter attitudes and behaviors were reported throughout the 1800s, one of the first references to bibliotherapy as a discipline was in a satirical article by Crothers (1916) that appeared in *The New Yorker*. Crothers highlighted an advertisement from the fictitious *Bibilopathic Institute*, to which was adjoined the *Young People's Lend-a-Thought Club* and a nursery where "tired mothers who are reading for health may leave their children" (p. 291). In remarks patterned after those in a dialogue by Plato, Crothers indicated his disdain for the purportedly scientific field of bibliotherapy. He wrote that "during the last year I have been working up a system of Biblio-therapeutics" in which "a book may be a stimulant or a sedative or an irritant or a soporific." He added waggishly that "a book may be of the nature of a soothing syrup or it may be of the nature of a mustard plaster" (p. 292). Although these remarks were patently humorous, the concept of employing books as a component of psychotherapy must have been sufficiently popular in 1916 for Crothers to not only be aware of it but to consider it a suitable, humorous subject to be presented to a general audience.

As bibliotherapy developed into a clinical strategy for helping persons solve their personal problems, it was viewed by many therapists as a specialized technique within psychology. Twenty-six years after Crothers has published his satirical article, Friedlaender (1942) recalled that "books for children have, even in the early days of Psychoanalysis, aroused its interest" (p. 129). Using the fairy tale as an example, she indicated that in this type of literature the child "meets again his own phantasies [sic]" and that "the fairy-tales' particular solutions for these conflicts appear to be a means for alleviating anxiety" (p. 129).

Writing about the "emotional nature of this [censorious] attitude of educational authorities towards children's literature," Friedlaender compared efforts by adults to regulate the materials that children read with attempts to suppress masturbation. She concluded the comparison by observing that "what strengthens the adult in his opinion that the reading of such literature should be forbidden, is the plain fact that instinctual gratification derived from it can clearly be observed in the child while reading or listening" (p. 146).

Friedlaender judged that not only learning to read but also the development of a healthy disposition were critically dependent on the synchrony of reading materials with children's stages of psychological development. She wrote candidly that "I do not think there is any value in introducing children too early to literature, which not only in its style of writing, but also in its contents, takes no account of the psychic stage of development of the child" and advised teachers to "let the child follow its inclinations, give at the same time such books which, while providing phantasies to correspond to its particular phase of development, yet combine with these the value of either being instructive or of having artistic merit" (p. 150).

Also writing during the 1940s, Kircher (1945) agreed with Friedlaender that books should be psychologically appropriate for children. To demonstrate the practicality of this principle, she developed a list of books to be used with children who exhibited behavior problems. In addition to providing summary annotations, she coded each entry in this bibliography with terms such as *adaptability, school, social understanding, detachment, obedience,* and *generosity.* In the introduction to Kircher's bibliography, Moore (1945) had observed that "the user of this list, who is concerned with the general character development of children, has a new tool that is of great help in dealing with behavior problems" (p. 11). He counseled that "one can introduce ideals and principles into the mind of the child much more easily by bibliotherapy than by verbal instruction and persuasion" because "the patient identifies himself with the hero and takes unto himself for a time at least the ideals and aspirations of the hero" (p. 11).

Tyson (1948) was also concerned that bibliotherapy needed to be appropriately understood. Reviewing ideas about bibliotherapy from psychologists and psychiatrists, she reported that several psychologists were wary of bibliotherapy because they feared that it might not have been adequately researched or that it might be an unregulated instance of self-analysis. But Tyson judged that most psychologists wished to "grant reading a place in psychotherapy" (p. 304). A year later Russell and Shrodes (1950) defined bibliotherapy as a dynamic interaction between readers and literature for the purpose of personality assessment, adjustment, and growth. They thought that the therapeutic effect of reading books resulted after readers had personally empathized with characters and situations in the stories that they had read.

Variable definitions of bibliotherapy by the practitioners in different academic fields had become increasingly noticeable when Tews (1962) surveyed 116 persons, including librarians and other persons knowledgeable about bibliotherapy. The respondents agreed that "good library service is beneficial, effective and valuable in the overall treatment and rehabilitation program of the patient" (p. 226). Tews reported that 90 percent of the respondents thought that reading could have a generally therapeutic character that was distinct from bibliotherapy and that reading could not be considered bibliotherapy "unless it is an adjunctive activity which is planned, guided, and controlled by skilled, trained librarians working in close cooperation and consultation with the medical team" (pp. 226-227).

After reviewing definitions of bibliotherapy from library science, social work, psychology, health, and health-related fields, Favazza (1966) concluded that professionals from each of these academic areas had defined bibliotherapy so as to highlight their own contributions. Similar to the recommendations that had been made four years earlier by Tews, he proposed a restrictive definition of bibliotherapy in which it was limited to physicians dealing with psychiatric patients.

After citing the extensive studies about bibliotherapy from library science, Brown (1975) noted that librarians had been concerned with it since the early 1920s and that they had "come close to achieving" goals that would transform it into a science. She was personally convinced that bibliotherapy could be a scientific process if it satisfied seven requirements, one of which was the assessment of a "patient's condition and needs by medical personnel" (p. 9) Brown wrote an entire chapter on "Education and Training for Bibliotherapy" in which she included appendices on certification for hospital-based bibliotherapy programs, standards for certification of poetry therapists, and even sample job descriptions for bibliotherapists.

Writing during this same period, Bettelheim (1975) adduced fairy tales as a type of material in which readers could discern fictional topics that corresponded to their personal problems. He wrote that "these stories speak to [a child's] budding ego and encourage its development" and that "they speak about his severe inner pressures in a way that the child unconsciously understands and without belittling the serious struggles that growing up entails" (pp. 50-51). A year later Bettelheim (1976) wrote that children judged fairy tales to be nonprescriptive because they "leave to the child's fantasizing whether and how to apply to himself what the story reveals about life and human nature" (p. 45). Because the psychologically useful information in fairy tales could be presented in formats that were less threatening than direct discussions of the actual problems children were confronting, he thought that the tales provided opportunities for emotional problems to be reflected upon or talked about openly and without feelings of guilt. Aware that fairy tales contained information about controversial topics, he admitted that "contrary to what takes place in many modern children's stories, in fairy tales evil is as omnipresent as virtue" (p. 8). Challenging those psychologists who thought that children should be diverted from psychologically troublesome issues, he warned that "such one-sided fare nourishes the mind only in a one-sided way, and real life is not all sunny" (p. 7).

Although many proponents of bibliotherapy remained convinced that it was a science, others were skeptical. This skepticism was predictable because so much of the literature in support of bibliotherapy had been sustained by anecdotal information. Brown (1975) lamented that from the 1920s through the early 1940s, most of the librarians who had investigated bibliotherapy were "unaided by scientific data and hypothesis" (p. 17). Reviewing the use of bibliotherapy with persons who were mentally ill, Junier (1962) noted that "from the literature one would observe that very little definitive work has been done" (p. 144). Five years later Kantrowitz (1967) examined data about the long-term therapeutic effects of bibliotherapy on children and concluded that the treatments had not had a discernible impact. In the foreword to a book about bibliotherapy, Monroe (1978) concluded that it "has not yet won widespread recognition, nor has it yet demonstrated the precision to which it aspires" (p. vii). Rubin (1978) thought it "obvious" that the current research on bibliotherapy was "conflicting and confusing" (p. 55).

NONSCIENTIFIC APPROACHES
TO BIBLIOTHERAPY

Shrodes (1955) was an advocate of the scientific approach to bibliotherapy who had observed a "parallel in substance and function" between bibliotherapy and the "primary phases of psychotherapy." She specified that these primary phases were identification of an individual's problem, catharsis, and insight by the individual about the etiology of the problem. She classified bibliotherapy as a "deep therapy" that could enable a person to "acquire a new perspective of his experience and of himself in relation to it, an insight that liberates him from the bondage it has imposed" (p. 25). However, she also observed that "for most students a therapeutic approach to reading will be of most benefit as a kind of preventative therapy" (p. 29). Writing 10 years after Shrodes, Cianciolo (1965) thought that bibliotherapy could be used to help students resolve a situation that otherwise might develop into a "hard case." To use bibliotherapy in a preventative fashion, she advised teachers to rely on "sound educational and psychological principles" as they selected good literature and shared this with their students.

Writing in the 1950s and 1960s, both Cianciolo and Shrodes were spokespersons for a movement that had begun decades earlier and that had a gradually increasing effect on bibliotherapy. This movement had emphasized the preventative as well as the remedial aspects of psychology and revealed opportunities for bibliotherapy to be applied in less structured formats. Brown (1975) was also a spokesperson for this movement. She described an approach to bibliotherapy that was less complicated than some of its precursors and that did not aspire to be scientific. She referred to this softer approach as the *art of bibliotherapy* and thought that only three requirements needed to be observed: pairing of a reader with a perceptive individual, access to a collection of relevant books, and establishment of a good rapport between the reader and the perceptive individual. From a similar perspective, Berry (1978) differentiated clinical bibliotherapy, which was to be employed by "a wide range of mental health professionals including psychiatrists, psychologists, social workers, counselors, ministers, nurses, [and] art therapists," from educational bibliotherapy, which was to be practiced by school counselors and teachers. Both the clinical and the educational versions of bibliotherapy were derived from the literature-based programs that had developed initially as part of an amorphous movement in which educators wished to acknowledge the contribution of books to students' maturity and education. Though some advocates of literature-based programs supported the attempts to transform their programs into scientific procedures, most of them progressively surrendered any aspirations toward scientific objectivity.

LITERATURE-BASED PROGRAMS IN THE SCHOOLS

When a connection between emotional disability and learning to read was established during the 1920s, initial investigations focused on the manner in which students' personalities had influenced the success of instruction. Not until the 1930s did a good number of educators turn their attention to the content of the passages read during instruction as a factor that could not only help students solve personal problems but influence their learning. However, several dramatic exceptions to these generalizations were apparent before the 1920s.

Precursors of Literature-Based Programs in the Schools—1800s

Henry Barnard was a contemporary of Horace Mann who occupied a position in Connecticut equivalent to that of Mann in Massachusetts. Barnard's (1965) progressive attitudes were revealed in his espousal of public reading rooms that would be "furnished with the periodical publications of the day, with maps and books of reference." As early as 1845 he had called for the use of nontraditional materials in education to motivate learners and to enhance comprehension.

Forty years later G. Stanley Hall published an influential monograph on teaching reading in which he noted that "though it by no means holds as a universal rule in education that there is no profit if there is no pleasure, yet pleasure always enhances the profit" and consequently "general knowledge of content, should as a rule precede" (p. 36). He also wrote that correct use of the English language "is taught best not by formal drill on enforced and uninteresting written theses, or treatises on style, but by first securing subject-matter that so deeply interests that style is left to form itself unconsciously in reaction upon content" (1897, p. 35).

Adler was a progressive educator who had established a laboratory school in Manhattan in 1878. A report in *Time* magazine ("Progressive's Progress," 1938) identified this school as the second progressive school in the United States, having been established three years after Francis Parker had developed the initial program in Massachusetts. At his laboratory school as well as in is writings on moral instruction, Adler encouraged the use of fairy tales that had not been bowdlerized. For example, Adler (1892) recommended that teachers "not take the moral plum out of the fairy-tale pudding, but let children enjoy it as a whole" (p. 68). He adjured them to use fairy tales not only because they developed a sense of morality but also because "they exercise and cultivate the imagination" (p. 64):

> As they follow intently the progress of the story, the young listeners are constantly called upon to place themselves in the situations in which they have never been, to imagine trials, dangers, difficulties, such as they have never experienced, to produce in themselves, for instance, such feeling as that of being alone in the wide world, of being separated from father's and mother's love, of being hungry and without bread, [and] exposed to enemies without protection (p. 64).

Toward the end of the nineteenth century, Wiggin (1892) recommended that the reading curriculum be expanded with books. But he cautioned that teachers should be careful because "no course of reading laid down by one person ever suits another, and the published 'lists of best books,' with their solemn platitudes in the way of advice are generally interesting only in their reflection of the writer's personality" (p. 83). Noting that stories could develop "familiarity with good English, cultivation of the imagination, development of sympathy, and clear impression of moral truth," Wiggin recommended a broad range of literature that included "the purely imaginative or fanciful, and here belongs the so-called fairy story" (pp. 94-95).

Precursors of Literature-Based Programs in the Schools—Early 1900s

In a chapter about the "class-room method in reading," McMurry (1903b) advised teachers that the "treadmill style of reading" should be replaced by "a rational, spirited, variegated method which arouses interest and variety of thought, and moves ever toward a conscious goal" (p. 127). He advised teachers to supplement classroom reading with library books because these could develop "deeper and wider views into life" (p. 132). He indicated that the teacher was "only a guide and interpreter" and that "his aim should be to best call the minds of the children into strong action through the stimulation of the author's thought" (p. 110). McMurry assured teachers that effective reading programs required that children "feel the force of ideas and of the emotions and convictions awakened by them" (p. 109). Especially when attempting to elicit emotions, he advised teachers to use myths, legends, and fairy tales. He wrote with passion that such materials enabled a child to become "a poet as he recreates the sparkling brightness of these simple pictures" and that "when a child has once suffered his fancy to soar to these mountain heights and ocean depths, it will no longer be possible to make his life entirely dull and prosaic" (1903a, pp. 106-107).

Although G. Stanley Hall had written about the importance of subject matter in the learning process during the 1800s, this concern emerged again in his writings from the early 1900s. In 1900 he published an extensive, topical bibliography of literary works that were likely to evoke the emotion of "pity" from readers (Saunders & Hall, 1900). Eleven years later he published a mammoth, two volume, 1,424-page textbook. This volume was unprecedented in its scope, containing long chapters on traditional subjects such as mathematics, history, civics, and music as well as adjurations to teachers to extend instruction to less familiar educational topics such as dance, pantomime, industrial training, and sex. Hall (1911b) observed that "one of the most significant culture movements of the last few years in this country is the invasion of the *library* upon the school" (p. 459). Although he included a 42-page section on "What to Read," most of his remarks may have revealed his own biases more than they did the situation in the schools. For example, he observed that "secret and clandestine reading of literature that is condemned, forbidden or disapproved, is more common among boys" and that "girls care far more for finesse" and that they "treat books better and are more amenable to library rules" (pp. 462-463). He also observed that the incorporation of books from libraries into reading programs had expanded the opportunities for learners in the schools to read children's books and adolescent literature.

Hall reported that the increasing use of trade books in the schools complemented an emerging "psycho-genetic theory" of reading. Admitting that the "details" of this new theory had not yet been worked out, he attempted to "roughly" outline its major assumptions:

> Fears are...educational possibilities of great worth and potency. Having explored them, the ideal educator can do very much by prescribing reading. Here is the crux of the whole problem and the art of the true physician of the soul will not be finished until he can prescribe aright. A book, or sometimes an article, at the right moment has often changed the current of a whole lifetime.... If a boy fears, e.g., earthquakes, this fact is a great and challenging opportunity to an insightful tutor. He must be told of and led to the very best, and for his stage, fittest literature on the subject, must read (but not unless he is strong) descriptions of the panic and horror of the great seismic catastrophes, volcanoes, floods, devastation, a little dynamic geology treating the cause, that his dread may deploy into the mental sphere, one function of which is to be a regulative of emotion.... Such a cure may seem to an over-tender parent too severe, and indeed it may easily be too drastic for those tainted with neuroticism. Hence, individual prescription must always be very circumspect and with constant watching at every stage. It involves long, persevering and detailed personal effort vastly beyond what is at present possible for the majority of children. But it is the ideal method or that of the future (pp. 483-484).

In a book on reading education, Klapper (1914) pointed to children's "natural cravings" that should be the basis for selecting the children's literature that would be incorporated into reading programs. One of these cravings was the child's "joy in telling as well as listening, in expressing what he feels most and loves best" (p. 161). Klapper assured his audience that appropriately selected books could satisfy this craving because the literature itself was the "product of these very emotions and yearnings" (p. 161). In a later edition of his textbook, Klapper (1926) recommended that "the primary requisite of the content of a primer or an early reader is that it should be good literature" (p. 112). Among the varied types of content that he judged to be suitable for reading textbooks were nursery rhymes, personal stories of class or school life, fairy tales, animal stories, folk tales, humorous stories, and fables. Klapper adjured teachers to select tales with morals while at the same time refraining from verbal moralizing. He wrote that "many an excellent story loses its appeal, fails to grip the children and provoke the designed response because of the moralizing indulged in by the teacher" (pp. 126-127).

Writing about vocational education, Davis (1914) advised teachers to build on the extracurricular interests of students when selecting topics for composition and reading. In a bibliography of materials that exhibited this character, he listed books such as *Boy's Book of Inventions, Lives of Girls Who Became Famous, Boys Who Became Famous, Great Men's Sons, Heroes of Everyday Life, Stories of Invention*, *Captains of Industry*, and *Making the Most of Ourselves*. In a later textbook on teaching reading in intermediate and high schools, Leonard (1922) also wrote about the opportunities to use the content of literary passages to enhance motivation. In a section about "the pleasures of danger, terror, and achievement against odds," he counseled teachers that "one of a child's earliest and most curious joys is the fascination of a fearful things—ogres and dragons and the like perils" (p. 91).

In their memoir about the educational program implemented in Illinois's Winnetka school district in 1919, Washburne and Marland (1963) described an instructional approach with "extensive reading" of books and with "the fitting of the books to the individual child" (p. 50). Writing about the same period, William Smith (1922) noted that reading textbook publishers had "gone so far as to admit considerable non-literary material [into their textbooks]" (p. 218). Although Smith indicated that "there is much to be said in favor of this departure," he agreed with many of his colleagues about the desirability of more conservative reading programs that relied on the "matter of fact content so essential for effective training in constructive thinking" and which supplied "the facts which children need for normal mental growth" (pp. 223-224).

In contrast to Smith, Brooks (1926) recommended that children read "good books and magazines" because these "provide highly impersonal, elevating recreation" and helped to form "high ideals of conduct" (p. 240). In an even more progressive spirit, Brooks recommended that teachers attempt to prescribe books that were sensitive to the characteristics of individual learners. For example, when dealing with "timid" children he suggested that "the materials should be so easy that the timid child will have little difficulty with them" (p. 221). He also advised that reading materials should be those in which the child would be "intensely interested" because this might persuade the learner to "forget his timidity."

Writing two years before Brooks, Uhl (1924) had published an entire book on the materials to be used during reading instruction. Because he believed that "economical teaching always takes account of the inclinations of the learner," he emphasized the "importance of consulting children in the selection and organization of courses in reading and literature" (p. 159). He reported about investigations of the "social worth" of reading that comprised "analyses of the subject matter of courses in reading, of the social situations in which pupils find or will find themselves, and of the traits of children." Uhl concluded that materials with social worth met two criteria: "first, reading materials must be interesting to the child, and second, it must impel the child to proceed toward a desirable objective" (p. 163). He also observed a connection between the content of materials read during reading instruction and the method of instruction that had been designated:

> Many of the older methods were very successful in the teaching of the mechanics of reading. They employed the formula, *Learning to read by not reading*. This formula has recently given way to the formula, *Learning to read by reading*. Recent investigations indicate that schools

must not only teach reading by having pupils read but that schools must also provide practice in the reading of materials designed especially to cultivate specific reading habits (p. 45).

Writing during that same year, Pennell and Cusack (1924) had also recommended that young children's books and adolescent literature be incorporated into reading instruction. They noted that though a child might seem to read for pleasure, "the child may be unconscious of the needs that drive him to books, but nevertheless books satisfy his vague longings and desires" (p. 5). Like Uhl, they were concerned about the selection of appropriate materials and provided extensive bibliographies to guide teachers. They counseled that "if reading is guided along right lines, a wealth of information and an enlargement of sympathies and understanding of life are gained, and ideals are formed that should result in social and individual progress" (p. 6).

Literature-Based Programs in the Schools—1930s

After examining 57 sociology textbooks that had been published between 1926 and 1945 and that contained information about educational methods, Hobbs (1951) noted that 40 of the texts criticized "the type of education which was prevalent in the United States in the past, but which has been considerably modified by 'progressive' doctrines in the last few decades" (p. 66). Hobbs defined the educational methods that were linked to these progressive doctrines as ones that were child-centered and that concentrated "on developing the creative interests of children, while traditional beliefs, disciplines, and training in moral principles are minimized or ignored." He emphasized that teachers using progressive approaches taught children "to learn from 'existing social situations' rather than from *a priori* principles" and that students in such programs concentrated on "'real life problems' in a self-directing manner which involves democratic give and take" (p. 67).

Pennell and Cusack (1935) were enthusiastic proponents of the progressive educational programs that had been developed during the period described by Hobbs. In the preface to their book on reading education, they quoted a famous statement from Kilpatrick in which he defined the school as "a place where pupils go, not primarily to acquire knowledge, but to carry on a way of life" (Kilpatrick, quoted by Pennell & Cusack, 1935, p. 2). As another indication of their support for the progressive attitudes on social reform with which Kilpatrick was associated, they titled their book *The Teaching of Reading for Better Living*. Despite their enthusiasm for progressive education, Pennell and Cusack conceded that "in most schools a basal reading series of readers is used at least throughout the primary grades because of its carefully graded vocabulary" (p. 19). But they observed a tendency "to have no basal series beyond the third grade." They adjured all teachers, even those who persisted in using basal readers, to recognize that "all grades should read many, many more books than the basal reader" (p. 19). To promote this goal, they provided extensive bibliographies that teachers, librarians, and parents could consult to help children in different grades "select wisely" the most appropriate books. For those teachers who insisted on adopting basal reading programs, they suggested that they follow guidelines, the first of which was an adjuration that "the materials for the first grade should be based on children's experiences and interests rather than on folk and fairy tales" (p. 20).

Five years earlier Hildreth (1930) had speculated about the relationship between reading and the subconscious mind. After reviewing details in a case study about a child who had entered school and exhibited reading problems, she concluded that emotional factors were restricting the child's success in reading individual words. She wrote that "nothing was more apparent in Peter's responses than the ease with which he learned words of a pleasant emotional tone and the difficulty that he experienced with words representing things feared or hated or words describing situations over which deep-seated emotional complexes might have developed" (p. 618). She explained these responses by this learner in terms of an "understanding of the part that emotional factors play in learning, partly as a result of Freudian researches on emotional complexes and the new objective psychology with its emphasis on fear and love as motivating factors in behavior" (p. 618). She gave a detailed example of the difficulty that the child in her report exhibited in the mastery of a single word:

> The word most difficult to learn, for no reason at first apparent, was "street." Peter's house was situated on a congested street only thirteen feet wide, the main artery of the village to the beach. A stout fence surrounded the house and yard, and nothing had been more firmly impressed on Peter's mind than the fact that he must never cross nor ever go near the street. Every day he would hang disconsolately on the fence, watching the cars go by. He greatly feared the street, much as it fascinated him. He had repeatedly been told that, if he ventured near the street, he would be severely injured or perhaps killed. From the first, it was apparent from Peter's reaction to the card that something was wrong with "street." Instead of looking at the word fixedly, as was his custom with other words, he turned away from it. This show of fear toward a white piece of cardboard on which some black letters were printed never wore off completely. He appeared, if any child ever did, practically "word-blind" toward this word (p. 618).

McKee (1934) described a program for elementary school reading that was similar to those for which progressive educators had been advocates. In this program the teaching of literature was combined with the teaching of reading so that the goals of the literature program were expanded beyond a simple appreciation for "good books." He explained that "the chief objective is to give the child through literature a wide variety of interesting and important experiences, interpretations of the ways of life, insights concerning human characteristics and relationships, and the like" (p. 475). In order to accomplish this goal, he recommended that books be presented in a fashion that would enable a learner to "feel, enjoy, and live through the episodes, the feeling, the descriptions offered in whatever good literature he may read" (p. 475).

Rosenblatt was a literary theorist and educator who also wrote about the reaction of adolescents to literature. In a book that she published originally in 1938, she argued that sensitivity to the personal needs of readers was essential to the effective teaching of a book because "the individual reader brings the pressure of his personality and needs to bear on the inextricably interwoven 'human' and 'formal' elements of the work" (1968, p. 51). Believing that "the student's primary experience of the work will have had meaning for him in these personal terms and no others," she wrote that "this will constitute the present meaning of the work for him" (p. 51). Rosenblatt anticipated that some critics would disapprove of the reader-centered approach she advocated because it might "incite the youth to rush into all sorts of untried modes of behavior." She dismissed this fear as one based on "Victorian moralism" and argued instead that "only in rare cases would the literary image of a new and aberrant interpretation of a personal role outweigh the influence of frequently encountered conventional images of that role" (p. 197).

Literature-Based Programs in the Schools—1940s and Beyond

Axline (1947) chronicled an experiment in which children with severe reading problems received "nondirective therapy" as they learned to read samples of their own writing, the writing of their peers, and books. The instruction provided an opportunity for the teachers to develop rapport with their learners and eventually to understand their emotional problems. Axline summarized the philosophy on which this approach was based when she wrote that "when we secure the confidence and trust of a little child and he shares his inner world with us, then we are impressed by the child's ability to cope with very serious problems" (p. 63).

During the preceding year Child, Potter, and Levine (1946) had published an influential monograph on children's textbooks and personality development for which they examined 914 stories within the third-grade books of 30 different reading series. They classified the stories in four categories: everyday events, tales of heroes, episodes with animal characters, and fairy tales. Though they supported the use of stories with everyday referents, they cautioned that "the probable function of fairy stories is not quite so clear" and might even be "serving as an outlet for the expression of anti-social needs" (p. 53). They questioned the therapeutic effect of fairy tales because "presentation of such behavior in very unrealistic circumstances fails to contribute to a child's learning ways for handling the similar anti-social tendencies he must cope with in everyday life" (p. 53). Writing an editorial that was inspired by this 1946 monograph, Cronbach (1948) criticized those reading textbooks that presented content based on "unrealistic optimism" and a "fairy-tale existence" in which "behavior which is fundamentally submissive or protective is almost always rewarded" (p. 197). This criticism of basal readers would recur frequently during the following decades.

Adams, Lillian Gray, and Reese (1949) included a 30-page chapter on "Reading, Mental Health, and Personality" in their general reading textbook. They explained that the information they reviewed had two emphases, deterring the psychological damage that could result when learners failed to read as well as "the exploration of the role of books and reading in enriching the child's personality and improving character" (p. 76). They concluded the chapter with a bibliography organized into categories about *nature, humor, hobbies, etiquette, travel, music,* and *art*. Three years later Witty (1952) reported that "reading to help pupils satisfy personal and social needs is an objective frequently stressed today by psychologists and by teachers" (p. 75). He indicated that a "defensible" reading program would involve systematic instruction in basic skills, integration of reading throughout the curriculum, and the connection of reading to students' interests and developmental needs.

Nine years after his 1952 report had appeared, Witty (1961) also advised teachers that they should gather information about the interests of the students in their classrooms and select topics for reading instruction that were based on this information. He described how one teacher had arranged individual interviews with children during which she asked them to state three wishes. The responses of some of the children "enabled the teacher to understand the pupils better and to provide the kind of school atmosphere in which happiness, successful achievement, and steady growth become possible" (p. 141). Writing during that same year, Burton and Larrick (1961) also highlighted the educational uses of literature. They wrote that literature enabled individuals to live vicariously through books, a goal they considered important because "the needs of the human organisms are so complex that no one can subsist on direct, actual experience alone" (p. 198). Advising teachers to carefully select books that would sensitize youth to the complexity of the human character and the demands of life, they warned that such insight could "never be achieved by the all too prevalent high-and-dry examination of supposed 'classics'" (p. 203). Instead, they recommended that selections "be chosen carefully in terms of the verisimilitude of experience portrayed" because "literature is preparation for experience" (p. 202).

Selecting Books for Literature-Based Programs in the Schools

Throughout the twentieth century educators argued that the selection of reading materials with appropriate content was critical to effective learning. In the 1920s Jordan (1926) had written that "if we could determine what the child's major interests are, be those interests good or bad, it would be possible to direct these forces along lines which are desirable" and that consequently "the importance of having boys and girls interested in books, stories, and poems cannot be overestimated" (p. 1).

Attitudes similar to Jordan's were apparent in the activities of educators decades later. For example, Spache (1969) compiled an annotated list of bibliographies that identified materials suitable for readers with problems. Although Brown (1975) also suggested books with topics that corresponded to problems persons might be experiencing, she embedded her bibliographies within chapters about special groups and special situations. For example, one of her chapters centered about programs for mental hospitals and "the mentally disturbed out-patient." Within this single chapter were compilations of books on a wide range of topics that included alcoholic parents, adolescence, adoption, boy-girl relationships, brain injury, conflict of values, courage, death, divorce, expression of self, family relationships, fathers in prison, single-parent homes, fears, foster homes, general conflict, greed, health, physical appearance, honesty, impatience, inferiority complex, introversion, jealously, laziness, lying, mental retardation, mental illness, orphans, persistence, psychological sex problems, rejection, religious conflict, responsibility, maturity, self-acceptance, selfishness, sex education, marriage, social responsibility, step-parents, temper, wealth, vocation, and war. Additional topical bibliographies that could be appropriate for adults were part of this chapter as well. Providing a synopsis of each book as well as information on the school grades for which it would be appropriate, Haldeman and Idstein (1977) also assembled a list of books that they divided into categories. Their categories included personal appearance, family situations, growing up, broken homes, new neighborhoods, physical handicaps, fears, and friendship.

Though many additional bibliographies were organized about topics corresponding to the problems that children were likely to experience, entire books of references with specialized areas of focus were published. For example, Rudman, Dunne-Gagne, and Bernstein (1993) assembled annotated lists of books intended to help children cope with separation and loss. The range of topics in their list varied from departure for camp to the death of a family member. Other specialized bibliographies concentrated exclusively on publications of fictional accounts of persons with disabilities (Robertson, 1992) or nonfiction accounts of individuals with disabilities (Brest-Friedberg, Mullins, & Weir-Sukeinnick, 1992).

Specialized bibliographies containing summaries of books appropriate for children at precisely defined stages of development were also available. For example, Thomas (1993) identified works suitable for children between the ages of four and eight. Gillespie and Naden (1989, 1993, 1994) assembled separate topical bibliographies for readers in narrow age ranges such as 8 to 12, 12 to 16, and 15 to 18. One of the most efficient ways for educators to access topical information about children's books was through a compact disc service, *Children's Reference PLUS* (Bowker, 1996). This annually up-dated set of discs contained book reviews as well as the information from 25 sets of bibliographical references. King (1995) suggested several sources of summary information that could be used to locate books, such as *The Book Finder*, a periodically up-dated compilation of children's literature in which problems and developmental needs were highlighted.

Once suitable materials had been identified, the books were to be presented to students in ways that encouraged them to read them. The most charismatic account of strategies with which to encourage teenagers to read books may have been that described by Fader (1966). After noting that the publication of trade books was based on a set of priorities different from that used in the production of textbooks, Fader wrote that "with the choice between market success and business failure, publishers, editors and writers know that survival depends on producing words that people *will* read." He added sardonically that the program he was advocating "advances the radical notion that students are people and should be treated accordingly" (p. 24). Because of the distinct publication priorities on which trade books were based and which he thought would be apparent to students, Fader recommended that school personnel "saturate" classrooms with newspapers, periodicals, and paperbacks. He observed that "school librarians should take a useful lesson from operators of paperbound bookstores, who have learned to let merchandise sell itself by arranging their stores so that customers are surrounded by colorful and highly descriptive paper covers" (p. 52). These creatively arranged materials could establish a bond between the learners and the world outside the classroom, encourage learners to develop strategies for dealing with personally meaningful problems, and help them realize that their peers were attempting to solve the same problems. Once learners were "saturated" with relevant reading materials in the classroom, Fader urged teachers to concentrate on "diffusion," which he defined somewhat amorphously as "the responsibility of every teacher in every classroom to make the house of literacy attractive" (p. 26).

A decade later Brown (1975) gave numerous examples of alternative classroom activities that might be suitable formats against which to advise students about books: distributing book lists, orally recommending books, displaying book jackets on bulletin boards, arranging table displays of books in classrooms, designating books to meet academic requirements in content-area classes, maintaining journals of books on a specified topic, encouraging students to recommend books to their peers, discussing books in student panels, illustrating incidents from books, encouraging students to create their own book jackets, circulating student-written synopses of books, displaying book posters made by students, circulating critical book reviews written by students, and encouraging students to compose simplified versions of books to be read by young learners.

STORYBOOK READING

Storybook reading has been a popular component of reading education programs throughout the twentieth century. McMurry (1903a) wrote that "the telling and reading of stories to children in early years, before they have mastered the art of reading, is of such importance as to awaken the serious thought of parents and teachers" (p. 1). He assured his readers that this technique "naturally begins at home, before the little ones are old enough for school" (pp. 1-2). McMurry was confident that "the oral speech through which the stories are given to children is completely familiar to them" and that "oral speech is, therefore, the natural channel through which stories should come in early years" (p. 5). He used a mixed metaphor that combined banking with agriculture to explain the effects of these early pre-reading experiences:

> In these early years the minds of children may be enriched with a furnishment of ideas of much value for all their future use, a sort of capital well invested, which will bring rich returns. Minds early fertilized with this variety of thought material become more flexible, productive, and acquisitive (p. 4).

Almost a century later Snow, Barnes, Chandler, Goodman, and Hemphill (1991) noted that *reading* often had a scholastic connotation of "successfully mastering a curriculum" (p. 175). They differentiated this restrictive connotation of the term *reading* from the less restrictive meaning of *literacy*, which connoted "participation in a culturally defined structure of knowledge and communication" (p. 175). Snow and her colleagues used the phrase *emergent literacy* to refer to pre-reading activities "such as pretend storybook reading, pretend writing, oral storytelling that shows literate traits, beliefs about literacy, production of certain oral language forms, and recognition of letters, logos, labels, and frequently encountered words" (p. 175). Giordano (1996) later referred to such behaviors as *patterned literacy* and illustrated how activities that promoted it could be effective not only with young children but with adults with developmental disabilities.

Storybook reading was a central component of emergent literacy programs. In a foreword to a book by Taylor and Strickland, Cullinan (1986) succinctly stated the rationale for storybook reading, noting that "children who do not hear stories will have fewer reasons for wanting to learn to read" (p. x). Taylor and Strickland (1986) defined the rationale for storybook reading more precisely as an activity that "grows with the interest [the participants] share in the content of the story and extends to their interest in the spoken and printed words the story contains" (p. 17).

Writing about the therapeutic value of storybook reading, Taylor and Strickland (1986) observed that "books are like lullabies: they caress a newborn baby, calm a fretful child, and help a nervous mother" (p. 23). Employing a rationale similar to that which had been summoned by champions of bibliotherapy, they judged that storybook reading could be an opportunity for children or their families to deal with the problems they were facing or with those that they might eventually confront. With regard to the preventative value of books, they wrote of materials dealing with death, divorce, and child abuse that "if you should come across such a book and find that it is well written and the topic is of interest to you and your child, don't hesitate to read it even though it may not have immediate significance to the events or problems in your own lives" (pp. 108-109).

Though it was not a formal set of pedagogical procedures, storybook reading was investigated by researchers who inquired about its impact on literacy, child development, and the pattern of interactions between parents and their children. For example, studies such as those by Ninio (1980), Sulzby (1985), and Roser and

Martinez (1985) indicated that the literacy progress that children made in response to storybook reading was correlated with the style of interaction that the parents or caregivers exhibited during the reading. Although Bus and Ijzendoorn (1988) also concluded that storybook reading's impact on the acquisition of literacy skills was likely to be influenced by the caregiver's style of interaction, they also noted a positive correlation with the age of children.

SUMMARY

Although educators had been aware of the psychoeducational characteristics of books for centuries, the organized use of books to nurture learning was a twentieth-century development. Literature-based programs, many of which were referred to as bibliotherapy, were founded on a conviction that books could help readers solve emotional problems. Initiatives within this interdisciplinary movement came not only from education but also from psychology, library science, and health care. Although some literature-based programs were implemented by teams on which educators and clinically trained therapists collaborated, this model became less popular than a preventative approach in which teachers selected materials that corresponded to the predictable emotional problems that students would encounter.

Chapter 10

TECHNOLOGY-BASED APPROACHES

First and foremost, the Teacher of Teachers must know that he shares equally with the Technologist in a new division of labor (Rugg, 1952).

Mechanical devices were used to teach reading toward the end of the 1800s. The technology connected to these activities was later supplanted by special electronic equipment designed to teach reading by radio, cinema, and television. However, the popularity of technology-based remedial reading activities increased most dramatically in the 1970s after efficient personal computers became accessible. Similar to earlier attempts to adapt reading instruction to various types of technology, the efforts to promote computers in education were resisted because of the limited types of lessons that could be implemented. However, computer-based instruction proliferated because it was practical and timesaving, especially when it was used to implement individualized instruction. Eventually, computer-based instruction was demonstrated to be compatible with all of the popular approaches to reading. The use of technology-based reading activities increased even more during the 1980s and 1990s when lessons were developed that took advantage of computers as tools for communication.

* * *

In his exhaustive study of the foundations for American education, Rugg (1947) indicated that the factor which had most influenced the transformation of America from the early 1890s "was the astonishing speed and efficiency with which the engineers perfected machine technology, and the business and financial men of six industrial countries built the modern corporation and organized a world-wide system of efficient enterprise" (p. 249). Rugg was not alone in this estimate about the pervasive influence of technology upon education.

In an early book on efficiency in education, Davenport (1911) wrote about his fascination with technology-based education because "while education is no relief from labor, or even drudgery, it ought, however, to lessen the totality of drudgery by the further utilization of mechanical energy and the more economic and intelligent direction of human effort" (p. 15). Despite his enthusiasm, Davenport noted that technology-based education was only a component in a general initiative to increase efficiency in the schools. He warned that neither technology nor the larger system of industrial education of which it was an element should be viewed outside the context of other educational issues:

> The first general principle to be recognized is this: That industrial education cannot be considered by itself alone any more than industrial people can live alone. It is at best but part of a general scheme of education that aims at a higher efficiency of all classes of people, and it is in this light that industrial education should be studied and its problems solved (p. 11).

Almost a century after Davenport had published the preceding remarks, Saettler (1990) agreed that educational technology should be viewed within a broad societal context. Defining educational technology as a process rather than a group of products, he argued that it had an origin that was not only well established by the 1800s but that preceded the invention of the printing press. He wrote that "educational technology, as a process, emerged out of the early technological tradition when a kind of knowledge began to be systematically applied to instruction" and that it was even apparent when "tribal priests systematized a body of knowledge and early cultures invented pictographs or sign writing to record and transmit information" (p. 4).

EARLY TECHNOLOGY

Systemization was a key component in the several hundred-year development of educational technology. In the specific case of reading education, systematized instruction had been a characteristic of skills-based approaches since the early 1800s. And systemization was an important element even during the inception of the remedial reading movement. Despite this tradition, the advent of technology in reading was often attributed to the electronic pacers and reading machines that became popular during the 1920s.

However, mechanical devices with features similar to later-developed electronic equipment had been used in reading education well before the twentieth century. In his history of nineteenth-century educational technology, Anderson (1961) wrote that "a significant evolution in attitude occurred" during the period after the Civil War and that early educational apparatuses once regarded as novelties, came to be regarded as necessary educational implements. He described several of the devices used to develop reading skills during the nineteenth century:

> [The Spelling Stick] consisted of a grooved piece of wood with a handle on it (like a window washer's squeezer) on which letters were stood upright. Single words or even simple sentences could be formed ("Let Me Try"). The class or individual then read the sentence back to the teacher.... A more complicated apparatus was "Baade's Permutation Reading Case" with a patent date of 1871.... Baade's device consisted of a wooden frame encasing three wooden

slots. Instead of numbers, there were words illustrated by cuts of animal, etc. Thus the teacher could flash individual words or whole sentences for the class to read.... Going a step further was "Jeffer's Panoramic Apparatus" of 1879. With this device, a picture, word, single letter, or entire sentence was depicted in a slot for the class to identify. The difference between this apparatus and its predecessors was that it was entirely mechanical. The teacher did not have to insert separate cards with words or pictures on them. Instead, two cranks at the side of the machine rolled the picture or object into view (pp. 50-51).

Figure 10.1 contains illustrations of early education technology.

Although some teachers' attitudes may have been positive toward the use of technology in reading education during the nineteenth century, the spread of the cumbersome and impractical reading devices that were available to schools was limited through most of the nineteenth and early twentieth century. This situation changed in the 1920s with the popularization of innovative electronic media.

EARLY TECHNOLOGY-BASED INSTRUCTIONAL STRATEGIES

Remarks made by enthusiasts of early educational technology and those made later by proponents of computer-based learning comprised a discernible strand that connected the technology through different eras. For example, Huey had anticipated later warnings about the degradation of books and the elevation of electronic technology when he cited predictions in 1908 by his contemporaries about the "displacement of much of reading, *in toto*, by some more direct means of recording and communicating" in which "an author may take his thought directly into some sort of gramophone–film book which will render it again to listeners, at will" (1968, p. 429). But Huey dismissed these predictions as "the wildest of speculations." Had he written these remarks two decades later, he might have been less confident about his negative prediction.

Radio-Based Education

In the early 1920s advocates for technology in the schools were distressed at the opposition to innovations, even those that had become common in other areas of society. Observing "the resistance of the public schools to any innovation," Irwin and Marks (1924) noted that "up to twelve years ago, there were no typewriters in the administration offices in New York City" and that "only within the last seven years has the telephone been used in these offices" (p. 1). They lamented that adding machines were only being installed at the time they were writing.

Despite accusations about the turgid schedule with which the schools were incorporating technology into their administration and curricula, reports from this period indicated receptivity of some schools to technology-based instructional innovations. For example, schools were experimenting with radio-based

Figure 10.1. Illustrations of Educational Technology from the 1800s

education as early as the 1920s. Lindop (1954) wrote that early enthusiasm about the spread of radio in the schools was in fact exaggerated to the point of being ridiculous:

No one knew what radio could do, and many educators made wild claims about the new medium. Radio was regarded as a sort of sovereign remedy for all educational ills; it would educate the general public so efficiently, it was thought, that institutions of higher learning would soon have no purpose or meaning. Radio would broadcast to every classroom, from kindergarten through graduate school, and do a much more efficient job than the regular teacher. Before long many teachers could be eliminated, and training—for adults or youngsters—directed entirely by radio (p. 123).

A 1942 report from the Wisconsin Research Project in School Broadcasting recounted details of an experiment in 1922 in which the University of Wisconsin had developed a program in musical appreciation. The report also chronicled a 1929 experiment by the university using radio to teach current events to upper elementary school students. The report concluded that these and subsequent radio lessons were "highly successful" and that radio-based education "may prove a means of equalizing educational opportunity" (p. 12).

Less than a decade later Nicholas Murray Butler (1931) delivered an NBC radio address to introduce a series of programs about economics and psychology. He advised his audience that "the amazing resources which modern science and modern engineering skill have put at the service of men are now to be used for the purpose of offering systematic instruction and interpretation concerning two intellectual interests and endeavors which are at the present time uppermost, and justly so, in the minds of the whole world" (1931, p. 1). But Butler also predicted that "we are only at the beginning of the new period in civilization which this new agency in education marks and accompanies" (p. 5). Two years later Willey and Rice (1933) observed that "the radio tends to promote cultural leveling" and gave the example of "Negroes barred from entering universities can receive instruction from the same institutions by radio" (p. 215). As an indication of how progressive such predictions were, Counts (1931) reported that the Soviet Union had developed an educational plan that included "the promotion of scientific research and technical laboratory investigation in the province of communication." However, the Soviet technical plan contained no reference to radio or cinema and instead advised that "the rôle of post and the telegraph in the cultural and educational development of the country will be enlarged extensively" (pp. 135-136). The Soviets also intended to extend telephone service and to encourage "the wide use of auto transport, the construction of better postal wagons, the broad utilization of air and waterways, and marked development of rural delivery" (p. 135).

Less emotional than some of his colleagues, Koon (1933) wrote that the radio was "simply a conveyor of sound" and that before it would become and invaluable aid to education, instructors "must master the art of teaching by radio" (p. 1). His motivation for writing an Office of Education Bulletin was to "make available to the educational profession what appear to be the best practices in teaching by radio" (p. 2). Koon classified the formats for educational radio presentations as talks, directed activities, live broadcasts, conversation, debates, music, and plays. He also included extensive advice on how educators could prepare for and then actually deliver effective broadcasts of lessons for radio. (As an indication of the precision of this advice, he included a six-page section on "microphone technique.")

Rightmire (1937), who was president of the Ohio State University, also assumed a less excited demeanor about radio. He made a series of four radio lectures about education which he represented as "an assembly" of ideas to be integrated with "the basic conception of Democracy." He apologized that "there are few new thoughts on Education today, but the old ones are worth frequent recasting" (p. 2). The four broadcasts respectively documented Rightmire's concerns about the history of the public schools, higher learning, state-supported higher education, and the Ohio State University.

Woelfel and Tyler (1942) were also concerned about the impact of radio on education in Ohio. Writing almost a decade after Rightmire had made his remarks, they reported the results of a 1941 survey which indicated that 55 percent of the schools in Ohio had radios. They not only judged this figure to be unacceptably low but cautioned that since "Ohio is unquestionably one of the foremost states in the development and extension of radio education...the figures for Ohio, low as they appear to be, are actually higher than would be found in most states" (p. 1). Noting that "there is nothing inherently good or evil in radio," Woelfel and Tyler recommended that educators "see to it that radio is used for human advancement and insure that goal by providing an American public which understands and appreciates radio's potentialities" (p. 176). They specified three precise uses of radio-based education: communication, motivation, and radio as a "subject matter worthy of serious and sometimes intensive study by the boys and girls in our schools" (p. 149).

In the introduction to a national educational yearbook, Ralph Tyler (1945) wrote that the military training programs developed during World War II had "demonstrated large potential values in a variety of training aids, such as motion pictures, records, models, and the like" and the "the incorporation of materials of this sort in the educational programs of the schools should also be carefully considered in the planning that goes on today" (p. 2).

In the foreword to a book on radio-based instructional strategies that was written a year later, Keith Tyler (1945), the director of radio education at Ohio State University, also expressed his conviction that "the radio has much to contribute to education." After observing that the "schools are lamentably backward in making use of this important instrument" he also noted more optimistically that "scattered here and there throughout the country are individual classrooms, single schools, and entire school systems which have realistically accepted the fact of radio and its tremendous influence and have adjusted the curriculum, teaching processes, and even administrative practices to take full advantage of this powerful learning aid" (p. v).

In the book for which Tyler had written the introduction, Levenson (1945) wrote that "so rapidly has modern broadcasting evolved that even to describe its current status, let alone to contemplate its future development, is an extremely difficult task" (p. 443). Levenson included a photo of children in a rural Kentucky school, beneath which was the caption "With Radio the Underprivileged School Becomes the Privileged One." This caption was similar to those that would be placed beneath illustrations of children with computers 40 years later. Another point of similarity with subsequent books on computer-based learning was the inclusion of a section on "Criteria for the Selection of Programs."

Identifying the educational advantages of radio-based instruction, Levenson indicated that this technology provided timely information, imparted a sense of participation to students, acted as an emotional force in the creation of desirable attitudes, added authority to learning, integrated learners' experiences, challenged dogmatic teaching, developed discrimination, eliminated limitations of distance, aided in continuous curriculum revision, improved teaching skills, and interpreted school activities to the public community. He also pointed out that "psychologists have noted that not all children learn equally well from the printed word" and that consequently "to these children, as well as to those with poor sight whose reading habits must be guarded, a school without a radio receiver is indeed 'an educational tragedy'" (p. 19).

Levenson's remarks complemented the conclusions in a 1942 report which advised teachers that "in certain areas of the curriculum, carefully planned and produced radio programs can be made of sufficient educational value to justify spending the time and money necessary for their production, and also using classroom time for their reception" (Wisconsin Research Project in School Broadcasting, 1942). Experiments in radio education were not restricted solely to audiences of students. Burris (1945) described how he had directed the "Institute of the Air" at a New Mexico university in an effort to train students by providing information to their teachers. He indicated that the institute had established radio "listening centers" in rural schools to assist the educators in those schools.

Writing in 1949 about the relationship of radio to reading, Nila Banton Smith disagreed with those persons who had predicted that radio listening would undermine children's motivation to read. But she was sympathetic to those critics who advised parents to exercise discretion in the types of programs to which they would allow their children to tune because of "the blood and thunder serials addressed to children with their slangy talk and highly melodramatic flavor" and because of "high-pressure sales talks" (p. 187).

Also writing about the effects of electronic media on moral values, the members of the National Education Association's Educational Policies Commission (1951) concluded that the effects of these media were "partly harmful, partly constructive, and partly neutral" but that "even the apparently 'neutral' effect should not be too quickly dismissed, for the mere consumption of vast amounts of time on trivialities is a matter for serious concern" (p. 92). Calculating that "some constructive cooperation" between the mass media and the schools had begun, they gave as an example "instruction in the evaluation of newspapers, magazines, motion pictures, and radio programs." They also noted with approval that "radio and television networks, sometimes with school cooperation, present some wholesome programs for children" and that "a few schools and colleges produce their own radio and television programs" (p. 92).

Television-Based Education

Lilian Gish, a famous star of silent movies, had written glowingly in the 1929 edition of the *Encyclopedia Britannica* that the "so-called educational moving picture has shown itself to be a form of informational Esperanto" (Gish, 1992, p. 421). However, just a year later Bagley (1930) observed that "moving pictures" had not had an impact as large as that which had been predicted. Bagley added parenthetically that "the development of the talkies, however, will very greatly increase the educational usefulness of the movies" and that "within a few years—perhaps even a shorter time—we may expect a wide range of talking films for school use" (p. 219). He also added prophetically that "of even richer promise to education is the combination of radio and television" (p. 219). Bagley speculated that radio might be limited as an instructional medium in the same way that silent movies had been. However he predicted that with the development of television "a much wider field of service will be opened" (p. 219). He suggested a format for instruction in which "the broadcasting teacher will himself have charge of a class, and that what the pupils of this class say and do will be projected upon the screen in thousands of classrooms" thereby creating "untold possibilities for the training of teachers in the educational talkies and in the television-radio" (p. 220). Bagley concluded sanguinely that just as textbooks had benefited by private enterprise, "in the same way, commercial competition in providing school radio programs may conceivably be the best method of refining the technic [sic] of educational broadcasting and of otherwise developing the educational possibilities inherent in the radio and in television" (p. 221).

Television did develop into a hardy industry during the decades that followed Bagley's prediction. Supportive remarks that had been made earlier about the value of radio-based learning were very similar to those that were made during the 1950s and 1960s about the unlimited future for television-based education. A report about televised teaching (Ford Foundation, 1961) began with the confident announcement that this date marked "the beginning of a new era in American education." Television was identified as "the most important new educational tool since the invention of movable type" and a medium which if used wisely "can bring to students educational experiences far beyond what is possible in the conventional classroom" (p. 68). Among the advantages of televised learning were observations that "televised instruction requires the student to accept more responsibility for his own learning than is the case with conventional methods of instruction," "students in television classes at the elementary and secondary level make more extensive use of the school library than students in regular classes," "televised courses have been much more carefully planned and organized than conventional courses," "the combination of the skills of the studio teacher and of the classroom teacher has made possible a cooperative teaching effort far better than either teacher could achieve alone," "the classroom teachers, relieved of the burden of planning and presenting the principal material in several different subjects during the course of a day, are free to concentrate on other important aspects of teaching," "a more effective use of teaching time and classroom space [results]," and "the use of superior teachers on television has proved an important means of upgrading the quality of other teachers" (pp. 11-13).

Nine years before the Ford Foundation report had been published, Du Mont (1952) had predicted that one of the "most fertile" markets for educational television was the "captive-audience" program in which closed-circuit channels were used to steer programs to special audiences. Du Mont wrote that "to be of any benefit, television should be able to provide better instruction" and that closed-circuit broadcasts "could utilize a better-than-average level of instruction" (p. 17). He was hopeful that televised instruction could simultaneously raise the level of teaching while reducing both the current educational costs and the amount of effort being expended by "local" teachers. Most of the reasons for employing television that had been listed in the Ford Foundation report referred to opportunities for improved instruction. For example, one of these opportunities was the benefit to instructors who adopted the careful planning endemic to television. Dale (1961) elaborated upon this point:

> Television, like radio, is broadcast under rigid limitations of time. Furthermore, its visual images appear on a relatively small screen area. Such physical restrictions compel those who prepare programs to organize auditory and visual content with great economy and care. They must develop a visual-verbal shorthand different from that required by radio or films. Television has already given birth to a new compressed form of communication, whose very succinctness brings clarity of explanation (pp. 201-202).

Despite such praise, Dale cautioned teachers to be vigilant because "whenever one is forced to condense an explanation, he may oversimplify" (p. 202).

Criticism of Radio-Based and Television-Based Education

After recalling the initial enthusiasm that met film-based education during the early 1920s, Wise (1939) admitted that this technology had failed to spread during the subsequent 15 years. He speculated that the failure could have resulted from a shortage of quality films, the high cost of equipment, technical problems with unsafe film, or limited access to portable projectors. He also discussed instructional factors that could enhance learning. For example, the instructional factors he identified that could influence the success of historical films in the classroom were the extent to which those films aroused interest, stimulated imagination, portrayed details not found in textbooks, aided retention, gave pleasure, re-created the atmosphere of the past, and engagingly rendered characters.

From a perspective similar to that from which Wise attempted to explain the failure of cinema in the classroom, other critics attempted to rationalize the limited effectiveness of radio. For example, Chase expressed misgivings about radio-based education in a 1937 paper he presented at a conference on educational broadcasting. He specifically had criticized "the unskilled manner in which the average educational program is presented" and cautioned that "if educational broadcasting is to be more successful, it is a field in which a vast deal of experimentation remains to be done" (p. 26).

Like Chase, Laine (1938) listened to radio programs that were "specially prepared and broadcast for schools" and worried that "probably there will never be complete correlation between a series of school broadcasts and the class work" (p. 111). However, she was not dismayed by this poor correlation because of her conviction that the greatest "contribution that the radio can make to education is undoubtedly that of introducing history in the making" (p. 93). She advised teachers to evaluate radio-based education "not only on the basis of its direct contribution to the curriculum, but also in terms of the interests it arouses, the activities it stimulates, and the attitudes it creates" (p. 111).

As early as the 1940s, school personnel contemplated a transition from radio-based to television-based instruction, a transition about which they were concerned because they did not wish to purchase equipment that would rapidly become obsolete. Dent (1942) advised school personnel that those "who may be hesitating to secure radio or motion-picture equipment for school use for fear of obsolescence due to rapid television development, may dismiss those fears and proceed with reasonable assurance that any up-to-date equipment installed this year or next, or during the nest several years, will be extremely useful for many years to come" (p. 178).

Educators had to consider not only the prospects of incorporating television into instruction, but also the issue of whether film would continue to be used. Lorang (1945) reported that questions about the enduring application of films in education had still not been resolved, even though "investigators report that the movies have great value in education; that they can be effective in character formation and in acquiring good habits" (p. 97). She speculated that the use of film in the classroom might be inadvertently promoting attendance at cinemas, which was undesirable because "there appears to be a common denominator in frequent movie attendance, poor home conditions, poor scholastic achievement, and emotional instability" (p. 103). Lorang concluded that "in a comparison of the motility during sleep caused by two cups of coffee and that caused by movie attendance, it was concluded that a serious effect on health might result from excessive attendance" (p. 103).

Television-based education became more popular during the 1950s. However, as its popularity increased, criticism of its use in education increased proportionately. As was the case with radio and film, this criticism examined not only the technology itself but also the limits of the format for televised instruction. Frazier (1959) complained that the format for educational television programs had been inappropriately derived from a model used in college teaching. Dissatisfied with the productions that had resulted, he referred to televised educational programs as "talking textbooks."

In contrast, Siepman (1958) expressed unqualified optimism for the future of television-based education after concluding that the radio had already "been perfected to an instrument of education" (p. 16). He alleged that 78 percent of schools used radio-based instruction and that television-based instruction, though it could not yet "boast" of such success, would be equally successful. He indicated that "whether we think of television as a neo-Marxist opiate of the masses, or as a formative influence of high cultural significance, any one of us is likely to concede that the public could have got along without it [but] it is the main purpose of this book to show that, by contrast, our educational system could not have done so and cannot now" (p. 2). Keeping in mind Siepman's enthusiasm for television-based education, examine the following description that he adduced as a model reading lesson:

> A standard 21-inch television set was wheeled into place on a desk-high stand. One child hung a sign on the door: "Don't enter—TV class in progress." Other children pulled down the blinds. The screen showed the hands of a clock. At exactly 9:45, the television teacher appeared. She greeted the children, introduced herself and began the prefatory remarks to her first lesson. She continued for twenty-five minutes. During that time, the classroom teacher observed pupils in order that she might solve individual problems during the supplementary period. When the television lesson was ended, the classroom teacher spent the remaining ten minutes of the period in answering questions, taking care of the individual differences in pupils, and reviewing what had been learned (p. 52).

Having reviewed televised instruction of this sort, Frazier (1959) concluded that "certainly most of us cannot accept the kind of thing being generally offered on television today" (p. 45). From a point of view similar to that from which Laine had criticized radio 21 years earlier, Frazier asked about "possibilities in simply looking at what can be done with creatively produced filmed materials, not in series or as courses, but as events in themselves, that can stimulate and inspire activity" (p. 44). In agreement with Frazier's critical observations, a National Education Association report published that same year expressed disappointment with many television-based programs. However, the authors advised that the best solution would recognize that "program makers cannot be technicians alone but must be part of a curriculum team" and that "television programs should be judged more clearly in terms of educational objectives than has been common in the past" (National Education Association, 1959, p. 36). The report specifically advised readers that educational programs "are good when their learning goals are sharply defined and poor when these goals are fuzzily conceived" (p. 37). Unlike

Frazier's suggestion to reduce the academic character of educational broadcasts, the NEA report recommended that those educational programs that were failing should require additional academic tailoring.

The evaluation of television-based education's effectiveness was compounded by the uncertainty of school administrators about the prospective longevity of television in the schools as well as the longevity of the other types of technology on which they might spend their limited funds. Although this uncertainty could be detected during the 1940s when television was initially becoming available, the indecision of administrators was still apparent two decades later. As an example, the issue of which types of equipment schools should select was considered in a 1960s report published by the National Educational Association (Finn, Perrin, & Campion, 1962). The report predicted that the country was in a state of transition from a "traditional" to a technological society and that to complete this transition "we view the build-up of audio-visual equipment and materials in education as one of the principal preconditions for a technological revolution in education" (p. 9). They were aware that teachers were confused about whether to purchase teaching machines, 8-mm sound projectors, cartridge loading projectors, computers, or other newly developed systems for distributing information. After responding that they did not wish "to elaborate on the advantages and disadvantages of means and/or media," the authors illogically advised that equipment spending should still proceed as long as funds "go into technological investment" (p. 72).

COMPUTER-BASED INSTRUCTIONAL STRATEGIES

In 1979 Dillingofski assembled an annotated bibliography of reports about computers and other "nonprint media" involved in reading instruction. She identified three areas in which the computer had been used for reading instruction: drill and practice, diagnosis, and tutorial instruction. Despite reports which indicated that computers benefited instruction in reading, Dillingofski (1979) concluded that "computers have not penetrated many school reading programs" (p. 27). As an explanation she suggested that "there is a dearth of validated programs for reading instruction," that "the cost per student continues to be prohibitive," and that "while computer programs can foster growth in word identification skills, they have not often been used to foster higher level cognitive strategies" (p. 27).

Kuchinskas (1983) reviewed professional literature on language-based instruction and concluded that "the value to students in easy access to their own writing production has been the essence of all language experience programs in reading" (p. 14). After noting that "recording student work in print has been time-consuming and has limited teachers' use of this valuable tool," Kuchinskas advised teachers to reduce the practical demands of language-based instruction through the use of computers. Also addressing potential objections from language-based instructors, Geoffrion and Geoffrion (1983) conceded that teachers might question why computers needed to be introduced into the reading classroom "when books serve reading so effectively." They responded that computers could motivate learners by novelty, allow texts to be tailored for instructional activities, introduce alternative formats for presenting materials, and integrate graphics with text. They also pointed out that computers could quickly perform the recording, sorting, and calculating tasks that might be required for learning activities. In addition to aiding teachers, computers could assist the learners themselves by equipping them with special tools such as a word processor, dictionary, glossary, thesaurus, or index.

Kinzer, Hynds, and Loofbourrow (1986) wrote about the special value of computers to those reading instructors who used language-based approaches. They were worried because "much reading software is little more than a high-technology workbook" (p. 215). Despite this weakness, they were confident that computers "do have the potential for advancing and improving reading instruction" and counseled that "existing software must be examined with a critical eye" so that "educators can use software originally designed for purposes besides reading instruction" (p. 216). The authors advised teachers that "simulation software, even if not intended specifically for reading instruction, can be used by reading teachers both in normal and content-area reading instruction" (pp. 218-219). They explicitly discussed how computers could be used to enhance language-based instruction:

> Computers can also be used to supplement the Language Experience Approach (LEA) in reading instruction. In this method, students recite stories to the teacher, who writes down what is dictated. The reading lesson then proceeds using the students' natural language. Using a computer, stories can be typed and later revised with a word processing program. Copies of the stories can be quickly printed and distributed to students. Specific lessons can also be developed easily based on a student's story. For example, if the teacher wanted to teach "–ing" words, those used by the student easily could be listed after the computer performs a word search. The computer could also keep records of the students' vocabularies for individualized word banks (1986, p. 219).

Despite these remarks, they still doubted the relative value of language-based exercises that were computer-assisted. They concluded that "the main advantage is in saving labor and time for the teacher" and that "a potential drawback is that young students may lose the benefit of watching the teacher form letters as the story is written" (p. 219).

Two years later Johnson (1988) described procedures by which advanced students could create their own materials using "an integrated software package." He wrote that he "was convinced that the ability to gather an array of information, organize that information, and develop it into meaningful and logical text is one of the most important things children need to learn" (p. 2). Using cumbersome language, he elaborated the details of such an instructional project:

> After gathering some information and organizing it into records and fields, the student would turn his attention to the word processor and a partially completed document. At certain points in the document the student would be asked to choose appropriate supportive information from the database. Similar, progressively more complex exercises could then follow, allowing the student to take more and more responsibility for the written work. Some templates could even take the student backward through the assimilation process, by starting with a theme sentence and going back to the raw data which become the supportive evidence. This could be done in a way that would demonstrate the process involved (p. 3).

Like Johnson, Polin (1993) gave examples of several experimental programs in which proponents of holistic approaches had integrated computers into their instruction, enabling those teachers to build on the "emergent literacy" of the learners:

> Students engaged "in a variety of patterns of use and forms of writing" at the computers. They used the graphics programs to draw, but also to "enact stories" and create illustrations for paper and pencil stories. They used the word-processing software to generate letter strings, whose patterns tended to echo the keyboard layout or environmental print in the room. Some letter strings were described as part of "playing typist" and others represented stories (p. 91).

Polin also wrote approvingly of an IBM project referred to as "Writing to Read." She noted that the approach "mixes reading, writing, listening, and speaking as mutually reinforcing literacy processes" (p. 93). Although she admitted that this project "does enact a good bit of what emergent literacy proponents find important for a young child to experience," Polin was not completely enthusiastic because "there are some places the project departs from emergent literacy, especially in its belief that using 42 phonemes (letter-sound combinations) as building blocks, children discover the sounds of speech can be made visible in writing" (p. 93). She cautioned that this latter premise "is not found among the views held by emergent literacy and whole language educators" (p. 93).

Also concerned about the integration of computers into language-based instruction, Searfoss and Readence (1994) suggested that instructors establish "print labs" in which students would learn to use computers both to read as well as to create printed materials that others would read. They advised that such applications could reduce the likelihood that computers would be restricted to "drill and practice" and become opportunities for communication.

During the 1990s educators who endorsed computer-based reading education attempted to disassociate themselves from that image in which computers were linked to drill activities. After noting that computerized lessons in reading had sometimes been referred to by the disparaging term *electronic drill sheets*, Collins and Cheek (1993) and Templeton (1995) highlighted opportunities to develop higher-order reading skills with computers. In a similar fashion, Gunning (1996) adjured teachers to resist the temptation to use computers as electronic textbooks and instead make them available to students who would "locate data, retrieve information, organize data, compose information, and present information" (p. 539).

Because drilling was frequently associated with technology-based learning, critics used this association as a demonstration that computers promoted the spread of unimportant activities in classrooms. However, not all educators conceded that drilling was unimportant to readers. Perfetti (1983) argued that computers presented an egress from a dilemma in which teachers were forced "to choose between the basic-but-dull and the complex-but-engaging" (p. 145). He pointed out that many teachers chose to design instructional activities for comprehension not because children would benefit more than they would from instruction in basic skills but rather because "it is more interesting to design tasks for comprehension" (p. 146). Convinced that development of fundamental skills was important to readers even though it might not be as professionally satisfying to teachers, Perfetti recommended that computers be used to make "the fundamental more engaging" (p. 161).

Also sure that drilling was useful for developing accuracy and "automaticity" in reading, Burns, Roe, and Ross (1996) recommended that computers be used as convenient tools with which to implement drills. They pointed out that the games that were typically integrated into those drills could motivate students by adding interest that would otherwise be lacking. Carnine, Silbert, and Kameenui (1996) suggested that teachers use computers for vocabulary instruction in reading because computers reduced the expenditure of teacher effort, enabled individualized instruction, and allowed teachers to systematize reviews and generalize concepts across academic areas. Grabe and Grabe (1996) had observed insightfully that those teachers who emphasized the learning of factual knowledge through drills were not responding to mandates from computers and would likely continue to use drill-like activities even should this technology be removed from their classrooms.

Using Computers to Individualize Instruction

While exploring the opportunities to individualize instruction through computers, Suppes (1967) had written that "this technology offers a possibility of individual fulfillment in education hardly conceivable fifty years ago" and that "for the first time since public education for everyone became a major goal of our society, individual instruction at a genuinely deep level is now a feasible goal" (p. 24). Writing in the same book as Suppes, Bushnell (1967) illustrated how learning could be integrated with games on computers. He explained that "in a computer game the student is presented with information about some situation and asked to make decisions" and that "his decisions are fed back into the system and result in a new set of facts, the consequences of his good or bad decisions, about which he must then make new decisions" (p. 62.)

Citing specific examples of the benefits of learning tasks that were integrated with games, Bushnell indicated that games could be related to the lives of the learners, made to reflect any problem area, formatted so that students had to cooperate in teams, orchestrated in a manner that was student-centered, and arranged to enhance motivation through competition with the computer or with other students.

Thirteen years later Bork (1980a) provided specific examples of procedures to enable computer-maintained records of instruction to be used as a means to improved instruction. As a consequence he hoped that "the learning experience for each student can be unique, tailored to the needs, desires, and moods of that student" (p. 60). In addition to the use of computer-maintained records to modify subsequent instruction, Bork highlighted advantages of technology-based learning that would not likely have been available to students who engaged in the identical activities through printed media. The control of pacing, time allocated for tasks, sequencing, and content were examples of these advantages.

After reviewing the professional literature on the relationship between technology and instructional methods, Nickerson (1988) noted that "the possibility of using computers and related technology for instructional purposes has been of interest to some researchers and educators for at least two decades." Despite this interest, he admitted that the "impact of technology on instruction and learning to date has not been great" (p. 7). Nonetheless, he examined the research literature and identified three general principles upon which he detected consensus. The first of these principles was that instruction should be individualized. Five years later Shanker (1993) described an "imperative" need for expanded technology because "all kinds of technology exist that can make individualized learning possible" (p. 618).

INSTRUCTION LINKED TO COMMUNICATION

Even though he realized that the ability to communicate through computers was limited in the early 1980s, Frude (1983) predicted that "the home will soon become a powerful information center, with the domestic computer, linked to telephone lines, able to gain access to a comprehensive, centralized store of knowledge and expertise" (p. 211). He described a futuristic vision in which "a user would be able to browse through vast library files, go on a trip through information pathways, and take short orientation courses on fringe and mainstream subjects." He even speculated that such information might be "'fully interactive,' and the mode of presentation might be chosen as visual or aural."

The impact of much of the criticism that had been directed toward technology-based instruction was deflected with the actualization of Frude's vision about expanded opportunities to employ computers as communication devices. However, the engineering that enabled widespread use of computer-based communication developed less rapidly than the other technologies associated with computers. A 1970 report indicated the extremely limited access to computer-based communication:

> There are an estimated 120 dial-access information-retrieval systems in schools, colleges, and universities across the country, enabling the teacher in the classroom and the individual student in the study carrel to retrieve, by dialing a number, limited amounts of instructional material....
> At some institutions, however, the effectiveness of dial-access has been slight. Hardware was developed without appropriate software, teachers were not sufficiently consulted, curricula were not revised to use the new media, and the dial-access equipment, often costing well over a hundred thousand dollars, has been left to gather dust (Commission on Instructional Technology, 1970, pp. 75-76).

Almost two decades later Flake, McClintock, Edson, Ellington, Mack, Sandon, and Urrutia (1987) reported that access to computer-based communication had changed. They advised that "telecommunications is a rapidly expanding area, with the potential of becoming one of the most important areas in computer education" (p. 168). They recommended that teachers purchase "a modem attached to your computer and connected to a telephone line" as well as "a software package to help you pass and receive files" (p. 168). As examples of communication activities that could be part of computer-based curricula, they provided several extremely simple projects, such as students transferring files between schools or playing a guessing game with a party in another location.

By the middle 1990s exciting changes in the computerized Internet had transpired. After pointing out that the term *cyberspace* had been employed originally in science fiction, Turkle (1995) observed that this word had been adapted to refer to the communicative characteristics of computers. She wrote that "in cyberspace, we can talk, exchange ideas, and assume personae of our creation" and that users "have the opportunity to build new kinds of communities, virtual communities in which we participate with people from all over the world, people with whom we converse daily, people with whom we may have fairly intimate relationships but whom we may never physically meet" (pp. 9-10).

A year earlier Miller (1994) indicated that the computerized Internet was an important resource available to students. Providing multiple examples of learning activities that could be implemented with Internet resources, Miller indicated that the Internet had increased during the years 1969 to 1994 from a system with four hosts to a network with more than two million host sites. Defining the Internet as a network of networks, the NRENAISSANCE Committee (1994) estimated the size of the Internet in 1994:

> Currently it consists of approximately 20,000 registered networks, some 2 million host computers, and 15 million users. Approximately half the networks are commercial...and half noncommercial; about one-third of the hosts are associated with research or educational institutions. Most of the Internet connections are in the United States, but 149 countries or national entities have connections of one sort or another to international computer networks, with about 63 countries possessing direct connections to the Internet (p. 21).

Citing statistics indicating that more than 20 million persons were using the Internet worldwide in 1994 and that the size of the Internet was increasing geometrically each year, Miller judged it as self-evident that "technology that affects so many people in so many countries cannot be dismissed" (p. 1). With similar confidence, Barron and Ivers (1996) advised teachers that "the typical classroom is no longer bound by four walls: it is open to students and experts from around the world" (p. xiii).

Nonetheless, some skeptics pointed to the similarly optimistic but unrealistic predictions that had been made about the benefits of other technologies. In a book with the derogatory title *Silicone Snake Oil*, Stoll (1995) chastised the individuals who had developed computerized networks for employing myths similar to those evoked by the developers of cable-television networks when they had promised to introduce diversity, culture, and novelty into television broadcasts. Two years earlier Postman had questioned the value of using computers to expand the amount of information to which learners had access when "children, like the rest of us, are now suffering from information glut, not information scarcity" (1993, p. 26).

Cronin (1996) wrote that the original government-oriented and research-based Internet was the "product of United States funding and technical resources" (p. 264). As recently as the late 1980s Internet connections outside the United Sates were largely restricted to universities and research institutions. During the late 1980s the National Science Foundation had supported the development of software that enabled the widespread use of the Internet that would take place during the early 1990s. Observing that commercial use of the Internet had mushroomed after the establishment of the Commercial Internet Exchange in 1991, Cronin wrote that the subsequent expansion of Internet connections around the world indicated its truly international character.

Serim and Koch (1996) provided many examples of learning projects that students could complete when they used the computer as a communicative device in conjunction with the Internet. To facilitate the arrangement of such projects, they provided an appendix of information sites useful to K-12 educators. They listed projects in which "students direct their learning by pursuing their interests and taking responsibility for managing their own projects" and in which "students are also strongly encouraged to collaborate with others" (p. 5).

Many of these sites identified by Serim and Koch were available through the World Wide Web. A government publication (U. S. Department of Education, 1996) defined the Web as a method of organizing the Internet with text, graphics, sound, and video. The report indicated that "the notable feature of the Web is its inter-linking of documents that enable you to go among and across a series of documents or pages simply by selecting a highlighted word or group of words called a 'link'" (p. 1). Ackermann (1996) estimated that the World Wide Web comprised conduits through which more than half of the information on the Internet was transferred to more than 20 million users. Cafolla, Kauffman, and Knee (1997) estimated that the number of World Wide Web sites as of July 1996 was 18 million and that more than 44 million persons were using Internet services throughout the world. They provided an annotated list of educational websites about topics such as the humanities, science, culture, current events, education, and media.

Miller (1994) had also provided an extensive list of websites appropriate for teachers. She warned them to promote their students' eventual success as workers and adult learners because "today's students must know how to use the Internet to communicate and to search and retrieve information" (p. 9). Barron and Ivers (1996) summarized the student advantages for the Internet when they noted that "it opens doors to real world learning experiences, invites higher-order thinking skills, and can help to increase motivation and writing skills" (p. 4). However, they warned instructors that "the quantity of educational resources available through these procedures and sources is overwhelming and it may be difficult for teachers to find the time to explore these resources and integrate them into their curricula" (p. xiii).

Heide and Stilborne (1996) supplied numerous examples of instructional activities in which students could send e-mail to persons throughout the world as well as engage in projects that centered about on-line computerized resources. They pointed to text-based resources on a wide range of topics as well as resources for "electronic field trips involving pictures, text, sound, and sometimes interactivity." In addition to formats for instructional activities, they provided electronic addresses for sites at which students could locate full-text books, magazines, reference materials, archives of historical information, and specialized data about multiple topics.

Sandholtz, Ringstaff, and Dwyer (1997) reported about a project that had used computers in classrooms since 1985. They indicated that their attitudes toward technology education had change over the period during which this project was being developed. They recounted that "in the beginning of the project, we thought that technology would be used to support individualized learning, self-expression through writing, and drill and practice" (p. 8). At the end of a decade of implementation, the staff "actively encouraged and supported teachers' efforts to create environments where technologies were used as knowledge-building tools for communication and collaboration, media-rich composition, and simulation and modeling across the curriculum" (p. 10).

Lockard, Abrams, and Many (1997) pointed out that, to some extent, all computerized activities that required the use of text could reinforce reading and language arts skills. However, they noted that communicative software provided a special opportunity to extend traditional classroom activities. For example, they explained that traditional readers' circles, in which students orally shared their impressions of materials that they had read, could be adapted so that persons at distant schools could participate through computers. They also provided a list of websites at which instructors and students could gain information about additional computer-based, communicative projects to develop language arts skills.

Though Frank Smith had been a vocal critic of computers in education, he conceded in 1997 that "electronic technology is here until some other technology supersedes it" and that the Internet's "possibilities and pitfalls are fundamentally no different from those of the rest of the world around us" (1997, p. 147). Although he still warned that computers could be abused by administrators and instructors who viewed them as teaching machines, Smith acknowledged the value of on-line communication technology that can "put children in touch with what they might want to read; it can tell them where to find particular books, magazines, and newspapers that they might desire or find interesting and useful; and it can present directly on its screen 'information' that they might find relevant to a purpose of their own" (p. 149).

In a critical article titled "The Computer Delusion," Oppenheimer (1997) summarized opinions by persons who were skeptical of the contributions that computers had made to education. Referring to computers as the filmstrip of the 1990s, he questioned whether the funds diverted to computers had diminished students' opportunities to avail themselves of more valuable areas in the curriculum. Even with this confrontational view, Oppenheimer gave several examples of imaginative learning projects that have been facilitated through the Internet and admitted that "the Internet, when used carefully, offers exciting academic prospects."

SUMMARY

Technology-based education originated well before computers had been placed in the schools. Having pointed to the problems that accompanied technologies such as radio and television after their introduction in education, some critics predicted that similar problems would accompany computers. Many of the problems that did develop originated with unreliable hardware and the regimented format of early instructional programs. Despite the pessimistic predictions, the number of computers in the schools increased noticeably during the 1980s. Because computers could individualize instruction and motivate learners, programs were developed to reduce the drudgery that teachers and students associated with reading drills. Word processing programs provided another benefit, enabling computers to be adapted for language-based instruction during which students created passages that were then used as their primary instructional material. Though the spread of computers in reading curricula was evident throughout the 1980s, the accessibility of the Internet during the 1990s escalated that development. The availability of limitless information and the opportunity for interaction between learners further secured the link between computers and reading education.

Chapter 11

TEACHING READING TO PERSONS WITH DISABILITIES

The process of decreasing retardation in the schools is merely a part of the more general one of adapting education to the capacities of children (Woodrow, 1923).

During the 1800s many persons with moderate and severe disabilities were placed in institutions. In spite of pioneering demonstrations that these individuals could develop literacy skills, most educators assumed that an appropriate curriculum for them would reinforce nonacademic learning, be implemented within institutionalized settings, and prepare them for tasks that were part of an institutionalized life. However, many children with learning problems could not be accommodated in institutions. Therefore, schools began to hire specially trained teachers to instruct students with disabilities in public school classrooms. Though the initial plan was to segregate the children with disabilities who were being instructed in public schools from their peers without disabilities, the number of persons with disabilities exceeded the opportunities for placements in segregated classrooms. Consequently, many children with disabilities had to be integrated into regular education classrooms, where they needed to become literate to benefit from the instruction. Although educators agreed that special literacy programs needed to be developed for these students, no consensus was apparent about which type of approach was in fact suitable. In their pursuit of effective programs, educators tried to designate the characteristics and causes of all disabilities that could interfere with reading. They paid special attention to a subtle problem that they referred to as dyslexia.

*   *   *

Descoeudres (1928) observed that various types of public special education programs had been initiated in England before the middle of the nineteenth century. However, determining the degree to which literacy was taught to persons with disabilities during the nineteenth century is complicated because of incomplete, and sometimes contradictory early reports. Despite Descoeudres's report,

293

Shuttleworth (1899) had recounted earlier that the first genuinely special education school in London was not opened until 1892. Earlier still, Ireland (1877) reported about programs for persons with disabilities in the United States. He indicated that "in 1818 the effort was begun, and continued for several years, at the American Asylum for the Deaf and Dumb, in Hartford, to instruct idiot children" (p. 292). Also writing about early programs in the United States, Frampton and Rowell (1938) noted that "a class for the training of idiots" had been started at the Blind Asylum at South Boston in 1837. A report about programs from this period that was actually written in the middle 1800s ("Schools in Lunatic Asylums," 1845), indicated that educational programs lasting for an hour each day had been developed within the New York State Lunatic Asylum at Utica.

Sylvester (1909) identified additional nineteenth-century programs in New York, Pennsylvania, Ohio, Connecticut, Kentucky, Illinois, Indiana, and New Jersey. By the late 1800s Fernald (1893) observed that "in this country the necessity and humanity of caring for and scientifically treating the insane, the deaf and dumb, and the blind had become the policy of many of our most progressive States" (p. 205). Despite Fernald's optimistic appraisal, Farrell (1908-1909) reported in her history of special schools in New York City that the first classes were not initiated until 1899. However, Holmes (1912) did report that just a decade later 99 cities in the United States had public school classes for "mentally defective pupils" and 220 had classes for "mentally backward children."

Although accounts of the educational programs used in nineteenth-century schools were sketchy, several literacy programs were documented. For example, Brockett (1856), who had taught adults with mental disabilities, recommended that reading be taught with a whole word approach rather than the alphabet method because "a *word* can be associated with an object, in the mind of a pupil, while letters can not" (p. 602). He also reviewed a case study about a nonverbal young adult who mastered initial reading skills with the aid of a textbook-centered approach.

Writing about "idiocy and imbecility" two decades later, Ireland (1877) included a chapter on education in which he concluded that the "best way to teach them to read is to teach them to recognize syllables before teaching them to know their letters" and that "for this purpose words should be selected" (p. 321). Unlike Brockett, Ireland discouraged the use of basal readers that systematically progressed from simple to complex lessons because he thought students with disabilities could not adapt to the schedules for such progressions.

At the end of the nineteenth century, Johnston (1898) described educational practices within Indiana institutions in which "simple reading" was taught by the "word method" to "high grade" learners. He also gave an example of a school for "middle grade" learners at which "each class gets but one half hour per day for reading, writing and arithmetic, all three" (p. 104). He explained that in these types of curricula "our aim here is to teach these children to read the simplest stories for their own amusement" as well as "to recognize groups to 10 or 15, and do a little writing to send their parents or guardians, as a source of pleasure to them" (p. 104). Johnston contrasted these academic approaches with that for "the lowest class," one which had been designed "with a view to giving them exercise—to rouse them out of themselves" (p. 105).

EARLY TWENTIETH-CENTURY LITERACY PROGRAMS

Though persons with disabilities who did receive an education were likely to receive it in public institutions like those Johnston had described, Pollock and Furbush (1917) reported that "the insane, feebleminded, epileptics and inebriates" were found not only in private institutions but in "almshouses, jails, reformatories and penal institutions" (p. 548). More than two decades earlier, Fernald (1893) had also admitted that "the class of helpless and neglected idiots who had no homes, as a rule were cared for in jails and poorhouses" (p. 205). However, Fernald wrote that when these persons were fortunate enough to be placed in appropriate institutions, they did receive educational as well as custodial care. He observed that "in the school department the children are instructed in the ordinary branches of the common schools" and that the education they received was "a difference of degree, and not of kind" (p. 216). Snedden (1907) estimated that more than 35,000 students were incarcerated at approximately 96 juvenile reform schools, many of which maintained both educational and corrective programs. He was convinced that educational programs were appropriate because "the children committed to the reform schools were far behind the normal child in point of intellectual attainments" (p. 19). He described the general format of programs in which "a system of education usually called literary" had been designed to "put the inmates somewhat on an equality with children outside" (p. 19).

Doll (1909) was a special education teacher in the Cincinnati schools who described case studies of students exhibiting "*slovenliness* in reading, writing, and in fact, in all work," and for whom she recommended reading activities involving phonics, spelling, and, in one case, the use of a typewriter to reinforce letter recognition. Among the 49 students she had instructed, "sixteen, after varying periods, were restored to their classes to take up the work with their normal mates; twenty were promoted to higher grades at the close of the school; ten others, who could not be so promoted, are prepared next year to perform intelligently and self-helpfully the work of the grade in which before they were floundering or helpless" (p. 34).

Publishing that same year, Devereux (1909) reported the results of a year-long experiment in which she taught 43 children with disabilities. Although she had initially intended to use manual activities such as woodwork, basketry, and sewing as the pretext for teaching academic skills, she abandoned this plan and "tried to make them see in every way what was the right thing to do, and not only to make them do it but to make them want to do it" (p. 47). She used the positive attitudes that resulted to facilitate instruction in reading, writing, and mathematics. Noting with pride that 29 of the 43 children in her class had returned to regular classrooms, she observed that "even now when they are returned to the grade, some still have a persistent defect but it does not mar their entire standing" (p. 47).

Two years later Sherlock (1911), a superintendent at a British asylum, wrote that "the feeble-minded" could be taught "with the help of a rhythmic arrangement" to repeat the letters of the alphabet. But he warned that the learners were "unable to say what letter comes before or after another taken at random, or what is the last letter, without running through the whole series" (pp. 304-305). Sherlock "questioned whether committing the alphabet to memory is the best preliminary to learning to read even in the case of normal children" and suggested instead that "the immediate purpose in teaching a child to read and write is to open up channels for conveying instruction" (pp. 305-306).

Many educators disagreed with their colleagues who were embarrassing literacy programs. Holmes (1915) recommended that teachers as well as their students be trained in nonacademic skills that "may seem appallingly but they are entirely reasonable":

> She should learn manual work, including bench work in carpentry, basket weaving, raffia work, clay-modeling, sand-modeling, drawing, water-color work and, what only a few teachers have yet attempted, enough knowledge of machinery to take apart a clock, odd bits of household plumbing, faucets, gas-cocks, electric bells, sewing-machines, phonographs, etc. Such an array of knowledge may seem formidable but she is not through yet. The expert teacher must add to her other accomplishments the art of physical culture encompassing the usual calisthenics, swimming, a number of indoor and outdoor games, and enough skill to follow the directions of a physician in corrective gymnastics. Closely allied to this is speech training, which so many of her pupils will need and on which so much mental development intimately depends (p. 227).

Although Anderson (1917) discouraged the routine incorporation of regular school subjects into the curricula of individuals with disabilities, she recognized that this practice was "so firmly grounded" that it was difficult to even locate alternative materials designed especially for students with disabilities. Anderson warned that reading, writing, and arithmetic should not be taught to all students because "with many a nervous child these studies have a definite tendency to increase the nervousness and have been known to cause insanity" (p. 72).

Literacy Programs After 1920

Burt (1922), a British psychologist, counseled instructors that "to teach reading in a special school to children whose mental ratio is less than 50 per cent is simply to squander time and energy" (p. 283). The nonacademic programs that were alternatives to literacy programs for persons with disabilities were generally referred to as manual training curricula. Nash and Porteus (1919) had questioned the value of such curricula when these were used exclusively. Though they conceded that manual educational programs facilitated individualized instruction and might even lead to successful careers, they also observed that "defectives vary in their abilities for manual work just as much as they do in their capacities for scholastic work" (p. 1). After describing the basket weaving and carpentry activities that had become prevalent in many programs, they outlined alternative instructional activities, some of which integrated academic and manual skills. As one example, they listed the advantages of teaching students to use a printing press that would require "exercise of patience, prudence, accuracy, and good judgment, combined with fair proficiency in English composition and spelling" (p. 15).

In the second edition of his book about "bright and dull" children, Woodrow (1923) indicated that the causes of retardation consisted not only in "traits of child nature" but with "causes lying within the school." Convinced that those children who were failing in reading were not receiving the most appropriate education, he recommended a reduction in the number of academic tasks that they would be expected to complete. Also concerned about failure in reading, Inskeep (1926) identified six possible reasons, one of which was mental retardation. She advised that "mentally slow children" be educated initially through language-based activities until they were ready for reading instruction. One reason that she advocated language-based materials was that "texts have not been written for dull and retarded children" and she judged that "it is doubtful whether such texts will ever be written" (p. 25). She gave detailed examples of procedures with which teachers could create other special materials:

> Let each child make an object reader by pasting little pictures, of a cat, a dog, or a top, and then later find the word *cat*, *dog*, or *top*, in a paper or in an advertisement, cut it out, and paste it beneath the picture. If he cannot find it in a paper or something from which he can cut it out, he prints it, copying it from the book where he has found it. Another sort of a reader can be made by pasting a picture, as of a drum, and having the children write the word under the picture several times. After a number of these pictures and words have been learned, a game can be formed by writing the words in one part of a square and asking the child to draw the picture that the word represents in another part of that square.... For mentally retarded children with language difficulties, especially those handicapped because no English is spoken in the home, a good plan is to take an old primer or first reader and cut out the pictures and a sentence or two to go with each picture. Give the child the picture and have him put it on his desk; cut up the sentence into words, mix these words up, and then let the child put the words in the proper order to make sense and place his sentence underneath the picture. If this is correct, let him paste the picture and the sentence in his loose-leaf language reader. After doing this with several pictures, encourage the child not only to paste the sentence words beneath the picture, but also to write some little sentences of his own about the picture. If the readers are exchanged, the children enjoy reading from each other's books (p. 71).

Descoeudres (1928) was a European educator who pioneered the use of games to teach reading to children with disabilities. In the second edition of her book, *The Education of Mentally Defective Children*, a chapter on reading instruction described two general approaches to instruction. Descoeudres observed that the analytical approach, which was particularly popular in Germany, Holland, and the United States, "starts with the word." She contrasted this with the "synthetic or alphabetical method, which starts with the sound" (p. 205). She recommended that instructors use the whole word approach because "it enables the teaching of reading to be joined more closely than other methods to the observation of things," "children of the visual type recognize a written name more quickly than a spoken one," and "the idea may even be associated with the written word without passing through the intervening stage of speech" (pp. 207-208). Although she was confident that whole word methods were "perfectly suited to children of the visual type," she cautioned that "other sensory types must also be taken into account" (p. 211). Despite her personal success with holistic learning strategies, she recounted honestly that "I have had many pupils thoroughly well equipped in the matter of hearing, and keenly interested in sounds, whose ability to grasp and retain shapes was very slight" (p. 211). Even though she provided an extensive discussion about the use of whole word strategies, she acknowledged the popularity of the phonetic method when she observed that "it is so well known that I need not describe it in detail" (p. 213).

Descoeudres was also a strong advocate of kinesthetic learning activities because "manual occupations invariably give pleasure, and the value of pleasure in the education of defectives cannot be exaggerated." She noted that "learners can be made to pick the letters, or embroider them; or they can form letters or syllables out of peas, sticks, or wires" (p. 215). During such exercises, children could be encouraged to recognize letters and words "by sight or touch, or do combined exercises in which both these senses are employed" (p. 215). Descoeudres also gave multiple examples of activities with "movable letters" such as dictation of sentences, copying of a handwritten text, or the juxtaposition of letters in order to create new words.

Literacy Programs After 1930

Writing in a U.S. Educational Bureau pamphlet that children with disabilities were to be found in every classroom, Martens (1934) gave specific examples of literacy lessons that were designed for children with disabilities who were being instructed in integrated settings. She wrote that the child with disabilities "can help in the building or in other manual work, he can take part in some of the class discussion, he can join in some of the musical or dramatic performances, he can accompany the group on their excursions" and as a result "all of these will be for him an incentive to redouble his efforts in learning to read about the things in which his interest has been aroused" (p. 29).

In 1940 Kirk devoted an entire book to the topic of teaching reading to "slow-learning" children. In a section on mental retardation he described approaches to literacy that could be employed with individuals whom he described in four categories: idiots, imbeciles, high-grade mental defectives, and borderline defectives. However, he recommended that persons with severe disabilities receive no type of literacy instruction since "the idiot is not trained in academic work" and "their education at home or in institutions consists primarily of training them to dress themselves, to keep themselves clean, and to eat discriminately" (pp. 13-14). Kirk reviewed popular approaches to instruction from the preceding decade that would enable reading activities to be adapted for individuals with mild disabilities. In the introduction to a set of drills on which he collaborated with Hegge and Winifred Kirk (Hegge, Kirk, & Kirk, 1940), he cautioned that older students could be embarrassed if they were required to read books in which the content was inappropriate.

A decade later Kirk and Johnson (1951) advised that instructional routines and schedules should not restrict teachers' creativity. They counseled teachers to play language games, expand children's experiences through field trips, arrange classroom activities to develop oral language, and involve students in activities in which they would illustrate passages or dramatize stories. They also advised teachers to prepare students for skills-based exercises through language-based activities, as well as through commercial reading textbooks and teacher-made materials. Noting that the U.S. Army had set fourth-grade reading achievement as the criterion for literacy among its recruits during World War II, they attempted to devise a reading program that would enable most individuals with disabilities to achieve literacy at the fourth-grade level.

Gates (1947) had judged the instructional techniques recommended by Kirk to be similar to the phonics approach developed by Marion Monroe and adapted by Samuel Orton. Worried that such a program was "undesirably formal and intricate" for persons with mental disabilities, he dismissed Kirk's approach. Gates himself had included chapters on teaching reading to the "non-reader" in the 1927, 1935, and 1947 editions of his textbook on remedial reading. In the preface to the 1935 edition he highlighted changes that included a chapter about "the teaching of reading to handicapped children—the dull, the deaf, the child with poor vision, defective motor control, nervous instability" (p. ix). Because Gates believed "the child of low intelligence enjoys substantially the same kinds of material as the average or brighter child," he recommended that the child with a disability "learns most effectively by a program similar in all essentials to that found to be most enjoyable and productive for other children (except that he needs more of it)" (pp. 403-404). He therefore advised teachers of students with disabilities to use remedial programs that had been designed for children without disabilities, but supplemented with special activities and materials. He summarized the advantages of such activities:

(1) The work book materials contain those pictures, words, and phrases and only those, which prepare the pupil to do the basal work in the course. (2) The planning of different re-uses of the materials is highly educative. (3) The activity provides the motivation which comes from permitting children to carry out their own purposes. (4) Each child will have his own material to work with. (5) Each child may work out individual projects to suit his own interests. (6) The

child is provided with natural incentives for many rereadings both of his own and other pupils' materials. (7) The plan gives pupils the satisfaction of developing something permanent which may be shown and reread, kept for other classes, bestowed as a gift, or otherwise used to satisfy good purposes. (8) Finally, a fact of greatest importance is that the materials are in regular book type and regular book sentence length and character. Thus they provide experiences identical with actual book reading (Gates, 1947, p. 408).

EARLY OPPONENTS OF SEGREGATED PROGRAMS

During the late nineteenth and early twentieth centuries educators debated whether persons with disabilities should learn to read. However, even those persons who were committed to developing literacy skills disagreed among themselves about the most effective approach. Another disagreement that drove special educators into factions was a concern about whether learning should transpire in segregated or integrated settings. Johnston (1898) was a proponent of segregated programs who explained that he had "no desire to make our child self-directing, as he must always be under the direction of the institution" (p. 98). Writing five years later, Lincoln (1903) described activities to substitute for the academic grade work of students with disabilities because those "who can be sent back to the grades to work successfully with fifty other children are the exceptional few" (p. 85).

Gilbert (1906) differentiated students who were "badly underdeveloped" from those that were "permanently defective." He allowed that the "badly underdeveloped" students should be "provided for in ungraded schools or ungraded rooms with carefully selected strong teachers" (p. 47). However, he was firm about the appropriate fate for "permanently defective" students, whom he thought "should, for their own good as well as for that of the school, be removed to some institution especially equipped to care for such" (p. 47). Despite his enthusiasm for segregated programs, Johnston (1908) recognized that "it is true that for many years there will be in the regular schools many children who should have special attention, and until the great body of citizens and educators learn to recognize the damage these children do and the loss of time they entail, there is but little likelihood of their being properly sequestered" (p. 1115).

Because of philosophic or pragmatic factors, some educators hesitated to endorse segregated programs for persons with disabilities. Huey (1912), who had written an influential book on the psychology of reading, later wrote a text about "backward and feeble-minded children." He observed that "the public schools receive and partially control, for a time, almost all of the individuals who will later trouble society as delinquents or dependents, or who will be troubled themselves by insanity or other forms of mental disturbance" (p. ix). Huey thought that many persons with disabilities could not be sent to institutions because their number greatly exceeded the capacities of the institutions intended to assist them. However, he was not distressed because he was sure that a "competent clinician-educator" could provide "the service of an institution superintendent in organizing the activities of defectives; and far more, for he can really save the state the cost of maintaining an additional institution for such cases" (p. x).

Huey had dedicated his book to Henry Goddard. In a book published originally in 1914, Goddard (1923) had recommended that children with disabilities "be placed under a distinct system which is not bound by the rules and regulations of the regular schools." Although he supported segregated programs, he was also aware of their limitations and even potential abuses. He warned that "it should always be easy to a child who has by some misunderstanding been placed in this group, but who shows ability, to get back into the normal grade at any time" (p. 61).

Groszmann (1917) wrote about the danger of placing children with disabilities in segregated environments when it might "appear as if the placing in any of these particular types of classes or schools were in the nature of a discrimination against a child" (pp. 483-484). Commenting specifically on learners with visual impairments, he advised teachers that they "should be trained in a manner which will give them from the start a habituation to natural conditions, so that they may be better equipped for conducting their life in the world of the non-defective" (p. 503).

Lewis Terman (1919), an influential psychologist who had done pioneering research on the use of tests to assess intelligence, also wrote about the disadvantages of teaching persons with disabilities in segregated classrooms. Emphasizing financial as well as instructional drawbacks, he protested that "even if the special classes were as effective educationally as its most enthusiastic champions claim, it would still be an impossible solution of the problem because of the prohibitive cost" (p. 131). Also writing in 1919, Best described an educational movement that challenged the placement of students with disabilities within restrictive programs because "the institution is more or less out of place in modern conceptions of child welfare, and is to be accepted only in the absence of anything better" (p. 308). An advocate for day care programs that would be placed in public schools, Best argued that such programs were effective because they would be supported by the families of children and because they were cost effective.

In a memoir about progressive practices that had been initiated in 1919 in the Winnetka school district, Washburne and Marland (1963) quoted a statement by Helen Brenton, the teacher of a class "for children of retarded mental development and others who for one reason or another could not do the regular classwork" (p. 109). The remarks were made "a year or two" after 1919, when a "special room" for children with disabilities had been established:

> I don't think we should have a special room for these children. They and their parents consider it a disgrace for them to be so segregated, and the other children look down on them. Now that our work in Winnetka is individualized, why can't these children be grouped with others of

their own age, and be assigned the individual work that they are ready for, even if it is much simpler than the work of others in the same class? Instead of teaching the special class, I could go to the classes where theses children are and give them and their teachers extra help (Brenton, quoted by Washburne & Marland, 1963, pp. 109-110).

Washburne and Marland indicated that Brenton's "idea had strong appeal" and that after it was implemented "everyone was happy about the result" (p. 110).

Gessell (1921) drew an analogy between the education of gifted learners and children with disabilities. Just as early intervention programs had benefited "superior children" in their development as future leaders, he pointed out that "likewise, we can give to the defective and incompletely constituted children the training and the external support which will in many instances make them amenable, and even contributive, members of society" (p. 6). Gessell's observation about the importance of preparing children with disabilities to live in society became a theme that recurred in later discussions about the desirability of establishing integrated instructional programs.

Writing about children with disabilities a year after Gessell had made these observations, Hollingworth (1922) was more cautious in her endorsement of integrated education. She noted that segregated programs, even with their disadvantages, enabled teachers to provide a highly specialized type of intervention that would not have been possible in less restrictive settings. Like Hollingworth, Reigart (1924) highlighted the advantages as well as the disadvantages of segregated programs, acknowledging that the placement of exceptional children in segregated classes had enabled them to receive special attention. But he still warned that segregated classes had "served to prove their limitations as a final solution of [these learners'] special problems" and identified integrated learning as one of several tendencies in education that "point in a more promising direction" (p. 327). In addition to integrated classrooms, Reigart highlighted the value of innovative practices that could be facilitated through classroom assistants, interdisciplinary teams of instructors, and specialists who would visit learners in their classrooms.

Recent Opposition to Segregated Programs

The early trends toward integration of learners with disabilities grew into the dominant practice during the last quarter of the twentieth century. However, that progress was graded. In the late 1890s Fernald (1893) had indicated that 6,315 "feeble-minded persons" had been placed in "special institutions." Two decades later Pollock and Furbish (1917) described a survey indicating that 34,404 "feebleminded persons" in the United States had been placed in public institutions and that another 2,816 resided in private institutions. However, the majority of persons who could have been institutionalized during this period were not. Pressey and Pressey (1926) identified over 300 institutions for persons with disabilities but questioned whether more than 10 percent of the "feeble-minded" who were eligible would "ever enter such an institution." The popularity of institutionalized programs had waned by the 1940s as a result of changes in the public's attitudes toward segregation and because of escalating costs. With regard to costs, Deutsch (1949) wrote that "to build institutions that could house all mental defectives, or even a considerable proportion of them (assuming that such a procedure was really desirable), would require gigantic financing that no administration or legislature would be willing or able to undertake" (p. 369).

Statistics from the second half of the twentieth century indicated the decrease in institutional placements for the growing population of individuals with disabilities. Even though the number of state-operated institutions for persons with disabilities had remained substantiality unchanged for a two-decade period beginning in the early 1970s, Braddock and Mitchell (1992) noted a dramatic change in the number of integrated, community-based facilities. Not only had community-based facilities proliferated, but the greatest growth had been among facilities with less than 16 residents. They noted that in 1977, 87 percent of the nation's 290,000 persons who had disabilities and who were in out-of-home residential placements lived in settings with 16 or more residents and that most lived in facilities with several hundred residents. Since most of these segregated facilities had been state-operated, the marked decrease in segregated placements was illustrated by the reduction of persons in state-operated institutions to less than 100,000 by 1988.

Twenty years later Seltzer, Krauss, and Janicki (1994) indicated that an overwhelming 85 percent of the living arrangements for persons who were mentally retarded had become family-centered. As the lifestyles of persons with disabilities became less restrictive, so did their educational opportunities. For example, Giordano (1996) described a full range of reading programs that had been devised for adults with developmental disabilities. In addition to programs for persons with moderate disabilities, he identified programs for persons with severe and profound disabilities that were modeled after those that had been used by adults without disabilities. Parallel to the changes in the lifestyle and education of adults with disabilities, programs for children became progressively integrated. Referred to with terms such as *mainstreamed education, the regular education initiative,* and *inclusive education,* academic programs for children with disabilities became more entwined with those of their peers without disabilities.

SPECIFIC LEARNING DISABILITY

In a nineteenth-century report Morgan (1896) described a 14-year-old boy who was "bright and of average intelligence in conversation." He indicated that the student could facilely multiply three digit numbers by each other and solve algebraic problems. However, the boy could not read adequately despite "laborious and persistent training." This child made errors while spelling his own name and could not read any of the words in a sentence from "an easy child's book." Morgan concluded that the child "seems to have no power of preserving and storing up the visual impression produced by words—hence the words though seen, have no significance for him" (p. 1378). A year later Kerr (1897) advised teachers that "besides the generally dull there are mentally exceptional, many quite suitable for ordinary school provided the teacher knows their peculiarities" and gave an example of "a boy with word blindness, [but] who can spell the separate letters" (p. 668). Wagner (1973) reported that Rudolph Berlin, a German ophthalmologist, had been the first person to use the term *dyslexia* in an 1887 publication in which he referred to a physically based disorder that prevented persons from reading passages of more than several words.

Twentieth-Century Reports

Reports similar to those published at the end of the nineteenth century continued to appear during the early 1920s. Hinshelwood (1900) published several case studies about reading disability, prefacing those reports with a parenthetic note that he had already authored four papers dealing with "distinct varieties of letter- and word-blindness" (p. 1506). Admitting that he was aware of only a limited number of cases, he was nonetheless convinced that "these are by no means so rare as the absence of recorded cases would lead us to infer." He argued that "it is a matter of the highest importance to recognize the cause and the true nature of this difficulty in learning to read which is experienced by these children, otherwise they may be harshly treated as imbeciles or incorrigibles and either neglected or flogged for a defect for which they are in no wise responsible" (p. 1508). Writing that same year, Nettleship (1901) indicated that "I have myself been familiar with the condition for many years, thinking and speaking of it as congenital want of power to acquire knowledge by printed signs."

Morgan (1914) included a chapter on "recurrent problems" among school children in which he indicated that "why teachers should constantly be finding children who read 'was' as 'saw'; why a child can write his name and then cannot read it; why he puts down '30' as '03,' are all puzzles and apparent inconsistencies which psychology, if it is to be practical, must explain" (p. 233). He then gave a detailed example of the interrelationship between phonics instruction and reading failure:

> [Phonics], instead of teaching children the alphabet at the very beginning, teaches them a number of whole words all at once, on the principle that since they must learn certain symbols which seem to them perfectly arbitrary, it makes the process less mechanical if the symbol represents an idea. So that they learn to recognize 'cat,' 'boy,' 'see,' together, with certain recurring combinations of letters and these root-words, as it were, are known as phonograms. Later when they come to longer words, it is urged that reading becomes easier because, for the

careful selection of the original phonogram, they recognize familiar syllables, and need only pronounce them together. The phonic system has much in its favour, especially for normal children; but it is largely responsible for the peculiar difficulty that modern teachers meet with when a child persists in reading his words backwards (pp. 241-242).

An inspector of "auxiliary classes" for the province of Ontario in Canada, Mac-Murchy (1915) wrote that "the word-blind child is often rather above the average in mental power, and only needs teaching and encouragement" (p. 37). She also reported that "word-blindness" was hereditary, more frequent among males than females, and exhibited most often among working-class children. She used multiply imbedded relative clauses to report "an interesting suggestion" about the possible cause and remedy for dyslexia:

> Since in right-handed persons the speech-centre used is that on the left side of the brain, and in left-handed persons that on the right side, it has been suggested that the special training of the left hand might stimulate the progress of some children who are word-blind, because it may be the speech-centre on the left side of the brain that is imperfect, and if so, the training of the left hand would help the speech-centre on the right side of the brain, which is possibly being used by the child, just as the training of the right hand helps the speech-centre on the left side of the brain (p. 39).

MacMurchy recommended a multi-modal approach to therapy because "three of the speech-centres out of four are nearly always good, and we must use the proper means to 'get into their heads' enough of word-memories to enable them to acquire an education" (p. 37). She illustrated a multi-modal lesson:

> Once the child has felt out the letters, watched himself say the letter sounds and the word in the looking-glass, and has written the word, attending to the way he makes his fingers go, a new path has been opened up in his brain, and his progress simply depends upon traveling this path so often that he feels confidence in is own power. Such a child specially needs short lessons, (1) often repeated, (2) with plenty of rest between, (3) by himself, (4) at home as well as at school (p. 37).

A year later Witmer (1916) reviewed a case study of a boy with "congenital aphasia" as a result of "congenital verbal amnesia." Witmer concluded that "just as one boy hasn't got an ear for music, because he hasn't got the kind of brain which stores up music, so this boy hasn't got the kind of brain which stores up memories of words and letters and sentences that are spoken to him" (p. 189). He added that this disability extended to other language modalities and that "some are beginning to recognize a condition in children that they call congenital illiteracy" (p. 189). In his book about the psychology of special disabilities, Bronner (1917) also reviewed case studies of persons with specific reading disabilities. He wrote that "with the ever increasing demand in education for recognition of the individual rather than the mass, it is remarkable that no attempt has been made as yet to formulate specifically the problems of specialized abilities and disabilities" and that in his writing he would focus on "particular disabilities in those who have normal general ability" (p. v). Writing during the same year as Bronner, Schmitt (1917-1918) indicated that the terms *congenital word blindness* and *dyslexia* were generally recognized references for a peculiar inability to learn to read. She defined *congenital word blindness* "as an extreme difficulty to learn to recognize printed or written language on the part of persons otherwise normally endowed mentally and without defect of vision or other physical defects of such gravity as to constitute an interference of the process of learning to read" (p. 680).

Reports After 1920

As a consensus developed about the reality of specific reading disabilities, educators gave progressively greater attention to their origin. White (1921) reviewed the literature about specific reading disability and concluded that "physical defects, unless very serious, cannot alone be causes of inability to read" (p. 18). Observing that low intelligence was not always correlated with low achievement in reading, he suggested that "a marked contrast between subjects with ability and inability to read is shown in learning tests of simple associative processes" and that "special methods based upon psychological principles be adapted to disability cases" (p. 18). Fields (1921) recorded three prevailing theories that had attempted to explain the etiology of "congenital word blindness":

(1) A theory which assumes the existence of definitely localized and circumscribed visual and auditory word-centres in the brain, the destruction or isolation of which will destroy language in either its visual or its auditory aspect;

(2) A theory which interprets word-blindness as only one symptom in a general lowering of mental ability; and

(3) One which attributes the condition to a more specialized lowering of power in the primary visual centres, rendering true visual perception of words and of other complex sense-data difficult (p. 286).

Fields concluded that the most likely explanation for word blindness was that this disability "is but one aspect of a more general, yet still in itself specific, defect in either the visual or auditory regions or in both" (p. 307). Four years later Samuel Orton (1925) published his initial paper on specific reading disabilities in which he lamented that "the views on 'congenital word-blindness' in the medical literature seem untenable as an explanation of these cases" and that "an hypothesis more in harmony with present conceptions of the aphasias and based on the structural relations and the probable physiologic activities with the visual cortices of the two hemispheres is offered" (p. 581).

The early twentieth-century interest of educators and psychologists in children who demonstrated a gap between their aptitude and their achievement continued throughout the 1930s. Wolf (1937) reported that though "there is a high correlation between intelligence and academic achievement as measured by standard tests," that many children "are within the range of normal intelligence, yet fail in their prescribed school subjects" (p. 304). As a further indication of the wide-spread concern about this problem, Wolf added that "much has been hypothesized as to the basic causes of normally intelligent children failing in academic school subjects" and that "these children constitute a major problem to educators and to parents" (p. 304). A year earlier Hamill (1936) had observed that "for several years cases of difficulty with reading have been reported" and that "children have been studied who seemed to have a specific difficulty with the recognition of printed or written words" (p. 1050). Stogdill (1938) also documented the enduring concern with specific learning disabilities when he noted that "educationists have long been concerned with children who appear to experience more difficulty with some branches of school work than with others" (p. 7).

Influence of Werner and Strauss

In a detailed account of an unsuccessful attempt to teach reading to a child with a mental deficiency, Sears (1935) indicated that though the child's "effort seems to have been good, Steve was still almost a total non-reader" (p. 136). Although pessimistic about the prospects for teaching reading to persons such as the child in his report, Sears noted that additional research was needed before conclusions could be drawn about the limits of either mental deficiency or reading disability.

In the same issue of the journal in which Sears had written, Hegge (1935) reported about a child with a comparably severe mental disability but who had demonstrated success in reading. Hegge described the person whom he had studied as physically "a perfect specimen" who "did not impress one in conversation as being feebleminded" with "poise and a pleasing personality" (p. 129). He added that "few who did not know his Binet rating and low education standing and who did not discover his lack of adequate vocabulary would rate him as low as he tested" (p. 129). Like Sears, Hegge recommended additional research to throw "more light on the hidden potentialities and the ultimate limits of scholastic trainability in the mentally deficient" (p. 134).

Sears and Hegge were researchers at the *Wayne County Training School* in Michigan, a cite for several other pioneering research studies. During this same period, Werner and Strauss were researchers at the identical school and studied the effects of instruction on those students who exhibited a peculiar inability to learn. Although they recognized the value of standardized tests, they were convinced that they needed to be supplemented by an analysis of the mental processes that supported achievements on tests. Their pursuit of a supplementary analysis evolved into the functional examination of individuals in critical situations that elicited impaired functions. Using this functional analytical technique, they were able to demonstrate that impaired spatial perception could account for learning problems in mathematics. They concluded that such underlying learning impairments were responsible for the academic problems revealed on standardized tests.

Four years later Strauss and Werner (1941) noted that the patterns of mental organization used by brain-injured children were not homogeneous. Children who exhibited hereditary mental problems and those who were injured as a result of physical lesions demonstrated distinct responses to different types of educational interventions. The group of disabled learners with physical lesions that Werner and Strauss discerned became the prototype for children with specific learning disabilities, which is to say children who had not suffered documented lesions but who exhibited some of the characteristics of children who had. Whereas disorders caused by documented lesions would be referred to as *alexia* or *aphasia*, disorders that appeared comparable but without documented causes came to be referred to as *dyslexia* or *dysphasia*.

In 1942 Werner and Strauss published a paper in which they illustrated the distinctive fashion in which children with neurological lesions responded to items on tests. They noted that the children in their study fixated pathologically upon "unessential details of objects or situations" and showed a "disregard for the more complex units of which such details forms [sic] only an element" (1978, pp. 306-307). They illustrated these mental traits by observing that "a child who relates the card with the word 'ball' to the picture of the bell has made his choice by isolating an element; he points to the pellet of the clapper as a ball, a relationship which a normal child, seeing the bell as a whole, would hardly perceive" (p. 307).

Although Strauss and Werner had provided the theoretical paradigm that could explain specific learning disabilities, specific learning disability was not used as a diagnostic category in the schools until the 1960s. Despite this delay, their contemporaries were aware of the fundamental concepts that Strauss and Werner advocated, concepts that did not allow refutation in the same straightforward manner as had the explanations for specific learning disabilities that were based on neurological or perceptual factors. But Werner and Strauss never themselves generalized their research about persons with demonstrated neurological lesions to persons without lesions. The assumption that the behaviors of persons without lesions which were like those of individuals with lesions were due to comparable neurological problems constituted a leap of faith that these methodical researchers did not attempt to make. However, some of their colleagues were less cautious.

Betts (1947) described "retarded readers characterized by associative learning disabilities" as "the least understood of all who experience difficulty in learning to read" (p. 406). Though he had dismissed remedial reading as the "fad of the 1930s" several years earlier, he estimated in 1947 that "approximately one to five per cent of the school population experience difficulty with reading because of associative learning disabilities" (p 406). Indicating that such persons had been described with terms such as "word-blindness, visual aphasia, alexia, and dyslexia," he added that "these individuals experience unusual difficulty in the establishment and retention of reading skills, especially when a visual-auditory approach is used." He identified eight "primary characteristics" of such cases:

1. Non-verbal intelligence tends to be significantly higher than verbal intelligence.
2. Visual-auditory associative learning tends to be higher than visual-visual.
3. Visual discrimination for word forms tends to be of a low order.
4. Hearing comprehension is significantly higher than visual, or reading comprehension.
5. Auditory memory span tends to be relatively higher than visual memory span.
6. Memory for related materials tends to be relatively higher than memory for unrelated material.
7. Oral re-reading tends to be as unrhythmical as oral reading at sight.
8. "Central" dominance tends to be confused (p. 406).

Eustis (1947) observed that "children who have not learned to read or to read fluently and with understanding are almost disgracefully numerous in our schools" (p. 243). He conceded that most educators and child psychologists "state emphatically that there is no single specific cause, but that causation must be sought in a composite of related conditions." Despite this consensus, he agreed with those "physicians and a few educators" who believed that specific reading disability was "a single factor that plays a large part in their reading difficulties." He defined specific reading disability as "an inherited sex-associated weakness of the language function combined with a tendency to ambidexterity" (p. 243). Convinced that children with specific reading disabilities required remedial activities distinct from those used by children without disabilities, Eustis railed against educators who homogeneously grouped all children for reading instruction.

Two years later Goodenough (1949) included a section on specialized educational deficiencies within a book on assessment in which she wrote that "it is necessary to make a sharp distinction between those forms of inability that are associated with, and may be considered the direct or indirect results of general mental backwardness, and those in which the lack of ability is limited to one or more single areas which are much out of line with the subject's general level of performance" (p. 354).

Link to Heredity

The influence of heredity upon specific reading disability was viewed from several different perspectives by researchers during the twentieth century. As an example, Thomas (1905) observed that congenital word blindness "is greater amongst the lower classes," that "the English cases hitherto recorded have been all boys," and that it "frequently assumes a family type" (p. 381). Stephenson (1907) reviewed six cases of congenital word blindness that affected three generations of one family. Like Thomas, he felt that his personal investigations established a genetic link "passing from the first to the second generation by an affected female, and from the second to the third generation by a female, herself unaffected" (p. 484). Rutherfurd (1909) reviewed the details of a 10-year-old female who was "smart at figures" but for whom "her reading in class is absolute nonsense, as she puts into the piece all sorts of words apparently for the sake of saying something rather than standing silent" (p. 485). After examining familial details of the case, Rutherfurd concluded that "a more perfect example could hardly be wished for to illustrate the effect of defective hereditary material in the causation of dyslexia congenita" (p. 487).

A year after Rutherford had published this report, Hinshelwood (1917) defined word blindness as "a congenital defect occurring in children with otherwise normal and undamaged brains characterized by a difficulty in learning to read so great that it is manifestly due to a pathological condition, and where the attempts to teach the child by the ordinary methods have completely failed" (p. 40). He cited excerpts from his correspondence with other pioneering researchers to confirm the continuity between their thoughts and his own. He included an entire chapter on heredity at the conclusion of which he remarked that though congenital word blindness "may be found in disease or injury at birth, I think it is probable that even in most of those isolated cases the condition is the result of defective development, just as in the hereditary form" (p. 73).

Seventeen years later Jastak (1934) developed an extensive report about "interferences in reading" in which he noted that reading problems might originate in visual, auditory, or motoric areas. However, he emphasized that "the hereditary nature of reading disabilities has been pointed out by practically all investigators" (p. 260). Although Marshall and Ferguson (1939) acknowledged that word blindness was "a well recognized clinical entity in the acquired and in the congenital forms," they disagreed with Jastak and the majority of researchers about the frequency with which the congenital form occurred, concluding that cases of "word-blindness" characterized by a "definite heredity are rare" (p. 164).

Despite the ardor of Marshall and Ferguson's convictions, the majority of researchers did not surrender their belief that specific reading disability was linked to heredity. More than a decade after their advice had been published, Hallgren (1950) made observations about persons with specific dyslexia. Describing how the sample of persons with dyslexia had been assembled for his study, he indicated that "in every case where the results of the tests indicated reading and writing disabilities, I required a positive history for a diagnosis of specific dyslexia" (p. 37). Such was Hallgren's impression of the role of heredity in dyslexia that he admitted "in certain cases, the diagnosis was made on the basis of the history alone" and that heredity "was taken as the most important diagnostic criterion" (p. 37). Almost two decades afterwards, Critchley (1968) remained convinced that dyslexia was hereditary. He wrote that data revealed "genetic determination" in the pattern of persons who became dyslexic and that "there can be no doubt that dyslexia is commoner in males than in females" (p. 17).

Continued Confusion about Specific Reading Disability

In a set of 1933 lectures on the "subnormal" mind, the British psychologist Cyril Burt noted sagaciously that "mental deficiency is a legal rather than a psychological term; and, as defined by law, it embraces a number of widely differing conditions" (1955, p. 63). He counseled that this term "must not be taken to describe any well-defined clinical entity" but that rather "it simply covers a group of individuals who, it may be from very different causes, are liable to be dealt with administratively under the various sections of the [British legislative Mental Deficiency] Acts" (p. 65). Burt pointed out that the principal criterion for identifying an individual as a "mental deficient" was "apparently an ineradicable maladjustment to the social environment, whatever that may be—to the school in the case of a child" (p. 65). He observed that such maladjustment could result from "temperamental peculiarities" just as readily as from intellectual limitations and that in many cases both factors were present simultaneously.

Had Burt's pragmatic advice from the early 1930s been extended to the concept of specific reading disability, much of the confusion about the characteristics of this disability might have been avoided. For the identity of specific reading disability, which was difficult to comprehend by itself, was further obfuscated by inconsistency in the terms that were used to identify it. This confusion was apparent in a passage by Hermann (1959):

> The term *congenital word-blindness* is used synonymously with *constitutional dyslexia*, or just *dyslexia*. In cases of acquired disturbance of language function (aphasia), *alexia* refers to the partial or complete loss of the ability to read, due to disease. Likewise, the term *agraphia* is applied to an acquired impairment of the ability to write (words as well as letters). Similarly, in regard to congenital word-blindness, one can speak of *dyslexia* as referring specifically to difficulties in reading, and of *dysgraphia* as referring to constitutionally determined difficulties in writing. As already mentioned, the term dyslexia is often used in such a way as to offer difficulties in both reading and writing in congenital word-blindness (the word "constitutional": being omitted)—but this is not wholly correct. Just as "word-blindness", strictly speaking, refers only to the defect of reading, but is used in everyday speech to include all the symbol disturbances which occur in this condition, so can dyslexia be used to designate the whole disorder (p. 18).

Park and Linden (1968) lamented that "innumerable terms" had been employed to describe the identical reading disabilities. The currently used terms they identified were "word-blindness, congenital symbolamblyopia, congenital typolexia, congenital alexia, amnesit visualis verbalis, congenital dyslexia, developmental alexia, analfebetia partialis, bradylexia, strephosymbolia, constitutional dyslexia, specific dyslexia and functional dyslexia" (pp. 318-319).

By the early 1960s the general term *learning disability* had superseded the term *specific reading disability*. Kirk (1962) indicated that "a child who has the intellectual capacity to learn to read but who does not learn after adequate instruction is classified as having a reading disability" (p. 263). However, he described reading disability as one instance within a broader category of disorders that he called *learning disabilities*. He wrote that the term *learning disabilities* could refer to "retardation, disorder, or delayed development in one or more of the processes of speech, language, reading, spelling, writing, or arithmetic resulting from a possible cerebral dysfunction and/or emotional or behavioral disturbance and not from mental retardation, sensory deprivation, or cultural or instructional factors" (p. 263).

Rawson (1968) also attempted to define some of the hermetic terms that had become associated with reading disability. She indicated that the term *dyslexia* had an "extended meaning" that was synonymous with *specific developmental language disability* and *strephosymbolia.* She defined these terms as appropriate for describing a person whose "spoken language, reading, spelling, penmanship, and perhaps other associated language skills, singly or in combination, falls appreciably below expectations based on his age, physical condition, intellectual ability (individual IQ test) and conventional educational opportunity" (p. 4).

Although other definitions of reading disabilities emerged during the period from the 1970s through the 1990s, most of these definitions continued to be erected on the foundation of principles that had been established in the late 1930s and early 1940s. Despite the fact that some theorists still maintained that cerebral dominance and laterality were the factors that could explain the origin of dyslexia, such theorists were a dwindling minority. After reviewing the research on laterality in their book on dyslexia, Goldberg and Schiffman (1972) had concluded that early in the 1970s "sufficient evidence has been accumulated to indicate that cerebral dominance and poorly defined laterality are not related to learning disorders." They added that the pattern of inconsistent dominance exhibited by many dyslexic learners was "merely a corollary associated with a central dysfunction or with the etiological factors" (p. 138). However, more than two decades later, Clark and Uhry (1995) reviewed the literature on biological correlates of dyslexia and still judged that, though "the research indicates that there is no significant link between eye preference and reading disability," questions about the relationship of handedness to dyslexia were "unresolved" and that "we lack enough substantial data to draw definitive conclusions" (p. 32).

Toward the end of the 1970s Rutter (1977) observed that two main hypotheses had been advanced to explain contemporary ideas about dyslexia. These hypotheses were that reading difficulties might "have many causes and encompass a variety of syndromes" or that "within the broader group of reading disabilities there are disorders due to some form of inherent biological deficit which is probably...genetic in origin" (p. 6). A year later Vellutino (1979) noted that theories had been proposed which attributed dyslexia to problems in visual perception, intersensory integration, ability to recall items in serial order, and verbal processing. Several years later Pavlidis and Fisher (1986) summarized a consensus about the origin of dyslexia by "neuroanatomists, pediatricians, neuropsychologists, neuroeducators, and others" when they defined it as "a form of learning disability related to reading, the recognition of words, and the interpretation of what is seen visually or heard auditorily which is the result of neurophysiological dysfunction" (p. xiv).

SUMMARY

In the early part of the nineteenth century special educators devised strategies for teaching reading to students with disabilities. As more educators recognized the advanced degrees of literacy that students with disabilities could attain, they experimented with techniques for instructing all learners, those without or with disabilities, including even learners with severe disabilities. An increasing number of advocates began to recommend that literacy be developed among students with disabilities who would be placed in integrated schools. Additionally, advocates argued for educational methods and materials that would be suitable for individuals with disabilities but that were still patterned after the pedagogical procedures used in traditional classrooms. Concomitant with the movement to reduce segregation and eccentric training programs, an awareness of milder forms of disabilities evolved. One of these milder disorders was dyslexia, a specific form of learning disability that had been studied since the late 1800s. However, popular awareness of dyslexia among the general public did not occur until the 1960s, after which it was widely diagnosed and became a focal point of many remedial reading programs.

Chapter 12

TEACHING READING TO MULTICULTURAL GROUPS

> Foreigners should be presented with lessons organized so as to keep constantly in the foreground the needs of the society in which the pupil is playing his part at the present moment, and in which his rôle will, with the years, become more and more important (Cohen, 1913).

Negative attitudes toward immigrants developed throughout the 1800s. These attitudes were partly the result of fears that unassimilated foreigners would undermine America's culture and government. Programs for adult immigrants were initiated as means of dealing with the problems that were contributing to such fears. These programs were designed to teach not only oral English but also American nationalism and literacy. The educational programs for the non-English-speaking children of immigrants reflected the identical learning objectives. Though some school districts developed plans for placing foreign students in segregated classrooms or special education programs, the number of students eligible for services exceeded the opportunities for restrictive placements. Consequently, most students were placed in regular education classrooms. In addition to disputes about the most suitable environment for instructing foreign students, early twentieth-century educators debated whether it was more effective for foreign students to begin reading instruction in English or in their native language. Educators also disagreed about the relative effectiveness of skills-based and language-based lessons. Encrusted with political implications, these educational issues remained unresolved throughout the twentieth century.

* * *

The difficulty of developing educational programs for ethnically diverse learners, many of whom did not speak English, was apparent during a lengthy period that began before the middle of the nineteenth century. The programs that were proposed during this era were influenced by the prevailing social attitudes, many of which turned unfriendly as the number of immigrants to the United States increased and their originating countries became more diverse. Not only were many immigrants viewed with hostility, but also the Catholic church, of which many of the new immigrants were members, was depicted as threatening the established educational and social institutions.

Animosity to both immigrants and Catholics was predictably evident in the rhetoric of xenophobic groups such as the Ku Klux Klan. In the proceedings from the first annual national meeting of the "Grand Dragons" of the Ku Klux Klan ("Knights of the Ku Klux Klan," 1923), a paper on immigration written by an author identified only as "the Grand Dragon of South Carolina" warned that "there are 14,000,000 foreign born in the United States, of whom more than 7,000,000 have never taken out naturalization papers, and who can neither speak nor read our language" ("The Regulation of Immigration," 1923, p. 70). A paper by the "Great Titan of the Realm of Texas" affirmed that the Klan's members confronted those "who would engender ill feeling among Protestants and weaken their church organizations" ("The Klan as a Civic Asset," 1923, pp. 68-69). Although he did not precisely estimate the size of the Ku Klux Klan, Woofter (1933) wrote in the report of the President's Research Committee on Social Trends that "the extent and intensity of the activities of the Ku Klux Klan manifested the amount of prejudice against alien groups which persists in the native mind" (p. 600). Ashmore (1954) wrote that the Ku Klux Klan "was not solely a Southern phenomenon; the movement, which now listed Jews and Catholics among its targets as well as Negroes, spread over much of the United States and became a prime symbol of the nation's post-World War I reaction" (p. 21). Williams and Ryan (1954) recounted activities of the Ku Klux Klan in Indianapolis during the 1920s:

> Indianapolis had integrated schools until, during the 1920's, the power of the Ku Klux Klan forced many of the Negro children into segregated schools. Having its headquarters in the city,...the Klan secured the erection of Crispus Attucks High School in 1927 and established it as a segregated school. In the same year a Klan-dominated school board initiated the policy of transporting Negroes away from the elementary school in their neighborhood to more distant schools for Negroes (p. 50).

HOSTILITY TO IMMIGRANTS DURING THE 1800s

Not restricted to explicitly racist organizations, anti-immigrant and anti-Catholic attitudes were apparent well before the early 1900s. Beale (1941) cited incidents during the 1840s such as the expulsion of Catholic children from a school in Boston and the burning of Catholic schools in Philadelphia by Protestants when he characterized this era as a time of "violent anti-Catholic feeling" (p. 101). His impression was confirmed by a mid-nineteenth-century editorial in *The Massachusetts Teacher*. This editorial in an educational journal had referred to the "down trodden, priest-ridden" Irish immigrants who were "degraded and ignorant" and among whom "the simple virtues of industry, temperance, and frugality are unknown" ("Immigration," 1851, p. 290). This editorialist concluded that "with the old not much can be done; but with their children, the great remedy is EDUCATION" ("Immigration," 1851, p. 290).

Several years after this editorial had appeared, Beecher (1855) referred to the Catholic church as the "Papal corporation" and accused its clergy of being "pecuniary agents" who had vowed their allegiance to a "foreign head of this corporation." Since Beecher was sure the Pope intended to subvert the democratic basis for government, he concluded by asking rhetorically "according to their own principles, then, are they not guilty of treason to the constitution of these United States—treason not in any declamatory sense, but in strict and legal verity?" (p. 401).

After chronicling seditious activities by the Catholic church, Dorchester (1888) advised "in the light of these facts, let American citizens seriously ponder the hostile attitudes of the Roman Catholic Church toward our public school system, and her pernicious influence upon the future prospects and citizenship of the multitude of children trained in her parochial schools" (p. 351). A year later Jay (1889) wrote that "the public school system, which is recognized at home and abroad by intelligent people of all creeds and parties as the chief basis of our government of the people, by the people, and for the people" was being threatened by "papal encyclicals, the decrees of provincial councils, and the ultramontane clericals, books and newspapers, denouncing the common school as a Godless and heathenish institution that must be destroyed" (pp. 152-153). Jay judged the political intrigues of the Catholic church to be so opprobrious that he discerned "growing opposition of loyal American Roman Catholics to the attempts to force them to withdraw their children from the public schools" (p. 153). King (1899) provided a sidebar on the title page of his book about the power and perils that were confronting the nation in which he indicated that "the POWER of Our Country, [has been] generated by Anglo-Saxon civilization and made effective through the American institutions of State, Church, and School" and that "the PERIL of Our Country, [has been] manifest in the claims of Politico-Ecclesiastical Romanism to universal dominion, and in its relations to political parties, politicians, platforms, legislation, schools, charities, labor, and war" (p. 1).

HOSTILITY TO IMMIGRANTS DURING THE EARLY 1900s

Shaw (1904b) wrote that not only children who attended Catholic schools but those enrolled in the parochial schools managed by other denominations were "weaker in moral and religious fiber, feebler in reasoning power and self-control, than the graduates of our public schools" (p. 4465). Writing about the same time in a book in which he highlighted the need to teach immigrants in English and discourage their use of homeland languages, Grose (1906) observed bitterly that, in Illinois, "it is not possible to pass a bill for compulsory education in the English language" because priests control the vote of the "foreign element in favor of the parochial schools" (p. 246). He described a parochial school in Pennsylvania where "English is not taught, and the children are growing up as thoroughly foreign and under priestly control as though they were in Bohemia or Galicia" (pp. 246-247). Fourteen years later Berkson (1920) warned that "undoubtedly the presence of the parochial school is an indication of the unsatisfactory state of adjustment between public and other education" and that society could not merely "suppress the parochial schools" but instead had to find the "root of the evil" (p. 165).

Although much of the criticism against immigrants was in the form of broadsides targeted at both Catholics and select ethnic groups, many writers relied on strictly political arguments. In a book with the title *Hindrances to Good Citizenship*, Bryce (1909) had written to Americans that it was important to integrate "the vast mass of immigrants, most of them ignorant of our language, still more of them ignorant, not only of your institutions, but of the general principles and habits of free government" (p. 122). He complimented his readers because "you are providing for all of them good schools, and their children will soon become Americans in speech and habits" (p. 122). A year earlier Gard (1908) had adjured teachers that "the American spirit is inculcated in this new young citizenship by the presence of the flag, obeisance to the flag, the singing of 'America' and other patriotic songs, and sentiment and story embracing love of country and humanity" and that "these make an impression never to be eradicated" (p. 684).

Other warnings about immigrants during the early part of the twentieth century appealed to fears about the dilution of the genetic base for future generations. For example, Burr (1922) warned that the "old immigrant stock" which had dominated entry into the United States before 1860 had shifted to a preponderance of "Italians, Spanish, Portuguese, white Mexicans, other Latin Americans, Provençals, Rumanians, other Latins and Greeks" (p. 115). In an article that appeared that same year in *Scientific Monthly*, Young (1922) agreed that "the influx of the foreigner into this country only became a serious problem with the shifting of the Old World source of the immigration from North to South Europe" (p. 417). Young recommended that "immigration should be controlled in the interest of national welfare" through physical and psychological tests that would "assist in rejecting those whom we do not want" (p. 433). In a study of "the possibilities of different immigrant groups, for adjustment to American standards of life," Bere (1924) noted that "the North European is of a higher calibre than the other groups" and that "the South European ranks lowest and is consistent with the opinion expressed in immigration reports" (p. 93).

In a study about nationalist groups that was published two years after that of Young, Huntington (1925) included a chapter about the "great races" of Europe. Referring to the terrain and climate of Norway, he judged that "natural selection would tend to preserve to a high degree the qualities of curiosity, individualism, introversion, self-assertion, and acquisitiveness." But he warned that "it is quite possible that some races, such as the Negroes, would be exterminated under such circumstances because they have already acquired opposite qualities under another environment" (p. 218). Among other groups that Huntington denigrated were the Italians, especially the Sicilians because "the climate of Sicily with its mild winters and long, hot, monotonous summers does not stimulate activity as does that of Norway, with its coolness, its storms, its variability, and yet its freedom from really severe extremes of temperature" (p. 219).

Huntington concluded that "many studies of eminent Americans leave little room for doubt that in spite of their relative decline in numbers the old American stocks whose ancestors were in the country before the Revolution still inherit a degree of ability which makes them dominant" (p. 314). He lamented those states which had not implemented judicious systems of immigration, such as New Mexico, where "the greater part of the people whom the census reckons as white in that State were actually Mexican, often with a large Indian admixture" (p. 315).

Fairchild (1926) judged that the immigrants who had come prior to 1882 had been primarily drawn from three sources: the United Kingdom, Germany, and the Scandinavian countries. However, in a chapter with the foreboding title, "A New Menace," he observed that "a marked change in the situation began to develop" with immigrants from less desirable countries such as "Italy, Austria-Hungary, and the Russian Empire and Finland" (p. 107). After noting that "no breeder would expect to improve his stock by random crossing with any variety that chanced to present itself," Fairchild explained that "the plant or animal breeder knows that the indiscriminate mixing of a large number of varieties can be expected to produce just one result—the mongrel" (p. 122).

Duncan (1933) referred to the span of years from 1882 to 1931 as a "modern period" of immigration characterized by an influx of persons from southern and eastern Europe. Aware that "Teutonic blood and culture predominate in the old immigration, and Latin and Slavic in the new," he expressed concern because "in general the Teutons are more vigorous and more progressive than the Latins and Slavs" (p. 481). Although Duncan judged that "the Teutons are culturally ascendant at present" he did caution that "this has not always been true and may not remain so" (p. 481).

PROGRAMS FOR ADULT IMMIGRANTS

Although established residents and employers supported the expansion of the schools as a strategy for helping immigrant adults and their children, they eventually concluded that the schools could not meet this challenge. Palmer (1905) reported that night schools had been started as early as 1833 in New York City. But the purpose of these early night schools was to train instructional apprentices who could assist teachers during the day. Palmer indicated that it was not until 1902 that a citywide "outline course of study for the teaching of English to foreigners was adopted" and "in that year there were eleven evening high schools and sixty-nine evening elementary schools" (p. 310).

A report written a year later contradicted Palmer's views. For the report ("The Education of the Immigrant," 1906) contained the remark that "with the exception of the provision of evening schools for foreigners in some of the larger cities of the Union, and the experimental work of lectures to immigrants in their native language conducted by the Department of Education of the City of New York, very little has been done in the way of educating the adult immigrant" (p. 164).

Moorhead (1908) reported about a school for adult Italian immigrants that was developed near Pittsburgh. She wrote that "the school was started as an experiment, in 1905, by the Society for Italian Immigrants, to which all credit is due for the conception and carrying out of the enterprise" (p. 500). Describing a curriculum to which reading was critical, she reported that "there is an English primer for those who are just learning to read, and Miss Moore's English-Italian Language Book for such as have already mastered the art in their own language" (p. 502).

Writing during the same year about Italian immigrants, May (1908) observed that "among all the cities in the United States perhaps the educational system of Boston is most generous in its provision for these 'strangers in a strange land,'" and that "during the past few years, evening classes for Italian adults have been organized in the public school buildings, settlements, missions and clubs, with more or less gratifying results" (p. 452). However, May suggested that the instruction in Boston's night schools would be improved if "teachers well-versed in both English and Italian were provided" (p. 452).

Although neither Moorhead nor May discussed the format of the instruction that was employed within their programs, O'Brien (1909) highlighted her effective use of skills-based lessons. In the introduction to her textbook she wrote that her experience "has shown that 80% of the foreigners who begin the study of English need objective work at first" (p. iv). She indicated that the lessons in her book "advance from simple and concrete to more abstract ideas" and that phonetic exercises were of the "utmost importance" because "English pronunciation is exceedingly difficult for foreigners." Including lessons on topics such as grocery stores, meat markets, shearing of sheep, cotton mills, manufacturing, coal mines, and steel mills, O'Brien thought that the content of reading passages should reflect activities in the learners' day-to-day lives. The following passage from her reading textbook described work in a meatpacking house:

> Many men work in the big stock-yards in Chicago. In these yards are gathered thousands of cattle and sheep. Let us go into one of the big packing houses. Here many men are working, too. They send us fresh beef cut from the flesh of these cattle. They send us fresh mutton cut from the flesh of sheep. Some of the meat they pack into cans. The workmen are very careful to keep themselves and the workroom clean and neat. From these packing-houses, meat is sent to all parts of the United States and to other countries. The bones of the animals are sold to factories to be manufactured into buttons and combs. What is done with the wool of the sheep? (1909, p. 85).

Night schools in both rural areas and large cities offered lessons for immigrants after they had completed their workdays. Colgrove (1916) described a night school for workers in the Iron Range of Minnesota that was designed to instruct adults who "have either one or both of two ambitions, to learn to read English newspapers and be able to pass an examination to become naturalized citizens" (p. 66). Loeb (1918) listed the benefits of urban night schools that were opportunities for the "foreign-born" to learn to speak and read English. But he also conceded that tired workers had found out that "sleep is a much more attractive prospect than spelling." He described innovative efforts to attract students to city night schools such as "advertising cards in street cars, printed appeals on pay envelopes, [and] announcements in foreign-language newspaper" (p. 426). But Loeb concluded that "the evening schools have failed singularly to interest any considerable proportion of our non-English-speaking population." A 1912 report about immigrants in Massachusetts (Commission on Immigration, 1914) recounted that "last year all illiterate persons between the ages of sixteen and twenty-one, who were living in towns or cities where public evening schools were maintained, were required by law to attend these classes regularly as a condition of the their legal employment at any kind of work" (p. 122). However, the report also noted that this law was "not well enforced." Loeb (1918) had recommended that "the most successful plan of education for the non-English speaking adult has been by means of classes in factories carried on voluntarily by the large employers" (p. 426). He indicated that in Chicago the school board had funded teachers to instruct persons in factories but that in most cities the classes were voluntary efforts by the employers.

Although he was not as pessimistic as Loeb in his evaluation of night schools, Thompson (1920) still qualified his enthusiasm when he wrote that "the best that can be said of the evening school is that it promises to continue to be the chief public means of providing education for the immigrant as long as we are restricted by our present laws and financial resources" (p. 98). Because he believed that "the immigrant is a more social being than is the native," Thompson did praise the programs in New York and Pittsburgh in which the instructors had made "significant and suggestive" efforts to socialize their evening classes. And like Loeb, Thompson was optimistic about the development of factory classes. Although he observed that "it is now certain that we shall see a substantial development of the factory class in the immediate future" he still cautioned that "as yet they do not rival the evening school" (p. 99).

Mahoney and Herlihy (1918) indicated that "presence in our country of such a large number of persons unable to speak the language of the country could constitute, even in the normal time of peace, a problem of deep national interest," but that as a result of the War "the very first step in making a unified people back of our fighting line, a zealous industrial army to augment our fighting forces, is to teach the foreigner English" (p. 23). But they warned that "there is a distinct pedagogy in this immigrant work, and a very distinct methodology" (p. 13). They emphasized that teachers should develop reading lessons in which they would help their students "read what they need to read in every-day life" and avoid "reading what is in a textbook, simply because it is there" (pp. 49-50).

Mahoney and Herlihy also gave detailed examples of methods by which teachers might effectively organize the lessons taught in the night schools. They advised that "the clever teacher, with the idea of getting class-activity, will shorten her reading-period, and have more of them, will select her pupils at random instead of allowing them to figure out their 'turns'; will match one group against another group to see who can imitate the teacher's model best, will insist that in every case each pupil read to the class as an audience" (p. 61). In addition to advice about the management of the classes, Mahoney and Herlihy stressed the essential role of skills-based instruction, which could "hammer home the vocabulary of a strange tongue so that it will 'stick'" (p. 63).

In a book written a year later about techniques for "schooling" adult immigrants, Thompson (1920) also argued that literacy programs should be functional. But unlike Mahoney and Herlihy, Thompson believed that phonics had been over-emphasized in most instructional programs. He was dismayed at a 1918 pamphlet published by the Bethlehem Steel Company that began with the advice that "the alphabet is the basis of the English Language, and should be used in forming the words of the beginner's vocabulary" (Bethlehem Steel Company Pamphlet, quoted by Thompson, p. 192). He suggested instead that "the standard for judging the worth of a lesson in English is the use to which the instruction may be put by the pupil to-day rather than to-morrow" (p. 211).

Thompson also recommended that children who spoke a foreign language should receive special instruction, patterned after that provided to students with mental disabilities, because "the immigrant child often has distinct handicaps in conditions which it is the purpose of Americanization to affect helpfully; he frequently suffers from the handicap of a foreign language in the household, and often from the inexperience of his parents in the American environment" (p. 74). He adjured his contemporaries to "rid themselves of two obsessions" in order to enhance education of immigrants: the beliefs "that native Americans constitute a superior race when compared with the foreign born, and second, that our institutions and aspirations are peculiar and distinctive to our own people and country" (p. 365). Thompson's pragmatism was based on a belief that "teachers to-day no longer hold the view that a single kind of procedure can accomplish the many purposes for which adults undergo hardships in learning our language; rather, they are guided in the selection of their methods by the conviction that these are unequal tools, to be used as occasion demands, and to be laid aside for other tools when necessity demands" (pp. 210-211).

Another recurring issue in discussions of immigrant education was the recruitment of students into programs in which they were to learn not only oral English and literacy skills but also cultural precepts. Horvath (1923) adjured that "the immigrant mother should learn not only to speak English, but should also learn the customs and laws of the country" (p. 682). Describing a program that had been developed in Cleveland, she suggested that public libraries become the sites for special female literacy clubs. MacLean (1924) described the efforts of the "Patriotic Education League of Lynn Massachusetts" to recruit persons into night classes that provided instruction not only about English but about "Americanization."

PROGRAMS FOR SCHOOL-AGE MULTICULTURAL GROUPS—PRIOR TO 1940

Educators wrote for more than a century and a half about the special problems of instructing adult immigrants. Discussions of these same problems recurred in the literature about the education of school-age multicultural groups. To illustrate the demographic proportions of this problem during the early part of the twentieth century, Abbott (1917) cited a survey indicating that half of the children in the elementary schools of Cleveland lived in homes in which a foreign language was spoken. She then referenced reports to indicate that these percentages were even higher in New York City, Chicago, and Boston. Wattenberg (1936) reported that Chicago's school population contained 30 nationalities, half of which were represented in significant numbers. Three years earlier Woofter (1933) had reported that two-thirds of the nation's counties had at least "1,000 members of a race other than the white, or 1,000 persons born outside the United States" (p. 553).

Taylor (1857) documented an 1839 program for bilingual children that enabled them to "attend a German school, if taught by a teacher duly qualified, and be entitled to receive from the local Directors an order for a proportionate share of the school money" (p. 201). He also described a provision of an 1853 Ohio educational act which stipulated that boards of education were "authorized to provide German schools for the instruction of such youths as may desire to study the German language, or the German and English languages together" (p. 225). In her history of Chicago, Pierce (1957) observed that "with a large foreign population holding political power, Chicago inevitably became the center of groups demanding the teaching of their native tongue" and that "other ethnic groups looked with jealous and resentful eye upon the favored position of the Germans" (p. 385).

Educators debated not only about the language that was suitable for instruction but also the methods that would be employed. Howerth (1908) wrote that the instructional methods used with the immigrant child "would not need to be especially different from those applied to American-born children" and that "he could be classified according to his mental development, regardless of his knowledge of the English language, and promoted according to is ability to carry on the work successfully" (p. 558). He was convinced that "in teaching these children we should make use of the value of their own experiences" because "they need something more than the so-called three R's" (p. 559). He counseled teachers of immigrants to "know their traits," "be familiar with their habits of life, their parentage, and their home influences," "know their home influences," "know their likes and dislikes," "be skilled in the object method of teaching," and to "be able, if possible, to speak and understand their language" (p. 559). As a final piece of practical advice, he suggested that schools "segregate the pupils of each nationality under a teacher who can speak that language."

Five years later a district superintendent in New York City (Maxwell, Haaren, Kidd, & Wade, 1913) agreed that the most effective type of instruction would be provided in ethnically segregated classrooms, with "the Jewish children being placed in one C class, and the Italian in another, for they differ radically" (p. 24). A report about problems of immigrants (Commission on Immigration, 1914) reported that "steamer classes" were being taught in 26 Massachusetts cities for children who did not speak English and who were too old to be placed in those elementary classrooms in which introductory lessons on English were being taught. Three years later Abbott (1917) also noted that "in most cities the only special provision made for immigrant children are the so-called 'steamer' classes" and that "occasionally, newly arrived immigrant children are put in classes organized for backward or subnormal children, or subnormal or backward children are put in the 'steamer' classes" (p. 224).

During the 1920s and 1930s educators questioned whether special instructional methods might not be more effective with immigrant children. For example, Zornow (1919) had suggested a program for Italian youth that simultaneously emphasized phonics and holistic comprehension. He wrote in support of "a composite method in which a maximum amount of attention shall be given to content and thought acquisition, but in which there shall be a co-ordinate emphasis on phonetic training" (p. 105). Reporting about the difficulty that Mexican children had adapting to standard curricula, Stanley (1920) recommended that "special schools" be established that would avoid "our present course of study with its emphasis on book study and on seat work" and instead emphasize the "skilled occupations for which they may be fitted" (p. 715).

Jones (1928) recounted efforts to educate the children of Chicago's Mexican immigrants during the 1920s in integrated programs where "the Mexicans were well able to keep up with the Slavs in their school work" (p. 594). Phillips (1931) reported about "tent schools" that had been developed in California to educate the children of immigrant Mexican farm workers through programs that were "far more fundamental and comprehensive than the 'Americanization' so common in the years immediately following the Great War" (p. 493). Two years later Meriam (1933) described a holistic "activity curriculum" that was devised for Los Angeles's Hispanic children and that was "positively not achievement in the traditional three R's" (p. 306).

Stone (1936) advised teachers that though the "language handicap" of foreign students did contribute to their reading failure in the elementary schools, it was only one of several contributing factors. He indicated various proposed solutions to such problems, which he stated as questions. For example, he asked "will the natural experience method with reading instruction integrated entirely in an activity program solve the problem of better reading that adapts learning conditions to the varying needs of children?" (p. 180). Burbeck (1939) was also concerned about the effectiveness of language-based instruction with bilingual learners. He used seven principles to summarize the key provisions of the multicultural, language-based approaches that were being implemented during the 1930s:

1. The teacher should first know the child, his background, and language.
2. The teacher should give the child many and varied experiences to develop an understanding of English.
3. The child should be able to speak English with some facility before reading is attempted.
4. Ear training in English sounds, the stress of words, intonation, and sentence melody should be given.
5. Defective pronunciation should be corrected before the child begins to read....
6. The curriculum must be flexible and the printed materials used should be easy enough to insure a reasonable amount of success for the child.
7. The standards of achievement must not be in terms of individual ability and the tasks undertaken, but in terms of the needs and interests of the child (Burbeck, 1939, p. 54).

PROGRAMS FOR SCHOOL-AGE MULTICULTURAL GROUPS—AFTER 1940

Vickery and Cole (1943) observed that "books, pamphlets, and magazines available to teachers engaged in intercultural education have increased in number and improved in quality in recent years" (p. 109). In a work published originally in 1949, Kandel (1974) wrote that "one of the striking movements in American education in the years immediately preceding and during the war was the widespread introduction in educational institutions at all levels of courses on the cultures of other peoples" (p. 9).

Twelve years earlier Munroe (1937) had called for a worldwide "disarmament of the mind" which he thought "depends upon good will to all other people; that this in turn depends upon the understanding of other peoples—their character, their situation, their ambitions, their objectives, and their needs; and that with such understanding would come the informed citizenship upon which would in turn be based a perfect international understanding as well as a true nationalism and valid patriotism" (p. 14). Munroe added that "it is now recognized that nationalism is based primarily upon unity of ideas, ideals, group purposes, and common group attitudes" and not upon "other characteristics of nationalism that until the present have been considered essential, such as race, religion, language, and territory" (p. 23). Munroe adjured teachers to expand the curriculum with "a vast amount of materials dealing with the social, economic, political, and cultural problems and characteristics not only of our own people but also in a lesser degree of various other peoples, so that a comprehensive, intelligent, and sympathetic attitude toward other peoples may be developed in school children" (p. 19).

Numerous articles and books from this era reported about opportunities to initiate and then expand multicultural education. A 1940 book form the National Education Association (Educational Policies Commission, 1940) described a program in which the Santa Barbara public schools established a "Community Cultural Studies Service" through which "teacher's wide contacts, cultural exhibits and programs are arranged, which enlist the participation of practically all the national and racial groups" and that as a result "the people of Santa Barbara, native-born and foreign-born alike, are helped to a better appreciation of one another's arts, handicrafts, music, dancing, and literature" (p. 301).

A 1942 anthology sponsored by several professional educational organizations (National Education Organization, 1942) contained 25 chapters illustrating practical activities that teachers could implement to promote multicultural sensitivity. In an introductory chapter, Wattenberg (1942) wrote that minority learners who participated in such a program could "encounter friendliness and learn what democracy can mean to them" and as a result "become a bulwark against Fifth Column activity" (p. 39). The alternative, he warned, was that "public hysteria makes them victims of unthinking persecution" and that "the bad feeling thus engendered may drive many into the camp of the enemy" (p. 40).

Stolle, Kidd, and Whitby (1942) described a "Spanish life class" in which students in Illinois explored other cultures instead of focusing on "the arid and meaningless pursuit of technical language skills" (p. 227). Additional chapters in this same book highlighted multicultural learning activities that had been designed for the diverse ethnic and racial groups that teachers might encounter in their classrooms. During that same year Mitchell and Boetz (1942) described multicultural experiences connected to trips, school jobs, and experiments and provided an extensive bibliography of multicultural materials intended to raise students' awareness of diverse cultural groups.

Brameld (1946) described a study about administrative policies and practices that had been developed in response to problems associated with multicultural learning. He gave details of a curriculum centered about "democratic living through developing appreciation of the way in which present culture groups make adjustment to the local community" and "appreciation of the way in which culture groups today, by comparison with former culture groups, carry on their functions" (p. 142).

Three years earlier Vickery and Cole (1943) had provided multiple examples of lessons that were functional, communicative, and designed to highlight the relevance of materials from which the students were learning. As such, the lessons that they recommended anticipated many of the characteristics of the language-based lessons that would be recommended decades later for use with multicultural groups. Language-based approaches were viewed as especially appropriate for bilingual learners because they enabled teachers to build on the communicative strengths that the learners already exhibited. Alternatives to language-based approaches might have compounded the problem of learning to read by requiring students to develop skills in English as the condition for learning to read. Or a program that was not language-based might have required children to learn to read in a language in which they had only limited proficiency. The debate about these issues persisted from the 1930s to the 1970s. Ching (1969) presented an annotated bibliography of studies beginning in 1939 and in which researchers had investigated children who spoke nonstandard English dialects or Spanish. She concluded that "English language development must be an integral part of the reading instruction of such children" (p. 622).

The attempt to designate the multicultural issues affecting literacy became focused on alternative dialects as well as alternative languages. Writing the same year as Ching but concentrating their attention exclusively on current data about dialects, Gladney and Leaverton (1968) counseled teachers to "respect and accept the children's established dialect" but also to "help the children recognize, learn, and hopefully begin to use standard English" (p. 761). Also addressing dialect, Venezky (1970) concluded that standard English was suitable for teaching children who spoke nonstandard dialects. But he gave this advice with three qualifications: "children whose dialects deviate markedly from standard English should be taught the standard brand before they are taught reading," "reading materials for beginning reading should...be as dialect free (and culture free) as possible," and "children should be allowed to translate from writing to that form of language from which they already obtain meaning" (pp. 342-343).

Separating himself from those educators who were recommending that all learners use standard English, Kenneth Goodman (1969b) argued for approaches that would preserve students' native languages. He wrote passionately that "language is not the private property of any one culture, society, nation, race, ethnic group or socioeconomic class" and that "each group's language is the best for its needs" (p. 124). Though Goodman used the term *language*, he was speaking about dialect as a distinctive property of language. Goodman (1969a) used a syllogism to explain why he thought dialect was a factor that could influence learning to read, writing that "since it is true that learning to read a foreign language is a more difficult task than learning to read a native language, it must follow that it is harder for a child to learn to read a dialect which is not his own than to learn to read his own dialect" (p. 14).

In contrast to Goodman, Stewart (1969) argued that the sound-spelling-meaning correspondences between black dialect and written standard English were not dramatically more irregular than the differences between spoken standard English and written standard English. He observed that "even relatively inexperienced readers seem to be able to cope with a fair amount of sound-spelling irregularity, provided that they are familiar with the spoken forms of the words and are able to get sufficient cues for associating the written and spoken form from the lexical and syntactic context" (p. 176). But Stewart did concede that grammatical differences between black and standard English were sufficient to cause comprehension problems. He recommended that these differences be addressed through a multistage type of instruction in which dialect was used initially to read passages but in which standard English was progressively edited into those passages.

A year later Rystrom (1970) attempted to discern changes in African-American students in elementary schools after they had read materials transcribed into black English. Not only did Rystrom fail to observe a significant increase in reading scores, but he actually observed a negative impact on the learners' decoding skills. He called for experimental testing of the assumption that African-American children would learn more easily and effectively if they were taught with dialect materials.

Writing about the instructional programs that had been proposed to help African-American youths who spoke nonstandard English, Burling (1973) candidly criticized the limitations of political solutions to complex educational problems. He wrote that "it is hardly fair to abandon a child with nothing but his nonstandard dialect if that will result in his permanent exclusion from full participation in our national life" (p. 132). After describing several flawed proposals intended to resolve this problem, he concluded that "we might at least try to teach standard speakers something *about* nonstandard English" because "we might encourage a greater tolerance among the privileged segment of out nation for dialect diversity" (p. 137).

Writing at the same time, O'Brien (1973) also addressed the issue of dialect diversity. She argued that dialect only became a hindrance to reading education if the grammar used by the speakers differed to a point that the readers lost interest, if phonology was so different as to cause frustration, if the speech of teachers or peers prevented learners from communicating, or if learners were required to read words and syntax that they had not yet heard or spoken. O'Brien identified two weaknesses of language experience approaches when these were used with "language-different" children. One weakness was that these approaches might assume a degree of language development in English that could be frustrating to the learners. The second problem could result from the disparity between the language that learners spoke and standard English. Although she acknowledged that these problems had not been resolved, she detected general agreement that though "primary children should be urged to express themselves freely in oral language without interruption or correction, there is general reluctance among many to see grammatical errors and spelling errors in print" (pp. 107-108).

Two years later Nila Banton Smith (1975) proposed a compromise position about teaching reading to children who spoke non Standard English dialects:

(1) Accept the child's dialect as his native language; (2) provide him opportunities to read in his own dialect as a precedent to or along with reading in Standard English; and (3) combine teacher guidance, appropriate materials, teacher and peer associations to aid him in acquiring ability to speak and read with increasing fluency in Standard English as a second language while maintaining his native language (p. 139).

One readily discerned drawback of those approaches that taught students exclusively in their dialects or in non-English languages was that these programs could inadvertently segregate children. In contrast, Smith wrote that a "strong oral language program in Standard English" could enable students to "associate freely with the teacher, other children and adults in the school who speak Standard English."

Reviewing the literature on second language learning, Bordie (1971) assumed that children who spoke a language other than English would eventually need to learn a second language. As such, he inquired about the ideal age at which such second language instruction should begin, concluding that the instruction could be postponed until the time of need, as early as possible when pronunciation skills were of significant social importance, or at virtually any time as long as that instruction involved a "continuous sequence of offerings" (p. 557). He also warned that the designation of any of the three suggestions would depend on "situational clarification before they can be applied."

The following year Eisenhardt (1972) described a linguistic approach for teaching bilingual reading that was based on two central premises. One of these was "a methodology which, in contrast to a dependence on the learner's passive acceptance of preconceived rules, offers opportunities for children to create knowledge based on their observations of language tested against their intuitive speech" (p. vi). The other premise was an emphasis on "the interrelationship of vocabulary, syntax, morphology and phonology as elements of meaning" (p. vi). The author warned those who "fear the climate of uncertainty and tentativeness as part of the process of inquiry" to turn away from the linguistic foundation supporting her book. Upon discerning these bold words, readers of the early 1970s might have anticipated a revolutionary approach to instruction. However, Eisenhardt's quite conventional approach was defined in her five goals for learners:

1. To want to learn standard dialect and to consider it his right rather than an obligation to the teacher and the school.
2. To develop the attitude that a language must be judged in terms of its appropriateness to the situation in which it is used.
3. To acquire a flexibility in language appropriate to a variety of needs and situations.
4. To gain respect for and an appreciation of linguistic variations which he considers *different* rather than *wrong*.
5. To master the basic sentence and intonation patterns with an ability to expand into a variety of complex sentences (1972, p. 114).

Also writing in 1972, Gumperz and Hernández-Chavez (1985) argued that the teaching of individuals who primarily spoke a language other than English was a sufficiently complex problem that a solution was unlikely to be achieved if instructors searched exclusively for optimal teaching aids and materials. They suggested an approach that made far greater demands on instructors than that being suggested by Eisenhardt. They recommended that teachers "become acquainted with code selection rules in formal and informal settings as well as with those themes of folk literature and folk art that form the input to these rules, so that they can diagnose their own communication problems and adapt methods to their children's background" (p. 106).

In contrast to Gumperz and Hernández-Chavez, Ramírez and Castañeda (1974) made suggestions for expanding the adaptability of learners rather than that of instructors. They counseled that a bilingual learner should "remain identified with the life style and values of his home and neighborhood while he becomes familiar with the life style and value system of the mainstream American middle class" (p. 35). Christian (1976) extended this argument to literacy, advocating "early and indefinitely continuing literacy in a minority home language, accompanied by literacy in a second language learned in school" (p. 17).

May and Eliot (1975) identified four approaches for teaching reading to students who spoke a primary language other than English. One approach required all students to learn in standard English, irrespective of their English language skills. Another approach provided instruction in oral English as the precursor to reading instruction with standard English materials. They identified a third approach in which students used materials that had been specially edited to eliminate features of English that could be unusually difficult for persons who spoke certain dialects or languages.

May and Eliot were especially sympathetic toward a fourth approach that encouraged children to learn to read initially in their mother tongue or oral language dialect and then learn English through art, music, and physical education. In this approach teachers would be responsible for instructing children in multiple dialects and languages. They did admit that it might be impractical to implement this model because of the difficulty of locating the talented teaching personnel and the linguistically diverse materials that were needed. Although they made no suggestions about where to locate personnel, they thought that language-based activities, which relied on passages that employed the distinctive language and experiences of learners, could be an instructional solution to the materials problem. Observing that children would inevitably use vocabulary and grammar that exhibited irregularities when their instructors employed language experience activities with them, May and Eliot recommended that the teachers refrain from editing the passages for fear that this would inhibit learners' creativity. Several decades earlier Ashton-Warner (1963) had used a comparable instructional approach as part of the program she had developed with native Maori children in a rural area of New Zealand.

Language-based approaches to reading were recommended frequently for multicultural groups during the last quarter of the twentieth century. Illustrating activities compatible with students' culture, traditions, and heritage, Diamond and Moore (1995) advised instructors to use multicultural literature, establish a culturally sensitive environment, and employ whole language. Like Diamond and Moore, Au (1993) had identified language-based activities as particularly effective for multicultural groups. She enthusiastically described the "constructive model" which supported language-based activities and which promoted sensitivity to learners' individual interests, background experiences, and cultures. She was less complimentary of the "transmission model" which she judged to be based upon beliefs that knowledge should be absorbed passively and that mainstream culture should be emphasized.

SUMMARY

The impact of reading education on linguistically diverse students was central to the deliberations of twentieth-century educators. During the early twentieth century the literacy programs that were developed for immigrant adults entailed many of the same issues that were being confronted by the teachers who were devising programs for immigrant children. For example, educators debated about the effectiveness of skills-based and language-based instruction, the suitability of non-English languages for instruction, the optimal length of any instruction that did take place using a language other than English, and the impact of literacy instruction on political, social, and cultural values. Although differences in opinion originated while educators were discussing children who spoke languages other than English, the ensuing controversies were generalized to children who spoke dialects other than standard English. Connected to political philosophies as well as instructional issues, the problems about multicultural literacy that had emerged during the early twentieth century remained unresolved at the end of the century.

REFERENCES

1,105,921 (1935). *Social Frontier, 1* (4), 5-6.

A new policy for a new times (1948). *Progressive Education, 25*, 41, 46, 58.

A rose is not a rose (1941). *Frontiers of Democracy, 7* (58), 100.

Abbott, G. (1917). *The immigrant and the community*. New York: Century.

Ackermann, E. (1996). *Learning to use the World Wide Web*. Wilsonville, OR: Franklin, Beedle.

Adams, C. F. (1880). Scientific common-school education. *Harper's New Monthly Magazine, 61*, 934-940.

Adams, F., Gray, L., & Reese, D. (1949). *Teaching children to read*. New York: Ronald.

Adams, J. (1897). Foreign-born children in the primary grades. In *National Education Association, Journal of Proceedings and Addresses of the Thirty-Sixth Annual Meeting* (pp. 104-112). Chicago: University of Chicago Press.

Adams, J. T. (1933). Can teachers bring about the new society: Comments on "A Call to the Teachers of the Nation." *Progressive Education, 10*, 310-313.

Adams, M. J. (1990). *Beginning to read: Thinking and learning about print*. Cambridge, MA: MIT Press.

Adler, F. (1892). *The moral instruction of children*. New York: Appleton.

Allen, J. (1890). *Temperament in education; also, success in teaching*. New York: Kellogg.

Allen, M. L. (1955). *Education or indoctrination*. Caldwell, ID: Caxton.

Allen, R. V. (1969). Individualizing with language experiences. In W. B. Barbe, R. V. Allen, & K. Smith, *Individualizing reading instruction* (pp. 9-14). Tucson, AZ: University of Arizona.

Allen, R. V. (1976). *Language experiences in communication*. Boston: Houghton Mifflin.

Allington, R., Guice, S., Michelson, N., Baker, K., & Li, S. (1996). Literature-based curricula in high-poverty schools. In M. Graves, P. Van Den Broek, & B. M. Taylor (Eds.), *The first R: Every child's right to read* (pp. 73-96). New York: Teachers College Press.

Allport, F. (1896). *The eye and its care*. Philadelphia: Lippincott.

Altbach, P. G. (1991). Textbooks: The international dimension. In M. W. Apple & L. K. Christian-Smith (Eds.), *The politics of the textbook* (pp. 242-258). New York: Routledge.

334 / *Twentieth-Century Reading Education*

American education and the war in Europe (1939). *National Education Association Journal, 28,* 225-228.

American Optical Company (1936–1937). *"Reading" in the class room: Teaching, diagnostic, and corrective techniques with the Ophthalm-O-Graph, a portable binocular eye-movement camera and the Metron-O-Scope, a triple shutter, short-exposure device for the practice of controlled reading.* Chicago, IL: Author.

Amidon, B. (1939). Over here. *Survey Graphic, 28,* 569.

Anderson, A. W. (1952). The cloak of respectability: The attackers and their methods. *Progressive Education, 100,* 66-81.

Anderson, C. (1961). *History of instructional technology, I: Technology in American education, 1650-1900* (Report prepared for the Technological Development Project, Occasional paper No. 1). Washington, DC: National Education Association.

Anderson, C. J., & Davidson, I. (1925). *Reading objectives: A guide book in the teaching of reading.* New York: Laurel.

Anderson, G. S. (1984). *A whole language approach to reading.* Lanham, MD: University Press of America.

Anderson, I. H., & Dearborn, W. F. (1952). *The psychology and teaching of reading.* New York: Ronald.

Anderson, M. L. (1917). *Education of defectives in the public schools.* Yonkers-on-Hudson, NY: World.

Andree, R. G. (1948). The menace of the comprehensive text. *Journal of Education, 151,* 54-55.

Apple, M. W. (1986). *Teachers and texts: A political economy of class and gender relations in education.* New York: Routledge.

Apple, M. W. (1996). *Cultural politics and education.* New York: Teachers College Press.

Archambault, R. D. (Ed.) (1974). *John Dewey on education: Selected writings.* Chicago: University of Chicago Press.

Armstrong, O. K. (1940, September). Treason in the textbooks. *American Legion Magazine,* 70-72.

Ashmore, H. S. (1954). *The Negro and the schools.* Chapel Hill, NC: University of North Carolina Press.

Ashton-Warner, S. (1963). *Teacher.* New York: Simon & Schuster.

Au, K. H. (1993). *Literacy instruction in multicultural settings.* Fort Worth, TX: Harcourt-Brace-Jovanovich.

Austin, M. C. (1953). Identifying readers who need corrective instruction. In H. M. Robinson (Ed.), *Corrective reading in classroom and clinic* (Supplementary Educational Monographs, Vol. 15, pp. 19-25). Chicago: University of Chicago Press.

Axline, V. M. (1947). Nondirective therapy for poor readers. *Journal of Consulting Psychology, 11* (2), 61-69.

Ayres, L. P. (1909). *Laggards in our schools: A study of retardation and elimination in city school systems.* New York: Russell Sage Foundation.

Bagley, W. C. (1916). *Classroom management: Its principles and technique.* New York: Macmillan.

Bagley, W. C. (1922). *The educative process.* New York: Macmillan. (Originally published in 1905)

Bagley, W. C. (1929). Discipline and dogma: A reply to professor Scholtz. *Educational Administration and Supervision, 15,* 561-573.

Bagley, W. C. (1930). The future of education in America. *Proceedings of the Sixty-Eighth Annual Meeting of the National Education Association, 68*, 218-225.

Bagley, W. C. (1931). The textbook and methods of teaching. In G. M. Whipple (Ed.), *The textbook in American education* (30th Yearbook of the National Society for the Study of Education, Part II, pp. 7-26). Bloomington, IL: Public School Publishing.

Bagley, W. C. (1938). An esesntialist's platform for the advancement of American education. *Educational Administration and Supervision, 224*, 241-256.

Baker, H. J. (1927). *Characteristic differences in bright and dull pupils: An interpretation of mental differences, with special reference to teaching procedures*. Indianapolis, IN: Public Schools Publishing.

Balmuth, M. (1982). *The roots of phonics: A historical introduction*. New York: McGraw-Hill.

Barnard, E. F. (1939). Before reading and writing. *Survey Graphic, 28*, 587-589.

Barnard, H. (1965). *Henry Barnard on education*. New York: Russell & Russell. (Original works published between 1839-1870)

Barnes, H. E. (1940). Should social change be consciously directed?: An historical survey. *Frontiers of Democracy, 6* (50), 106-110.

Barney, H. H. (1857). Introduction. In J. W. Taylor, *A manual of the Ohio School System; Consisting of an historical view of its progress, and a republication of the school laws in force* (pp. iii-x). Cincinnati, OH: Derby.

Barron, A. E., & Ivers, K. S. (1996). *The internet and instruction activities and ideas*. Englewood, CO: Libraries Unlimited.

Bartoli, J. S. (1995). *Unequal opportunity: Learning to read in the U.S.A.* New York: Teachers College Press.

Barzun, J. (1988). *Teacher in America*. Indianapolis, IN: Liberty. (Originally published in 1945)

Basler, R. (1947). Life adjustment education for youth: Commission to develop program for universal secondary education. *School and Society, 30* (2), 3-6.

Bayles, E. E. (1966). *Pragmatism in education*. New York: Harper & Row.

Beale, H. K. (1936). *Are American teachers free?: An analysis of the restrains upon the freedom of teaching in American schools* (Report of the Commission on the Social Studies, Part 12). New York: Scribner's.

Beale, H. K. (1941). *A history of freedom of teaching in American schools*. New York: Scribner's.

Beard, C. A. (1923). *The economic basis of politics*. New York: Knopf.

Beard, C. A. (1932). *The myth of rugged American individualism* (John Day Pamphlet No. 6). New York: Day.

Beard, C. A. (1934). Property and democracy. *Social Frontier, 1* (2), 13-15.

Beck, I. L. (1984). Developing comprehension: The impact of the directed reading lesson. In R. C. Anderson, J. Osborn, & R. J. Tierney (Eds.), *Learning to read in American schools: Basal readers and the content texts* (pp. 3-20). Hillsdale, NJ: Erlbaum.

Beck, I. L., McCaslin, E. S., & McKeown, A. (1981). Basal readers' purpose for story reading: Smoothly paving the road or setting up a detour? *Elementary School Journal, 81*, 156-161.

Beecher, E. (1855). *The papal conspiracy exposed: And Protestantism defended, in the light of reason, history, and scripture*. New York: Dodd.

Beiswanger, G. W. (1936). The atrophy of education. *Social Frontier, 1* (3), 246-248.

Bell, B. I. (1949). *Crisis in education: A challenge to American complacency*. New York: Whittlesey.

Benne, K. D. (1949). Democratic ethics in social engineering. *Progressive Education, 26,* 201-207.

Bennett, C. C. (1938). *An inquiry into the genesis of poor reading* (Teachers College Contributions to Education, No. 755). New York: Teachers College Press.

Bennett, H. E. (1940, March). Fifty years of school seating. *American School Board Journal, 100,* 41-43, 125.

Bere, M. (1924). *A comparative study of the mental capacity of children of foreign parentage*. New York: Teachers College Press.

Berkaman, A. (1936, June). Sociology of the comic strip. *American Spectator, 4,* 51-54.

Berkson, I. B. (1920). *Theories of Americanization: A critical study, with special reference to the Jewish group*. New York: Teachers College Press.

Berliner, D. C., & Biddle, B. J. (1997). *The manufactured crisis: Myths, fraud, and the attack on America's public schools*. New York: Longman.

Berry, F. M. (1978). Contemporary bibliotherapy: Systematizing the field. In R. J. Rubin (Ed.), *Bibliotherapy sourcebook* (pp. 185-190). Phoenix, AZ: Oryx.

Best, H. (1919). *The blind: Their condition and the work being done for them in the United States*. New York: Macmillan.

Bestor, A. (1953). Anti-intellectualism in the schools. *New Republic, 128* (3), 11-13.

Bestor, A. (1985). *Educational wastelands: The retreat from learning in our public schools* (2nd ed.). Urbana, IL: University of Illinois Press.

Bettelheim, B. (1975, December 8). The uses of enchantment. *The New Yorker, 51,* pp. 50-114.

Bettelheim, B. (1976). *The uses of enchantment: The meaning and importance of fairy tales*. New York: Knopf.

Bettelheim, B., & Zelan, K. (1982). *On learning to read: The child's fascination with meaning*. New York: Knopf.

Betts, E. A. (1936). *The prevention and correction of reading difficulties*. New York: Row, Peterson.

Betts, E. A. (1946). *Foundations of reading instruction*. New York: American.

Blackhurst, J. H. (1922). Educational research and statistics. *School and Society, 16,* 697-700.

Blair, G. M. (1946). *Diagnostic and remedial teaching in secondary schools*. New York: Macmillan.

Blair, G. M. (1956). *Diagnostic and remedial teaching: A guide to practice in elementary and secondary schools*. New York: Macmillan.

Bloom, B. (1976). *Human characteristics and school learning*. New York: McGraw-Hill.

Bloomfield, L. (1933). *Language*. New York: Holt.

Bode, B. H. (1930, June 4). The new education ten years after: Apprenticeship or freedom? *New Republic, 59,* 61-64.

Bode, B. H. (1933). The confusion in present-day education. In W. H. Kilpatrick (Ed.), *The educational frontier* (pp. 3-31). New York: Appleton-Century.

Bode, B. H. (1935). Dr. Bode replies. *Social Frontier, 2* (2), 42-43.

Bode, B. H. (1938). *Progressive education at the crossroads*. New York: Newson.

Bode, B. H. (1940). *How we learn*. Boston: Heath.

Bogardus, E. S. (1928). *Immigration and race attitudes*. Boston: Heath.

Bond, G. L., & Tinker, M. A. (1957). *Reading difficulties: Their diagnosis and correction.* New York: Appleton-Century-Crofts.

Bond, G. L., Tinker, M. A., & Wasson, B. B. (1979). *Reading difficulties: Their diagnosis and correction* (4th ed.). Englewood Cliffs, NJ: Prentice-Hall.

Book burnings. (1940, September 9). *Time, 34*, pp. 64-65.

Boorstin, D. J. (1981). Introduction. In J. Y. Cole & T. G. Sticht (Eds.), *The textbook in American society: A volume based on a conference at the Library of Congress on May 2–3, 1979* (pp. ix-x). Washington, DC: Library of Congress.

Bordie, J. G. (1971). When should instruction in a second language or dialect begin? *Elementary English, 48*, 551-554.

Bork, A (1980a). Interactive learning. In R. Taylor (Ed.), *The computer in the school: Tutor, tool, tutee* (pp. 53-66). New York: Teachers College Press.

Bork, A (1980b). Preparing student-computer dialogs: Advice to teachers. In R. Taylor (Ed.), *The computer in the school: Tutor, tool, tutee* (pp. 15-52). New York: Teachers College Press.

Borrowman, M. L. (1956). *The liberal and technical in teacher education: A historical survey of American thought.* Westport, CT: Greenwood.

Bowers, C. A. (1969). *The progressive educator and the depression: The radical years.* New York: Random House.

Bowker, R. R. (1996). *Children's reference PLUS.* New Providence, NJ: Author.

Bowmar Publishers (1970). *Breakthrough to literacy: An introduction* [Brochure]. Glendale, CA: Author.

Boyer, C. C. (1908). *Modern methods for teachers: A twentieth century hand-book for American teachers, normal schools, and teachers' reading circles.* Philadelphia: Lippincott.

Bracey, G. W. (1991). Why can't they be like we were? *Phi Delta Kappan, 73*, 104-117.

Bracey, G. W. (1992). The second Bracey report on the condition of education. *Phi Delta Kappan, 74*, 104-117.

Bracey, G. W. (1993). The third Bracey report on the condition of education. *Phi Delta Kappan, 75*, 104-117.

Bracey, G. W. (1994). The fourth Bracey report on the condition of education. *Phi Delta Kappan, 76*, 114-127.

Braddock, D., & Mitchell, D. (1992). *Residential services and developmental disabilities in the United States: A national survey of staff compensation, turnover and related issues.* Washington, DC: American Association on Mental Retardation.

Brameld, T. (1935). Karl Marx and the American teacher. *Social Frontier, 2*, 53-56.

Brameld, T. (1936). American education and the social struggle. *Science and Society, 1*, 1-17.

Brameld, T. (1946). *Minority problems in the public schools: A study of administrative policies and practices in seven school systems.* New York: Harper.

Brameld, T. (1950). *Patterns of educational philosophy: A democratic interpretation.* Yonkers-on-Hudson, NY: World.

Brameld, T. (1951, December 15). The battle for free schools: Four-point agenda for education. *Nation, 173*, 523-526.

Branham, A. F. (1930). The development of the American school textbook. *American School Board Journal, 91* (2), 58,-59, 122, 125.

Brest-Friedberg, J. Mullins, J. B., & Weir-Sukeinnick, A. (1992). *Portraying persons with disabilities: An annotated bibliography.* New Providence, NJ: Bowker.

Briggs, T. H. (1940). *Pragmatism and pedagogy.* New York: Macmillan.

Briggs, T. H., & Coffman, L. D. (1911). *Reading in public schools* (Rev. ed.). Chicago: Row, Peterson.

Britton, B. K. (1986). Capturing art to improve text quality. *Educational Psychologist, 21,* 333-356.

Brockett, L. P. (1856, May). Idiots and institutions for their training. *American Journal of Education,* 601-608.

Bronner, A. F. (1917). *The psychology of special abilities and disabilities.* Boston: Little, Brown.

Browder, E. (1935). Education—An ally in the workers' struggle. *Social Frontier, 1* (4), 22-24.

Brown, E. F. (1975). *Bibliotherapy and its widening applications.* Metuchen, NJ: Scarecrow.

Brown, J. F. (1909). *The American high school.* New York: Macmillan.

Brown, J. F. (1922a). School textbooks from an editor's point of view, *Journal of Education, 96,* 380-383.

Brown, J. F. (1922b). Textbooks and publishers. *Elementary School Journal, 19,* 382-388.

Brown, R. (1931). Vocabularies of history and reading textbooks. *Elementary School Principal, 10,* 408-411.

Brown, S. I., & Finn, M. E. (Eds.) (1988). *Readings from Progressive Education: A movement and its professional journal* (Vol. 1). New York: University Press of America.

Brueckner, L. J., & Melby, E. O. (1931). *Diagnostic and remedial teaching.* Boston: Houghton Mifflin.

Bruner, J. S. (1973). Culture, politics, and pedagogy. In F. A. Ianni & E. Storey (Eds.), *Cultural relevance and educational issues* (pp. 463-476). Boston: Little-Brown.

Bryce, J. (1909). *The hindrances to good citizenship.* New Haven, CT: Yale University Press.

Bryson, L. (1937). What are readable books? *Educational Forum, 1,* 397-402.

Budenz, L. F. (1951, November). Do colleges have to hire red professors? *American Legion Magazine,* 168-173.

Budenz, L. F. (1954). *The techniques of communism.* Chicago: Regnery.

Burbeck, E. (1939). Problems presented to teachers of bilingual pupils. *California Journal of Elementary Education, 8,* 49-54.

Burgess, M. (1921). *The measurement of silent reading.* New York: Russell Sage Foundation.

Burling, R. (1973). *English in black and white.* New York: Holt, Rinhehart, & Winston.

Burnham, J. C. (1960). Psychiatry, psychology and the progressive movement. *American Quarterly, 12,* 457-465.

Burns, P. C., Roe, B. D., & Ross, E. P. (1996). *Teaching reading in today's elementary schools.* Boston: Houghton Mifflin.

Burr, C. S. (1922). *America's race heritage: An account of the diffusion of ancestral stocks in the United States during three centuries of national expansion and a discussion of its significance.* New York: National Historical Society.

Burstall, S. A. (1909). *Impressions of American education in 1908*. New York: Longman, Green.

Burt, C. (1922). *Mental and scholastic tests*. London: King.

Burt, C. (1955). *The subnormal mind* (3rd ed.). London: Oxford University Press.

Burton, D. L., & Larrick, N. (1961). Literature for children and youth. In N. B. Henry (Ed.), *Development in and through reading* (60th Yearbook of the National Society for the Study of Education, Part I, pp. 189-208). Chicago: University of Chicago Press.

Burton, W. (1929). *The district school as it was: By one who went to it*. New York: Crowell (Originally published in 1833).

Bus, A. G., & Van Ijzendoorn, M. H. (1988). Mother-child interactions, attachment, and emergent literacy: A cross sectional study. *Child Development, 59*, 1262-1272.

Bushnell, D. D. (1967). Applications of computer technology to the improvement of learning. In D. D. Bushnell & D. W. Allen (Eds.), *The computer in American education* (pp. 59-76). New York: Wiley.

Buswell, G. T. (1922). *Fundamental reading habits: A study of their development*. Chicago: University of Chicago Press.

Buswell, G. T. (1923). The school treatment of mentally exceptional children. *Elementary School Journal, 23*, 683-693.

Butcher, T. W. (1919). Some difficulties attending the work of a textbook commission. *Elementary School Journal, 19*, 500-505.

Butler, J. D. (1951). *Four philosophies and their practice in education and religion*. New York: Harper.

Butler, N. M. (1931). *Radio's new opportunity in education*. Chicago: University of Chicago Press.

Butts, R. F. (1947). *A cultural history of education: Reassessing our educational traditions*. New York: McGraw-Hill.

Butts, R. F., & Cremin, L. A. (1953). *A history of education in American culture*. New York: Holt.

Cafolla, R., Kauffman, D., & Knee, R. (1997). *World Wide Web for teachers: An interactive guide*. Needham Heights, MA: Allyn and Bacon.

Caine. S. P. (1974). The origins of progressivism. In L. L. Gould (Ed.), *The progressive era* (pp. 11-34). Syracuse, NY: Syracuse University Press.

Caldwell, O. W., & Courtis, S. A. (1925). *Then & now in education, 1845–1923: A message of encouragement from the past to the present*. Yonkers-on-Hudson, NY: World.

California Curriculum Commission (1931). *The activity program and the teaching of reading: Manual for kindergarten and primary teachers* (Office of Education Bulletin No. 2). Washington, DC: Government Printing Office.

Cambourne, B. (1989). *The whole story: Natural learning and the acquisition of literacy in the classroom*. Auckland, New Zealand: Aston Scholastic.

Carnine, D., Silbert, J., & Kameenui, E. J. (1990). *Direct instruction reading* (2nd ed.). Columbus, OH: Merrill.

Carnine, D., Silbert, J., & Kameenui, E. J. (1996). *Direct instruction reading* (3rd ed.). Columbus, OH: Merrill.

Carnoy, M. (1974). *Education as cultural imperialism*. New York: McKay.

Carpenter, C. (1963). *History of American schoolbooks*. Philadelphia: University of Pennsylvania Press.

Carroll, J. (1964). A model of school learning. *Teachers College Record, 64*, 723-733.

Cast, G. C. (1919). Selecting text-books. *Elementary School Journal, 19*, 468-472.

Caswell, H. L., & Campbell, D. S. (1935). *Curriculum development*. New York: American.

Cecil, N. L. (1989). *Teaching to the heart: An affective approach to literacy instruction*. Salem, WI: Sheffield.

Chadsey, C. E. (1924). Editor's introduction. In J. L. Horn, *The education of exceptional children* (pp. v-viii). New York: Century.

Chall, J. S. (1958). *Readability: An appraisal of research and application* (Bureau of Educational Research Monograph No. 34). Columbus, OH: Bureau of Educational Research.

Chall, J. S. (1967). *Learning to read: The grate debate*. New York: McGraw-Hill.

Chall, J. S., & Conard, S. S. (1991). *Should textbooks challenge students?—The case for easier or harder textbooks*. New York: Teachers College Press.

Chamberlain, J. (1939). Our jobless youth: A warning. *Survey Graphic, 28*, 579-582.

Chancellor, W. E. (1913). The state publication question. *School Journal, 80*, 218-220.

Chancellor, W. E. (1914). The government publication of school Books. *School Journal, 81*, 161-164.

Charters, W. W. (1913). *Teaching the common branches: A textbook for teachers of rural and graded schools* (pp. 139-164). Cambridge, MA: Houghton Mifflin.

Chase, H. W. (1937). The viewpoint of education. In C. S. Marsh (Ed.), *Educational broadcasting 1937* (Proceeding of the Second National Conference on Educational Broadcasting, pp. 24-26). Chicago: University of Chicago Press.

Chase, S. (1931). *Out of the depression—And after: A prophecy* (John Day Pamphlet No. 2). New York: Day.

Child, I. L., Potter, E. H., & Levine, E. M. (1946). *Children's textbooks and personality development: An exploration in the social psychology of education* (Psychological Monograph, Vol. 60, No. 3) Washington, DC: American Psychological Association.

Childs, J. L. (1931). *Education and the philosophy of experimentalism*. New York: Appleton–Century.

Childs, J. L. (1936). Can teachers stay out of the class struggle? *Social Frontier, 2* (7), 219-222.

Childs, J. L. (1942, March). Teachers and boards of education in a war period. *Frontiers of Democracy, 8* (68), 166.

Childs, J. L. (1954). Education and the crisis in American democracy: A review of education and social integration. *Progressive Education, 31*, 91-97.

Childs, J. L. (1956). *American pragmatism and education: An interpretation and criticism*. New York: Holt.

Ching, D. (1969). Reading, language, and the bilingual child: An annotated bibliography. *Elementary English, 46*, 622-629.

Chonchol, J. (1973). Preface to "Extension or communication." In P. Freire, *Education for critical consciousness* (M. Bergman-Ramos, Trans., pp. 87-89). New York: Continuum.

Christian, C. C. (1976). Social and psychological implications of bilingual literacy. In A. Simões (Ed.), *The bilingual child: Research and analysis of existing educational themes* (pp. 17-40). New York: Academic Press.

Church, S. M. (1996). *The future of whole language: Reconstruction or self-destruction?* Portsmouth, NH: Heinemann.

Cianciolo, P. J. (1965). Children's literature can affect coping behavior. *Personnel and Guidance Journal, 43,* 897-903.

Ciborowski, J. (1992). *Textbooks and the students who can't read them: A guide to teaching content.* Brookline, MA: Brookline.

Clark, D. B., & Uhry, J. K. (1995). *Dyslexia: Theory & practice of remedial instruction* (2nd ed.). Baltimore: York Press.

Clay, M. M. (1993). *Reading recovery: A guidebook for teachers in training.* Portsmouth, NH: Heinemann.

Clifton, J. L. (1933). *Ten famous American educators.* Columbus, OH: Adams.

Cobb, S. (1934). *New horizons for the child.* Washington, DC: Avalon.

Cockerell, T. D. A. (1911). Text-books and reviewing. *Science, 34,* 561-562.

Cohen, H. L. (1913). The foreigner in our schools: Some aspects of the problem in New York. *English Journal, 2,* 618-629.

Cohen, H. L. (1919). Americanization by classroom practice. *Teachers College Record, 20,* 238-249.

Cohen, S. (1964). *Progressives and urban school reform: The public education association of New York City, 1895-1954.* New York: Teachers College.

Cole, L. (1934). *Psychology of the elementary school subjects.* New York: Farrar & Rinehart.

Cole, L. (1938). *The improvement of reading: With special reference to remedial instruction.* New York: Farrar & Rinehart.

Cole, M., & Griffen, P. (1986). A sociohistorical approach to remediation: A reader. In S. De Castell, A. Luke, & K. Egan (Eds.), *Literacy, society, and schooling* (pp. 110-131). Cambridge, England: Cambridge University Press.

Colgrove, P. P. (1916). Night schools of the Iron Range of Minnesota. *Immigrant in America Review, 1* (4), 65-69.

Collectivism and collectivism (1934). *Social Frontier, 1* (2), 3-4.

Collins, E. (1933). Learning the fundamentals in the activity curriculum. *Journal of Experimental Education, 1,* 309-315.

Collins, M. D., & Cheek, E. H. (1993). *Diagnostic-prescriptive reading instruction: A guide for classroom teachers* (4th ed.). Dubuque: IA: Brown & Benchmark.

Commager, H. S. (1950). *The American mind: An interpretation of American thought and character since the 1880's.* New Haven. CT: Yale University Press.

Commission on Immigration (1914). *The problem of immigration in Massachusetts.* Boston: Wright & Potter.

Commission on Industrial and Technical Education (1906). *Report of the commission on industrial and technical education.* New York: Teachers College Press.

Commission on Instructional Technology (1970). The status of instructional technology today. In S. G. Tickton (Ed.), *To improve learning: An evaluation of instructional technology* (Vol. I, Part One, Report of the Commission on Instructional Technology, pp. 65-76). New York: Bowker.

Commission on Reading of the National Council Teachers of English (1989). Basal readers and the state of American reading instruction: A call for action. *Language Arts, 66,* 896-898.

Commission on the Social Studies (1934). *Conclusions and recommendations of the commission: Report of the commission on the Social Studies.* New York: Scribner's Sons.

Committee of the Progressive Education Association on Social and Economic Problems (1933). *A call to the teachers of the nation* (John Day Pamphlets No. 30). New York: Day.

Conant, J. B. (1959). *The American high school today: A first report to interested citizens.* New York: McGraw-Hill.

Confessions of public school teachers (1896, July). *Atlantic Monthly, 78,* 97-110.

Conkin, P. K. (1976). *Puritans and pragmatists: Eight eminent American thinkers.* Bloomington, IL: Illinois University Press.

Cooke, F. J. (1926). Fundamental considerations underlying the curriculum of the Francis W. Parker School. In G. M. Whipple (Ed.), *The foundations and technique of curriculum-construction* (26th Yearbook of the National Society for the Study of Education, Part 1, pp. 305-314). Bloomington, IL: Public School Publishing.

Copperman, P. (1978). *The literacy hoax: The decline of reading, writing, and learning in the public schools and what we can do about it.* New York: Morrow.

Cottrell, M. J. (1948). Essential equipment for basic instruction in reading: In the primary grades. In W. S. Gray (Ed.), *Basic Instruction in reading in elementary and high schools* (Supplemental Educational Monographs, Vol. X, pp. 102-106). Chicago: University of Chicago Press.

Counts, G. S. (1931). *The soviet challenge to America.* New York: Day.

Counts, G. S. (1932). *Dare the school build a new social order?* (John Day Pamphlet No. 11). New York: Day.

Counts, G. S. (1971). *School and society in Chicago.* New York: Arno. (Originally published in 1926)

Courtis, S. A. (1915). Standards in rates of reading. In S. C. Parker (Ed.), *Minimum essentials in elementary-school subjects—Standards and current practices* (14th Yearbook of the National Society for the Study of Education, Part 1, pp. 44-68). Chicago: University of Chicago Press.

Courtis, S. A. (1921). Analysis of reading ability. *Journal of Educational Research, 4,* 287-293.

Cremin, L. A. (1969). *The transformation of the school: Progressivism in American education, 1876–1957.* New York: Knopf.

Critchley, M. (1968). Isolation of the specific dyslexic. In A. H. Keeney & V. T. Keeney (Eds.), *Dyslexia: Diagnosis and treatment of reading disorders* (pp. 17-20). St. Louis, MO: Mosby.

Cronbach, L. J. (1948). Values in textbooks. *School Review, 56,* 196-198.

Cronbach, L. J. (1955). The text in use. In L. J. Cronbach (Ed.), *Text materials in modern education* (pp. 188-216). Urbana, IL: University of Illinois Press.

Cronin, M. J. (1996). *Global advantage on the internet.* New York: Van Nostrand Reinhold.

Crothers, S. M. (1916, August). A literacy clinic. *The New Yorker, 41,* pp. 299-301.

Cuban, L. (1984). *How teachers taught: Constancy and change in American classrooms 1890–1980.* New York: Longman.

Cubberly, E. P. (1947). *Public education in the United States: A study and interpretation of American educational history*. Cambridge, MA: Houghton Mifflin.

Cullinan, B. E. (1986). Foreword. In D. Taylor & D. S. Strickland, *Family storybook reading* (pp. ix-x). Portsmouth, NH: Heinemann.

Curti, M. (1935). *The social ideas of American educators*. New York: Scribners.

Curtis, F. D. (1922). More from our textbooks. *School Review, 30*, 770-776.

Curtis, S. J. (1967). *History of education in Great Britain* (7th ed.). London: University Tutorial Press.

Dale, E. (1961). *Audio-visual methods in teaching* (Rev. ed.). New York: Holt, Rinehart, & Winston.

Dale, E., & Chall, J. (1949). The concept of readability. *Elementary English, 26*, 19-26.

Dale, E., & Tyler, R. W. (1934). A study of the factors influencing the difficulty of reading materials for adults of limited reading ability. *Library Quarterly, 4*, 384-412.

Davenport, E. (1911). *Education for efficiency: A discussion of certain phases of the problem of universal education with special reference to academic ideals and methods*. Boston: Heath.

Davis, B. (1985, January 3). Many forces shape making and marketing of a new schoolbook: Houghton Mifflin consulted teachers and minorities before publishing a text. *Wall Street Journal, 105*, p. 1, 8.

Davis, J. (1930). *Contemporary social movements*. New York: Century.

Davis, J. B. (1914). *Vocational and moral guidance*. Boston: Ginn.

De Castell, S., & Luke, A. (1989). Literacy instruction: Technology and technique. In S. De Castell, A. Luke, & C. Luke (Eds.), *Language, authority and criticism: Readings on the school textbook* (pp. 77-95). Philadelphia: Falmer.

Dearborn, W. F. (1928). *Intelligence tests: Their significance for school and society*. Boston: Houghton Mifflin.

Dearborn, W. F. (1939). The nature and treatment of reading disability: The nature and causation of disabilities in reading. In W. S. Gray (Ed.), *Recent trends in reading* (Supplementary Educational Monographs, I, pp. 103-110). Chicago: University of Chicago Press.

Dearden, R. F. (1980). Education and politics. *Journal of Philosophy of Education, 14*, 149-156.

DeBoer, J. J. (1945). Forward progressives! *Progressive Education, 25*, 225, 251.

Delacato, C. (1959). *The treatment and prevention of reading problems*. Springfield, IL: Thomas.

Delacato, C. (1963). *The diagnosis and treatment of speech and reading problems*. Springfield, IL: Thomas.

DelFattore, J. (1992). *What Johnny shouldn't read*. New Haven, CT: Yale University Press.

Delgado, L. , Hilley, M. J., Bowie, M., & Allen, J. (1995). Whole language, media centers, and classroom libraries: Research in action. In J. Allen, M., Cary, & L. Delgado (Eds.), *Exploring blue highways: Literacy reform, school change, and the creation of learning communities* (pp. 127-144) New York: Teachers College Press.

DeLima, A. (1942). *The little red school house*. New York: Macmillan.

Demiashkevich, M. J. (1935a). *An introduction to the philosophy of education*. New York: American.

Demiashkevich, M. J. (1935b). Some doubts about the activity movement. *Harvard Teachers Record, 3*, 170-178.

Denison, D. (1912). *Helping school children: Suggestions for efficient cooperation with the public schools.* New York: Harper.

Dent, E. C. (1942). *The audio-visual handbook.* Chicago: Society of Visual Education.

Descoeudres, A. (1928). *The education of mentally defective children: Psychological observations and practical suggestions* (E. F. Row, Trans., 2nd ed.). Boston: Heath.

Deutsch, A. (1949). *The mentally ill in America: A history of their care and treatment from colonial times* (2nd ed.). New York: Columbia University Press.

Devereux, H. T. (1909, April). Report of a year's work on defectives in a public school. *The Psychological Clinic: A Journal for the Study and Treatment of Mental Retardation and Deviation, 3*, 45-48.

Deweese, T. A. (1902). Two years' progress in the Chicago public schools. *Educational Review, 24*, 325-328.

Dewey, J. (1898). The primary education fetich. *Forum, 25*, 315-328.

Dewey. J. (1907). *The school and society: Being three lectures by John Dewey, supplemented by a statement of the university elementary school.* New York: McClure, Philips.

Dewey, J. (1915, May 15). Education vs. trade-training—Dr. Dewey's reply. *New Republic, 3*, 42.

Dewey, J. (1916). *Democracy and education.* New York: Macmillan.

Dewey, J. (1928a). Progressive education and the science of education. *Progressive Education, 5*, 197-204.

Dewey, J. (1928b, December 12). Impressions of Soviet Russia, V: New schools for a new era. *New Republic, 57*, 91-94.

Dewey, J. (1934). Can education share in social reconstruction? *Social Frontier, 1* (1), 11-12.

Dewey, J. (1936). Class struggle and the democratic way. *Social Frontier, 2*, 241-242.

Dewey, J. (1938). *Experience and education.* New York: Macmillan.

Diamond, B. J., & Moore, M. A. (1995). *Multicultural literacy: Mirroring the reality of the classroom.* White Plains, NY: Longman.

Dilling, E. (1935). *The red network: A "who's who" and handbook of radicalism for patriots.* Chicago: Author.

Dillingofski, M. S. (1979). *Nonprint medial and reading: An annotated bibliography.* Newark, DE: International Reading Association.

Division of Secondary Education/Division of Vocational Education (1947). *Life adjustment education for every youth.* Washington, DC: U. S. Government Printing Office.

Dix, L. (1939). *A charter for progressive education.* New York: Bureau of Publications.

Dixon, C. N. (1976). Teaching strategies for the Mexican American child. *Reading Teacher, 30*, 141-145.

Dodge, R. (1900). Visual perception during eye movement. *Psychological Review, 7*, 454-465

Dogherty, M. A. (1943). *'Scusa me teacher.* Francestown, NH: Marshall Jones.

Dolch, E. W. (1930). Sampling of reading matter. *Journal of Educational Research, 22*, 213-215.

Dolch, E. W. (1939). *A manual for remedial reading.* Champaign, IL: Garrard.

Doll, L. M. (1909, April). A Cincinnati special class. *The Psychological Clinic: A Journal for the Study and Treatment of Mental Retardation and Deviation, 3*, 34-44.

Donahue, M. R. (1975). *The child and the English language arts* (2nd ed.). Dubuque, IA: Brown.

Donovan. H. L. (1924). How to select textbooks. *Peabody Journal of Education, 2* (1), 1-11.

Dorchester, D. (1888). *Romanism versus the public school system.* New York: Philips & Hunt.

Dougherty, M. L. (1923). *How to teach phonics.* Boston: Houghton Mifflin.

Down, A. G. (1988). Preface. In H. Tyson-Berstein, *A conspiracy of good intentions: America's textbook fiasco* (pp. vii-xii). Washington, DC: Council for Basic Education.

Downing, J. (1979). *Reading and reasoning.* New York: Spring-Verlag.

Doyle, D. P. (1984). Unsacred texts: Market forces that work too well. *American Educator, 8* (2), 8-13.

Du Mont, A. B. (1952). Educational television. In C. V. Newsom (Ed.), *A television policy for education* (Proceeding of the Television Programs Institute, pp. 13-21). Washington, DC: American Council on Education.

Duncan, H. G. (1933). *Immigration and assimilation.* Boston: Heath.

Duncan, J. (1953). *Backwardness in reading: Remedies and prevention.* London: Harrap.

Dunn, F. W. (1921). *Interest factors in primary reading material.* New York: Teachers College Press.

Durrell, D. D. (1940). *Improvement of basic reading abilities.* New York: World.

Durrell, D. D. (1968). Phonics in beginning reading. In J. Allen Figurel (Ed.), *Forging ahead in reading* (pp. 19-25). Newark, DE: International Reading Association.

Dutton, S. T. (1900). *Social phases of education in the school and the home.* New York: Macmillan.

Dutton, S. T., & Snedden, D. (1908). *The administration of public education in the United States.* New York: Macmillan.

Educating for tomorrow (1934). *Social Frontier, 1* (1), 5-7.

Education and the defense of American democracy (1940). *National Education Association Journal, 29*, 161-168.

Education Policies Commission (1938). *The purposes of education in American democracy.* Washington, DC: National Education Association/American Association of School Administrators.

Education Policies Commission (1940). *Learning the ways of democracy: A case book of civic education.* Washington, DC: National Education Association/American Association of School Administrators.

Educational Policies Commission (1943). *What the school should teach in wartime.* Washington, DC: National Education Association.

Edwards, N., & Richey, H. G. (1963). *The school in the American social order* (2nd ed.). Boston: Houghton Mifflin.

Eggleston, E. (1889). *The Hoosier school-master: A novel.* New York: Orange Judd.

Eisenhardt, C. (1972). *Applying linguistics in the teaching of reading and the language arts.* Columbus, OH: Merrill.

Eliot, C. W. (1892). Undesirable and desirable uniformity in schools. *Addresses and Proceedings of the National Education Association, 31*, 82-95.

Eliot, C. W. (1898). *Educational reform: Essays and addresses.* New York: Century.

Ernst, F. (1953, May). How dangerous is John Dewey? *Atlantic Monthly,* pp. 59-62.

Eustis, R. S. (1947). Specific reading disability: A familial syndrome associated with ambidexterity and speech defects and a frequent cause of problem behavior. *New England Journal of Medicine, 237,* 243-249.

Evans, H. M. (1949). The social character of problem solving. *Progressive Education, 26,* 161-165.

Evans, L. B. (1914, June). State publication of text books. *School and Homes, 6,* 7-10.

Fader, D. (1966). *Hooked on books.* New York: Putnam.

Fairchild, H. P. (1926). *The melting-pot mistake.* Boston: Little, Brown.

Fairchild, H. P. (1934). A sociologist views the New Deal. *Social Frontier, 1* (1), 15-18.

Fang, I. E. (1967). The "easy listening formula." *Journal of Broadcasting, 11* (1), 63-68.

Farkas, G. (1996). *Human capital or cultural capital? Ethnicity and poverty groups in an urban school district.* New York: De Gruyter.

Farnham, G. L. (1895). *The sentence method of reading.* Syracuse, NY: Bardeen. (Originally published in 1881)

Farrell, E. K. (1908-1909). Special classes in the New York City schools. *Journal of Psycho-Asthenics, 13,* 91-96.

Favazza, A. R. (1966). Bibliotherapy: A critique of the literature. *Bulletin of the Medical Library Association, 54,* 138-141.

Feffer, A. (1993). *The Chicago pragmatists and American progressivism.* Ithica, NY: Cornell University Press.

Fernald, G. (1943). *Remedial techniques in basic school subjects.* New York: McGraw-Hill.

Fernald, G. M., & Keller, H. (1921). The effect of kinaesthetic factors in the development of word recognition in the case of non-readers. *Journal of Educational Research, 4,* 355-377.

Fernald, W. E. (1893). The history of the treatment of the feeble-minded. *Proceeding of the National Conference of Charities and Correction, 20,* 205-221.

Fields, L. G. (1921). A psychological inquiry into the nature of the condition known as congenital word-blindness. *Brain, 44,* 286-307.

Fine, B. (1947). *Our children are cheated: The crisis in American education.* New York: Holt.

Finkelstein, B. (1989). *Governing the young: Teacher behavior in popular primary schools in nineteenth-century United States.* New York: Falmer.

Finley, I. E. (1913). *Blackboard work in reading.* Boston: Sanborn.

Finn, J. D., Perrin, D. G., & Campion, L. E. (1962). *Studies in the growth of instructional technology, I: Audio-visual instrumentation for instruction in the public schools, 1930–1960, a basis for take-off* (Technological Development Project, Occasional Paper No. 6). Washington, DC: National Education Association.

Finney, R. L. (1928). *A sociological philosophy of education.* New York: Macmillan.

Flake, J. L., McClintock, C. E., Edson, L., Ellington, K., Mack, F., Sandon, M. L., & Urrutia, J. (1987). *Classroom activities for computer education.* Belmont, CA: Wadsworth.

Flesch, R. (1951). *How to test readability.* New York: Harper & Brothers.

Flesch, R. (1955). *Why Johnny can't read—And what you can do about it.* New York: Harper & Row.

Flesch, R. (1981). *Why Johnny still can't read.* New York: Harper & Row.

Ford Foundation (1961). *Teaching by television*. New York: Author.

Frampton, M. E., & Rowell, H. G. (1938). *Education of the handicapped* (Vol. 1). Yonkers-on-Hudson, NY: World.

Frank, T. (1997). *The conquest of cool: Business culture, counterculture, and the rise of hip consumerism*. Chicago: University of Chicago Press.

Frazier, A. (1959). We need more than talking textbooks. In A. Frazier & H. E. Wigren (Eds.), *Opportunities for learning: Guidelines for television* (pp. 42-45). Washington, DC: National Education Association.

Freeman, F. N. (1916). *Experimental education: Laboratory manual and typical results*. Boston, MA: Houghton Mifflin.

Freeman, Y. S., & Freeman, D. E. (1992). *Whole language for second language learners*. Portsmouth, NH: Heinemann.

Freire, P. (1970a). *Cultural action for freedom* (L. Slover, Trans.). Cambridge, MA: Center for the Study of Development and Social Change.

Freire, P. (1970b). *Pedagogy of the oppressed* (M. Bergman, Trans.). New York: Herder & Herder.

Freire, P. (1973). *Education for critical consciousness* (M. Bergman-Ramos, Trans.). New York: Continuum.

Freire, P. (1985). *The politics of education: Culture, power, and liberation* (D. Macedo, Trans.). South Hadley, MA: Bergin & Garvery.

Friedlaender, K. (1942). Children's books and their function in latency and puberty. *American Imago, 3*, 129-150.

Fries, C. C. (1963). *Linguistics and reading*. New York: Holt, Rinehart, & Winston.

Froese, V. (1991). Introduction to whole-language teaching and learning. In V. Froese (Ed.), *Whole-language: practice and theory* (pp. 1-16). Needham Heights, MA: Allyn & Bacon.

Fromm, E. (1960). Foreword. In A. S. Neill, *Summerhill: A radical approach to child rearing* (pp. ix-xvi). New York: Hart.

Frostig, M., & Horne, D. (1964). *The Frostig program for the development of visual perception*. Chicago: Follett.

Frostig, M., & Maslow, P. (1973). *Learning problems in the classroom: Prevention and remediation*. New York: Grune & Stratton.

Frude, N. (1983). *The intimate machine: Close encounters with computers and robots*. New York: New American Library.

Fry, E. (1968). A readability formula that saves time. *Journal of Reading, 11*, 513-516, 575-578.

Fuller, H. J. (1951). The emperor's new clothes, or prius dementat. *Scientific Monthly, 72*, 32-41.

Fuller, W. E. (1982). *The old country school: The story of rural education in the middle west*. Chicago: University of Chicago Press.

Fullerton, H. S. (1927, November 26). That guy McGuffey. *Saturday Evening Post*, 14-15, p. 54.

Fullerton, H. S. (1936). Preface. In H. C. Minnich (Ed.), *Old favorites from the McGuffey readers* (pp. v-vi). New York: American.

Gaffney, J. S., & Anderson, R. C. (1991). Two-tiered scaffolding: Congruent process of teaching and learning. In E. H. Hiebert (Ed.), *Literacy for a diverse society: Perspectives, practices, and policies* (pp. 184-198). New York: Teachers College Press.

Gagnon, P. (1987). *Democracy's untold story: What world history textbooks neglect.* Washington, DC: American Federation of Teachers.

Gans, R. (1941). *Guiding children's reading through experiences.* New York: Bureau of Publications—Teachers College Press.

Gard, E. D. (1908). The foreign pupil. *Journal of Education, 67,* 683-684.

Gardiner, R. A. (1958). Alfred A. Strauss, 1897–1957. *Exceptional Children, 24,* 373-375.

Gardner, D. E. M. (1942). *Testing results in the infant school.* London: Methuen.

Gates, A. I. (1927). *The improvement of reading: A program of diagnostic and remedial methods.* New York: Macmillan.

Gates, A. I. (1935). *The improvement of reading: A program of diagnostic & remedial methods* (Rev. ed.). New York: Macmillan.

Gates, A. I. (1941). The role of personality maladjustment in reading disability. *Journal of Genetic Psychology, 59,* 77-83.

Gates, A. I. (1947). *The improvement of reading: A program of diagnostic & remedial methods* (3rd ed.). New York: Macmillan.

Gates, A. I. (1971). An autobiography. In R. J. Havighurst (Ed.), *Leaders in American Education* (70th Yearbook of the National Society for the Study of Education, Part II, pp. 189-217). Chicago: National Society for the Study of Education.

Geoffrion, L. D., & Geoffrion, O. P. (1983). *Computers and reading instruction.* Reading, MA: Addison-Wesley.

Gessell, A. (1921). *Exceptional children and public school policy: Including a mental survey of the New Haven elementary schools.* New Haven, CT: Yale University Press.

Get adjusted (1947, December 15). *Time,* p. 64.

Gibson, D. (1943, February). Pedagogues and pedagese. *American Scholar, 22,* 92-104.

Gilbert, C. B. (1906). *The school and its life: A brief discussion of the principles of school management and organization.* New York: Silver, Burdett.

Gillespie, J. T., & Naden, C. J. (1989). *Seniorplots: A book talk guide for use with readers ages 15-18.* New Providence, NJ: Bowker.

Gillespie, J. T., & Naden, C. J. (1993). *Juniorplots 4: A book talk guide for use with readers ages 15-18.* New Providence, NJ: Bowker.

Gillespie, J. T., & Naden, C. J. (1994). *Middleplots 4: A book talk guide for use with readers ages 8-12.* New Providence, NJ: Bowker.

Gillette, J. M. (1910). *Vocational education.* New York: American.

Gillingham, A., & Stillman, B. W. (1940). *Remedial training for children with specific disability in reading, spelling, and penmanship.* New York: Sackett & Wilhelms.

Ginsburg, M. B., Kamat, S., Raghu, R., & Weaver, J. (1995). Educators and politics: Interpretations, involvement, and implications. In M. B. Ginsburg (Ed.), *The politics of educators' work and lives* (pp. 3-54). New York: Garland.

Giordano, G. (1996). *Literacy programs for adults with developmental disabilities.* San Diego, CA: Singular.

Gish, L. (1992). The silver screen. In C. Fadiman (Ed.), *The treasury of the Encyclopedia Britannica: More than two centuries of facts, curiosities, and discoveries from the most distinguished reference work of all time* (pp. 420-422). New York: Penguin.

Gladney, M. R., & Leaverton, L. (1968). A model for teaching standard English to non-standard English speakers. *Elementary English, 45,* 758-763.

Goddard, H. H. (1923). *School training of defective children*. Yonkers-on-Hudson, NY: World. (Originally published in 1914)

Goddard, N. (1974). *Literacy: Language-experience approaches*. London: Macmillan.

Gold, J. (1975). A word to the wise. In J. Gold (Ed.), *In the name of language!* (pp. 1-17). Canada: Macmillan.

Goldberg, H. K., & Schiffman, G. B. (1972). *Dyslexia: Problems of reading disabilities*. New York: Grune & Stratton.

Goodenough, F. L. (1949). *Mental testing: Its history, principles, and applications*. New York: Rinehart.

Goodman, K. S. (1965). Cues and miscues in reading: A linguistic study. *Elementary English, 42*, 635-642.

Goodman, K. S. (1969a). Dialect barriers to reading comprehension. In J. C. Baratz & R. W. Shuy (Eds.), *Teaching black children to read* (pp. 14-28). Washington, DC: Center for Applied Linguistics.

Goodman, K. S. (1969b). On valuing diversity in language. *Childhood Education, 46*, 123-125.

Goodman, K. S. (1986). *What's whole in whole language*. Portsmouth, NH: Heinemann.

Goodman, K. S. (1993). *Phonics phacts*. Portsmouth, NH: Heinemann.

Goodman, P. (1960). *Growing up absurd*. New York: Vintage.

Goodman, P. (1970). *New reformation: Notes of a Neolithic conservative*. New York: Random House.

Goodson, I. F., & Marsh, C. J. (1996). *Studying school subjects*. Washington, DC: Falmer.

Gordon, P., & Lawton, D. (1978). *Curriculum change in the nineteenth and twentieth centuries*. New York: Holmes & Meier.

Gould. L. L. (1974). Introduction: The progressive era. In L. L. Gould (Ed.), *The progressive era* (pp. 1-10). Syracuse, NY: Syracuse University Press.

Goulet, D. (1973). Introduction. In P. Freire, *Education for critical consciousness* (M. Bergman-Ramos, Trans., pp. vii-xiv). New York: Continuum.

Grabe, M., & Grabe, C. (1996). *Integrating technology for meaningful learning*. Boston: Houghton Mifflin.

Graff, H. J. (1991). *The legacies of literacy: Continuities and contradictions in western culture and society*. Bloomington, IN: Indiana University Press.

Graham, P. A. (1967). *Progressive education: From Arcady to academe*. New York: Teachers College Press.

Gray, C. T. (1913). Relation of breathing to oral reading. *Journal of Educational Psychology, 4*, 39-41.

Gray, C. T. (1922). *Deficiencies in reading ability: Their diagnosis and remedies*. Boston: Heath.

Gray, W. S. (1916a). Methods of testing reading—I. *Elementary School Journal, 16*, 231-246.

Gray, W. S. (1916b). Methods of testing reading— II. *Elementary School Journal, 16*, 281-298.

Gray, W. S. (1919). Principles of method in teaching reading, as derived from scientific investigation. In G. M. Whipple (Ed.), *Fourth report of the committee on economy of time in education* (18th yearbook of the National Society for the Study of Education, Part 2, pp. 26-51). Bloomington, IL: Public School Publishing.

Gray, W. S. (1922). *Remedial cases in reading: Their diagnosis and treatment.* Chicago: University of Chicago Press.

Gray, W. S. (1925). *Summary of investigations relating to reading.* Chicago: University of Chicago Press.

Gray, W. S. (1939). The value and place of reading in general education: The nature of reading problems in general education. In W. S. Gray (Ed.), *Recent trends in reading* (Supplementary Educational Monographs, Vol. I, pp. 3-8). Chicago: University of Chicago Press.

Gray, W. S. (1946). Preface. In H. M. Robinson, *Why pupils fail in reading: A study of causes and remedial treatment* (pp. i-xii). Chicago: University of Chicago Press.

Gray, W. S. (1960). *On their own in reading: How to give children independence in analyzing new words* (Rev. ed.). Chicago: Scott Foresman.

Gray, W. S., & Ayer, A. M. (1934). Controversial issues. In G. M. Whipple (Ed.), *The activity movement* (33rd Yearbook of the National Society for the Study of Education, Part 2, pp. 167-182). Bloomington, IL: Public School Publishing.

Gray, W. S., & Leary, B. (1935). *What makes a book readable: With special reference to adults of limited reading ability—An initial study.* Chicago: University of Chicago Press.

Gray, W. S., & Leary, B. (1939). Reading instruction in elementary schools. In L. J. Brueckner, *The changing elementary school* (pp. 282-305). New York: Inor.

Greene, M. (1978). *Landscapes of learning.* New York: Teachers College Press.

Greer, C. (1972). *The great school legend: A revisionist interpretation of American public education.* New York: Basic.

Greer, T. H. (1949). *American social reform moments: Their pattern since 1865.* New York: Prentice-Hall.

Grose, H. B. (1906). *Aliens or Americans?* New York: Young People's Missionary Movement.

Groszmann, M. P. E. (1913, October). A tentative classification of exceptional children. *Child, 4,* 33-39.

Groszmann, M. P. E. (1917). *The exceptional child.* New York: Scribner.

Gumperz, J. J., & Hernández-Chavez, E. (1985). Bilingualism, bidialectalism, and classroom interaction. In C. B. Cazden, V. P. John, & D. Hymes (Eds.), *Functional of language in the classroom* (pp. 84-108). Prospect Heights, IL: Waveland. (Originally published in 1972)

Gunning, T. G. (1996). *Creating reading instruction for all children* (2nd ed.). Needham Heights, MA: Allyn & Bacon.

Gunter, M. A., Estes, T. H., & Schwab, J. (1995). *Instruction: A models approach* (2nd ed.). Needham Heights, MA: Allyn & Bacon.

Gurko, L. (1947). *The angry decade.* New York: Dodd, Mead.

Haldeman, E. G., & Idstein, S. (1977). *Bibliotherapy.* Washington, DC: University Press of America.

Hale, E. E. (1927). *A New England boyhood.* Boston: Little, Brown. (Originally published in 1893)

Hall, G. S. (1897). *How to teach reading and what to read in school.* Boston: Heath. (Originally published in 1886)

Hall, G. S. (1911a). *Educational problems* (Vol. I). New York: Appleton.

Hall, G. S. (1911b). *Educational problems* (Vol. II). New York: Appleton.

Hall, G. S. (1924). *Life and confessions of a psychologist*. New York: Appleton.

Hall, M. (1972). *The language experience approach for the culturally disadvantaged*. Newark, DE: International Reading Association.

Hall, M. (1976). *Teaching reading as a language experience* (2nd ed.). Columbus, OH: Merrill.

Hall, M. (1978). *The language experience approach for teaching reading: A research perspective*. Newark, DE: International Reading Association.

Hall, M. R. (1940). *Children can see life whole: A study of some progressive schools in action*. New York: Association Press.

Hall-Quest, A. L. (1920). *The textbook: How to use and judge it*. New York: Macmillan.

Hall-Quest, A. L. (1923). Preface. In A. L. McGregor, *Supervised study in English: For junior high school grades* (pp. ii-xii). New York: Macmillan.

Hall-Quest, A. L. (1940). Editorial introduction. In T. H. Briggs, *Pragmatism and pedagogy* (pp. vii-xi). New York: Macmillan.

Hallgren, B. (1950). *Specific dyslexia ("congenital word-blindness"): A clinical and genetic study* (E. Odelberg, Trans., Supplement 62). Stockholm, Sweden: Acta Psychiatrica et Neuolgica.

Halliday, M. A. K. (1970). Forword. In D. Mackay, B. Thompson, & P. Schaub, *Breakthrough to literacy: Teacher's manual* (pp. iii-viii). London: Longman (for the Schools Council).

Halliday, M. A. K. (1979). Forword. In D. Mackay, B. Thompson, & P. Schaub, *Breakthrough to literacy: Teacher's manual* (2nd ed., pp. 1-3). London: Longman (for the Schools Council).

Hamill, R. C. (1936). Emotional factors in mental retardation. *Archives Neurology and Psychiatry, 36*, 1049-1067.

Hamilton, G. E. (1954). Tachistoscopes and their use. In Kinder, J. S., & McClusky, F. D. (Eds.), *Audio-visual reader* (pp. 151-155). Dubuque, IA: Brown.

Hanus, P. H. (1913a). Editor's preface. In F. M. McMurry, *Elementary school standards: Instruction, course of study, supervision, applied to New York City schools* (pp. vii-viii). Yonkers-on-Hudson, NY: World.

Hanus, P. H. (1913b). *School efficiency: A constructive study applied to New York City, being a summary and interpretation of the report on educational aspects of the school inquiry*. Yonkers-on-Hudson, NY: World.

Harap, H. (1934). *The technique of curriculum making*. New York: Macmillan.

Harper, C. A. (1939). *A century of public teacher education: The story of the state teachers colleges as they evolved from the normal schools*. Washington, DC: National Education Association.

Harris, A. J. (1940). *How to increase reading ability: A guide to developmental and remedial methods*. New York: Longman, Greene.

Harris, A. J. (1968). Five decades of remedial reading. In J. Allen Figurel (Ed.), *Forging ahead in reading* (pp. 25-34). Newark, DE: International Reading Association.

Harris, A. J., & Sipay, E. R. (1980). *How to increase reading ability: A guide to developmental and remedial methods* (7th ed.). New York: Longman.

Harris, J. M., Donovan, H. L., & Alexander, T. (1927). *Supervision and teaching of reading*. Richmond, VA: Johnson.

Harris, W. T. (1892). Editor's preface. In F. Adler, *The moral instruction of children* (pp. v-x). New York: Appleton.

Harris, W. T. (1902). Editor's preface. In G. H. Martin, *The evolution of the Massachusetts public school system: A historical sketch* (pp. v-xv). New York: Appleton. (Originally published in 1894)

Harris, W. T. (1914). The importance of the text-book. *Journal of Education, 80*, 317.

Harrison, M. L. (1936). *Reading readiness*. Boston: Houghton Mifflin.

Healy, W. (1917). *The individual delinquent: A text-book of diagnosis and prognosis for all concerned in understanding offenders*. Boston: Little, Brown.

Heberle, R. (1951). *Social movements: An introduction to political sociology*. New York: Appleton–Century–Crofts.

Hegge, T. G. (1935). Results of remedial reading at the middle moron level: A case study. *Journal of Juvenile Research, 19*, 128-134.

Hegge, T. G., Kirk, S. A., & Kirk, W. D. (1940). *Remedial reading drills*. Ann Arbor, MI: Wahr.

Heide, A., & Stilborne, L. (1996). *The teacher's complete & easy guide to the Internet*. Toronto: Trifolium.

Henderson, C. H. (1902). *Education and the larger life*. Boston: Houghton Mifflin.

Henry, J. M. (1991). Reading recovery through reading and writing. In J. T. Freeley, D. S. Strickland, & S. B. Wepner (Eds.), *Process reading and writing: A literature-based approach* (pp. 171-180). New York: Teachers College Press.

Hermann, K. (1959). *Reading disability: A medial study of word-blindness and related handicaps* (P. G. Aungle, Trans.). Springfield, IL: Thomas.

Herrick, V. E., Anderson, D., & Pierstorff, L. (1961). Basal instructional materials in reading. In N. B. Henry (Ed.), *Development in and through reading* (60th Yearbook of the National Society for the Study of Education, Part I, pp. 165-188). Chicago: University of Chicago Press.

Hesseltine, W. B. (1936). *A history of the South, 1607–1936*. New York: Prentice-Hall.

Hickman, L. A. (1990). *John Dewey's pragmatic technology*. Bloomington, IN: Indiana University Press.

Hicks, G. (1935). The captive school. *Social Frontier, 2* (1), 10-12.

High school overhaul (1947, December 15). *Newsweek*, p. 86.

Hildreth, G. (1928). A survey of educational research. *Journal of Educational Research, 23*, 1-14.

Hildreth, G. (1934). Reversals in reading and writing. *Journal of Educational Psychology, 25*, 1-20.

Hildreth, G. (1936). *Learning the three R's: A modern interpretation*. Minneapolis, MN: Educational Publishers.

Hildreth, G. (1949). Reading programs in grades II and III. In N. D. Henry (Ed.), *Reading in the elementary school* (48th Yearbook of the National Society for the Study of Education, Part 2, pp. 54-126). Chicago: University of Chicago Press.

Hildreth, J. R. (1965). Experience related reading for school beginners. *Elementary English, 42*, 280-297.

Hinsdale, B. A. (1896). *Teaching the language arts: Speech, reading, composition*. New York: Appleton.

Hinshelwood, J. (1900). Congenital Word-blindness. *Lancet, 1*, 1506-1508.

Hinshelwood, J. (1917). *Congenital word-blindness*. London: Lewis.

Hobbs, A. H. (1951). *The claims of sociology: A critique of textbooks*. Harrisburg: PA: Stackpole.

Hoffer, E. (1966). *The true believer: Thoughts on the nature of mass movements.* New York: Perennial. (Originally published in 1951)

Hofstadter, R. (1963). *Anti-intellectualism in American life.* New York: Vintage.

Hollingworth, L. S. (1922). *The psychology of subnormal children.* New York: Macmillan.

Hollingworth, L. S. (1923). *Special talents and defects: Their significance for education.* New York: Macmillan.

Holmes, A. (1912). *The conservation of the child: A manual of clinical psychology presenting the examination and treatment of backward children.* Philadelphia: Lippincott.

Holmes, A. (1915). *Backward children.* Indianapolis, IN: Bobbs-Merrill.

Hood, W. J. (1991). Preface. In Y. M. Goodman, W. J. Hood, & K. S. Goodman (Eds.), *Organizing for whole language* (pp. xiii-xiv). Portsmouth, NH: Heinemann.

Hook, S. (1973a). Foreword. In C. J. Troost (Ed.), *Radical school reform: Critique and alternatives* (pp. vii-xiii). Boston: Little, Brown.

Hook, S. (1973b). John Dewey and his betrayers. In C. J. Troost (Ed.), *Radical school reform: Critique and alternatives* (pp. 57-66). Boston: Little, Brown.

Horn, E. (1920). The selection of silent reading textbooks. *Journal of Educational Research, 2,* 615-619.

Horn, E. (1922a). Foreword. In E. Watkins, *How to teach silent reading to beginners* (pp. i-vii). Philadelphia: Lippincott.

Horn, E. (1922b). Introduction. In R. H. Franzen & F. B. Knight, *Textbook selection* (pp. 5-8). Baltimore: Warwick & York.

Horvath, H. (1923). The pleas of an immigrant—Abstract. In *Addresses and proceeding of the sixty-first annual meeting of the National Education Association, Oakland-San Franciso* (Vol. 61, pp. 680-682). Washington, DC: National Education Association.

Hosic, J. F. (1920). The content of school reading books. *School and Society, 11,* 179-180.

Howerth, J. (1908). The foreign child in the public schools. *Pennsylvania School Journal, 56,* 558-560.

Huey, E. B. (1912). *Backward and feeble-minded children: Clinical studies in the psychology of defectives, with a syllabus for the clinical examination and testing of children.* Baltimore: Warwick & York.

Huey, E. B. (1968). *The psychology and pedagogy of reading: With a review of the history of reading and writing and of methods, texts, and hygiene in reading.* Cambridge, MA: MIT. (Originally published in 1908)

Hughes, F. (1950). *Prejudice and the press: A restatement of the principle of freedom of the press with specific reference to the Hutchins-Luce Commission.* New York: Devein-Adair.

Hughes, J. L. (1912). *Teaching to read.* New York: Barnes.

Hughes, R. E. (1902). *The making of citizens: A study in comparative education.* New York: Scribner's.

Hulburd, D. (1951). *This happened in Pasadena.* New York: Macmillan.

Huntington, E. (1925). *The character of races: As influenced by physical environment, natural selection and historical development.* New York: Scribner's Sons.

Illuminating Engineering Society (1914). Diffusing media III: Papers and ink. *Transactions of the Illuminating Engineering Society, 10,* 379-387.

Immigration (1851, October). *Massachusetts Teacher, 4,* 289-291.

Inskeep, A. D. (1926). *Teaching dull and retarded children.* New York: Macmillan.

Inskeep, A. D. (1930). *Child adjustment in relation to growth and development.* New York: Appleton.

Introductory remarks on indoctrination (1935). *Social Frontier, 1,* 8-9.

Ireland, W. W. (1877). *On idiocy and imbecility.* London: Churchill.

Irvine, R. (1941). An ocular policy for public schools. *American Journal of Ophthalmology, 24,* 779-787.

Irwin, E. A., & Marks, L. A. (1924). *Fitting the school to the child: A experiment in public education.* New York: Macmillan.

Iversen, R. W. (1959). *The communists & the schools.* New York: Harcourt, Brace.

Iversen, S., & Tunmer, W. E. (1993). Phonological processing skills and the reading recovery program. *Journal of Educational Psychology, 85,* 112-126.

James, W. (1907a). *Pragmatism and the meaning of truth.* Cambridge, MA: Harvard.

James, W. (1907b). *Pragmatism: A new name for some old ways of thinking.* New York: Longmans, Green.

James, W. (1925). *The philosophy of William James.* New York: Modern Library.

James, W. (1958). *Talks to teachers on psychology: And to students on some of life's ideals.* New York: Norton. (Originally published in 1892)

Jastak, J. (1934). Interferences in reading. *Psychological Bulletin, 31,* 244-272.

Jay, J. (1889). Public and parochial schools. *Addresses and Proceedings of the National Education Association, 28,* 152-179.

Jennings, F. G. (1967, September 16). The revolution in education: It didn't start with Sputnik. *Saturday Review, 50,* 77-79, 95-97.

Jensen, F. A. (1931). *Current procedure in selecting textbooks.* Philadelphia: Lippincott.

Jersild, A. T., Goldman, B., Jersild, C. L., & Loftus, J. J. (1941). Studies of elementary school classes in action: A comparative study of the daily occupations of pupils in "activity" and "non-activity" schools. *Journal of Experimental Education, 9,* 295-302.

Johnson, C. (1935). *Old-time schools and school-books.* New York: Smith.

Johnson, D. L. (1988). The computer as a tool for teaching writing. *Computers in the Schools, 5* (1/2), 1-3.

Johnson, F. W. (1925). A checking list for the selection of high school textbooks. *Teachers College Record, 27,* 104-108.

Johnson, G. R. (1930). An objective method of determining reading difficulty. *Journal of Educational Research, 21,* 283-287.

Johnson, M. (1931). Standards and the child. *Progressive Education, 8,* 692-694.

Johnston, E. R. (1898). What we do and how we do it. *Journal of Psycho-Asthenics, 2,* 98-105.

Johnston, E. R. (1908). The functions of the special class. In *National Education Association Journal of Proceedings and Addresses of the 46th Annual Meeting,* 1114-1118.

Joint Committee of the National Education Association and the American Textbook Publishers Institute (1963). *Guidelines for textbook selection.* Washington, DC: National Education Association.

Jones, A. E. (1928). Mexican colonies in Chicago. *Social Service Review, 2,* 579-597.

Jones, K., & Oliver, R. (1956). *Progressive education is REDucation.* Boston: Meador.

Jones, R. G. (1915). Standard vocabularies. In S. C. Parker (Ed.), *Minimum essentials in elementary-school subjects—Standards and current practices* (14th Yearbook of the

National Society for the Study of Education, Part 1, pp. 37-43). Chicago: University of Chicago Press.

Jordan, A. M. (1926). *Children's interests in reading* (Rev. ed.). Chapel Hill, NC: University of North Carolina Press.

Judd, C. H. (1918a). Analyzing Text-books. *Elementary School Journal, 19*, 143-154.

Judd, C. H. (1918b). *Reading: Its nature and development* (Supplementary Educational Monographs, Vol. II). Chicago: University of Chicago Press.

Judd, C. H. (1933). Education. In *Recent social trends in the United States: Report of the President's Research Committee on Social Trends* (pp. 325-381). New York: McGraw-Hill.

Junier, A. J. (1962). Bibliotherapy: Projects and studies with the mentally ill patient. *Library Trends, 2*, 136-146.

Kahrhoff, R. E. (1952). *This farce called education*. New York: Exposition.

Kandel, I. L. (1947). Adjustment to life. *School and Society, 65*, 372.

Kandel, I. L. (1957). *American education in the twentieth century*. Cambridge, MA: Harvard University Press.

Kandel, I. L. (1974). *The impact of the war upon American education*. Wesport, CT: Greenwood. (Originally published in 1949)

Kantrowitz, V. (1967). Bibliotherapy with retarded readers. *Journal of Reading, 11*, 136-146.

Karier, C., Violas, P. C., & Spring, J. (1973). *Roots of Crisis: American education in the twentieth century*. Chicago: Rand McNally.

Katz, M. B. (1971). *Class, bureaucracy, and schools: The illusion of educational change in America*. New York: Praeger.

Kearney, N. C. (1953). *Elementary school objectives: A report for the Mid-Century Committee on Outcomes in Elementary Education*. New York: Russell Sage Foundation.

Keboch, F. D. (1927). Variability of word difficulty in five American history texts. *Journal of Educational Research, 15*, 22-26.

Keifer, M. (1948). *American children through their books: 1700-1835*. Philadelphia: University of Pennsylvania Press.

Kendall, C. N., & Mirick, G. A. (1915). *The elementary school subjects: How to teach the fundamental subjects* (Vol. 1). Cambridge, MA: Houghton Mifflin.

Kendrick, B. B., & Arnett, A. M. (1971). *The south looks at its past*. New York: Russell & Russell. (Originally published in 1935)

Kephart, N. (1960). *The slow learner in the classroom*. Columbus, OH: Merrill.

Kerr. J. (1897). School hygiene in its mental, oral, and physical aspects. *Journal and Proceedings of the Royal Statistical Society, 60*, 613-680.

Kerschensteiner, G. (1911). *Education for citizenship* (A. J. Pressland, Trans.). Chicago: Rand McNally.

Kilpatrick, W. H. (1932). *Education and the social crisis: A proposed program*. New York: Liveright.

Kilpatrick, W. H. (1936). High Marxism defined and rejected. *Social Frontier, 2*, 272-274.

Kilpatrick, W. H. (1942a). Education in wartime. *Frontiers of Democracy, 8* (69), 198-199.

Kilpatrick, W. H. (1942b, March). Our schools and the war. *Frontiers of Democracy, 8* (68), 166-167.

King, I. (1914). *Social aspects of education: A book of sources and original discussions with annotated bibliographies*. New York: Macmillan.

King, J. M. (1899). *Facing the twentieth century: Our country, its power and peril.* New York: American Union League Society.

King, R. P. (1995). The school library media specialist's role in bibliotherapy. In C. L. Wesson & M. J. Keefe (Eds.), *Serving special needs students in the school library media center* (pp. 97-110). Westport, CT: Greenwood.

Kingston, A. J., & Weaver, W. W. (1967). Recent developments in readability. *Journal of Reading, 11*, 44-47.

Kinzer, C. K., Hynds, S., & Loofbourrow, M. C. (1986). Applications in reading and writing instruction. In C. K. Kinzer, R. D. Sherwood, & J. D. Bransford (Eds.), *Computer strategies for education: Foundations and content-area applications* (pp. 213-252). Columbus, OH: Merrill.

Kircher, C. J. (1945). *Character formation through books: A bibliography—An application of bibliotherapy to the behavior problems of childhood.* Washington, DC: Catholic University of America Press.

Kirk, R. (1954). *A program for conservatives.* Chicago: Regnery.

Kirk, S. A, & Johnson, G. O. (1951). *Educating the retarded child.* Cambridge, MA: Houghton Mifflin.

Kirk, S. A. (1940). *Teaching reading to slow-learning children.* Cambridge, MA: Houghton Mifflin.

Kirk, S. A. (1962). *Educating exceptional children.* Boston: Houghton Mifflin.

Kirst, M. W. (1984). Choosing textbooks: Reflections of a state board president. *American Educator, 8* (2), 18-23.

Klapper, P. (1914). *Teaching children to read.* New York: Appleton.

Klapper, P. (1926). *Teaching children to read: A manual of method for elementary and junior high schools* (4th ed.). New York: Appleton.

Kliebard, H. M. (1986). *The struggle for the American curriculum, 1893–1958.* Boston: Routledge.

Knight, E. W. (1916). *Public school education in North Carolina.* Boston: Houghton Mifflin.

Knight, E. W. (1952). *Fifty years of American education: A historical review and critical appraisal.* New York: Ronald.

Knights of the Ku Klux Klan: Papers read at the meeting of Grand Dragons at their first annual meeting—With other articles of interest to Klansmen (1923). Ashevill, NC: Ku Klux Klan.

Knowlton, P. A. (1948). Materials for basic reading instruction: Recent trends in the improvement of basic reading materials. In W. S. Gray (Ed.), *Basic Instruction in reading in elementary and high schools* (Supplemental Educational Monographs, Vol. x, pp. 92-96). Chicago: University of Chicago Press.

Koerner, J. D. (1963). *The miseducation of American teachers.* Boston: Houghton Mifflin.

Koerner, J. D. (1968). *Who controls American education? A guide for laymen.* Boston: Beacon.

Koon, C. M. (1933). *The art of teaching by radio* (Office of Education Bulletin No. 4). Washington, DC: Government Printing Office.

Kottmeyer, W. (1947). *Handbook for remedial reading.* St. Louis: Webster.

Krause, L. W. (1941). What principles of modern and progressive education are practiced in intermediate-grade classrooms? *Journal of Educational Research, 35*, 251-262.

Kuchinskas, G. (1983). 22 ways to use a microcomputer in reading & language arts classes. *Computers, Reading, and Language Arts, 1* (1), 11-16.

Kuhn, I. C. (1952, April). Your child is their target. *American Legion Magazine,* 18-19, 54-60.

Kurtz, P. (Ed.) (1966). *American philosophy in the twentieth century: A sourcebook from pragmatism to philosophical analysis.* New York: Macmillan.

Laine, E. (1938). *Motion pictures and radio: Modern techniques for education.* New York: McGraw Hill.

Lamoreaux, L. A., & Lee, D. M. (1943). *Learning to read through experience.* New York: Appleton-Century-Crofts.

Langford, H. D. (1936). *Education and the social conflict.* New York: Macmillan.

Lasch, C. (1965). *The new radicalism in America (1889–1963): The intellectual as a social type.* New York: Knopf.

Lawler, T. B. (1938). *Seventy years of textbook publishing: A history of Ginn and Company.* Boston: Ginn.

Lazar, M. (1942a). *A diagnostic approach to the reading program: Part I* (Educational Research Bulletin). New York: Board of Education of the City of New York.

Lazar, M. (1942b). *A diagnostic approach to the reading program: Part II* (Educational Research Bulletin). New York: Board of Education of the City of New York.

Lazar, M. (Ed.) (1952). *The retarded reader in the junior high school: A guide for supervisors and teachers.* New York: New York Board of Education—Bureau of Educational Research.

Lee, J. M., & Lee, D. M. (1940). *The child and his curriculum.* New York: Appleton-Century.

Leonard, S. A. (1922). *Essential principles of teaching reading and literature in the intermediate grades and the high school.* Philadelphia: Lippincott.

Levenson, W. B. (1945). *Teaching through radio.* New York: Farrar & Rinehart.

Lewerenz, A. S. (1935). A vocabulary grade placement formula. *Journal of Experimental Education, 3,* 236.

Lincoln, D. F. (1903). Special classes for feeble-minded children in the Boston Public Schools. *Journal of Psycho-Asthenics, 7,* 83-93.

Lindberg, S. L. (1976). *The annotated McGuffey: Selections from the McGuffey Eclectic Readers 1836-1920.* New York: Van Nostrand-Reinhold.

Lindeman, E. C. (1939). The goal of American education. *Survey Graphic, 28,* 570-576.

Lindop, B. E. (1954). Radio education in historical perspective. In J. S. Kinder & F. D. McClusky (Eds.), *Audio-visual reader* (pp. 122-127). Dubuque, IA: Brown.

Lindsay, B., & Ginsburg, M. B. (1995). Transforming teacher education, schooling, and society: Lessons learned and political commitments. In M. B. Ginsburg & B. Lindsay (Eds.), *The political dimension in teacher education: Comparative perspectives on policy formation, socialization and society* (pp. 265-276). Washington, DC: Falmer.

Lippmann, W. (1931). *Notes on the crisis* (John Day Pamphlet No. 5). New York: Day.

Lively, B. A., & Pressey, S. L. (1923). A method for measuring the "vocabulary burden" of textbooks. *Educational Administration and Supervision, 9,* 389-398.

Lockard, J., Abrams, P. D., & Many, W. A. (1997). *Microcomputers for twenty-first century educators* (4th ed.). New York: Longman.

Loeb, M. (1918). Compulsory English for foreign-born. *Survey, 41,* 426-427.

Lohmann, V. L. (1953). Eliminating obstacles to effective reading: In clinics. In H. M. Robinson (Ed.), *Corrective reading in classroom and Clinic* (Supplementary Educational Monographs, Vol. XV, pp. 75-79). Chicago: University of Chicago Press.

Lorang, M. C. (1945). *The effect of reading on moral conduct and emotional experience.* Washington, DC: Catholic University Press.

Lord, E. E., Carmichael, L., & Dearborn, W. F. (1925). *Special disabilities in learning to read and write* (Harvard Monographs in Education, No. 6). Cambridge, MA: Harvard University Press.

Lorge, I. (1939). Predicting reading difficulty of selections for children. *Elementary English Review, 16*, 229-233.

Lorge, I. (1948). Predicting readability. *School and Society, 47*, 404-419.

Lowe, H. R. (1961). The whole-word and word-guessing fallacy. In C. C. Walcutt (Ed.), *Tomorrow's illiterates: The state of reading instruction today* (pp. 85-114). Boston: Little, Brown.

Luke, A. (1991). The secular word: Catholic reconstructions of Dick and Jane. In M. W. Apple & L. Christian-Smith (Eds.), *The politics of the textbook* (pp. 166-190). New York: Routledge.

Luke, E. (1931). *The teaching of reading by the sentence method.* London: Methuen.

Lund, F. (1947). The dynamics of behavior and reading difficulties. *Education, 67,* 416-421.

Lynd, A. (1953). *Quackery in the public schools.* Boston: Little-Brown.

Lynd, R. S., & Lynd, H. M. (1929). *Middletown: A study in American culture.* New York: Harcourt-Brace.

Lynd, R. S., & Lynd, H. M. (1937). *Middletown in transition: A study in cultural conflicts.* New York: Harcourt-Brace.

Lyons, C. A., & Beaver, J. (1995). Reducing retention and learning disability placement through reading recovery: An educationally sound, cost-effective choice. In R. L. Allington & S. A. Walmsley (Eds.), *No quick fix: Rethinking literacy programs in America's elementary schools* (pp. 116-136). New York: Teachers College Press.

Lyons, C. A., Pinnell, G. S., & DeFord, D. E. (1993). *Partners in learning: Teachers and children in reading recovery.* New York: Teachers College Press.

MacLean, I. D. (1924). The patriotic education League of Lynn Massachusetts. In *Addresses and proceeding of the sixty-second annual meeting of the National Education Association, Washington, DC* (Vol. 62, pp. 570-572). Washington, DC: National Education Association.

MacMurchy, H. (1915). *Organization and management of auxiliary classes* (Ontario Department of Education Pamphlet No. 7). Ontario, Canada: Cameron.

Maddox, W. A. (1924). Development of method. In I. L. Dandel (Ed.), *Twenty-five years of American education: Collected essays* (pp. 141-176). New York: Macmillan.

Mahoney, J. J., & Herlihy, C. M. (1918). *First steps in Americanization: A handbook for teachers.* Boston: Houghton Mifflin.

Manguel, A. (1996). *A history of reading.* New York: Viking.

Mark, H. T. (1901). *Individuality and the moral aim in American education: The Gilchrist report presented to the Victoria University.* London: Longmans, Green.

Marshall, W., & Ferguson, J. H. (1939). Hereditary word-blindness as a defect of selective association, with case report. *Journal of Nervous and Mental Diseases, 89*, 164-173.

Martens, E. H. (1934). *Teachers' problems with exceptional children, III: Mentally retarded children* (U. S. Department of Education Pamphlet No. 49). Washington, DC: U. S. Government Printing Office.

Martin, G. H. (1902). *The evolution of the Massachusetts public school system: A historical sketch.* New York: Appleton. (Originally published in 1894)

Martin, L. (1951, September 8). Denver, Colo. *Saturday Review of Literature,* 9-10, 31.

Mathews, M. M. (1966). *Teaching to read: Historically considered.* Chicago: University of Chicago Press.

Maxwell, C. R. (1919). The selection of text-books. *School and Society, 9,* 44-52.

Maxwell, W. H., Haaren, J. H., Kidd, C. A., & Wade, J. H. (1913). Education of the immigrant child. In *Education of the immigrant: Abstracts of papers read at a public conference under the auspices of the New York-New Jersey Committee of the North American Civic League for Immigrants, held at New York City, May 16 and 17, 1913* (United States Bureau of Education, Bulletin No. 51, pp. 18-24). Washington, DC: Government Printing Office.

May, E. (1908). Italian education and immigration. *Education, 28,* 450-453.

May, F. B., & Eliot, S. B. (1975). *To help children read: Mastery performance modules for teachers in training* (2nd ed.). Columbus, OH: Merrill.

Mayer, M. (1961). *The schools.* New York: Harper.

Mayhew, K. C., & Edwards, A. C. (1936). *The Dewey school: The laboratory school of the University of Chicago, 1896–1903.* New York: Atherton. (Originally published in 1936)

McAndrew, W. (1878). Educational review: Matters of moment. *School and Society, 28,* 551-558.

McCall, W. A. (1923). *How to measure in education.* New York: Macmillan.

McCallister, J. M. (1936). *Remedial and corrective instruction in reading: A program for the upper grades and high school.* New York: Appleton-Century.

McCaul, R. L. (1959). Dewey's Chicago. *School Review, 67,* 258-259.

McClusky, H. V. (1934). A quantitative analysis of the difficulty of reading materials. *Journal of Educational Research, 28,* 276-282.

McCracken, G. (1952). Have we overemphasized the readiness factor? *Elementary English, 29,* 271-276.

McFee, N. N. (1918). *The teacher, the school, and the community.* New York: American.

McGregor, A. L. (1923). *Supervised study in English: For junior high school grades.* New York: Macmillan.

McGuffey-Ruggles, A. (1950). *The story of the McGuffeys.* New York: American.

McKee, P. (1934). *Reading and literature in the elementary school.* Boston: Houghton Mifflin.

McLaughlin, G. H. (1969). SMOG grading—A new readability formula. *Journal of Reading, 12,* 639-646.

McManis, J. T. (1916). *Ella Flagg Young: And a half-century of the Chicago public schools.* Chicago: McClurg.

McMurray, F. M. (1913). *Elementary school standards: Instruction, course of study, supervision, applied to New York City schools.* Yonkers-on-Hudson, NY: World.

McMurray, F., & Cronbach, L. J. (1955a). The controversial past and present of the text. In L. J. Cronbach (Ed.), *Text materials in modern education* (pp. 9-27). Urbana, IL: University of Illinois Press.

McMurray, F., & Cronbach, L. J. (1955b). The proper function of text materials. In L. J. Cronbach (Ed.), *Text materials in modern education* (pp. 28-58). Urbana, IL: University of Illinois Press.

McMurry, C. A. (1903a). *Special method in primary reading and oral work with stories.* New York: Macmillan.

McMurry, C. A. (1903b). *Special method in the reading of complete English classics in the grades of the common school.* New York: Macmillan.

Mearns, H. (1958). *Creative power: The education of youth in the creative arts* (2nd ed.). New York: Dover.

Meriam, J. L. (1930). Avoiding difficulties in learning to read. *Educational Method, 13,* 413-419.

Meriam, J. L. (1933). An activity curriculum in a school of Mexican children. *Journal of Experimental Education, 1,* 304-308.

Miller, D. S. (1946). Beloved psychologist. In H. Peterson (Ed.), *Great teachers: Portrayed by those who studies under them* (pp. 223-228). New Brunswick, NJ: Rutgers University Press.

Miller, E. B. (1994). *The internet resource directory for K-12 teachers and librarians, 94/ 95 edition.* Englewood, CO: Libraries Unlimited.

Minnich, H. C. (1936). *William Holmes McGuffey and his readers.* New York: American.

Mirick, G. A. (1923). *Progressive education.* Boston: Houghton Mifflin.

Misak, C. (1994). American pragmatism—Peirce. In C. L. Ten (Ed.), *The nineteenth century* (pp. 357-380). New York: London.

Mitchell, B. (1934). The choice before us. *Social Frontier, 1* (2), 13-16.

Mitchell, L. S., & Boetz, J. (1942). *The people of the U.S.A.: Their place in the school curriculum.* New York: Progressive Education Association.

Monroe, M. (1932). *Children who cannot read: The analysis of reading disabilities and the use of diagnostic tests in the instruction of retarded readers.* Chicago: University of Chicago Press.

Monroe, M. (1935). Diagnosis and treatment of reading disabilities. In G. M. Whipple (Ed.), *Educational diagnosis* (34th Yearbook of the National Society for the Study of Education, pp. 201-228). Bloomington, IL: Public School Publishing.

Monroe, M. E. (1978). Foreword. In R. J. Rubin, *Using bibliotherapy: A guide to theory and practice* (pp. vii-ix). Phoenix, AZ: Oryx.

Monroe, M., & Backus, B. (1937). *Remedial reading.* Boston: Houghton Mifflin.

Monroe, P. (1905). *A text-book in the history of education.* New York: Macmillan.

Montgomery, H. L. (1932). English teachers awake. *Education Worker, 2* (3), 3.

Moore, T. V. (1945). Preface. In C. J. Kircher, *Character formation through books: A bibliography—An application of bibliotherapy to the behavior problems of childhood* (pp. 3-11). Washington, DC: Catholic University of America Press.

Moorhead, E. (1908, February 29). A school for Italian laborers. *Outlook, 88,* 499-504.

Moreo, D. W. (1996). *Schools in the great depression.* New York: Garland.

Morgan, B. S. (1914). *The backward child: A study of he psychology and treatment of backwardness, a practical manual for teachers and students.* New York: Putnam's Sons.

Morgan, M. B. (1896). A case of congenital word blindness. *British Medical Journal, 2,* 1378.

Morse, A. D. (1951, September). Who's trying to ruin our schools? *McCall's, 78*, pp. 26-27, 94, 102, 108.

Mort, P. R., & Gates, A. I. (1932). *The acceptable uses of achievement tests: A manual for test users.* New York: New York City Bureau of Publications/Teachers College Press.

Mossman, L. C. (1934). Statement of the problem. In G. M. Whipple (Ed.), *The activity movement* (33rd Yearbook of the National Society for the Study of Education, Part 2, pp. 1-8). Bloomington, IL: Public School Publishing.

Mowry, W. A. (1908). *Recollections of a New England educator, 1838–1908: Reminiscences—Biographical, pedagogical, historical.* New York: Silver, Burdett

Mulcahy, P., & Samuels, S. J. (1987). Three hundred years of illustrations in American textbooks. In H. A. Houghton & D. M. Willows (Eds.), *The psychology of illustration* (Vol. 2, pp. 2-52). New York: Springer-Verlag.

Munroe, J. P. (1911). *The educational ideal: An outline of its growth in modern times.* Boston: Heath.

Munroe, J. P. (1912). *New demands in education.* Garden City, NY: Doubleday, Page.

Munroe, P. (1937). Nationalism, patriotism, informed citizenship and international understanding. In I. L. Kandel & G. M. Whipple (Eds.), *International understanding through the public-school curriculum* (Part 2, 36th Yearbook of the National Society for the Study of Education, pp. 13-24). Bloomington, IL: Public School Publishing.

Must teachers sink without a struggle?—An imaginary conversation (1932–1933, December, January). *Progressive Education, 9*, 3-7.

Nash, A. M., & Porteus, S. D. (1919). *Educational treatment of defectives* (Training School Bulletin No. 18). Vineland, NJ: Vineland Training School.

National Education Association (1942). *Americans all: Studies in intercultural education.* Washington, DC: Author.

National Education Association (1959). *Interaction in learning: Implications for television.* Washington, DC: Author.

Neill, A. S. (1960). *Summerhill: A radical approach to child rearing.* New York: Hart.

Neill, A. S. (1967). *Talking of Summerhill.* London: Gollancz.

Neill, A. S. (1972). *"Neill! Neill! Orange peel!": An autobiography.* New York: Hart.

Neilson, W. A. (1939). Education can't be better than the teachers. *Survey Graphic, 28*, 610-613.

Nettleship, E. (1901). Cases of congenital word-blindness (inability to learn to read). *Ophthalmic Review, 20*, 61-67.

Newman, J. M. (1985). Introduction. In J. M. Newman (Ed.), *Whole language: Theory in use* (pp. 1-6). Portsmouth, NH: Heinemann.

Nickell, V. (1949). How can we develop an effective program of education for life adjustment? *Bulletin of the National Association of Secondary School Principals, 33*, 153-157.

Nickerson, R. (1988). Technology in education in 2020: Thinking about the not-distant future. In R. S. Nickerson & P. P. Zodhiates (Eds.), *Technology in education: Looking toward 2020* (pp. 1-10). Hillsdale, NJ: Erlbaum.

Nietz, J. A. (1961). *Old textbooks: Spelling, grammar, reading, arithmetic, geography, American history, civil government, physiology, penmanship, art, music—As taught in the common schools from colonial days to 1900.* Pittsburgh, PA: University of Pittsburgh Press.

Ninio, A. (1980). Picture-book reading in mother-infants dyads belonging to two subgroups in Israel. *Child Development, 51*, 587-590.

Notes on the convention (1932). *Progressive Education, 9*, 201-302.

Novack, G. (1975). *Pragmatism versus Marxism: An appraisal of John Dewey's philosophy.* New York: Pathfinder.

NRENAISSANCE Committee (1994). *Realizing the information future: The internet and beyond.* Washington, DC: National Academy Press.

O'Brien, C. A. (1973). *Teaching the language-different child to read.* Columbus, OH: Merrill.

O'Brien, J. A. (1921). *Silent reading: With special reference to methods for developing speed, a study in the psychology and pedagogy of reading.* New York: Macmillan.

O'Brien, S. R. (1909). *English for foreigners: Book one.* Boston: Houghton Mifflin.

O'Shea, M. V. (1924). Editor's introduction. In E. A. Irwin & L. A. Marks, *Fitting the school to the child: An experiment in public education* (pp. xxiii-xxvi). New York: Macmillan.

Ohmann, R. (1976, October 25). The decline in literacy is a fiction, if not a hoax. *Chronicle of Higher Education*, 32.

Oppenheimer, T. (1997). The computer delusion. *Atlantic Monthly, 280*, pp. 45-62.

Orientation (1934). *Social Frontier, 1* (1), 3-5.

Orton, J. L. (1966). The Orton-Gillingham approach. In J. Money (Ed.), *The disabled reader: Education of the dyslexic child* (pp. 119-145). Baltimore: Johns Hopkins Press.

Orton, S. T. (1925). "Word-blindness" in school children. *Archives of Neurology and Psychiatry, 14*, 581-615.

Orton, S. T. (1989). *Reading, writing, and speech problems in children and selected papers.* Austin, TX: PRO-ED. (Originally published in 1939)

Otis, E. M. (1923). A textbook score card. *Journal of Educational Research, 7*, 132-136.

Otto, W., McMenemy, R. A., & Smith, R. J. (1973). *Corrective and remedial teaching* (2nd ed.). Boston: Houghton Mifflin.

Overstreet, H. A. (1929). Educating for the new age. *Progressive Education, 6*, 61-65.

Packard, V. (1974, April). Are we becoming a nation of illiterates? *Readers Digest*, pp. 81-85.

Page, D. P. (1885). *Theory and practice of teaching: The motives and methods* (Rev. ed. by W. H. Payne). New York: American.

Painter, F. V. N. (1901). *A history of education.* New York: Appleton. (Originally published in 1886)

Palmer, A. F. (1905). *The New York public school: Being a history of free education in the city of New York.* New York: Macmillan.

Palmer, G. H., & Palmer, A. F. (1908). *The teacher: Essays and addresses on education.* Boston: Houghton Mifflin.

Park, G. E. & Linden, J. E. (1968). The etiology of reading disabilities: An historical perspective. *Journal of Learning Disabilities, 1*, 318-332.

Parker, F. W. (1895). Discussion on report of Dr. Harris. *Journal of Education, 41*, 165-167.

Parker, F. W. (1937). *Talks on pedagogics: An outline of the theory of concentration.* New York: Day. (Originally published in 1891)

Parker, S. C. (1912). *A textbook in the history of modern elementary education: With emphasis on school practice in relation to social conditions*. Boston: Ginn.

Parker, S. C. (1923). *Types of elementary teaching and learning: Including practical technique and scientific evidence*. Boston: Ginn.

Patri, A. (1921). *A schoolmaster of the great city*. New York: Macmillan.

Patty, W. W., & Painter, W. I. (1931). Improving our method of selecting high-school textbooks. *Journal of Educational Research, 24*, 23-32.

Pavlidis G. T., & Fisher, D. F. (Eds.) (1986). *Dyslexia: Its neuropsychology and treatment*. New York: Wiley.

Peabody, E. P. (1836). *Record of a school: Exemplifying the general principles of spiritual culture* (2nd ed.). Boston: Russell, Shattuck.

Pennell, M. E., & Cusack, A. M. (1924). *How to teach reading*. Boston: Houghton Mifflin.

Pennell, M. E., & Cusack, A. M. (1935). *The teaching of reading for better living*. Boston: Hougton Mifflin.

Perfetti, C. A. (1983). Reading, vocabulary, and writing; Implications for computer-based instruction. In A. C. Wilkinson (Ed.), *Classroom computers and cognitive science* (pp. 145-161). New York: Academic.

Phillips, H. (1931). The school follows the child. *Survey, 66*, 493-495, 524-525.

Pierce, B. L. (1957). *A history of Chicago: The rise of a modern city, 1871–1893* (Vol. 3). New York: Knopf.

Pikulski, J. J. (1994). Preventing reading failure: A review of five effective programs. *Reading Teacher, 48*, 30-39.

Polin, L. (1993). Young children, literacy, and computers In T. Cannings & L. Finkel (Eds.), *The technology age classroom* (pp. 90-93). Wilsonville, OR: Franklin, Beedle.

Pollock, H. M., & Furbush, E. M. (1917). Insane, feebleminded, epileptics and inebriates in institutions in the United States, January 1, 1917. *Mental Hygiene, 1*, 548-566.

Postman, N. (1993). Of luddites, learning, and life. *Technos, 2* (4), 24-26.

Potter, M. (1953). Discovering retarded readers: In clinics. In H. M. Robinson (Ed.), *Corrective reading in classroom and clinic* (Supplementary Educational Monographs, Vol. XV, pp. 43-48). Chicago: University of Chicago Press.

Powdermaker, H., & Storen, H. F. (1944). *Probing our prejudices: A unit for high school students*. New York: Harper.

Power, E. J. (1996). *Educational philosophy: A history from the ancient world to modern America*. New York: Garland.

Pressey, S. L., & Pressey, L. C. (1926). *Mental abnormality and deficiency*. New York: Macmillan.

Progressive's progress. (1938, October 31). *Time, 32*, 31-37.

Purves, A. C. (1990). *The scribal society: An essay on literacy and schooling in the information age*. New York: Longman.

Quality and cost of textbooks (1915). *Journal of Education, 81*, 681-683.

Quantz, R. A. (1985). The complex visions of female teachers and the failure of unionization in the 1930s: An oral history. *History of Education Quarterly, 25*, 439-458.

Rafferty, M. (1972). *1972 supplement to Col. A. G. Rudd's "Bending the twig."* New York: New York Chapter of the Sons of the American Revolution.

Ramírez, M., & Castañeda, A. (1974). *Cultural democracy, bicognitive development, and education*. New York: Academic Press.

Ravitch, D. (1978). *The revisionists revised: A critique of the radical attack on the schools.* New York: Basic Books.

Ravitch, D. (1995). The search for order and the rejection of conformity: Standards in American education. In D. Ravitch & M. A. Vinovskis (Eds.), *Learning from the past: What history teaches us about school reform* (pp. 167-190). Baltimore: Johns Hopkins Press.

Rawson, M. B. (1968). *Developmental language disability: Adult accomplishments of dyslexic boys.* Baltimore, MD: Johns Hopkins Press.

Reason, R., & Boote, R. (1994). *Helping children with reading and spelling.* New York: Routledge.

Redding, M. F. (1963). *Revolution in the textbook publishing industry* (Occasional Paper No. 9, Report of the Technological Development Project). Washington, DC: National Education Association.

Redefer, F. L. (1949). Resolutions, reactions, and reminiscences. *Progressive Education, 26,* 187-191.

Reeder, R. R. (1900). *The historical development of school readers and method in teaching reading.* New York: Macmillan.

Reigart, J. F. (1916). *The Lancasterian system of instruction in the schools of New York city.* New York: Teachers College Press.

Reigart, J. F. (1924). Education of exceptional children. In I. L. Dandel (Ed.), *Twenty-five years of American education: Collected essays* (pp. 307-332). New York: Macmillan.

Rice, J. M. (1893). The public schools of Chicago and St. Paul. *Forum, 15,* 200-215.

Richey, H. G. (1931). The professional status of textbook authors. In G. M. Whipple (Ed.), *The textbook in American education* (30th Yearbook of the National Society for the Study of Education, Part II, pp. 67-77). Bloomington, IL: Public School Publishing.

Richman, J. (1905). The immigrant child. *Addresses and Proceedings of the National Education Association, 44,* 113-121.

Rickover, H. G. (1957a, December 6). A size-up of what's wrong with American schools. *U. S. News and World Report, 43,* pp. 86-91.

Rickover, H. G. (1957b, March 2). Let's stop wasting our greatest resource. *Saturday Evening Post, 229,* pp. 19, 108-109, 111.

Rickover, H. G. (1959). *Education and freedom.* New York: Dutton.

Rightmire, G. W. (1937). *Education in Ohio: Lower and higher.* Columbus, OH: Ohio State University.

Robb, L. (1994). *Whole language, whole learners: Creating a literature-centered classroom.* New York: Morrow.

Robertson, D. (1992). *Portraying persons with disabilities: An annotated bibliography of fiction for children and teenagers.* New Providence, NJ: Bowker.

Robinson, H. M. (1946). *Why pupils fail in reading: A study of causes and remedial treatment.* Chicago: University of Chicago Press.

Robinson, H. M. (Ed.) (1953). *Corrective reading in classroom and clinic* (Supplemental Educational Monographs, Vol. xv). Chicago: University of Chicago Press.

Robinson, H. M. (1961). Corrective and remedial instruction. In N. B. Henry (Ed.), *Development in and through reading* (60th Yearbook of the National Society for the Study of Education, Part I, pp. 357-375). Chicago: University of Chicago Press.

Robinson, H. M. (1985). William S. Gray: The scholar. In J. A. Stevenson (Ed.), *William S. Gray: Teacher, scholar, leader* (pp. 24-36). Newark, DE: International Reading Association.

Robinson, R. R. (1930). *Two centuries of change in the content of school readers.* Nashville, TN: Peabody College Press.

Roseboom, E. H., & Weisenburger, F. P. (1934). *A history of Ohio.* New York: Prentice-Hall.

Rosenblatt, L. M. (1968). *Literature as exploration* (Rev. ed.). New York: Noble & Noble.

Roser, N., & Martinez, M. (1985). Roles adults play in preschool responses to literature. *Language Arts, 62,* 485-490.

Roswell, F., & Natchez, G. (1971). *Reading disability: Diagnosis and treatment* (2nd ed.). New York: Basic.

Roswell, F., & Natchez, G. (1977). *Reading disability: Diagnosis and treatment* (3rd ed.). New York: Basic.

Routman, R. (1996). *Literacy at the crossroads: Crucial talk about reading, writing, and other teaching dilemmas.* Portsmouth, NH: Heinemann.

Rubin, R. J. (1978). *Using bibliotherapy: A guide to theory and practice.* Phoenix, AZ: Oryx.

Rudd, A. G. (1957). *Bending the twig: The revolution in education and its effect on our children.* New York: New York Chapter of the Sons of the American Revolution.

Rudman, M. K., Dunne-Gagne, K. D., & Bernstein, J. E. (1993). *Books to help children cope with separation and loss: An annotated bibliography* (4th ed.). New Providence, NJ: Bowker.

Ruediger, W. C. (1910). *The principles of education.* Boston: Houghton Mifflin.

Ruediger, W. C. (1932). *Teaching procedures.* Boston: Houghton Mifflin.

Rugg, H. (1921). Is the rating of human character practicable? *Journal of Educational Psychology, 12,* 425-438.

Rugg, H. (1926). The school curriculum and the drama of American life. In G. M. Whipple (Ed.), *The school curriculum, 1825-1890* (26th Yearbook of the National Society for the Study of Education, Part I, pp. 3-32). Bloomington, IL: Public School Publishing.

Rugg, H. (1936). The American mind and the "class" problem. *Social Frontier, 2,* 138-142.

Rugg, H. (1941). *That men may understand: An American in the long armistice.* New York: Doubleday, Doran.

Rugg, H. (1943). The year of decision 1943–1944: The people must make up their minds, FRONTIERS' position and program. *Frontiers of Democracy, 10* (79), 3-5.

Rugg, H. (1947). *Foundations for American education.* Yonkers-on-Hudson, NY: World.

Rugg, H. (1952). *The teacher of teachers: Frontiers of theory and practice in teacher education.* New York: Harper.

Rugg, H., & Shumaker, A. (1928). *The child-centered school: An appraisal of the new education.* New York: World.

Russell, B. (1932). *Education and the modern world.* New York: Norton.

Russell, D. H., & Shrodes, C. (1950). Contributions of research in bibliotherapy to the language-arts program: I. *School Review, 58,* 335-342.

Russell, D. H., Karp, E. E., & Kelly, E. I. (1938). *Reading aids through the grades: Two hundred and twenty-five remedial reading activities.* New York: Teachers College Press.

Rutherfurd, W. J. (1909). The aetiology of congenital word-blindness; with an example. *The British Journal of Children's Diseases, 6*, 484-488.

Rutter, M. (1977). Prevalence and types of dyslexia. In A. L. Benton & D. Pearl (Eds.), *Dyslexia: An appraisal of current knowledge* (pp. 5-28). New York: Oxford University Press.

Ryan, W. C. (1939). Announcement. *Social Frontier, 5*, 259-260.

Rystrom, R. (1970). Dialect training and reading: A further look. *Reading Research Quarterly, 4*, 581-599.

Saettler, P. (1990). *The evolution of American educational technology*. Englewood, CO: Libraries Unlimited.

Sandholtz, J. H., Ringstaff, C., & Dwyer, D. C. (1997). *Teaching with technology: Creating student-centered classrooms*. New York: Teachers College Press.

Sangren, P. V. (1932). *Improvement of reading through the use of tests*. Kalamazoo, MI: Western State Teachers College.

Saunders, F. H. & Hall, G. S. (1900). Pity. *American Journal of Psychology, 13*, 534-591.

Schaack, M. J. (1889). *Anarchy and anarchists: A history of the red terror and the social revolution in America and Europe—Communism, socialism, and nihilism in doctrine and in deed—The Chicago Haymarket conspiracy, and the detection and trial of the conspirators*. Chicago: Schulte.

Scheffler, I. (1974). *Four pragmatists: A critical introduction to Peirce, James, Mead, and Dewey*. New York: Humanities Press.

Schmidt, C. C. (1929). *Teaching and learning the common branches*. New York: Appleton.

Schmitt, C. (1917-1918). Developmental alexia: Congenital word-blindness or inability to learn to read. *Elementary School Journal, 18*, 680-700.

Schonell, F. J. (1945). *The psychology and teaching of reading*. London: Oliver & Boyd.

Schonell, F. J. (1961). *The psychology and teaching of reading* (4th ed.). New York: Philosophical Library.

Schools in lunatic asylums (1845). *American Journal of Insanity, 1*, 326-340.

Schorling, R., & Edmonson, J. B. (1931). The techniques of textbook authors. In G. M. Whipple (Ed.), *The textbook in American education* (30th Yearbook of the National Society for the Study of Education, Part II, pp. 27-66). Bloomington, IL: Public School Publishing.

Schuster, E. H. (1985, March 6). Textbooks: "There has never been a golden age." *Education Week*, p. 40.

Schwab, J. J. (1959). The impossible role of the teacher in progressive education. *School Review, 67*, 139-159.

Scott, C. A. (1908). *Social education*. Boston: Ginn.

Scott, C. W., & Hill, C. M. (1954). *Public education under criticism*. New York: Prentice-Hall.

Scott, D. H. (1964). *Roads to literacy*. Glascow, Great Britain: Holmes.

Search, P. W. (1905). *An ideal school: Or, looking forward*. New York: Appleton.

Searfoss, L. W., & Readence, J. E. (1994). *Helping children learn to read* (3rd ed.). Needham Heights, MA: Allyn & Bacon.

Sears, R. (1935). Characteristics and trainability of a case of special reading disability at the moron level. *Journal of Juvenile Research, 19*, 135-145.

Selke, E., & Selke, G. A. (1922). A study of the vocabularies of beginning books in twelve reading methods. *Elementary School Journal, 22*, 745-749.

Seltzer, C. A. (1933). *Lateral dominance and visual fusion: Their application to difficulties in reading, writing, spelling, and speech* (Harvard Monographs in Education, No. 12). Cambridge, MA: Harvard University Press.

Seltzer, M. M., Krauss, M. W., & Janicki, M. (Eds.) (1994). *Life course perspectives on adulthood and old age*. Washington, DC: American Association on Mental Retardation.

Serim, F., & Koch, M. (1996). *NetLearning: Why teachers use the internet*. Sebastopol, CA: Songline.

Shaler, N. S. (1904). *The citizen: A study of the individual and the government*. Boston: Hougton Mifflin.

Shanker, A. (1993). Technology is imperative for school restructuring In T. Cannings & L. Finkel (Eds.), *The technology age classroom* (pp. 618-619). Wilsonville, OR: Franklin, Beedle.

Shanon, P. (1989). *Broken promises: Reading instruction in twentieth-century America*. New York: Bergin & Garvey.

Shanon, P. (1992). Introduction: Why become political? In P. Shanon (Ed.), *Becoming political: Readings and writings in the politics of literacy education* (pp. 1-11). Portsmouth, NH: Hienemann.

Shapiro, J. (1991). Research perspectives on whole-language. In V. Froese (Ed.), *Whole-language: practice and theory* (pp. 313-356). Needham Heights, MA: Allyn & Bacon.

Sharpless, I. (1902). *English education in the elementary and secondary schools*. New York: Appleton.

Shaw, A. M. (1903). The true character of New York public schools. *World's Work, 7*, 4204-4221.

Shaw, A. M. (1904a). Common sense country schools. *World's Work, 8*, 4883-4894.

Shaw, A. M. (1904b). The public schools of a boss-ridden city. *World's Work, 8*, 4460-4466.

Shaw, E. R. (1901). *School hygiene*. New York: Macmillan.

Sheldon, E. A. (1911). *Autobiography of Edward Austin Sheldon*. New York: Ives-Butler.

Sheldon, H. D. (1901). *Student life and customs*. New York: Appleton.

Sherlock, E. B. (1911). *The feeble-minded: A guide to study and practice*. London: Macmillan.

Shor, I. (1986). *Culture wars: School and society in the conservative restoration 1969–1984*. Boston: Routledge.

Shoup, W. J. (1891). *The history and science of education: For institutes, normal, schools, reading circles and the private self-instruction of teachers*. New York: American Book Company.

Shrodes, C. (1955). Bibliotherapy. *Reading Teacher, 9* (10), 24-29.

Shuttleworth, G. E. (1899). The elementary education of defective children by "special classes" in London. *Journal of Psycho-asthenics, 4*, 58-64.

Siepman, C. A. (1958). *TV and our school crisis*. New York: Dodd, Mead.

Sinclair, U. (1906). *The jungle*. New York: Grosset & Dunlap.

Sinclair, U. (1922). *The goose-step: A study of American education*. Pasadena, CA: Author.

Singer, H. (1975). The SEER technique. *Journal of Reading Behavior, 7*, 255-267.

Smelser, N. J. (1962). *Theory of collective behavior*. New York: Free Press.

Smith, B. O., Stanley, W. O., & Shores, J. H. (1950). *Fundamentals of curriculum development*. New York: World.

Smith, B. O., Stanley, W. O., & Shores, J. H. (1957). *Fundamentals of curriculum development* (Rev. ed.). New York: World.

Smith, B. R. (1943). Improvement of instruction in the wartime emergency. *Curriculum Journal, 14*, 224-225.

Smith, D. E. P., & Carrigan, P. M. (1959). *The nature of reading disability*. New York: Harcourt Brace.

Smith, D. V. (1949). Literature and personal reading. In N. B. Henry (Ed.), *Reading in the elementary school* (48th Yearbook of the National Society for the Study of Education, Part 2, pp. 205-232). Chicago: University of Chicago Press.

Smith, F. (1986). *Insult to intelligence: The bureaucratic invasion of our classrooms*. New York: Arbor House.

Smith, F. (1997). *Reading without nonsense* (3rd ed.). New York: Teachers College Press.

Smith, M. (1954). *The diminished mind: A study of planned mediocrity in our public schools*. Chicago: IL: Regency.

Smith, N. B. (1934). *American reading instruction: Its development and its significance in gaining a perspective on current practices in reading*. New York: Silver, Burdett.

Smith, N. B. (1954). Can reading withstand the competition? In J. S. Kinder & F. D. McClusky (Eds.), *Audio-visual reader* (pp. 186-188). Dubuque, IA: Brown.

Smith, N. B. (1975). Cultural dialects: Current problems and solutions. *Reading Teacher, 29*, 137-141.

Smith, R. E. (1924). *Education moves ahead: A survey of progressive methods*. Boston: Atlantic Monthly Press.

Smith, W. A. (1922). *The reading process*. New York: Macmillan.

Smith, W. H. (1884). *The evolution of Dodd: A pedagogical story*. Chicago: Rand-McNally.

Snedden, D. (1907). *Administration and educational work of American juvenile reform schools* (Columbia University Contribution to Education No. 12). New York: Teachers College Press.

Snitzer, H. (1968). *Living at Summerhill*. Toronto: Collier.

Snow, C. E., Barnes, W. S. Chandler, J., Goodman, I. F., & Hemphill, L. (1991). *Unfulfilled expectations: Home and school influences on literacy*. Cambridge, MA: Harvard University Press.

Some educators define their goals (1939). *Survey Graphic, 28*, 576-577.

Spache, G. (1953a). A new readability formula for primary grade reading materials. *Elementary School Journal, 53*, 410-413.

Spache, G. (1953b). Factors which produce defective reading. In H. M. Robinson (Ed.), *Corrective reading in classroom and clinic* (Supplemental Educational Monographs, Vol. XV, pp. 49-57). Chicago: University of Chicago Press.

Spache, G. (1969). *Sources of good books for poor readers: An annotated bibliography*. Newark, DE: International Reading Association.

Spalding, W. (1955). The selection and distribution of printed materials. In L. J. Cronbach (Ed.), *Text materials in modern education* (pp. 166-187). Urbana, IL: University of Illinois Press.

Spring, J. (1972). *Education and the rise of the corporate state*. Boston: Beacon.

Spring, J. (1986). *The American School 1642–1985: Varieties of historical interpretation of the foundations and development of American education.* New York: Longman.

Squire, J. R., & Morgan, R. T. (1990). The elementary and high school textbook market today. In D. L. Elliott & A. Woodward (Eds.), *Textbooks and schooling in the United States* (89th Yearbook of the National Society for the Study of Education, Part 1, pp. 107-126). Chicago: University of Chicago Press.

Stableton, J. K. (1900). *Diary of a western schoolmaster.* Chicago: Ainsworth.

Staff of the Maury School (1941). *Teaching reading in the elementary school.* New York: Service Center of the Progressive Education Association.

Stahl, S. A., & Miller, P. D. (1989). Whole language and language experience approaches for beginning reading: A quantitative research synthesis. *Review of Educational Research, 59,* 87-116.

Stanger, M. A., & Donahue, E. K. (1937). *Prediction and prevention of reading difficulties.* New York: Oxford University Press.

Stanley, G. C. (1920). Special schools for Mexicans. *Survey, 44,* 714-715.

Stauffer, R. G. (1947). A clinical approach to personality and the disabled reader. *Education, 67,* 427-435.

Stauffer, R. G. (1953). Basic problems in correcting reading difficulties. In H. M. Robinson (Ed.), *Corrective reading in classroom and clinic* (Supplementary Educational Monographs, Vol. XV, pp. 118-126). Chicago: University of Chicago Press.

Stauffer, R. G. (1970). *The language experience approach to the teaching of reading.* New York: Harper & Row.

Stead, W. T. (1964). *If Christ came to Chicago.* New York: Living Books. (Originally published in 1894)

Stearns, M. M. (1939). "Subjects" or children? *Survey Graphic, 28,* 579-582.

Steiner, R. (1928). *The story of my life.* New York: Anthroposophic Press.

Steiner, R. (1969). *Education as a social problem: Six lectures* (L. D. Monges & D. M. Bugbey, Trans.). New York: Anthroposophic Press (Originally published in 1919).

Steiner, R. (1972a). *A modern art of education: Fourteen lectures given in Likey, Yorkshire, 5th-17th August, 1923* (J. Darrell, Trans.). London: Rudolf Steiner Press.

Steiner, R. (1972b). *An outline of occult science* (M. Monges, H. B. Monges, & L. D. Monges, Trans.). Spring Valley, NY: Anthroposophic Press (Originally published in 1925).

Steiner, R. (1986). *Soul economy and Waldorf education.* Spring Valley, NY: Anthroposophic Press (Original lectures delivered between 1921 and 1922).

Stephenson, S. (1907). Six cases of congenital word-blindness affecting three generations of one family. *Ophthalmoscope, 5,* 482-484.

Stevenson, J. A. (1921). *The project method of teaching.* New York: Macmillan.

Stewart, W. A. (1969). On the use of Negro dialect in the teaching of reading. In J. C. Baratz & R. W. Shuy (Eds.), *Teaching black children to read* (pp. 156-219). Washington, DC: Center for Applied Linguistics.

Stewig, J. W., & Buege, C. (1994). *Dramatizing literature in whole language classrooms* (2nd ed.). New York: Teachers College Press.

Stogdill, G. S. (1938). Subject disabilities: A symptom. *Understanding the Child, 7,* 7-9.

Stoll, C. (1995). *Silicon snake oil: Second thoughts on the information highway.* New York: Doubleday.

Stolle, H., Kidd, E., & Whitby, H. (1942) Spanish life class. In *Americans all: Studies in intercultural education* (pp. 227-237). Washington, DC: National Education Association.

Stone, C. R. (1935). The current-experience method in beginning reading. *Elementary School Journal, 36*, 105-109.

Stone, C. R. (1936). *Better primary reading: How to adapt reading instruction to the varying needs of the children*. St. Louis, MO: Webster.

Stone, C. R. (1937). *Better advanced reading*. St. Louis, MO: Webster.

Stone, L. (1931). How I teach beginning reading. *Progressive Education, 8*, 564-569.

Storm, G. E., & Smith, N. B. (1930). *Reading activities in the primary grades*. Boston: Ginn.

Strang, R., & Kendall-Bracken, D. (1957). *Making better readers*. Boston: Heath.

Strang, R., McCullough, C. M., & Traxler, A. E. (1961). *The improvement of reading*. New York: McGraw-Hill.

Strauss, A. A., & Werner, H. (1941). The mental organization of the brain-injured mentally defective child (The crippled child). *American Journal of Psychiatry, 97*, 1194-1203.

Strickland, D. S., & Cullinan, B. (1990). Afterword. In M. J. Adams, *Beginning to read: Thinking and learning about print*. (pp. 425-434). Cambridge, MA: MIT Press.

Stuart, D. C. (1910). One way of making textbooks. *Nation, 90*, 428-429.

Sullivan, M. (1927). *Our times: The United States 1900-1925—The turn of the century*. New York: Scribner.

Sulzby, E. (1985). Children's emergent reading of favorite storybooks: A developmental study. *Reading Research Quarterly, 20*, 458-481.

Suppes, P. (1967). On using computers to individualize instruction. In D. D. Bushnell & D. W. Allen (Eds.), *The computer in American education* (pp. 11-24). New York: Wiley.

Sutherland, A. H. (1922). Correcting school disabilities in reading. *Elementary School Journal, 23*, 37-42.

Swett, J. (1911). *Public education in California: Its origin and development, with personal reminiscences of half a century*. New York: American.

Swift, E. J. (1916). *Youth and the race: A study of psychology of adolescence*. New York: Scribner's Sons.

Sylvester, E. (1909). The education of exceptional children in the United States. In B. Maennel (Ed.), *Auxiliary education: The training of backward children* (E. Sylvester, Trans., pp. 200-243). New York: Doubleday & Page.

Taylor, B., Short, R., Shearer, B., & Frye, B. (1995). First grade teachers provide early reading intervention in the classroom. In R. L. Allington & S. A. Walmsley (Eds.), *No quick fix: Rethinking literacy programs in America's elementary schools* (pp. 159-176). New York: Teachers College Press.

Taylor, D., & Strickland, D. S. (1986). *Family storybook reading*. Portsmouth, NH: Heinemann.

Taylor, E. A. (1937). *Controlled reading: A correlation of diagnostic, teaching, and corrective techniques*. Chicago: University of Chicago Press.

Taylor, J. W. (1857). *A manual of the Ohio school system; Consisting of an historical view of its progress, and a republication of the school laws in force*. Cincinnati, OH: Derby.

Taylor, W. L. (1953). "Cloze procedure": A new tool for measuring readability. *Journalism Quarterly, 30,* 415-433.

Teachers and the class struggle (1935, November). *Social Frontier, 2* (2), 39-40.

Templeton, S. (1995). *Children's literacy: Contexts for meaningful learning.* Boston: Houghton Mifflin.

Terman, L. (1919). *The intelligence of school children: How children differ in ability the use of mental tests in school grading and the proper education of exceptional children.* Boston: Houghton Mifflin.

Terman, L. (1943). Foreword. In G. Fernald, *Remedial techniques in basic school subjects* (pp. ii-xv). New York: McGraw-Hill.

Tews, R. M. (1962). Bibliotherapy. *Library Trends, 11,* 97-105.

Thayer, H. S. (1981). *Meaning and action: A critical history of pragmatism* (2nd ed.). Indianapolis, IN: Hackett.

Thayer, V. T. (1928). *The passing of the recitation.* Boston: Heath.

The California text-book plan (1909). *Journal of Education, 69,* 173-180.

The education of the immigrant (1906, September). *Journal of Social Science, 4,* 163-174.

The Klan as a civic asset (1923). In *Knights of the Ku Klux Klan: Papers read at the meeting of Grand Dragons at their first annual meeting—With other articles of interest to Klansmen* (pp. 69-74). Ashevill, NC: Ku Klux Klan.

The mission of education in this war: A statement by the board of editors (1942). *Frontiers of Democracy, 9* (73), 68-70.

The model school (1896, January 16). *University of Chicago Weekly,* 707.

The nation's biggest business (1939). *Survey Graphic, 28,* 583-586.

The position of the Social Frontier (1935). *Social Frontier, 1* (4), 30-33.

The regulation of immigration (1923). In *Knights of the Ku Klux Klan: Papers read at the meeting of Grand Dragons at their first annual meeting—With other articles of interest to Klansmen* (pp. 66-69). Ashevill, NC: Ku Klux Klan.

This war and America: A statement to the educational profession by twelve of the fourteen members of the board of editors of Frontiers of Democracy (1941). *Frontiers of Democracy, 8* (63), 10-11.

This war and American education: An editorial (1942). *Frontiers of Democracy, 8* (66), 1.

Thomas, C. J. (1905). Congenital word-blindness and its treatment. *Ophthalmoscope, 3,* 380-385.

Thomas, R. L. (1993). *Primaryplots 2: A book talk guide for use with readers ages 4-8.* New Providence, NJ: Bowker.

Thompson, D. P. (1853). *Locke Amsden, or the schoolmaster: A tale.* Boston: Mussey.

Thompson, F. (1920). *Schooling of the immigrant.* New York: Harper.

Thorndike, E. L. (1913). *An introduction to the theory of mental and social measurements* (2nd ed.). New York: Teachers College Press.

Thorndike, E. L. (1921). *The teacher's word book.* New York: Teachers College Press.

Thorndike, E. L. (1932). *A teacher's word book of 20,000 words.* New York: Bureau of Publications—Teachers College Press.

Thorndike, E. L. (1973). *Education: A first book.* New York: Arno. (Originally published in 1912)

Thorndike, E. L., & Gates, A. I. (1929). *Elementary principles of education.* New York: Macmillan.

Thorndike, E. L., & Lorge, I. (1944). *The teacher's word book of 30,000 words*. New York: Bureau of Publications—Teachers College Press.

Tiles, J. E. (1994). American pragmatism—James. In C. L. Ten (Ed.), *The nineteenth century* (pp. 381-407). New York: London.

Todd, E. J., & Powell, E. (1899). *How to teach reading: A treatise showing the relation of reading to the work of education*. New York: Silver, Burdett.

Tompkins, P. (1997). Lost Atlantis. *Harper's, 294* (277), pp. 76-83.

Trace, A. S. (1961, May 27). Can Ivan read better than Johnny? *Saturday Evening Post, 234*, pp. 30, 67-68.

Traxler, A. E. (1941). *Ten years of research in reading: Summary and bibliography* (Educational Records Bulletin No. 32). New York: Educational Records Bureau.

Treacherous teaching (1939, August 15). *Forbes*, p. 8.

Truswell, H. A. (1975). *Made in Summerhill*. New York: Hawthorn.

Tulchin, S. H. (1935). Emotional factors in reading disabilities in school children. *Journal of Educational Psychology, 26*, 443-454.

Turkle, S. (1995). *Life on the screen: Identity in the age of the internet*. New York: Simon & Shuster.

Tyler, I. K. (1945). Foreword. In W. B. Levenson, *Teaching through radio* (pp. v-vi). New York: Farrar & Rinehart.

Tyler, R. W. (1945). Introduction. In N. B. Henry, *American education in the postwar period: Curriculum reconstruction* (44th Yearbook of the National Society for the Study of Education, Part 1, pp. 1-4), Chicago, IL: University of Chicago Press.

Tymocozko, D. (1996). The nitrous oxide philosopher. *Atlantic Monthly, 227* (5), pp. 93-101.

Tyson, R. (1948). The validation of mental hygiene literature. *Journal of Clinical Psychology, 4*, 304-306.

Tyson-Bernstein, H. (1988). *A conspiracy of good intentions: America's textbook fiasco*. Washington, DC: Council for Basic Education.

U. S. Department of Education (1996). *Using the Internet: World Wide Web pages featuring education* (Consumer Guide, No. 15). Washington, DC: Author.

Uhl, W. L. (1916). The use of the results of reading tests as a basis for planning remedial work. *Elementary School Journal, 17*, 266-275.

Uhl, W. L. (1924). *The materials of reading: Their selection and organization*. New York: Silver-Burdett.

Ulich, R. (1968). *History of educational thought* (Rev. ed.). New York: Van Nostrand Reinhold.

Vail, H. H. (1911). *A history of the McGuffey readers*. Cleveland, OH: Burrows.

Vandewalker, N. C. (1908). *The kindergarten in American education*. New York: MacMillan.

Veatch, J., Sawaki, F., Elliot, G., Flake, E., & Blakey, J. (1979). *Key words to reading: The language experience approach begins* (2nd ed.). Columbus, OH: Merrill.

Vellutino, F. R. (1979). *Dyslexia: Theory and research*. Cambridge, MA: MIT Press.

Venezky, R. L. (1970). Nonstandard language and reading. *Elementary English, 47*, 334-345.

Venezky, R. L. (1987). A history of the American reading textbook. *Elementary School Journal, 87*, 247-265.

Vernon, M. D. (1931). *The experimental study of reading.* Cambridge, Great Britain: Cambridge University Press.

Vernon, M. D. (1957). *Backwardness in reading: A study of its nature and origin.* London: Cambridge University Press.

Vickery, W. E., & Cole, S. G. (1943). *Intercultural education in American schools: Proposed objectives and methods.* New York: Harper.

Vogel, M., & Washburne, C. (1928). An objective method of determining grade placement of children's reading material. *Elementary School Journal, 28,* 373-381.

Wagner, R. B. (1989). *Accountability in education: A philosophical inquiry.* New York: Routledge.

Wagner, R. F. (1973). Rudolph Berlin: Originator of the term dyslexia. *Bulletin of the Orton Society, 23,* 57-63.

Walcutt, C. C. (1961). Phonic systems: Proved and available. In C. C. Walcutt (Ed.). *Tomorrow's illiterates: The state of reading instruction today.* Boston: Little, Brown.

Walmsley, S. A., & Allington, R. L. (1995). Redefining and reforming instructional support programs for at-risk students. In R. L. Allington & S. A. Walmsley (Eds.), *No quick fix: Rethinking literacy programs in America's elementary schools* (pp. 19-44). New York: Teachers College Press.

Walp, T. P., & Walmsley, S. A. (1995). Scoring well on tests or becoming genuinely literate: Rethinking remediation in a small rural school. In R. L. Allington & S. A. Walmsley (Eds.), *No quick fix: Rethinking literacy programs in America's elementary schools* (pp. 177-196). New York: Teachers College Press.

Ware, C. F. (1935). *Greenwich Village, 1920—1930: A comment on American civilization in the post-war years.* Boston: Houghton Mifflin.

Ware, F. (1901). *Educational foundations of trade and industry.* New York: Appleton.

Warner, F. (1897). *The study of children and their school training.* New York: Macmillan.

Wartime Commission of the U. S. Office of Education (1942). Educational policy concerning young children and the war. *National Elementary Principal, 21,* 198.

Washburne, C. (1924). Merits of the individual plan of instruction. *School Life, 9,* 179.

Washburne, C. (1926). *New schools in the old world.* New York: Day.

Washburne, C. (1932). *Adjusting the school to the child: Practical first steps.* Yonkers-on-Hudson, NY: World.

Washburne, C. (1936). Ripeness. *Progressive Education, 13,* 125-130.

Washburne, C., & Marland, S. P. (1963). *Winnetka: The history and significance of an educational experiment.* Englewood Cliffs, NJ: Prentice-Hall.

Washburne, C., & Morphett, M. V. (1938). Grade placement of children's books. *Elementary School Journal, 38,* 355-364.

Watkins, E. (1922). *How to teach silent reading to beginners.* Philadelphia: Lippincott.

Watson, D. (1989). Defining and describing whole language. *Elementary School Journal, 90,* 129-141.

Watson, D., & Crowley, P. (1988). How can we implement a whole-language approach? In C. Weaver (Ed.), *Reading process and practice: From socio-psycholinguistics to whole language* (pp. 232-279). Portsmouth, NH: Heinemann.

Wattenberg, W. W. (1936). *On the educational front: The reactions of teachers associations in New York and Chicago.* Morningside Heights, NY: Columbia University Press.

Wattenberg, W. W. (1942). Forming attitudes. In *Americans all: Studies in intercultural education* (pp. 25-44). Washington, DC: National Education Association.

Weaver, C. (1990). *Understanding whole language: From principles to practice.* Portsmouth, NH: Heinemann.

Weber, O. F. (1926). Educational research and statistics: Methods used in the analysis of text-books. *School and Society, 24,* 678-684.

Wells, G. F. (1915). Some significant facts in the history of reading as a school subject. *Education, 36,* 585-588.

Welter, R. (1962). *Popular education and democratic thought in America.* New York: Columbia University Press.

Werner, H., & Strauss, A. A. (1978). Disorders of conceptual thinking in the brain-injured child. In S. S. Barten & M. B. Franklin (Eds.), *Developmental processes: Heinz Werner's selected writings* (Vol. 2, pp. 283-309). New York: International Universities Press. (Originally published in 1942)

Wesbury, I. (1990). Textbooks, textbook publishers, and the quality of schooling. In D. L. Elliott & A. Woodward (Eds.), *Textbooks and schooling in the United States* (89th Yearbook of the National Society for the Study of Education, Part 1, pp. 1-22). Chicago: University of Chicago Press.

What shall we do about reading today? A symposium (1942). *Elementary English Review (Special Topical Issue), 29,* 225-256.

Wheat, H. G. (1923). *The teaching of reading: A textbook of principles and methods.* Boston: Ginn.

Whipple, G. M. (Ed.) (1920). *New materials of instruction* (19th Yearbook of the National Society for the Study of Education, Part 1). Bloomington, IL: Public School Publishing.

Whipple, G. M. (Ed.) (1924). *Report of the national committee on reading* (24th Yearbook of the National Society for the Study of Education, Part 1). Bloomington, IL: Public School Publishing.

White, A. (1921). *Reading ability and disability of subnormal children.* New York: Department of Public Welfare.

White, E. E. (1886). *The elements of pedagogy: A manual for teachers, normal schools, normal institutes, teachers' reading circles, and all persons interested in school education.* New York: American.

Wickersham, J. P. (1886). *A history of education in Pennsylvania: Private and public, elementary and higher, from the time the Swedes settled on the Delaware to the present day.* Lancaster, PA: Author.

Wiggin, K. D. (1892). *Children's rights: A book of nursery logic.* Boston: Houghton Mifflin.

Willey, M. M., & Rice, S. A. (1933). The agencies of communication. In *Recent social trends in the United States: Report of the President's Research Committee on Social Trends* (pp. 167-217). New York: McGraw-Hill.

Williams, R. (1961). *The long revolution.* Westport, CT: Greenwood.

Williams, R. M., & Ryan, M. W. (Eds.) (1954). *Schools in transition: Community experiences in desegregation.* Chapel Hill, NC: University of North Carolina Press.

Williamson, J. H. (1981). Textbook publishing: Facts and myths. In J. Y. Cole & T. G. Sticht (Eds.), *The textbook in American society: A volume based on a conference at the Library of Congress on May 2–3, 1979* (pp. 38-40). Washington, DC: Library of Congress.

Wilson, G. M., & Hoke, K. J. (1921). *How to measure.* New York: Macmillan.

Wilson, K. G., & Daviss, B. (1994). *Redesigning education.* New York: Holt.

Wilson, S. (1958). It's time to close our carnival. *Life, 44,* pp. 37-38.

Winch, C. (1990). *Language, ability and educational achievement.* New York: Routledge.

Winch, W. H. (1925). *Teaching beginners to read in England: Its methods, results, and psychological bases.* Bloomington, IL: Public School Publishing.

Winship, A. E. (1915a). Quality and virility of American school books. *School Journal, 82,* 255-258.

Winship, A. E. (1915b). Text-books—Educational, commercial and political. *School Journal, 81,* 285-288.

Wirth, A. G. (1972). *Education the technological society: The vocational-liberal studies controversy in the early twentieth century.* Scranton, PA: Intext.

Wisconsin Research Project in School Broadcasting (1942). *Radio in the classroom: Experimental studies in the production and classroom use of lessons broadcast by radio.* Madison, WI: University of Wisconsin Press.

Wise, H. A. (1939). *Motion pictures as an aid in teaching American history.* New Haven, CT: Yale University Press.

Wise, J. E. (1964). *The history of education: An analytic survey from the age of Homer to the present.* New York: Sheed & Ward.

Witmer, L. (1916). Congenital aphasia and feeblemindedness—A clinical diagnosis. *Psychological Clinic, 10,* 181-191.

Witty, P. (1952). Reading to meet emotional needs. *Elementary English, 29,* 75-84.

Witty, P. A. (1961). The role of interest. In N. B. Henry (Ed.), *Development in and through reading* (60th Yearbook of the National Society for the Study of Education, Part I, pp. 127-143). Chicago: University of Chicago Press.

Witty, P., & Kopel, D. (1939). *Reading and the educative process.* Boston: Ginn.

Woelfel, N. (1933). *Molders of the American mind: A critical review of the social attitudes of seventeen leaders in American education.* New York: Columbia University Press.

Woelfel, N., & Tyler, I. K. (Eds.) (1942). *Radio and the school: A guidebook for teachers and administrators.* Yonkers-on-Hudson, NY: World.

Woellner, R. C., & Lyman, R. L. (1930). Evaluating books on vocational guidance. *School Review, 38,* 191-198.

Wolf, S. J. (1937). A comparative study of two groups of girls of relatively equal intelligence but differing markedly in achievement. *Journal of Applied Psychology, 21,* 304-310.

Woodring, P. (1953). *Let's talk sense about our schools.* New York: Mcgraw-Hill.

Woodring, P. (1957, September 2). Reform plan for schools. *Life, 43,* pp. 123-136.

Woodring, P. (1958). Introduction. In W. James, *Talks to teachers* (pp. 6-17). New York: Norton.

Woodrow, H. (1923). *Brightness and dullness in children* (2nd ed.). Philadelphia: Lippincott.

Woodward, A., & Elliott, D. L. (1990a). Textbooks, curriculum, and school improvement. In D. L. Elliott & A. Woodward (Eds.), *Textbooks and schooling in the United States* (89th Yearbook of the National Society for the Study of Education, Part 1, pp. 222-232). Chicago: University of Chicago Press.

Woodward, A., & Elliott, D. L. (1990b). Textbooks: Consensus and controversy. In D. L. Elliott & A. Woodward (Eds.), *Textbooks and schooling in the United States* (89th Yearbook of the National Society for the Study of Education, Part 1, pp. 146-161). Chicago: University of Chicago Press.

Woodward, A., Elliott, D. L., & Nagel, K. C. (1988). *Textbooks in school and society: An annotated bibliography and guide to research.* New York: Garland.

Woody, T. (1934). Historical sketch of activism. In G. M. Whipple (Ed.), *The activity movement* (33rd Yearbook of the National Society for the Study of Education, Part 2, pp. 9-43). Bloomington, IL: Public School Publishing.

Woofter, T. J. (1933). The status of racial and ethnic groups. In *Recent social trends in the United States: Report of the President's Research Committee on Social Trends* (pp. 553-601). New York: McGraw-Hill.

Wrightstone, J. W. (1951). Research related to experience records and basal readers. *Bulletin—International Council for the Improvement of Reading Instruction, 5,* 5-7, 17.

Wyer, J. S. (1914). Text-books and some others. *School Journal, 80,* 427-428.

Yoakam, G. A. (1955). *Basal reading instruction.* New York: McGraw-Hill.

Young, K, (1922). Intelligence tests of certain immigrant groups. *Scientific Monthly, 15,* 417-434.

Zilversmit, A. (1976). The failure of progressive education, 1920-1940. In L. Stone (Ed.), *Schooling and society: Studies in the history of education* (pp. 252-263). Baltimore: John Hopkins University Press.

Zirbes, L. (1918). Diagnostic measurement as a basis for procedure. *Elementary School Journal, 18,* 505-522.

Zirbes, L. (1940). What is a modern reading program? *Educational Method, 20,* 151-155.

Zirbes, L. (1949). Gaps in curriculum research. *Educational Leadership, 7,* 187-192.

Zirbes, L. (1951). The experience approach in reading. *Bulletin—International Council for the Improvement of Reading Instruction, 5,* 1-2, 15.

Zornow, T. A. (1919). The use of the Gray oral reading test in a Rochester school and some deductions from the results. *Journal of the New York State Teachers' Association, 67,* 99-107.

AUTHOR INDEX

SUBJECT INDEX